ADVANCE PRAISE FOR *SOVEREIGN, SETTLER, LEAKER, LIE: FORMS OF THE SECRET IN US POLITICAL RHETORIC*

"Much work on the secret skirts its rhetorical form and associated tropes, but Hallsby has written a rigorous, capacious, and highly engaging account that situates the secret historically and culturally. Essential reading for those interested in the politics and aesthetics of secrecy."
—Clare Birchall, author of *Radical Secrecy: The Ends of Transparency in Datafied America*

"Presented from a psychoanalytic perspective that refuses to collapse into binaries of suspicion and faith, *Sovereign, Settler, Leaker, Lie* is both reassuring for its ability to 'name' contemporary rhetorical dynamics and sobering because, as Freud once put it, we are not masters of our own house."
—Joshua Gunn, author of *Political Perversion: Rhetorical Aberration in the Time of Trumpeteering*

"Smart, playful, and theoretically sophisticated, *Sovereign, Settler, Leaker, Lie* introduces us to the hard truths of secrecy in American politics. A one-of-a-kind book."
—Joshua Reeves, coauthor of *The Prison House of the Circuit: Politics of Control from Analog to Digital*

"*Sovereign, Settler, Leaker, Lie* generatively brings rhetorical studies into conversation with surveillance studies to offer important expansions and correctives to the study of secrecy. Drawing on a rich historical archive that includes figures like Alan Turing, Saul D. Alinsky, Valerie Plame Wilson, and Chelsea Manning, Hallsby powerfully illustrates how secrets are not just in but of discourse. In so doing, he importantly foregrounds the secret's material impacts and entanglements with racial, sexual, colonial, and gendered violences."
—Mia Fischer, author of *Terrorizing Gender: Transgender Visibility and the Surveillance Practices of the U.S. Security State*

"This analytically sophisticated book offers a captivating exploration of the often-destructive role of political secrets in society. Whether found in conspiracy theories, national security leaks, or fabrications supporting war, as Atilla Hallsby shows, secrets powerfully shape collective knowledge and legitimize forms of violence."
—Torin Monahan, author of *Crisis Vision: Race and the Cultural Production of Surveillance*

SOVEREIGN, SETTLER, LEAKER, LIE

NEW DIRECTIONS IN RHETORIC AND MATERIALITY
Allison L. Rowland, Christa Teston, and Shui-yin Sharon Yam, Series Editors

SOVEREIGN, SETTLER, LEAKER, LIE

FORMS OF THE SECRET IN US POLITICAL RHETORIC

Atilla Hallsby

THE OHIO STATE UNIVERSITY PRESS
COLUMBUS

Copyright © 2026 by The Ohio State University.
All rights reserved.
Use of this material to train AI is prohibited without the express permission of the publisher.

This book is freely available in an open access edition thanks to TOME (Toward an Open Monograph Ecosystem)—a collaboration of the Association of American Universities, the Association of University Presses, and the Association of Research Libraries—and the generous support of the University of Minnesota Libraries. Learn more at the TOME website, available at openmonographs.org.

Attribution-NonCommercial-NoDerivatives 4.0 International (CC BY-NC-ND 4.0), https://creativecommons.org/licenses/by-nc-nd/4.0/legalcode.en

Library of Congress Cataloging-in-Publication Data

Names: Hallsby, Atilla, author.

Title: Sovereign, settler, leaker, lie : forms of the secret in US political rhetoric / Atilla Hallsby.

Other titles: New directions in rhetoric and materiality

Description: Columbus : The Ohio State University Press, [2026] | Series: New directions in rhetoric and materiality | Includes bibliographical references and index. | Summary: "Analyzes the role of the secret in twenty-first-century US political discourse, theorizing different forms of the secret across presidential scandals, detective narratives, national security leaks, and racist dog whistles"—Provided by publisher.

Identifiers: LCCN 2025043760 | ISBN 9780814216057 hardback | ISBN 0814216056 hardback | ISBN 9780814284780 ebook | ISBN 0814284787 ebook

Subjects: LCSH: Secrecy—Political aspects—United States | Official secrets—United States | Official secrets—United States—History—21st century | Rhetoric—Political aspects—United States

Classification: LCC JF1525.S4 H35 2026

LC record available at https://lccn.loc.gov/2025043760

Other identifiers: ISBN 9780814259726 (paperback) | ISBN 0814259723 (paperback)

Cover design by Brad Norr
Text composition by Stuart Rodriguez
Type set in Minion Pro

∞ The paper used in this publication meets the minimum requirements of the American National Standard for Information Sciences—Permanence of Paper for Printed Library Materials. ANSI Z39.48-1992.

CONTENTS

List of Illustrations		vi
Preface	This Page Left Intentionally Blank	vii
INTRODUCTION	The Secret's Forms	1
CHAPTER 1	The Secret Episteme: A Genealogy of Political Crisis	22
CHAPTER 2	The Secret in and of Discourse: Hidden Depths and Open Surfaces	57
CHAPTER 3	The Scandal: George W. Bush and the Exposure of Valerie Plame Wilson	82
CHAPTER 4	The Dog Whistle: Weaponizing Saul Alinsky in the Obama Years	108
CHAPTER 5	The Leak: Sexual Caricature and the National Security State	140
CHAPTER 6	The Detective: Settler Subjects and Neocolonial Warfare	174
CHAPTER 7	Twisted Endings: The Secret in and of the Deep State	208
Acknowledgments		227
Bibliography		233
Index		273

ILLUSTRATIONS

FIGURES

FIGURE 2.1	Hans Holbein the Younger, *The Ambassadors*	78
FIGURE 3.1	Repetition, caesura, and synecdoche	91
FIGURE 5.1	Megethos, or the masculine (phallic) logic of leaks	150
FIGURE 5.2	Apophasis, or the feminine (phatic) logic of leaks	161
FIGURE 6.1	Detective analepsis	185
FIGURE 6.2	Settler analepsis	186
FIGURE 6.3	Paralipsis of the other	193
FIGURE 6.4	Paralipsis of the settler	196
FIGURE 6.5	The *nazar bonçuk*	206

TABLES

TABLE 5.1	Sexualized logics of the NSS leak	147
TABLE 6.1	Tropes of the settler-detective	183
TABLE 7.1	The secret's two principles	211

PREFACE

This Page Left Intentionally Blank

The phrase "this page intentionally left blank" is a common sight on classified documents and inside printed books. In the context of classification, it ensures that every page is accounted for and no extraneous material has been added in after the fact. In the realm of printed books, the phrase assures readers that empty pages were not included by mistake. Mass production often involves mechanical folding processes that require blank pages for spacing. Updated editions sometimes require them to account for formatting alterations. Blanks may even be included in digital documents for accurate double-sided printing. Although intentionally blank pages may be easily overlooked, they are crucial in lending a balanced form to files and bound books.

In *Sovereign, Settler, Leaker, Lie,* the secret assumes a role that is analogous to the blank page. It, too, is structural and calls attention to its own invisibility. Both organize the form and feel of discourse in ways that seem essential, contradictory, and confounding. Both communicate nothing, yet "are part of what the reader 'reads' or 'sees' without reference to the maker's purpose."[1] Both are puzzling contradictions: In the case of "this page left intentionally blank," the words deny their own presence, saying, "Nothing to see here! Look the other way! Just pretend this message doesn't exist." If "this page left intentionally

---

1. Michaels, *Shape of the Signifier,* 6.

blank" alerts the reader to something beyond their perception, this book does something similar: It aims to give the secret a recognizable form.

The first way that the secret makes itself known is through *names*. The names we give it mark what is beyond knowing, attuning public audiences to the fact that information is esoteric or inaccessible. Designations like "top secret" and "classified," for instance, draw our attention to information as knowledge that carries different degrees of risk if exposed.[2] Names for a pervasive shroud of institutional secrecy, like "the deep state," conjure a political realm beyond public life.[3] Other times, proper names like the Manchurian Candidate, "Jason Bourne," and "James Bond" evoke fictional legitimacy for official secrets.[4] Even when the secret amounts to nothing more than false flags, stovepiped signals, paranoid conspiracies, or deliberate disinformation, names are the shorthand that allow the secret to hover between openness and mystery. Enunciatively, they express "I know what I'm seeing here" by extending the promise that naming grants the knower *some* control over what is beyond their ability to access. In this book, names like *scandal, dog whistle, leaker,* and *detective* capture unique forms of knowing-but-also-not-knowing, each one promising to diminish the powerlessness that accompanies being on the secret's outside.

The second way that the secret rises to the level of perceptibility is as a banal, quotidian *trope*. We know we are in the presence of the secret when we see redactions covering the printed text of a document, take note of someone's casual use of a hateful dog whistle, or hear the subtle signifiers of gossip leaking beyond the boundaries of an intimate conversation. The commonest form of the secret is the paradox: Spread this message no further, even if I break this rule by telling it to you.[5] *Sovereign, Settler, Leaker, Lie* asks the reader to notice the tension between action and retroaction, or between what the secret says in the moment and what it does with the benefit of hindsight. As "that which is generally known, but cannot be articulated," the secret can assume many forms, allowing one to know when they have achieved intimacy with a fellow traveler or to pass unnoticed while under a surveillant gaze.[6]

In this book, I use a number of rhetorical tropes to attach a familiar structure to the political secret. Etymologically, the word *trope* refers to a turn, most often, a turn of phrase. Some readers will come to this book with an understanding of tropes as an obsolete catalog of figures and writerly choices that

---

2. Galison, "Removing Knowledge," 41–45.
3. Lofgren, *Deep State*.
4. Melley, *Covert Sphere*, 18.
5. Bellman, "Paradox of Secrecy," 9.
6. Taussig, *Defacement*, 5.

lie somewhere between embellishment and eloquence. However, tropes can be so much more: They are deliberately used figures (e.g., anaphora or simile), general thematic categories (e.g., the trope of X, where X is a placeholder for any number of signifiers, such as "war," "social justice," or "radicalization"), or epistemic rules that play a key role "in the discovery and description of the truth."[7] A fourth and final sense moves us away from understanding tropes as always intentional or deliberate ways of organizing language. This way of understanding trope does not allow us to choose the arrangement of our discourse; instead, discourse's rules speak through us, exceeding conscious choice. Whereas some tropes signal an intending agent who leaves their mark *in* language, others are patterns *of* discourse that only rise to perception retroactively, after the fact.

Finally, the secret's many appearances in political discourse have a characteristic *blankness,* a state of being-out-in-the-open and ignorable. Erasing histories of white racial hegemony, gender discrimination, and colonial violence, blankness renders history as it happened secret. It favors versions of past events that are universalizing, homogeneous, and whitewashed, prioritizing "moves to innocence," the bad-faith play of political whataboutism, and transcendentalizing claims of racial purity or sexual objectivity.[8] Consider, for instance, the infamous book burnings of World War II. The secret isn't that the books were destroyed but that the burnings erased the public memory of Magnus Hirschfeld's Institute for Sexology and decades of research on transgender medicine, further naturalizing cisgender normativity as unmarked.[9] Understood in these terms, the secret is a totem of the present age, marking what goes unmentioned despite its pivotal importance.[10] From destructive conspiracies to the promise of transparency, *Sovereign, Settler, Leaker, Lie* takes stock of the secret as an attack upon the collective social body waged under the guise of protecting it.

In *The Gay Science,* Nietzsche dedicates one of his many aphorisms to the powerful desire to communicate what cannot—or should not—be communicated: "There is nothing we like so much to impart to others as the seal of secrecy—along with what is under it."[11] This book is no exception. Readers

---

7. Lundberg, "Enjoying God's Death," 389; and Rowland, *Zoetropes,* 5–6.
8. Nakayama and Krizek, "Whiteness," 293; and Tuck and Yang, "Decolonization."
9. "Although the film footage of this book burning and the 1995 construction of a memorial on the spot where it took place has made this event famous, the fact that it was Hirschfield's library that burned was not well known until recently. In 2008, Ranier Herrn curated an exhibition to clarify this history: *Sex Burns—Magnus Hirschfeld and the Nazi Book Burnings,* which was staged at the Medizinhistorisches Museum of the Charité in Berlin." Timm, "Introduction," 8.
10. Derrida, "White Mythology."
11. Nietzsche, *Gay Science,* 140.

may have already noted the title's sonic resemblance to that of John le Carré's famous novel about Cold War–era secrecy, *Tinker, Tailor, Soldier, Spy*.[12] If this book recodes Le Carré, then each of the four case-driven chapters also recodes the title's featured terms: the *Sovereign* scandal, the *Settler* detective, the national security *Leaker*, and the dog whistle's *Lie*. Ultimately, this book is both *about* secrets and seeks to *perform* the experience of coming upon epistemic ephemera. I hope that it contains what you are looking for, and that you enjoy learning about the secret it divulges.

---

12. Le Carré, *Tinker, Tailor, Soldier, Spy*.

INTRODUCTION

The Secret's Forms

> The thief hides the purloined letter, in Edgar Allan Poe's story, by placing it in plain sight. His theft is overlooked because no attempt is made to conceal it. The crimes of the postmodern American empire, I want to suggest, are concealed in the same way. Covert operations actually function as spectacle. So let us begin like Poe's Inspector Dupin, and attend to the evidence before our eyes.
> —Michael Rogin, "'Make My Day!'" (99)

The Secrecy Antecedent

In the years just before and after September 11, 2001, humanists and social scientists began to establish an area of research focused on *secrecy*. Advancing an interdisciplinary approach, they brought together the history and sociology of science, anthropology, and legal studies to argue that secrecy was a pervasive but invisible force that saturated many domains of public, political, and intellectual life. In the short time that secrecy studies flashed into existence, scholars coined new terms and headings for academic research, including *anti-epistemology, blackboxing,* and *defacement*.[1] They argued that secrecy organized the conduct of international diplomacy, the transformation of conspiracy theories into popular narratives, government classification procedures, the handling and disposal of radioactive materials, and the academic peer-review process.[2]

---

1. Galison, "Removing Knowledge"; Latour, *Pandora's Hope*, 304; and Taussig, *Defacement*.
2. Der Derian, *Antidiplomacy*; Melley, *Empire of Conspiracy*; Galison, "Removing Knowledge"; van Wyck, *Signs of Danger*; and Jasanoff, "Transparency in Public Science."

In the years after the 9/11 attack on the World Trade Center, however, the study of secrecy gave way to another organizing category: *surveillance*.[3] We might attribute this transition to many interlinked events: the American wars on Afghanistan (2001) and Iraq (2003) initiated by George W. Bush's presidential administration; the passage and reauthorization of the USA Patriot Act (2001 and 2005), which instituted novel restrictions on Fourth Amendment rights and limited the presumptive right to privacy among citizens and noncitizens; landmark national security leaks by Edward Snowden (2013) that demonstrated how surveillance programs in the United States were far more directed at the body politic than was acknowledged by the US federal government or reported by the Fourth Estate; the normalization of police body cameras, drone strikes, and cyberweapons; and the list goes on.

Of course, there were many echoes of the academic call to investigate secrecy in the years after September 11. In the final years of George W. Bush's presidency, Jack Bratich turned his attention to secrecy as the immanentizing force animating the new national security state.[4] Catherine Squires theorized "enclave public spheres" as a necessary revision to public sphere theory, positing different spaces for resistive activity rooted in the prosocial and self-protective activities of Black folk.[5] In the chapter "Freedom Is a Secret," Katherine McKittrick argued that the Underground Railroad, far from a discrete or mappable geographic space, was "unwritten and unmapped" out of fugitive necessity:

> Primarily identified through famous conductors and escapees (Harriet Tubman, Henry "Box" Brown) and secret messages (hidden in constellations, quilts, landmarks, songs, enigmatic newspaper advertisements) the Underground Railroad was considered to be unwritten and unmapped. Disclosure of routes and places would curtail, often violently, black freedoms. The subversion was a radical spatial act, an explicit reconfiguration of the spaces of white supremacy and a socio-spatial resistance that, if discovered, would incite death, bodily violence, and a return to enslavement.[6]

Early twentieth century secrecy studies attended to invisible, material excesses of presidential power, practical communication strategies used by Black publics to hide "counterhegemonic ideas and strategies in order to survive and

---

3. On the prevalence of *surveillance* as a centralizing term, see also (presented chronologically) Marx, *Undercover*; Andrejevic, *I Spy*; Browne, *Dark Matters*; Ohl, "Nothing to See or Fear"; Reeves, *Citizen Spies*; Y. Levine, *Surveillance Valley*; Zuboff, *Age of Surveillance Capitalism*; Fischer, *Terrorizing Gender*; Monahan, *Crisis Vision*; Hochman, *Listeners*; and Kelly, *Caught on Tape*.
4. Bratich, "Public Secrecy."
5. Squires, "Rethinking the Black Public Sphere."
6. McKittrick, "Freedom Is a Secret."

avoid sanctions," and North American memories of resistance to chattel slavery.[7] In 2016, Susan Maret, seeking to enshrine secrecy studies as a discrete area of inquiry, opened the inaugural volume of *Secrecy and Society* by calling secrecy out as a "wicked problem": complex, without easy resolution, symptomatic of other problems, and defiant of efforts to delineate boundaries or limits.[8] In my home discipline of rhetorical studies, secrecy scholarship has slowed to a trickle, largely continuing under the heading of *occultatio*, a thematic-tropological category for the strategic use of omission and elision in official political discourse.[9] Scholarship on occultatio also coincided with the publication of Davin Allen Grindstaff's 2013 *Rhetorical Secrets*, which situated secrecy at the intersections of ideological criticism and queer theory.[10]

The rise of surveillance as an interdisciplinary "order-word" did not mean that the pervasive influence of secrecy upon public culture disappeared.[11] On the contrary, it intensified. Recalling the infamous secret societies of the eighteenth- and nineteenth-century American republic, the dark money pooled by anonymous billionaires increasingly exercises an undue influence on the trajectory of American elections.[12] The recent rise of conspiracy theories on topics ranging from COVID-19 to QAnon may be seen as an amplified version of more than a century of politicized paranoia, strumming a chord that has long functioned as a reactionary defense on behalf of white, masculine, and heteronormative hegemonies within the United States.[13] In computer science, the discipline of sand (silicon) and lightning (electrons), "perfect secrecy" remains a topic of practical interest, referring to an ever more technical cryptographic problem whereby an attacker with unlimited resources cannot gain information about the contents of a message.[14] Whether as political capital, disinformation, or emergent technology, secrecy remains an important foundation. Even if secrecy studies' status as a pivotal antecedent to surveillance scholarship has received little attention, the secret is more pervasive than ever. We may have lost track of it, but it certainly has not lost track of us.

---

7. Squires, "Rethinking the Black Public Sphere," 448.
8. Maret, "Charm of Secrecy," 3.
9. Gunn, *Modern Occult Rhetoric*; and Conley and Saas, "*Occultatio.*"
10. Grindstaff, *Rhetorical Secrets*.
11. "Order-words do not concern commands only, but every act that is linked to statements by a 'social obligation.' Every statement displays this link, directly or indirectly. Questions, promises are order-words. The only possible definition of language is the set of all order-words, implicit presuppositions, or speech acts current in a language at a given moment." Deleuze and Guattari, *Thousand Plateaus*, 79.
12. Mayer, *Dark Money*.
13. Hofstadter, *Paranoid Style in American Politics*.
14. Simeall and Spring, "Resistance Strategies." I also credit Karl Hallsby with describing computer science as a discipline of sand (i.e., silicon) and lightning (i.e., electricity).

Sovereign, Settler, Leaker, Lie is an encomium to secrecy studies, a rhetorical rescue of an under-noticed but necessary interdisciplinary project that need not be quietly abandoned in the twenty-first century.[15] We are, after all, still in the throes of a secrecy crisis. It existed before we were born and will likely outlast us. Although surveillance may seem like the organizing force of the digital age, neoliberal governance, and insurgent fascism, the secret is its patterned precursor.

Situation, Episteme, Spectacle

Another way of framing the pervasiveness of the secret in our current moment might be to say that *the secret determines our situation*. This phrase has rhetorical implications, given how rhetoric is bonded to the word *situation*. As Lloyd Bitzer put it, "rhetorical discourse comes into existence as a response to situation, in the same sense that an answer comes into existence in response to a question, or a solution in response to a problem."[16] Rhetoric's connection to a determining situation is frequently attributed to Aristotle, who defines rhetoric as "the faculty of discerning the possible means of persuasion in each particular case."[17] In the late twentieth-century United States, *situation* became a rhetorical term of art associated with the confluence of factors shaping a singular speech event. However, this framework alone may be ill-suited to describing the secret, for several reasons. First, the secret is not a singular

---

15. I attribute this understanding of the encomium to Gorgias of Leontini's "Encomium of Helen," which offered a sophistic demonstration of improvisational oratorical skills and the power of persuasive speech under the pretense of rescuing Helen of Troy from her once-prevalent reputation of initiating the Trojan War. As employed here, encomium also loosely connotes what Debra Hawhee describes in reference to animals as the "paradoxical encomium," a rhetorical form that seeks to praise "the unpraisable," the "trivial," and the "base." My topics match these criteria: whereas secrecy studies is under-noticed (or "trivial"), the secret has the reputation of being unrescuable (or "base"). My wish is to restore the sense that humanists can and should seriously engage with both. Gorgias, *Encomium of Helen*; and Hawhee, *Rhetoric in Tooth and Claw*, 95–97.

16. Bitzer, "Rhetorical Situation," 5.

17. The definition cited in the text is drawn from Aristotle, *Art of Rhetoric*, xxxvi. This definition is phrased differently elsewhere in the same book: "the faculty of *discovering* the possible means of persuasion *in reference to any subject whatever*" (15; italics added). The latter clause takes the place of the indefinite "cases" referenced by the former and, therefore, also of the "situations" to which it might refer. George Kennedy's translation of Aristotle's *Rhetoric* makes other substitutions: "Let rhetoric be [defined as] an ability, in each [particular] case, to see the available means of persuasion" (Aristotle, *On Rhetoric*, 36). The significance of these substitutions is twofold: (1) Replacing "discovering" with "seeing" or "observing" connects the study of rhetoric to "ocularcentric" Greek "theory" (*theoria/theorein*) (Jay, *Downcast Eyes*, 23). (2) Replacing "any subject whatever" with "each particular case" justifies rhetoric's twentieth- and twenty-first-century emphases on situations or specific contexts where rhetoric transpires.

situation but an evental plurality, akin to a cacophony that traverses many domains of public life and spans vast timescales. To say that the secret determines our situation means that it permeates public culture in ways that make it invisible, structural, and quotidian. Second, the rhetorical situation framework has consistently bracketed embodied, spatial, and discursive forms of materiality when theorizing rhetoric's effects. The consequence of such bracketing is to make the framework incapable of addressing recurring emergencies concerning racial capitalism and planetary destruction.[18] To paraphrase Bitzer, a speaker cannot convince a hurricane to divert from its path of devastation.[19] Be that as it may, the secret is both rhetorical and material, being thoroughly entangled with histories of racial, colonial, and gendered violence. Refusing to engage with material aspects of a shared social and symbolic reality would limit our imagination of the secret's effects, just as confining it to a single moment in time would leave out the secret's many historical antecedents.

A first way we might supplement our understanding of the secret's rhetoricity is to consider it as the object of an *episteme*. An episteme is a formation of knowledge, discourse, and power that ruptures neat categories of linear time. It elaborates "the conditions of thought under which what was written could be written. We could think of these conditions as unconscious to the text, or as its unstated, because invisible, a priori."[20] Epistemes are organized around a focal object that seeps beyond its earliest identifiable moment of emergence. Situated as the object of an ongoing episteme, the secret describes an evolving formation of power and knowledge whose primary aim is the concealment of knowledge. Set in these terms, the secret would elaborate a form of memory that "dwell[s] in the present" and engages "the simultaneous action of remembering and forgetting."[21] It would describe both the immanentizing forces within a discourse formation and their tendency to aim at a metadiscursive account of knowledge and power, no matter how impossible such an account might be. It would, finally, describe how the secret (re)produces itself as a tool of governance, even if every attempt to fully capture its essence inevitably falls short.[22]

A second way to rethink the secrecy situation concerns the *spectacle*, a mediated assemblage of racial capitalism, neoliberal governance, and civic spectatorship. In his 1988 sequel to *Society of the Spectacle* (1967), Guy Debord

---

18. Ochieng, "Limit Formations," 333.
19. "An exigence which cannot be modified is not rhetorical; thus, whatever comes about of necessity and cannot be changed—death, winter, and some natural disasters, for instance—are exigences to be sure, but they are not rhetorical." Bitzer, "Rhetorical Situation," 6.
20. Cousins and Hussein, *Michel Foucault*, 30.
21. Stormer, "Recursivity," 30.
22. Lundberg, *Lacan in Public*, 3.

asserts that the secret has always been the spectacle's beating heart.[23] The questions Debord poses in this book remain timely: "Since the spectacle today is certainly more powerful than it was before, what is it doing with this additional power? What point has it reached, that it had not reached previously? What, in short, are its present *lines of advance*?"[24]

The twenty-first-century spectacle has gathered many new forms. Television programs and popular fiction evoke dual processes of "agency panic," or "intense anxiety about an apparent loss of autonomy or self-control" at the hands of controlling organizations—and masculine fantasies about the "covert sphere," a "cultural imaginary shaped by both institutional secrecy and public fascination with the secret work of the state."[25] Even those carceral, policing, and intelligence functions of the state that seem entirely covert must be understood as "a form of power and not simply window dressing that diverts attention from the secret substance of American foreign policy."[26] As Michael Rogin suggests (see epigraph at the start of this chapter), the spectacle conceals the crimes of postmodern America by constantly producing public discourse about these inaccessible goods. The spectacle not only encourages anxious, conspiratorial rumination but it justifies the national security state's undemocratic and extrajudicial actions by convincing spectators, the "public supposed to believe" in the all-seeing, all-knowing authority of governing institutions, that there is little they can do about it.[27]

The spectacle is further intensified by post-racial fantasy, which continuously repeats the figure of a Black biothreat as a figural response to "a disturbance in the symbolic order—like the election of the first Black president."[28] Post-racial fantasies are infused by a "phenomenal forgetting" in which "major social ills—economic inequality, police brutality, systemic racism, mass murder"—are displaced from popular narratives that would otherwise furnish social allegories for ongoing structural harms. Agency panic, the covert sphere, and post-racial fantasy make social ills palatable, ignorable, and popular: They transform "what is commemorated" into something that forgets its racial, sexual, and colonial baggage, making whiteness, heteronormative masculinity, and orientalism "*feel* right, *good*, the way it *should* be."[29] As Steven Martinot and Jared Sexton explain:

---

23. Debord, *Treatise on Secrets*, 11–12.
24. Debord, *Treatise on Secrets*, 4.
25. Melley, "Agency Panic," 62; and Melley, *Covert Sphere*, 7.
26. Rogin, "'Make My Day!,'" 100.
27. J. Dean, *Publicity's Secret*, 19–20.
28. Watts, *Postracial Fantasies and Zombies*, 7.
29. Watts, *Postracial Fantasies and Zombies*, 27.

> Spectacle is a form of camouflage. It does not conceal anything; it simply renders it unrecognizable. One looks at it and does not see it. It appears in disguise. . . . Camouflage is a relationship between the one dissimulating their appearance and the one who is fooled, who looks and cannot see.[30]

Spectacle, in other words, names how the secret has been normalized, fashioned into a centuries-long rhetoric that continues to organize everyday life. It conceals nothing because one can look directly at the secret and still not see what is going on. In the words of Casey Ryan Kelly, the secret is appealing because the spectacle organizes it as "a stumbling block to the fulfillment of democratic fantasies; hence, the need to perpetually reveal more."[31] Whereas the spectacle falsely promises that the next revelation will, finally, be the one to bring everything into the light, the secret is its prime commodity, its most renewable resource.

Sovereign, Settler, Leaker, Lie extends the above insights in chapter 1, which highlights how the secret is an embedded, ignorable, and durable feature of the American status quo. Although it may be tempting to create a moral binary in which "the secret" accrues a universally negative connotation as the opposite of "transparency," I would caution that such binaries are oversimplified. These terms carry within themselves the capacity to reinforce hegemonic power dynamics (in the case of the secret) or encourage endless self-exposure to make oneself more governable (in the case of transparency). Each also carries the capacity to foster protective community intimacy (in the case of the secret) and to circumvent exploitative power hierarchies (in the case of transparency). Simone Browne theorizes a similar dynamic when arguing that the secret has yielded conditions of totalizing oppression and resistive "dark sousveillance," that is, tactics that appropriate the tools of social controllers and refuse white supremacy's tendency to go ignored, by bringing its tactics to the spectacle's surface.[32] This book adopts a similar outlook: Rhetoric offers a way to look back upon the secret's past, putting its patterns on display for audiences who might otherwise become its passive spectators in the present.

The Secret and/as Rhetoric

Although this book is about the secret's spectacular and epistemic forms, this emphasis does not deny the existence of *secret* secrets, that is, truly hidden information that goes undisclosed because it has been erased or is permanently

---

30. Martinot and Sexton, "White Supremacy," 174.
31. Kelly, *Caught on Tape*, 19.
32. Browne, *Dark Matters*, 21.

sealed. The process of creating real or actual secrets is what Peter Galison terms "anti-epistemology," a highly codified set of practices concerned with "how knowledge can be covered and obscured."[33] Anti-epistemology describes the iconoclastic destruction of knowledge, the deliberate withdrawal of information from public circulation, as well as the compartmentalized categories and protocols that render this data inaccessible, beyond retrieval. The counterpart to the public-facing spectacle, anti-epistemology is the name for how secrets get made, perpetuating a status quo in which the amount of open knowledge that exists in the world pales in comparison to the volume of classified information tucked away by governing actors and institutions. As Galison explains:

> Whether one figures by acquisition rate, by holding size, or by contributors, the classified universe is, as best I can estimate, on the order of five to ten times larger than the open literature that finds its way to our libraries. Our commonsense picture may well be far too sanguine, even inverted. The closed world is not a small strongbox in the corner of our collective house of codified and stored knowledge. It is we in the open world—we who study the world lodged in our libraries, from aardvarks to zymurgy, we who are living in a modest information booth facing outwards, our unseeing backs to a vast and classified empire we barely know.[34]

The solution cannot be "no more secrets" or to make other universal, categorical-imperative-y, holds-in-all-cases pronouncements. Nor is it to embrace the false belief that "knowing" the secret will change this status quo, that some ideal of transparency has all the answers. There are communal forms of hiddenness that nurture and protect, just as there are disingenuous acts of transparency whose aim is to denude, expose, and destroy.[35] Embracing this complexity, this book makes a rhetorical distinction between the secret *in* and *of* discourse. The secret *in* discourse is akin to information hidden in an esoteric text or forgotten archive. It is often the product of anti-epistemologies

---

33. Galison, "Removing Knowledge," 45.
34. Galison "Removing Knowledge," 39.
35. One well-documented example of transparency's destructive potential concerns the post-9/11 Transportation Security Administration (TSA) injunction for airline passengers to render themselves transparent to searches and body scanners as a rhetoric of able-bodied whiteness. As Rachel Hall explains, such appeals to transparency falsely presume the existence of homogeneously raced and gendered bodies: "Built into the aesthetics of transparency as it is currently mobilized by the US security state is the desire for a generalizable body type which can be easily recognized as innocent or nonthreatening and thus efficiently be 'cleared' for take-off." Hall, "Terror and the Female Grotesque," 133. For other instances of destructive transparency rhetoric, see also Birchall, *Radical Secrecy*, 69–92; Hall, *Transparent Traveler*; and Hallsby, "Resisting the Demand for Transparency."

of the kind that Galison describes. Its counterpart, the secret *of* discourse, describes how the spectacle places everything in plain sight, creating the secret as a retroactive rhetorical form.

The secret *in* and *of* discourse, developed in chapter 2, builds substantially on other rhetorical scholars' theorizing. When other rhetoricians have theorized the secret, rhetoric's definitional scope has varied significantly:

1. Rhetoric may concern *techniques of spoken persuasion and visual inference*, in which the creative and intentional use of language and discourse is connected to a field of objective, material, and social circumstances in ways that defy simple explanations of cause and effect.
2. Rhetoric may concern *the production, reception, and articulation of symbols and representations*. Both a hermeneutics (i.e., an interpretive method) and a strategy of mapping complex relations of power, rhetoric informs how publics mobilize subjectivity, aesthetics, knowledge, signification, and belief.
3. Rhetoric is *a framework of pre-figurative rules*. Informing many traditions (e.g., affect theory, genealogy, psychoanalysis, assemblage theory), this way of understanding rhetoric positions contingent "rules" that organize discourse as the structural precursor for any utterance whatsoever. Rhetoric in this last sense is not something one may learn to excel as a speaker or use to read a symbol. Existing "beyond" language and representation, it organizes discourse prior to the subject's encounter with it.

This crescendo from speech to onto-epistemology may seem vertiginously open-ended. These categories are intended as ways of delimiting how rhetoric may be defined, rather than what rhetoric must be, once and for all. They also illustrate how, when scholars profess to study rhetoric, the object of their criticism often slides to signifiers like *speech, matter, aesthetics,* or *affect*. In the sections below, I take each of these terms up as examples of how rhetoricians and other cultural critics have theorized the secret. Whether rhetoric is concerned with deceptive speech, absent representations, or an affective-aesthetic-material "beyond," the secret is there.

The Secret as Speech

One way to understand the secret's rhetoricity is through established frameworks of speech and public address. Delimited by a specific kind of situation, rhetoric is a spoken art of managing contingency that is necessary to ameliorate a given exigency, or "imperfection marked by urgency."[36] For rhetoricians, secrecy has been a long-standing rhetorical exigency in the United States. In 1988, rhetorical theorist Edwin Black argued that secrecy and disclosure were essential *topoi* of American democracy.[37] Black's pivotal theory of the second persona deployed a scathing analysis of the hateful, conspiracy-driven John Birch Society.[38] Elsewhere, he cited the World War II–era slogan "loose lips sink ships" as making "judicious secrecy . . . a civic obligation."[39] The phrase warned laboring Americans that military victory required keeping quiet about wartime work. More contemporary expressions like "snitches get stitches" and "see something say something" carry similar weight, urging resistance to—or compliance with—police surveillance.[40] As speech, rhetoric may be a pithy maxim or meticulously worded oration. Crafted to produce effects upon an audience, rhetoric communicates something about the secrecy culture in which we live: when to keep information hidden, when to spill the beans, and how each reinforces collective belonging and shared identity.

The framework of rhetoric-as-addressivity also describes the secret as a covert signification, whereby a speech carries distinct meanings for different audiences. Spoken aloud, the secret may be a double entendre or a dog whistle; it splits audiences into dupes and insiders to create community and sow division. Charles E. Morris III, for instance, recalls how FBI director J. Edgar Hoover (1924–72) made use of a "pink herring" to constitute a "silent, savvy, but discreet audience" in his tough-on-crime public address. Employing subtle "textual winks," Hoover affirmed his homosexuality to those who were in the know and whose silence, in turn, made his "duplicitous utterances appear legitimate."[41] His duped audiences failed to hear his speeches in this confessional register, keeping his sexual orientation a well-protected secret.

A related way of understanding the relationship between the secret and speech is as a style of spoken concealment, one designed to reveal nothing to a public audience. In 2010, Donovan Conley and William O. Saas suggested an addition to the stylistic triad of necessity, spectacle, and affection Robert Hariman proposed to account for the rhetorical artistry of imperial power. Adapting Joshua Gunn's formulation of occultatio, Conley and Saas set out to describe how speech could be stylized to produce suspicion through purposeful elision and silence: "We mean to refashion the classical figures of *praeteritio*,

---

36. Bitzer, "Rhetorical Situation," 6.
37. Black, "Secrecy and Disclosure."
38. Black, "Second Persona."
39. Black, *Rhetorical Questions*, 79.
40. Reeves, "'Lateral Surveillance.'"
41. Morris, "Hoover's Sex Crime Panic," 241.

paralepsis, parasiopesis, and occupation into a single rhetorical form—*occultatio*—that designates not merely a play of words but rather a set of habituated performances."[42] As an umbrella term for tropes that "name through coyly refusing to name," occultatio offered an account of the George W. Bush Administration's political style by attending to how the administration had undone decades of government transparency with executive orders and complicated legal language.[43] Taken together, rhetoricians who have theorized the secret as speech have argued that it is a way of codifying cultural norms and constituting collusive audiences, using double meanings and deflection tactics to obscure what a speaker does not wish to divulge.

The Material Secret

A second way rhetoric has engaged the secret is via theories of rhetoric's polymorphous materiality. After Robert L. Scott's pivotal 1967 essay, "On Viewing Rhetoric as Epistemic," rhetoricians began to conceive of rhetoric's relationship to an objective and external world in varied ways.[44] Most immediately, two competing positions arose: Rhetoric was either a constitutive-constructive force that created social reality through speech acts and language, or rhetoric was a way of assuming different perspectives relative to objective and context-invariant knowledge, a partial reflection of the world's inflexible material constants.[45] Stances on materiality subsequently branched and evolved into sub-disciplinary areas ranging from the rhetoric of inquiry[46] (later known as the rhetoric of science) to the tradition of rhetorical materialism, which coupled insights drawn from the linguistic turn with Marxist analyses of rhetoric.[47]

Getting to the bottom of what it means for rhetoric to be material often requires a certain amount of detective work. Rhetoric's materiality has described the recalcitrant objectivity that underwrites scientific inquiry; recurring historical patterns of class stratification; apparatuses that manufacture persuasion via cultural, legal, financial, and governing institutions; a

---

42. Gunn, *Modern Occult Rhetoric*; and Conley and Saas, "*Bush Administration's Rhetorical War,*" 332.
43. Conley and Saas, "*Bush Administration's Rhetorical War,*" 331.
44. Scott, "On Viewing Rhetoric as Epistemic."
45. Brummett, "Some Implications of 'Process' or 'Intersubjectivity'"; and Cherwitz and Hikins, "Rhetorical Perspectivism."
46. Railsback, "Beyond Rhetorical Relativism"; and Nelson, Megill, and McCloskey, "Rhetoric of Inquiry."
47. McGee, "Materialist's Conception of Rhetoric."

fractalated orientation to the agentic vibrancy of the nonhuman; and a theory of the signifier in which rhetoric pre-figures perceptions of the external world.[48] Drawing fragments from these sources, this book adopts a threefold understanding of the secret's materiality:

1. First, the "material" refers to *interlocking and systemic conditions of social harm*. The open and public character of these harms and the lack of recognition accorded to them enables such material realities as racism, gender discrimination, and colonialism to carry on in perpetuity and in plain sight. This understanding of materiality evokes an external, sensuous world as the source of speech and language, which, in turn, participates in the ordering of social reality.[49] By focusing on different faces of systemic social harm, this book prioritizes the role of an "external" material world that exercises undue influence over the rhetorical production of the secret as speech, language, and discourse.
2. Second, the "material" refers to *the signifier's materiality*, as theorized by Lacanian psychoanalysis and adjacent psychoanalytic traditions. The materiality of the signifier refers to the theory that the *form* of what is said—most traditionally, the form of the spoken or written sound-image, the sonic compression of air, or the graphic mark that establishes a connection with an external, material world—has a vibrant life independent of the content that it may carry at a given time. One example rooted in the psychoanalytic tradition concerns the retroactivity of the talking cure: Upon meeting a patient, the analyst cannot take the meaning of what they say at face value. This is because the signifiers a given patient (or analysand) uses carry singular meaning *for them alone*. What a patient means emerges as their signifiers repeat across different sessions, enabling the analyst to gauge their precise inflection. This signifier acquires depth and weight belatedly, over many sessions, and analysis consists in the analysand's dawning realization that their words carry a surplus weight; it is a secret kept by and from the subject who speaks it aloud. Abstracted from the session to the public and the social, this kind of weight is attached to words, phrases, images, and discourse that appear inconspicuous at first glance but have a precise meaning that is solidified through the related processes of repetition and retroaction.

---

48. A. Gross, "Rhetoric of Science *Is* Epistemic Rhetoric," 304–6; Cloud, "Materiality of Discourse as Oxymoron"; Greene, "Rhetorical Capital"; Stormer, "Rhetoric's Diverse Materiality"; and Biesecker, "Rhetorical Studies."

49. Cloud, *Reality Bites*, 22–23, 73–74.

3. Finally, the "material" refers to those forms I would call *tropes of the secret*. Both the material world of systemic oppressions and the materiality of the signifier are connected by recurring patterns of discourse, which I align with caesura, synecdoche, catachresis, irony, apophasis, paralepsis, and other rhetorical terms of art. Tropes, I argue, capture the recurrent patterns of speech, language, and discourse; they function as sub- and superjacent structures upholding systemic violence. That is why, for example, we can talk about the rhetorical form of dog whistles or acts of uncloseting perpetrated by the national security state as distinct and determinable. In each case, a new phrase, code word, or leak is fed into a tropological process that speaks the subject into existence.

Sovereign, Settler, Leaker, Lie conceives of materiality as objectively real and discursively produced. Material is the stuff of bodies and institutions as well as what comes to matter, rising to the level of salience or significance. It encompasses the rule-like formal-tropological patterning of discourse that turns code words, coloniality, and conspiracy into aspects of quotidian life.

This book is not the first to approach the secret as a multiply material rhetoric. In the tradition of rhetorical materialism, the secret is the discursive effect structure of a governing apparatus, "a complex field of practical reasoning that invents, circulates, and regulates public problems."[50] Rhetorically, the apparatus functions as a multipronged articulation of institutions and discourse. Its description exceeds a suspicious orientation to superstructure, which assumes that interests "are hidden, distorted, or revealed by that speaker's rhetorical choices."[51] Instead, the apparatus foregrounds rhetoric's emergence through conflict, competition, and contradiction, manifesting as a contingent articulation among nations, public institutions, technologies, and private entities.[52] Within this complex articulation, the secret is a lure for reasons similar to why Michel Foucault called visibility a "trap."[53] It is a category of rhetorical production that makes the governed subject into a subject who knows, or who airs the secret to feel seen and known. Of course, this kind of secret also has the effect of making oneself eminently visible, quantifiable, and governable.[54] For that reason, the governing apparatus enlists the secret as part of its biopolitical system of surveillance, which is designed to "police a

---

50. Greene, "Another Materialist Rhetoric," 22.
51. Greene, "Another Materialist Rhetoric," 38.
52. See also Hayes, *Violent Subjects*.
53. Foucault, *Discipline and Punish*, 200.
54. Greene, "Another Materialist Rhetoric," 31.

population, space, and/or object by articulating an ensemble of human technologies into a network of power to improve public welfare."[55]

Guttural, physical, and somatic, the signifier is the material support of language, and key to *Sovereign, Settler, Leaker, Lie*'s account of materiality.[56] As the articulation of sound and graphic image, the signifier is a mark divorced from representation and reference. If it is common sense to imagine speaking subjects as using signifiers to communicate their intended meanings, a Lacanian psychoanalytic perspective inverts this common sense: *You do not control the signifier, because the signifier controls you*. Thus assembled, materiality refers to "the materiality of the signifier" as well as to invariant social and systemic circumstances that have entrenched taken-for-granted ways of being in the world. This is the secret as material and discursive: It has real effects and achieves significance in ways that exceed conscious intent.

The Aesthetic Secret

A third avenue for theorizing the secret's rhetoricity is via aesthetics, which describes how articulations of form and sensation lend dynamics of concealment and revelation an affirmative presence. As Clare Birchall writes, an aesthetic frame can "interrupt the containment strategies of communicative capitalism/democracy" by refusing the typical tendency to think in terms of "the *hermeneutics* of the secret, which set up the secret as a problem to be solved through revelation and interpretation."[57] An aesthetic reframing instead seeks to situate "the secret 'itself' within a distributive regime" that makes "collectivities and subjectivities" available. Drawing upon Jacques Rancière's formulation of aesthetics as "the system of *a priori* forms determining what presents itself to sense experience," Birchall's explanation of the secret is one in which the hidden "resists cognitive judgment," is "available to all," and constitutes a continuum that includes revelation, the lost or rendered invisible, the open or half-secret, and finally, the secret, which resists both aestheticization and knowing.[58] Most notably, when examined in this register, criticism most often emerges through artistic interventions that offer "a different vantage point from which to consider a contemporary politics of the secret."[59]

---

55. Greene, "Another Materialist Rhetoric," 22.
56. Barthes, *Elements of Semiology*, 47.
57. Birchall, "Aesthetics of the Secret," 26.
58. Rancière, *Politics of Aesthetics*, 8; and Birchall, "Aesthetics of the Secret," 28–30. See also Birchall, *Radical Secrecy*, 119–46.
59. Birchall, "Aesthetics of the Secret," 30.

Sovereign, Settler, Leaker, Lie is most sympathetic to the aesthetic position's emphasis on the secret's pre-figurative forms, here rendered as a rhetorical tropology that anticipates and shapes the secret across a range of public and political contexts in the United States. Aesthetics, in other words, furnishes complex sites of resistance to and complicity with extractive surveillance regimes that rely on the secret as their core currency. Indeed, "artistic counter-archives" can display the dangers of transparency, reproduce dynamics of policing and interpellation, or something in between, agitating "from within or from the margins of the perceptible."[60] Or, to borrow Ronak K. Kapadia's formulation, aesthetics captures a dual capacity to represent surveillance power in ways that make the imperial state visible and safeguard its violent hegemony. Materializing a "paradox of transparency and opacity," such aesthetics characterize both "the gendered racialization of contemporary Arab Muslim and South Asian immigrant and refugee communities in the US" and the "insurgent aesthetic works which cast light on the manifold unseen and disembodying technologies of secrecy and terror that define the forever war."[61] The aesthetics of the secret, in other words, evoke a wicked push and pull between resistive "trespass, fugitivity, and ungovernability" and the fortification of ideological power vis-à-vis the warmongering state.

Beyond the reflexive and resistive work of art, the aesthetics of the secret may also function as a banal backdrop that lends a documentary quality to moments of revelation, generating visual, verbal, and physical surfaces that present themselves as commensurate with the real by "minimizing resistance or hesitation to the claims of transparency and authenticity."[62] Such aesthetics are ignorable because they are entwined with the everyday, wordlessly communicating that a secret is being kept or revealed. They furnish the viewer, reader, or listener with a sense of knowing that they are in the presence of the deliberately hidden, using familiar "cues and codes": the whir of photocopiers, animations of redaction and unredaction, the familiar *click* of a wiretap, plaintext language that turns into enciphered code (and vice versa). Architecturally, the aesthetics of the secret often announces itself through a style of bland neutrality characterized by open, empty spaces, congested bureaucracies, overstuffed filing cabinets, dim halogen lights, and brutalist concrete. Such features evoke what Bill Nichols describes as the "epistephilia" of documentary realism, an alluring "pleasure in knowing" that invites the viewer "to confront a topic, issue, situation, or event that bears the mark of the historically real."[63]

---

60. Monahan, *Crisis Vision*, 73.
61. Kapadia, *Insurgent Aesthetics*, 189.
62. Nichols, *Representing Reality*, 165.
63. Nichols, *Representing Reality*, 178.

A collection of forms that alludes to the fact of concealment, the aesthetics of the secret is highly ambivalent. Because it may be applied to any content, it equally lends the secret and the nonsecret the sensorial quality of documentary revelation.

The Affective Secret

Affect and the secret have long been silent partners. Affect is both a surplus of signification and an ephemeral sensation that precedes linguistic capture, for instance as a spoken emotion or a known feeling. One of Teresa Brennan's famous examples from the opening pages of *The Transmission of Affect* concerns the affective quality of a secret. Upon entering a room, she reports sensing an unsettling atmosphere and intuits that something is off.[64] Gregory Seigworth and Matthew Tiessen suggest that the secret is affective through and through, describing it as a hidden "pocket" of knowledge, a depersonalized "pool" of data, and a "plasma"-like dispersion of leaked information.[65] Even affect's rich companion terms, emotion and *pathos*, have achieved a secret-like status due to their historical subordination to reason, rationality, and *logos*.[66]

A related cadre of theories likens the secret to the assemblage, a threefold layering of content, form, and expression. As Gilles Deleuze and Félix Guattari assert in *A Thousand Plateaus*, "Every secret is a collective assemblage." Like Seigworth and Tiessen's pockets, pools, and plasma, the secret may be a hidden content (e.g., the envelope in Edgar Allan Poe's "The Purloined Letter"), a formal pattern of secretive behavior (e.g., the secret agent's identity management), and an uncontrolled viral expression (e.g., information leaks).[67] Assemblage theorists and affect scholars often characterize the secret affirmatively: Rather than a lack, absence, or lacuna, it takes shape as a surplus, an emergent quantity, or an effect greater than its cause. For instance, when Jennifer Row describes "the musical paradigm for . . . visible secrecy," it takes the form of a harmonic, a sound that exceeds the sum of its parts:

> A musical paradigm for this visible secrecy, or the open secret, might be the *overtone* or *harmonic* in music. When two instruments play notes in perfect harmony, an unexpected, higher extra pitch is generated. Importantly, the

---

64. Brennan, *Transmission of Affect*, 3.
65. Seigworth and Tiessen, "Mobile Affects," 54–70.
66. Gross, *Secret History of Emotion*.
67. Deleuze and Guattari, *Thousand Plateaus*, 286–87.

harmonic tone is not actually "played" by the musicians but produced as a supplementary product of the perfect matching of two notes. The supplementary sonic pleasure can only be grasped through perfected articulation. Instead of being sounded marginally or edged out, such desire is apparent, in plain sight, but only caught by the trained ear to the unexpected, lingering overtones.[68]

Per Row's account, the secret inhabits an affective register because it is a resonant production, not an intentional act of hiding. Even beyond its specifically musical presentations, the affective secret may be understood as a synthetic and supplementary third term, inseparable from the complementary relationships that birth it. Becoming aware of this secret puts an audience in contact with something beyond a reasoned intention: It marks a singular experience or encounter that defies capture by language.

Affective encounters with the secret can take many forms. Sometimes, affect breaks through speech as something that escapes the speaker's best intentions: "Human speech harbors an inherent riskiness—that one will say something she doesn't mean, that someone will misunderstand, that others will hear things in our voices that we would rather keep secret."[69] Such affective eruptions are secrets that defy the speaker's control, saying more than what they mean to communicate. Other times, the affective secret materializes as a fixed orientation to criticism or ideological baggage that the ordinary reader cannot easily shake. This understanding of affect informs both Eve Sedgwick's account of paranoid criticism, where every text is suspected of ideological concealment, and Jodi Dean's account of "publicity's secret," which argues that the digital age conditions us to become conspiracy theorists by promising that the hidden truth will always be a click away.[70] Whether understood as suspicion, paranoia, or conspiratorial rumination, affect anticipates the encounter with discourse. It may arise as the expectation that discourse conceals something that must be exposed or erupts when one reads between the lines or at the margins. "Trauma . . . is as much the name of a collection of rhetorical forms as it is an affective phenomenon," writes Lee Pierce. "That's not to say that trauma isn't real, but rather to say that it is both a form and a feeling."[71] To understand the secret as having affective dimensions means that the secret is always something more than an act of concealment. It is also a form and a feeling. Whether the secret betrays the existence of injustice

---

68. Row, *Queer Velocities*, 119.
69. Gunn, "On Speech and Public Release," 189.
70. Sedgwick, *Touching Feeling*, 123–51; and Dean, *Publicity's Secret*, 47–78.
71. Pierce, *Tense Times*, 49.

or facilitates protective intimacy, its affective dimensions texture how it is experienced, expressed, and shared.

The Secret as Rhetorical Form

A final way to frame the secret is as form. Forms can be many things. They can describe how a speaker purposefully arranges their oratory (e.g., exordium, narration, partition, confirmation, refutatio, peroration), a specific articulation of capital and class interest (e.g., as ideology or governmentality), the ritual presentation of stylistic features (mise-en-scène), or an affect that erupts "as duration, rhythm, absences, elisions, ruptures, gaps, and points of contradiction."[72] The vocabulary of form unifies an array of rhetorical objects and discourses. It can describe a "multiplicity of speakers, speeches, and occasions," the "antecedent genres" that guide a "rhetor toward a response consonant with situational demands," and the tropes that translate a crisis of white masculinity into allegories of innocence, sacrifice, and victimage.[73] Form, in other words, draws together such distinct domains as speech, materiality, aesthetics, and affect as having related rhetorical modulations.

As developed in this book, rhetoric is *the active and retroactive organization of discourse,* a mode of formal arrangement that enables audiences to observe the secret as an insistent, after-the-fact patterning of everyday life. Both generative and repressive, the secret happens to an audience who senses that they did not perceive the subtending order of things until too late. The name for this belatedly perceived "order" is trope. Trope, as Allison L. Rowland explains, is "a fundamental condition of language 'inexpungable from discourse' . . . that makes existents and their worlds."[74] With respect to the secret, tropes are not just deliberately chosen figures of speech or strategies of intentional concealment. They also lend political discourse suspense by leaving us waiting to find out the next thing that we did not already know. That is how the secret "makes existents and their worlds." Deeply hidden *in* discourse and a recurring effect *of* discourse, the secret's tropological patterns exceed the observational faculties of a person or public and condition them to expect future revelations.

Importantly, the secret, secrecy, and secrets are not interchangeable but comprise a field of related terms. Whereas secrecy is the historical, legal, and

---

72. Brinkema, *Forms of the Affects,* 37.
73. Griffin, "Rhetoric of Historical Movements," 184; Jamieson, "Antecedent Genre," 414; Gunn, "Death by Publicity"; and Sisco King, *Washed in Blood,* 12.
74. Rowland, *Zoetropes,* 5.

institutional ambiance that lends value to information whose public circulation is prohibited, secrets are those specific nuggets of hidden information that come in and out of focus at a given moment. My insistence on "the secret" signals its status as a third term: Stationed between generalized secrecy and particular secrets, it describes both a common rhetorical-tropological (material, affective, and aesthetic) structure and specific instances of discourse that lend the secret singularity and urgency. These features comprise "a constellation of substantive, stylistic, and situational characteristics" that illuminate the secret's iterability across time and context, within and beyond a given situation.[75]

Form lends the secret its power because it instills complacency and felt mastery in its audiences. Here, the reader may feel implicated at a paratextual level. A book that takes the secret as its object, such as this one, may make the reader feel they have unlocked something others cannot see, sense, or read. This self-congratulatory outlook is not a sign that we have mastered the secret, but a symptom of the secret's grip upon us. My hope is that by attending to the secret's distinct tropological forms, we may become more attuned to how seemingly novel moments of revelation are often patterned repetitions of the past. Even if we acknowledge that there is always a hidden content (or "beyond") to the secret, attending to its form reveals that there is just as often no secret at all.

Precis of the Chapters

Sovereign, Settler, Leaker, Lie tells two stories. The first concerns the epistemic, historical, and rhetorical precedents for the secret's prolonged crises. This story is laid out in chapters 1–2, which address the secret as an object and as a method, respectively. Chapter 1 ("The Secret Episteme") recounts a genealogy of the secret, arguing for it as a form of knowledge whose primary conceit is the concealment of knowledge. Emphasizing the secret's etymological, social, disciplinary, and popular transformation, this chapter foregrounds the etymologies, social practices, disciplines, and governmentality that multiplied the secret's force between the seventeenth and the twenty-first centuries. The threads begun in this chapter are woven through the later chapters, offering an epistemic context for contemporary presidential scandals, racist dog whistles, national security leaks, and settler-detective narratives.

---

75. K. Campbell and Jamieson, "Form and Genre," 401.

Chapter 2 ("The Secret in and of Discourse") furnishes the theoretical grounding for this book and introduces the phrasing "*in* and *of* discourse" to point to the secret's divided structure. After reviewing a key debate over rhetoric's materiality, I explore the rootedness of my prepositional reading strategy in the literary-philosophical traditions of "depth" and "surface" reading. The final section deconstructs this distinction, enlisting *trope* as a term that displaces the presumptive opposition between depth (i.e., the secret *in* discourse) and surface reading (i.e., *of* discourse). The final section introduces naming and retroaction as two functions of this dyadic reading strategy. These functions are a continuous thread in the remaining chapters, which repeat the secret with a difference vis-à-vis distinct names (i.e., scandal, dog whistle, leak, and detective) and tropes of retroactive signification.

The second story concerns the secret and its formal variations in the early twenty-first century and features the scandal, dog whistle, leaker, and detective. These chapters pair a specific variation of the secret with a distinct hegemonic context: the scandal centers sovereign power and white supremacy, the dog whistle foregrounds racism and anti-Blackness, the leaker features heterosexual and cisgender normativity, and the detective highlights the pervasiveness of settler colonialism in popular and political culture. My choice of contexts, cases, and sequence (i.e., as "first" or "last") are not intended to reproduce a dynamic in which hegemonic forms of systemic violence must compete for attention or page space. The placement of these chapters is instead intended to perform the intensification of the secret over time and across different domains of US political discourse. Beginning with George W. Bush and ending with Joseph R. Biden, these chapters are semi-chronological and seek to reflect on the secret's forms as precedent for Donald Trump's first and second presidential administrations.

Chapter 3 ("The Scandal") is a provisional starting point: the George W. Bush administration and its handling of the Valerie Plame Wilson Affair. Plame Wilson, a former counterproliferation expert, had her covert identity exposed by members of George W. Bush's executive branch following the American declaration of war in Iraq. Routed through repetition, caesura, and synecdoche, the multiyear unfolding of the story of the Bush administration's role in her exposure demonstrates how the use and abuse of the presidential secret set a clear precedent for subsequent Trump-era scandals.

Chapter 4 ("The Dog Whistle") returns us to the late twentieth-century story of Chicago-based community organizer Saul D. Alinsky, as told through his published works and the community leaders he organized. After covering his reception by Chicago's Woodlawn community in the 1960s and '70s, I turn to the appropriation of his name as a dog whistle used to attack President

Barack Obama. There, I highlight how catachresis and irony reshaped Alinsky's name into an expression of anti-Black racism, paying particular attention to Alinsky's uptake among the Tea Party, antiabortion advocates, and conservative pseudojournalists.

Chapter 5 ("The Leak") foregrounds the simultaneous rise to public prominence of several leakers—Julian Assange, Edward Snowden, Chelsea Manning, and Alan Turing. Information leaking is animated by carceral sexualities that blur the distinction between gender expression and the porous boundaries of a national security enclosure. The focal tropes of this chapter are megethos, a trope of enormity and excess, and apophasis, a trope of unstated taboo and omission. Whereas the former describes the empty promises of the masculine megaleaker, the latter accounts for the rhetorical crossover between the feminization of the closeted leaker and the discovery of national security vulnerabilities.

Chapter 6 ("The Detective") examines three organizing tropes of the "settler-detective," a frequent protagonist in neocolonial narratives. The function of this subject is to foster identifications with a detector of atrocities who disavows their known complicity with the violence they uncover. Drawing on analepsis (past), paralipsis (present), and prolepsis (future), I align each with a psychoanalytic register—the Symbolic, Imaginary, and Real—to demonstrate the settler-detective's pervasiveness across fictional and real renderings of contemporary, high-tech war.

The final chapter ("Twisted Endings") revisits the secret *in* and *of* discourse to discuss the emergent conspiracy culture of the twenty-first century. There, I trace the emergence of the Trump-era phrase "the deep state" as a conspiracy theory that has distorted the political signification of transparency. No longer a quest for accountability, Trump-era transparency has become a quest for retribution clothed in accusations of secrecy. This concluding example both describes the imperative to return to hidden figures and encourages the reader to again consider the secret's past trajectories as its forms return to haunt public life.

CHAPTER 1

The Secret Episteme

A Genealogy of Political Crisis

> If the genealogist refuses to extend his faith in metaphysics, if he listens to history, he finds that there is "something altogether different" behind things: not a timeless and essential secret, but the secret that they have no essence or that their essence was fabricated in a piecemeal fashion from alien forms.
> —Michel Foucault, "Nietzsche, Genealogy, History" (142)

The Secret as Episteme

The *secret episteme* is an invention of the premodern era that has intensified over many generations. Its focal knowledge object, the secret, carries overlapping and contradictory functions. At its most particular, the secret references historically specific articulations of violence, and knowledge about the concealment of knowledge. Over centuries, it has shaped theories of imperial sovereignty, emancipatory self-government, the enforcement of racial hierarchy, the production of specialized academic knowledge, and the cultivation of a vibrant and contradictory social paranoia. The nonlinear progression of the secret's discursive formations suggests that new iterations of the secret did not simply displace its earlier versions. Rather, the secret built upon its own foundations in ways that revised, recombined, and perpetuated its earliest forms. At its most general, the secret aspires to the status of a historical metadiscourse, describing a cyclical movement of history whereby the agencies of power continuously make and remake governing knowledge before consigning it to obscurity by design, necessity, or forgetting.[1]

This chapter offers a truncated genealogy of the secret, tracing its patterns of emergence and descent through a series of epistemic breaks,

---

1. Stormer, "Recursivity," 31.

governing contradictions, and discursive transformations. Naming the secret as a material-discursive object does not mean it has only a substantial, fixed, or positive definitional content. On the contrary, the secret is an evolving answer to historically specific problems of governance, knowledge, and identity.[2] To borrow Michel Foucault's phrasing, the secret allegedly uncovered by genealogy does not have an essential meaning or transcendental shape. It has not had the same function, use, or purpose for the different epochs, ruling regimes, and populations that have put it to work. "Assembled in piecemeal fashion from alien forms," the secret reveals the contingencies of history rather than the timeless character of an essential thing.[3] Glimpsed in this half-light, the secret generates recombinant and overlapping functions in service of power each time it is brought forth.

I note that my account of this episteme is "truncated" because it leaves certain scholarly and historical articulations of the secret un- or under-examined. Absent, for instance, is the thread that would link the secret to private finance capital, the academic professionalization of cryptography vis-à-vis computer science, the emergence of the military-industrial complex, and with it, the whole class of secrets associated with nuclear science. These connections run alongside this genealogy; they are extensively accounted for elsewhere and in greater detail than could be accomplished here.[4] Peter Galison's "Secrecy in Three Acts," for instance, takes us on a journey that links the 1917 Espionage Act, the 1946 Atomic Energy Act, and the 2001 Patriot Act. This chapter shares his sensibility that the secret was legally codified in ways to respond to distinct political, scientific, and infrastructural contingencies especially salient at the moment of their institutionalization.[5] Other archivally rich histories like Sarah E. Igo's *The Known Citizen* and Brian Hochman's *The Listeners* address concurrent developments that inform the political and media evolution of the secret as a rhetorical form in the twentieth and twenty-first centuries.[6] Despite the complementarity between that scholarship and this chapter, they receive only brief mention here because my object is the secret, whereas these other

---

2. Whereas the abstract noun *secrecy* accounts for an ambience (such as when hiddenness achieves the status of a public or institutional norm), the plural noun *secrets* describes instances of concealed knowledge. A noun phrase, "the secret" is the formal-rhetorical condition of possibility for both, toggling between the general "secrecy" and particular "secrets." Because all of these terms are used in this chapter (and throughout this book), they need to be read with the above-described inflections when the reader encounters them.

3. Foucault, "Nietzsche, Genealogy, History," 142.

4. See, for instance, Kahn, *Codebreakers*; Mayer, *Dark Money*; Matheson, *Desiring the Bomb*; and Wellerstein, *Restricted Data*.

5. Galison, "Secrecy in Three Acts."

6. Igo, *Known Citizen*; and Hochman, *Listeners*.

scholars place privacy or surveillance at the center of their respective historical investigations.

Below, I consider five transitional scenes of the secret's emergence. The opening section, "The Secret Before the Letter," recounts the premodern etymological field that lent the secret specificity in the sixteenth and seventeenth centuries. "The Secret Society" explains eighteenth- and nineteenth-century secret societies as resistance to sovereign power. "The Secret as Disciplinary Knowledge" and "The Secret as 'Civic' Paranoia" survey the secret in the nineteenth and twentieth centuries, attending to its academic codifications and its articulation to an anxious and insurgent white nationalism, respectively. "Transparency's Rise" discusses the late twentieth-century emergence of the injunction to disclose US government secrets.

This genealogy also provides crucial context for the different cases to be considered in this book. As discussed in the later chapters, the secret has become entangled with endlessly prolonged authoritarian spectacles (i.e., the scandal), reactionary forms of political organizing (i.e., the dog whistle), narrative commonplaces that make policing palatable (i.e., the detective), and paranoid affects that make it seem as though the enemy other is everywhere and nowhere, all at once (i.e., the leak and the conspiracy). As these examples suggest, the secret is not one concept, idea, or invention. It is a recurring feature of "the polycrisis," or what Ira J. Allen calls that "heap of crises that will be the end of one world, an accumulating and mutually amplifying collection of deferred costs that cannot be paid."[7] Amid this wide array of entangled crises, the secret is a signifier for one possible common denominator, a name for something that changes shape but whose mutations have staying power across generations. As the recurring fissure between the known and the unknown, the secret is a polymorphic object, one whose many forms converge and intensify at the horizon of a fleeting, crisis-driven political present.

---

7. I. Allen, *Panic Now?*, ix, 166. Allen's account of the polycrisis, drawn from Edgar Morin and Anne Brigitte Kern's *Homeland Earth*, differs in some respects from the genealogy presented here. His approach, rooted in the historical-material assemblage of capitalism, climate change, and colonialism (or CaCaCo), resonates with many of the episodes recounted in this and other chapters of this book. Allen also leaves open the possibility of other, related genealogies, as undertaken here. In his words, "an alternate, equally reasonable, genealogy would trace our planetary woes to the emergence of whiteness, colonialism, capitalism, and chattel slavery in the 16th century." As argued here, the secret is, in many ways, a rhetorical adhesive among the historical and material forces that Allen references, one that continuously disperses and reproduces political crisis.

The Secret Before the Letter

Before the word *secret* was coined, other signs codified the function and presentation of hidden knowledge. Hence "the secret before the letter": Something like the secret existed prior to the coining of *secret* as a sign of informational concealment. Two antecedents, *steganos* and *cryptos*, are retained in still-common terms like *steganography* and *cryptography* and were once exclusively associated with practices of hidden writing as strategies for managing sensitive wartime information.[8] The fifth-century Greek term *steganos* loosely signifies "cover-up" and captures the practice of veiling a message's presence by making it inconspicuous to onlookers. It allows a person to have a secret message in their presence but not know that it is concealed below or behind another surface. Herodotus, for instance, describes how the Persian double agent Histiaeus tattooed a message inciting rebellion against Darius I upon an unnamed enslaved person's head, allowing their hair to grow back before dispatching the message for delivery.[9] Likewise, the Greek exile Demaratus, who had gained Xerxes's favor, engraved his message warning the Lacedaemonians of an impending Persian attack "on a tablet, which he afterwards covered with wax: that, if intercepted, no characters might appear."[10] If steganos enables the writer to veil a message's presence in more and less dehumanizing ways, then *cryptos* references the concealment of a message's substance using a calculated transposition of words and characters, making writing illegible without the proper cipher.[11] Unlike steganos, cryptos is indifferent to whether the person who carries a secret knows they have sensitive information. Instead, it prevents the secret from being read, even when intercepted. Between 1069 and 1092 CE, poet and King Al Moetamid Ibn Abad employed cryptography by substituting the letters of a secret message with "an ordered set of bird names. Then, he would compose poetry where he would quote the names of birds obtained by the transformation of the message, in the same order."[12] Together, *steganos* and *cryptos* named the secret well before the common Latin root for the word *secret* came into being, offering a practical and poetic terminology for the arts of deliberate concealment.

Etymological relatives to the Roman imperial-era *secret* similarly named ways that common access to knowledge was restricted or prohibited. Terms

---

8. Kahn, *Codebreakers*; and Singh, *Code Book* (2002).
9. Herodotus, *Histories*, book 5, 420–21. See also Macrakis, *Prisoners, Lovers, and Spies*, 50.
10. Polyaenus, *Stratagems of War*, book 2, 80. See also Sheldon, *Ambush*.
11. Al-Kadi, "Origins of Cryptography," 97. See also Schwartz, "From Text to Technological Context."
12. Azizi and Azizi, "Arabic Cryptography in Morocco," 49.

like *mysterium, arcanum,* and *secretum* (from which the contemporary *secret* derives) described knowledge held apart from what was more widely known. Respectively, these terms denote (*mysterium*) "a dimension of the unknowable, a religious or cultic secret, the inscrutability of God, nature, or the human soul"; (*arca/arcanum*) a "chest, coffin, or treasury" that "is not available because it has been put under wraps and is thus removed (by lid or lock) from visibility or use"; and (*secretus/secretum*) "something that has to be sought out, found out . . . a relation between the known and the unknown, between those who suspect and those who are supposed to know."[13] Of these terms, the latter two, *arcanum* and *secretum*, have a clear rhetorical point of origin. Each initially referenced a physical object or material, which was then catachrestically transposed as a name for more ephemeral knowledge-management strategies. The sealed contents of the chest (*arca*) became information permanently sealed away; the seepage of matter through a sieve (*secretus*) became valuable information caught at the uppermost patrician echelons while its detritus flowed downward in a controlled manner for plebian consumption.

Most importantly, each term—*mysterium, arcanum, secretum*—denotes a well-documented art of governing. The phrase "mysteries of State" during the late Middle Ages accounts for the transfer of pastoral religious authority to a secular monarch, whereby the prince stepped "into the pontifical shoes of Pope and Bishop."[14] The phrase *arcanum imperii*, most often attributed to first-century Roman historian Publius Cornelius Tacitus, described proper princely conduct vis-à-vis "social techniques designed to hide a person's thoughts or intentions" while restricting "politically relevant knowledge to the smallest possible group."[15] Even the word *secretary*, derived from *secretum*, references a rich history of proxy communication, letter locking, and complex cryptography employed by aristocratic envoys in western Europe, who used clandestine missives to avoid the prying gaze of neighboring fiefs. The word *secret* is a distant cousin, signifying a sifting of the known from the unknown that reserves signs of value for only a governing few. In subsequent centuries, the secret continued to evolve with the advent of new technologies and social forms, each of which sought to preserve the narrow aperture through which sensitive information could be dammed from a wider public.

Michel Foucault briefly mentions the evolving lexical and practical aspects of the secret in his lectures on governmentality. He most overtly aligns it with the late sixteenth- and early seventeenth-century invention of *raison d'état*, a conceptual novelty of postfeudal European sovereignty and an "extraordinary

---

13. Horn, "Logics of Political Secrecy," 108–9.
14. Kantorowicz, "Mysteries of State," 67, quoted in Arendt, *On Revolution*, 146.
15. Horn, "Logics of Political Secrecy," 111.

re-investment" in Roman political thought. In his words, raison d'état was "an innovation and scandal" that sought to remedy "the problem of the management of states."[16] His sole discussion of the secret centers on statistics as one of the arts of governance whose publication was prohibited and describes the rationale for this censorship as rooted in Tacitus's *arcana imperii*. Statistics was not just an innovation that made for the expeditious management of populations; it was a "secret of state" locked away in fear that grave harm might otherwise come to the western European inheritors of imperial Rome's political doctrines.[17] As a category of governing reason, raison d'état captured a corpus of politically sensitive knowledge that specified "what is necessary and sufficient for the state to exist and maintain itself in its integrity if, in the event of it being damaged, it is necessary to re-establish this integrity."[18] When faced with the possibility of revolt and sedition, the architects of raison d'état specified the likely source of threats to the state's authority and, correspondingly, the proper conduct of princes, the economy, and the opinion of the governed.[19] The secret—understood as knowledge of the concealment of knowledge—had to remain secret because it betrayed the absence of an authority that guaranteed the law, which otherwise resided in the sovereign's duality as both a proxy for the divine and an embodiment of mortal law. Of course, the sixteenth- and seventeenth-century conceptions of raison d'état did not identically reproduce first-century ideas with perfect fidelity. These earlier ideas provided a framework and justification for incorporating the secret as essential to the arts of sovereign government while enabling new apertures for resistance to sovereign power.

The Secret Society

Secret societies in the eighteenth and nineteenth centuries brought forth new formulations of self-governance, set a precedent for enforcing white racial hierarchies in emerging democracies, and offered a key antecedent for the twentieth-century forms of administrative and bureaucratic secrecy.[20] Whereas eighteenth-century secret societies like the Freemasons were primarily legible

---

16. Foucault, *Security, Territory, Population*, 240–41.
17. Foucault, *Security, Territory, Population*, 275.
18. Foucault, *Security, Territory, Population*, 257–58.
19. Foucault, *Security, Territory, Population*, 267–73.
20. On the European reemergence of Freemasonry in the eighteenth century, see also Hamill, *History of English Freemasonry*; Stevenson, *Origins of Freemasonry*; and Jacob, *Living the Enlightenment*.

in terms of "forms of religious dissidence," those in the nineteenth century were less populated by "revolutionary Puritans" than by "revolutionary philosophes" whose "secular political religious agenda" was the embodiment of "the Enlightenment fanaticized."[21] The nineteenth-century societies "[took] on clearer political objectives—plots, political or social revolutions—but always with an aspect of the pursuit of a different form of conduct: to be led differently, by other men, and towards other objectives than those proposed by the apparent and visible official governmentality of society."[22]

The secret society is vital to Jürgen Habermas's theory of the bourgeois public sphere because, at least in his famous late twentieth-century account, it presaged self-governance as an alternative to princely rule. Such societies, he maintains, provided crucial resources for later revolutionary forms of rational-critical deliberation.[23] Citing Immanuel Kant, he argues that eighteenth-century Masonic lodges embraced "the 'popular will that has its source in reason'; for laws empirically had their origin in the 'public agreement' of the public engaged in critical debate."[24] Even as secret societies constructed protective microcosmoses of Enlightenment rationality and laboratories of self-governance, they also embraced *arcana* in a manner that strangely resembled the secret kept by both the sovereign and the Church. However, even as they were organized around hermetically sealed knowledge, rituals, and artifacts, these societies adopted an internal dynamic that eschewed sovereign and ecclesiastic models of governing hierarchy.[25] "Bound together through the secret" and imbued "with the aura of the unknown," Freemasons created a state within and beyond the state, which threatened the sovereign's policing power precisely because it was within and beyond their capacity to rule. Consider, for instance, Margaret C. Jacob's account of those arrested during a 1744 raid on a lodge by the Parisian police, who were particularly "alarmed" by the fact that the members, who represented all manner of class strata, took on roles such as "legislators" and "constitution-makers."[26]

> The problem was that some of the men present were of the most ordinary status: a lapidary (or jeweler), a minor official of the poultry market, a gardener, a tapestry merchant, worse still, an actor in the Comédie Italienne, and perhaps most remarkable of all, "a Negro who serves as a trumpeter in

---

21. Jacob, *Living the Enlightenment*, 10.
22. Foucault, *Security, Territory, Population*, 199.
23. Habermas, *Structural Transformation*, 35.
24. Habermas, *Structural Transformation*, 107.
25. Dean, *Publicity's Secret*, 25–26. See also Gunn, "Death by Publicity," 249–51.
26. Jacob, *Living the Enlightenment*, 3–4.

the King's Guard." There were also a wine merchant as master of the lodge, army officers, a secretary to a nobleman, three Benedictine priests, a valet at court, a "gentleman," a "bourgeois," a surgeon; and, on the raid conducted in June 1744, four women, unmarried, were also rounded up. Such a wide range of occupations and status conforms to other masonic records from the 1730s. In them we find accountants, a black musketeer, merchants, and an official of a provincial tax court who was also a prominent champagne merchant.[27]

Secret societies mimicked and undermined state authority because their law- and constitution-making powers were enacted by a constituency that defied the representational hierarchies of sovereign governance. In doing so, they also fostered a mode of self-organization that appeared to be under the law's authority and at the same level as the law.[28] Whereas the lodge system's secrecy countered "the representational power of the sovereign with its own mysterious authority," their use of public reason was increasingly legible as the manifestation of an insurrectionary political will that threatened the princely state from within.[29]

In the United States, the Masonic tradition is often traced to the premier Grand Lodge of England in 1717 and Freemasonry's subsequent spread in pre–Revolutionary War America.[30] Sometimes credited to Benjamin Franklin, the migration of Masonic secret societies into the early United States "helped provincial elites separate themselves from the common people and build solidarity in a time of often bitter factionalism."[31] During the Revolutionary period, "lesser men appropriated the fraternity, spreading it to inland leaders as well as Continental army officers." Both European and American traditions of Freemasonry sought moral and philosophical grounding by falsely, factiously,

---

27. Jacob, *Living the Enlightenment*, 4.

28. The characteristic duality of the secret society (i.e., as "within" and "apart" from governance) mirrors the characteristic duality of the sovereign "as a public person and . . . as a private person," which, by the account of John of Salisbury in 1159, is "in the office itself." This distinction specifically refers to the prince's status as both "under the law, *legibus alligatus*," and "above the law, *legibus solutus*." Kantorowicz, *King's Two Bodies*, 96.

29. Dean, *Publicity's Secret*, 25–26.

30. Walker, *Noble Fight*, vii; Hackett, *That Religion in Which All Men Agree*, 23; Bullock, *Revolutionary Brotherhood*, 9–49.

31. Although Jacob attributes the American variant of Freemasonry to Benjamin Franklin, Bullock notes the contested nature of Franklin's leadership over the Philadelphia Freemasons. For instance, in the three decades that Franklin lived abroad, his Masonic successors labeled themselves "ancient" (as opposed to Franklin's preferred London-derived naming of the organization as "modern") and refused to attend Franklin's 1790 funeral. Jacob, *Living the Enlightenment*, 158; Bullock, *Revolutionary Brotherhood*, 2, 85.

and retroactively attributing strong pro-Masonic sentiments to Enlightenment thinkers like Locke, Voltaire, and Rousseau:[32]

> The revival of Locke's name in masonic circles increasingly during the 1770s signals a willingness to invoke an author associated with republican conspiracy and the justification of revolution, as his *Two Treatises of Government* (1690) was believed to have offered. Masonic writers asserted, on the basis of weak, if not spurious evidence, that Locke had been initiated as a freemason and "that the favourable opinion this philosopher conceived of the society of masons before his admission, was sufficiently confirmed after his initiation."[33]

There was also an extensive political and academic backlash to masonry, including accusations that Freemasons had not just anticipated but orchestrated the French Revolution.[34] Additionally, "with the significant exception of women's participation" in 1770s France, such societies were significantly less egalitarian and more exclusionary than is often presumed, to the point that "some lodges were almost authoritarian in their governance."[35]

Despite accounts that European Freemasons "tended to be more tolerant or at least remained indifferent" with respect to race, gender, political affiliation, and social status, US colonial and post-Revolutionary secret societies were at least as strongly prohibitive with respect to their membership. According to Cécile Révauger, "race was obviously an acute problem in the United States and in Caribbean countries," as white colonial-era lodges explicitly prohibited Black membership.[36] For that reason, we may read the tradition of Black Freemasonry as concomitant with and a counterpart to the establishment of white Masonic lodges in the United States. The former exemplifies characteristic practices of an "enclave public sphere," a space that maintained "safe spaces, hidden communication networks, and group memory to guard against unwanted publicity of the group's true opinions, ideas, and tactics for survival."[37]

The creation of Black lodges in the United States is typically attributed to Prince Hall, formerly enslaved founder of the Prince Hall African Lodge. Hall

---

32. Jacob, *Living the Enlightenment*, 16, 96, 158; and Bullock, *Revolutionary Brotherhood*, 85, 141.
33. Jacob, *Living the Enlightenment*, 63–64.
34. Jacob, *Living the Enlightenment*, 213–14.
35. Burke and Jacob, "French Freemasonry"; and Jacob, *Living the Enlightenment*, 17–19.
36. Révauger, "Freemasonry and Blacks," 422; and Jacob, *Living the Enlightenment*, 4, 29.
37. Squires, "Rethinking the Black Public Sphere," 458.

initially had his request to establish an inaugural charter for Black Freemasons in the United States denied by Massachusetts authorities on allegedly procedural grounds. As Joanna Brooks explains, "Many claimed that Prince Hall's 1775 initiation into an Irish Military Lodge was invalid because Irish Freemasonry itself was illegitimate. In the 1720s, working-class Irish masons living in London were barred from entry to the city's more aristocratic lodges."[38] Nonetheless, his lodge was issued a provisional permit from an Irish military lodge in 1775, received an official charter from the Grand Lodge of England in 1787, and was cut off from the British lodge system in 1827 before finally being reacknowledged by British Masonic authorities in 1996.[39] Corey D. B. Walker cites the following passage from Rev. William H. Grimshaw regarding the charter for African Lodge No. 459:

> Prince Hall, then twenty-seven years of age, wended his way to the quarters of General Gage, on Copp's Hill, Boston Harbor, Mass. The purpose of his visit was the insatiable desire to become a Mason. He feared nothing, not even in the enemy's camp, but with a firm trust in God, knocked and the door of Masonry was opened to him—thus his eyes beheld for the first time the form and beauty of a military Lodge. In that traveling British Lodge, No. 58, before the first blood had flowed upon the green grass at Lexington, he received the light of Masonry, and was raised to the sublime degree of Master Mason—the first one of African descent who had been initiated into the order in the American Colonies.[40]

The Prince Hall tradition cultivated notions of universal brotherhood that contested the Jeffersonian view "of the African as essentially alien."[41] Hall's lodge also leveraged "its Masonic connections to political purposes," submitting petitions for emancipation and transit to Africa.[42] Within this "enclave of black self-governance," the secret was crucial to communication among brothers, as members employed signal gestures that would oblige "fellow Masons

---

38. Brooks, "Prince Hall, Freemasonry, and Genealogy," 199–200. See also Bullock, *Revolutionary Brotherhood*, 159; Dumenil, *Freemasonry and American Culture*, 10; Muraskin, *Prince Hall Freemasonry*; and Williams, *Black Freemasonry*.
39. Révauger, "Freemasonry and Blacks," 425; Brooks, "Prince Hall, Freemasonry, and Genealogy," 199; Kantrowitz, "African American Freemasonry," 1005–6; and Walker, *Noble Fight*, viii.
40. Walker, *Noble Fight*, 48.
41. Brooks, "Prince Hall, Freemasonry, and Genealogy," 199.
42. Brooks, "Prince Hall, Freemasonry, and Genealogy," 199–200.

to come to the aid of a 'Brother.'"[43] Such forms were reinforced by American segregation, as other, similarly named organizations called "African Societies" were populated exclusively by "anti-slavery whites."[44] Hall's African Lodge also distinguished the secret at its core from that of white Freemasons by laying claim to a more authentic connection to other lodges' conventional *arcana*, including the use of "signs and tokens" that would enable members to recognize one another as belonging to the same fraternal organization.

> Masons worldwide claimed that their ritual practices—secrecy, ceremony, hierarchy—derived from an ancient Egyptian order, a history to which the members of the African Lodge could make a double claim. The occluded or "occult" character of this history lent itself to active speculation and creative elaboration. Thus, the Egyptian "roots" of the Order came to be a recognized and celebrated dimension of Prince Hall Freemasonry.[45]

Although there are documented instances of antebellum allyship between white and Black masons, secret societies overwhelmingly made whiteness a mandatory requirement for membership.[46] Whereas "black Masonic intellectuals considered Freemasonry a powerful weapon against racial caste," they ran against significant resistance as "white Masonic bodies repeatedly labeled black Masons 'counterfeit' or 'clandestine,' 'irregular' and 'fraudulent.'"[47] During the late nineteenth-century period of Reconstruction, other phrases like "social equality" were coded to obliquely reference Black sexual monstrosity, constructing "a shibboleth of white supremacy" to reject appeals originating from Black Masons.[48] Black lodges in the tradition of Prince Hall were therefore enclaves that fulfilled a range of protective, social, and financial functions for their members. As W. E. B. Du Bois wrote in 1899:

> [From] general observation and the available figures, it seems fairly certain that at least four thousand Negroes belong to secret orders, and that these orders annually collect at least $25,000, part of which is paid out in sick and death benefits, and part invested. . . . The function of the secret society is partly social intercourse and partly insurance. They furnish pastime

---

43. Brooks, "Prince Hall, Freemasonry, and Genealogy," 200. See also Brooks, "Early American Public Sphere"; Dunbar, "Hidden in Plain Sight."
44. Brooks, "Prince Hall, Freemasonry, and Genealogy," 201.
45. Brooks, "Prince Hall, Freemasonry, and Genealogy," 201.
46. Hernandez, *Ku Klux Klan and Freemasonry*, 38–39.
47. Kantrowitz, "African American Freemasonry," 1014–15.
48. Kantrowitz, "African American Freemasonry," 1025.

from the monotony of work, a field for ambition and intrigue, a chance for parade, and insurance against misfortune. Next to the church they are the most popular organizations among Negroes.[49]

In other words, Black Masons' use of the secret went beyond the use of signs and tokens. To offer some measure of protection from ubiquitous white supremacy, these organizations created and preserved esoteric histories, fostered social and professional connections, and offered their members a modicum of financial security.

Historians and rhetorical scholars often mark the tipping point of white secret societies' decline with a specific moment: a groundswell of hostile popular opinion known as the anti-Masonic movement.[50] From 1826 until approximately 1838, the anti-Masonic movement grew in popularity due to a scandal known as the William Morgan affair, in which Morgan, a white bricklayer and former member of a Batavia, New York, lodge, had threatened to publicize his order's secrets.[51] He was imprisoned on a false charge, kidnapped to Rochester, and transported to an abandoned fort above Niagara Falls, "where, from that moment, all historical trace of him vanishes."[52] Morgan's disappearance inaugurated a series of statewide, citizen-led committees in Massachusetts, Connecticut, Michigan, and Vermont that sought to unmask Freemasons generally as demonic seeds of corruption.[53] Well after the scandal, "anti-masonic sentiment persisted longer, effectively blocking the fraternity's growth for many years" while intensifying the demand for secret-keeping among Masonic organizations.[54] By the 1840s, chapters in newly settled states like Indiana "began to use financial and administrative management practices" to preserve these organizations' longevity by binding their wealth to emergent forms of finance capital.[55] However, public memory of the Morgan scandal remained strong.[56] As Hackett explains, mistrust of masons evolved into an anti-Christian conspiracy theory: "Seen from the perspective of Anti-Masonry . . . the

---

49. Du Bois and Eaton, *Philadelphia Negro*, 224, quoted in Putnam, *Bowling Alone*, 391.
50. Hofstadter, *Paranoid Style in American Politics*, 14–18. See also Hackett, *That Religion in Which All Men Agree*, 112–13; Bullock, *Revolutionary Brotherhood*, 277–79; Dumenil, *Freemasonry and American Culture*, 5–7; and D. Davis, *Fear of Conspiracy*, 74.
51. Bullock, *Revolutionary Brotherhood*, 277.
52. Griffin, "Antimasonic Movement," 148.
53. Bullock, *Revolutionary Brotherhood*, 281.
54. Dumenil, *Freemasonry and American Culture*, 7.
55. Popielarz, "Freemasonry and Finance Capitalism," 658–59.
56. Smith, "Voice from the Past," 154–55.

brotherhood was a secret cabal of politically connected, secularizing, affluent men deeply threatening to the common man and evangelical Christianity."[57]

The more gradual twentieth-century decline in Masonic membership is complex, having multiple causes that include significant transformations in American civil society. Despite the organization's efforts at reinvention in the 1920s, "it suffered heavy losses during the Depression, as many men dropped out or were suspended and few new members joined."[58] Its conventional function of expressing "the religious and moral values of the Victorian middle class" no longer served the same social function.[59] The surge in fraternal membership before and after World War I could not be sustained, and radical increases in the size of the middle class after World War II traded off with membership in Masonic lodges as alternate modes of bourgeois socialization displaced such societies.[60] By the end of the twentieth century, the popularization of masons in film and television put increased pressure upon lodges to publicize their rituals, infelicitously leading to the further diminishment of their ranks. The inversely proportional relationship between Masons' increasing penchant for disclosing their *arcana* and their declining membership leads Joshua Gunn to theorize "the inexhaustible secret": "the formal and relational dimensions of that which brings a public into being" in which the indefinite preservation of broadly social-democratic *arcana imperii* "generates the curiosity that leads to its continued existence."[61] Without the secret, there was neither pull nor purpose to sustain the Masonic publics in the way they had once existed.

The Secret as Discipline

In the last decade of the nineteenth century, Georg Simmel and Sigmund Freud independently situated the secret at the core of the then-emerging disciplines of sociology and psychology. However, like many white Masonic societies, Simmel and Freud centered the perspectives, experiences, and institutions of white, affluent, and cisgender male Europeans while drawing on evolutionary myths that situated Indigenous tribalism as a precursor to Westerners' rational and civilized behavior. For instance, Freud's anthropology of taboo—which famously culminates with his myth of the primal horde—drew

---

57. Hackett, *That Religion in Which All Men Agree*, 111.
58. Dumenil, *Freemasonry and American Culture*, 218.
59. Dumenil, *Freemasonry and American Culture*, 219.
60. Putnam, *Bowling Alone*, 388–91.
61. Gunn, "Death by Publicity," 253–61.

upon quasi-ethnographic accounts of Indigenous groups to theorize the psychic foundations of the law-abiding ego.[62] Simmel took a similar stance when echoing eugenicist Gustave Le Bon's conception of crowds, both of them maintaining that collective consciousness drew forth humans' lowest instincts and most primitive being.[63] Both Freud and Simmel leveraged the secret that civilized humans—unconsciously or collectively—retained "primitive" characteristics, and thereby advanced their respective approaches to the errors of speech and socialization, contrasting the early twentieth-century stage of civilization with the existence of global subjects who were de facto presumed developmentally stunted.[64] A key divergence between the early social and psychological sciences concerned their respective emphases on social space or psychological time. Whereas Simmel grounded his theories in notions of social spaces external to the individual subject, Freud described the secret via the strange temporality of the subject's psychic interior, recounting quasi-fictional ancestral myths and memories of trauma to explain his psychoanalytic technique.

Simmel opens "The Sociology of Secrecy and of Secret Societies" by explaining how all relationships are textured by the partial knowledge that an individual has of their social other. It reflected upon not only the past century and a half of Freemasonry but also the marketplace and the Church, such that the relationships described included those between Mason and nonmember, customer and merchant, clergy and lay public.[65] Often arguing that discrete spaces were a determinant of social behavior, Simmel's writings evoked a dynamic whereby an individual would presume to know something about their social others based on characteristics that the latter revealed "through word and deed."[66] One's conscious sense of a mutually veiled presence is, Simmel writes, "the first precondition of having anything to do with another." Elsewhere, he describes a prototypical subject he calls "the stranger," who, because they are "near and far at the same time," embodies the limit upon mutual knowledge.[67] Across the twentieth century, Simmel's theories found continuous uptake among linguistic pragmatists, phenomenologists, sociologists, and analytic philosophers.[68] Erving Goffman, for instance, cites Simmel's

---

62. Freud, *Totem and Taboo*, 176–77. See also Khanna, *Dark Continents*.
63. Simmel, "Stranger," 32. See also Le Bon, *Crowd*.
64. In similar fashion, Freud claimed that verbal tics or parapraxes—errors of speech—effected a separation between repressed unconscious content and the conscious mind. Simmel, "Sociology of Secrets," 441–43; Freud, *Psychopathology of Everyday Life*; and Freud, "Parapraxes."
65. Simmel, "Sociology of Secrets," 471, 479.
66. Simmel, "Sociology of Secrets," 441.
67. Simmel, "Stranger"; Scaff, "Simmel on Time," 6.
68. M. Davis, "Simmel and Goffman," 370; and Blank, "Two Schools for Secrecy," 67.

spatial formula of the "ideal sphere that lies around every human being" to describe the social distance that separates performers from their audiences.[69] Goffman's Simmel-informed work has, in turn, been widely taken up as both a theoretical foundation for interpersonal communication and even as a practical primer for interrogations, which also appear in Goffman's own work as a "background, topic, and resource" for social analysis.[70]

Conversely, for Freud, the secret described an inaccessible element coextensive with the unconscious, repressed memory, and the inaccessible "navel" of the dream.[71] This inscrutable quantity could only be partially reconstructed through a retroactive temporal sequence. In *The Interpretation of Dreams*, for instance, Freud explains that secrets abide by the rule of *Nachträglichkeit* (frequently translated as "retroaction," "belatedness," "afterwardsness," or "deferred effect"). This temporality makes the dreamwork into a "rebus" or puzzle of symbols whose meanings can only be partially apprehended after the fact, while the truly repressed knot of the dream could not be recovered:

> Suppose I have a picture-puzzle, a rebus, before me: a house with a boat on its roof, then a single letter of the alphabet, then a running figure with his head conjured away, and the like. Now I could fall into the trap of objecting that this combination and its constituent parts are nonsense. . . . The dream is a picture-puzzle of this kind, and our predecessors in the field of dream-interpretation made the mistake of judging the rebus as if it were a pictorial composition. As such, it seemed to them to have no meaning or value.[72]

Freud departed from predecessor traditions of dream interpretation by claiming that the encrypted symbols encountered in dreams were only retroactively available to the analyst or the dreamer and required decipherment to elicit their hidden signification. Although one could describe and know denotatively what such symbols were, their meaning would remain opaque. Analysis consisted in the reflective work of elaborating how dreamt symbols were protective substitutes for traumatic, real-world referents in the patient's life (i.e., displacement) and the subtending logic that linked the symbols of the

---

69. Goffman, *Presentation of Self*, 69.

70. Goffman, *Strategic Interaction*, 34, 52; Petronio, *Boundaries of Privacy*, 189; and Jaworski, *Goffman and the Cold War*, 127.

71. "The best-interpreted dreams often have a passage that has to be left in the dark, because we notice in the course of interpretation that a knot of dream-thoughts shows itself just there, refusing to be unravelled, but also making no further contribution to the dream content. This is the dream's navel, and the place beneath which lies the Unknown." Freud, *Interpretation of Dreams*, 341.

72. Freud, *Interpretation of Dreams*, 211–12.

dreamwork together (i.e., condensation). Freud's interpretive methods were taken up by subsequent traditions of psychoanalysis, such as object relations theory and Lacanian linguistics.[73] Lacan's revision of Freud is especially noteworthy for the way that he, in a Simmelesque gesture, situates the unconscious on the subject's outside, or as a function of the autonomously circulating signifiers beyond the subject's psychic interior or their cognitive control.[74] Per his "graph of desire," any given signifier acquires its signification retroactively, much as the significance of a dream could only be apprehended after the fact.[75] In an analytic session, this means that the analyst attends to how certain signifiers repeat in search of what the analysand (i.e., patient) is "aiming at in behavior that could be strange even to himself."[76] Rather than taking for granted that both analyst and analysand know and share the meaning of what is spoken, the signifier's recursion within and across sessions enables the analyst to take stock of the analysand's singular attachments, which would otherwise go unobserved as they are enunciated, remaining secret from the patient even as they speak them aloud. It is only in retrospect that the meaning the analysand aims for—a significance entirely separate from literal reference or denotation—becomes apparent to either party.

At approximately the same moment as Lacan's writing, Freud's writings were themselves retroactively re-signified as instruments of racist US governance, allowing American legislators to adopt the stance of a suspicious

---

73. Winnicott, "Communicating and Not Communicating"; Abraham and Torok, *Wolf Man's Magic Word*; and Abraham and Torok, "Topography of Reality."

74. "The unconscious is on the outside" is a widely cited but rarely attributed phrase associated with Lacanian psychoanalysis. However, Jacques Lacan makes many statements that resemble this one. In *Écrits*, for instance, he emphasizes how the purloined letter of Poe's story is significant for its circulation out in the diegetic world rather than for its "inner" contents, which remain unknown to the reader ("Seminar on the 'Purloined Letter,'" 43). He also writes that "the fact that the symbolic is located outside of man is the very notion of the unconscious" ("Situation of Psychoanalysis," 392). Elsewhere, he writes of the death drive: "To say that this mortal meaning reveals in speech a center that is outside of language is more than a metaphor—it manifests a structure" ("Function and Field," 263). As taken up by other adherents of the Lacanian tradition, "the unconscious is on the outside" can also be specified in at least five additional ways: (1) The unconscious so often presumed "inside" the subject of the psyche is, in fact, routinely exteriorized by its discourse. (2) There is no "discourse outside of discourse" available to cognition that can approximate the total structure of language or the unconscious (Fink, *Lacan to the Letter*, 123). (3) The structural position of the Other of discourse is "outside" a given social and symbolic order. (4) The relation of "extimacy" (as opposed to *intimacy*) is determinative of the subject's relationship to itself, and "causes the subject to appear to itself as culpable, as guilty of hiding something" (Copjec, *Read My Desire*, 27). (5) Psychoanalytic topologies are generally concerned with the play of outside and inside, of exteriors that appear in interior spaces and of interiors that are transformed into exteriors (Brinkema, *Forms of the Affects*, 24).

75. Lacan, "Subversion of the Subject," 681–82.
76. Miller, "Much Ado About What?," 22.

analyst who mistrusted their analysand's own account of their experience. A key text in this regard is the 1965 Moynihan Report, which held racist caricatures of Black mothers and fathers responsible for systemic poverty and education deficits in the wake of post–Civil War Reconstruction.[77] Drawing heavily on Freudian Oedipal motifs, the Report held Black families responsible for having produced a "tangle of pathologies" that entrenched Black poverty, which persisted because of a lack of "training and skills." Mid-century psychoanalysis was, in other words, weaponized in service of a bootstrapping rhetoric that proclaimed Black Americans unable to know (how to help) themselves, which in turn offered a key rationale for refusing reparations as a viable policy solution to debilitating racial and economic inequality.

Examples of resistance to twentieth-century social and psychological theories of the secret might be found in the postcolonial critiques leveraged by Martinique contemporaries Frantz Fanon and Édouard Glissant. Although Simmel and Freud are not consistent foils for their respective writings, Fanon regularly criticized European-centric psychoanalysis (if not also Freud himself), while Glissant's *Poetics of Relation* challenged the normative and rational presumptions associated with colonial governance, specifically taking issue with the normalization of subjective self-exposure as a base criterion for social interaction. Fanon and Glissant also centered the secret when theorizing the experiences and resistance practices of historically colonized African and Afro-Caribbean communities. Fanon's references to the secret in the 1952 *Black Skin, White Masks* include the introvert's "secret area of bitter, disillusioned resentments," primitivist characterizations of African "magico-social structure" as a secret society, and the suspicion directed at Fanon by a white professor after he broke free of the "acquisitive relation" that had defined their intellectual exchange.[78] Fanon, a practicing psychiatrist, criticized the individual-focused Freudian paradigm while also borrowing the language of psychotherapy as a tool for dismantling the master's house. For instance, he diagnosed the "juxtaposition of the white and black races" as having created "a massive psycho-existential complex," which he aimed to destroy through his analyses.[79] Correspondingly, Glissant transcoded notions of the secret by enlisting *opacity* as his focal term. Opacity reversed the conventional valences of the secret as a tool for policing, touting opacity as the "self-defense" of postcolonial subjects "against both the standardization of globalization and the transparency-seeking epistemologies of the West and its historic functionaries:

---

77. Moynihan, *Negro Family*; Hill Collins, "Comparison of Two Works"; and Klug, "Moynihan Report Resurrected."
78. Fanon, *Black Skin, White Masks*, 73, 79, 125–26, 128.
79. Fanon, *Black Skin, White Masks*, 13–14.

anthropologists, philosophers, diplomats, aid workers, and so on."[80] As Saidiya Hartman explains of African diasporic identity, "the search for roots can only exacerbate one's sense of being estranged, intensify the exilic consciousness, and confirm the impossibility of reversion."[81] A similar "obsession with discovering what lies at the bottom of natures" prompts Édouard Glissant to posit *the right to opacity*, which captures "that which protects the Diverse" by refusing the categorization of subjects, bodies, cultures, and communities into observable, quantifiable, and more easily governable entities.[82] The traditions of "undersight" exemplified by Fanon and Glissant thus furnished theoretical, practical, and poetic modes of resistance to settler-colonial and white supremacist "oversight," assembling resistive potentialities out of the secret "tactics employed to render one's self out of sight . . . and strategies used in the flight to freedom from slavery."[83]

Within the imperial-colonial context of the United States, the sociological and psychological traditions of the secret eventually converged in the administrative bureaucracy, which was infused with more and less veiled forms of anti-Blackness. As described by Woodrow Wilson in 1887, the study of public administration was a practical social science concerned with the optimal hierarchy of organizations, institutions, and governments.[84] The unstated though ever-present aim of Wilsonian administration was white racial purity. In his writings on Reconstruction, for instance, Wilson described those who had newly been freed as "looking for pleasure and gratuitous fortune," while applauding the white patrols who "took the law into their own hands" and did "by secret and association what they could not do in avowed parties."[85] Upon ascending to the presidency in 1913, Wilson made good on the tacit promise of his writings, firing most Black government appointees of the Taft administration while providing pretext for white officials to report that they could not possibly work with Black colleagues or under their supervision.[86] Under the Wilson presidency, the Post Office, Navy, and Treasury likewise underwent restructuring to enforce segregationist policies under the pretense of protecting white women from Black men.[87] It was not until Franklin D. Roosevelt's 1941 Executive Order 8802 that US presidential administrations

---

80. B. Davis, "Glissant's Right to Opacity," 65.
81. Hartman, "Time of Slavery," 766.
82. Glissant, *Poetics of Relation*, 62, 189–90. Cited in Davis, "Glissant's Right to Opacity," 65. See also Monahan, *Crisis Vision*, 41, 143.
83. Browne, *Dark Matters*, 21–22. See also K. Ross, "White Oversight," 46–71.
84. Wilson, *Study of Public Administration*.
85. Skowronek, "Reassociation of Ideas and Purposes," 391.
86. McLaughlin Green, *Secret City*, 171. See also Benbow, "Birth of a Quotation."
87. McLaughlin Green, *Secret City*, 172–73.

sought to "directly address racial discrimination in the workplace," gathering attention from "at least three federal commissions" and "individual agencies" that were tasked with investigating "their own internal affairs." Initially driven by the "wartime labor demand" of the defense industry in World War II, until 1981, "every president except Gerald Ford issued an executive order to directly address racial discrimination in the workplace," including the introduction of "new or refined grievance measures" that cited "the sensitive and symbolic nature of federal service and its high visibility."[88]

In 1920, the study of public administration underwent a further evolution with German sociologist Max Weber's novel theory of bureaucracy, in which secrecy was a regulation that "prescribes what the citizen may know."[89] Despite the theory's auspicious beginnings, it later became a key vehicle for genocidal horror during the Holocaust. One of Weber's under-recognized contributions was to repopularize "bureaucracy" as an efficient and egalitarian form of administration. In his view, bureaucracy's primary function was to collate and distribute secrets across hierarchies, preventing disruptive unilateral action by any one agent.[90] His ideal bureaucracy enshrined Marxist notions of a revolutionary division of labor: "bureaucratic organization is technically the most highly developed means of power," one that left "the absolute monarch . . . powerless."[91] However, after World War II, the promise of a revolutionary bureaucracy also clashed with the harsh reality that the mode of secret administration enlisted by Nazi Germany had been used to perpetrate unspeakable evil. In *Eichmann in Jerusalem*, for instance, Hannah Arendt reported on the Holocaust trial of Nazi official Adolf Eichmann, referring to him by his official title, *Geheimnisträger*, or "bearer of secrets."[92] As she explains, the court that sentenced Eichmann acknowledged that his criminality was inextricable from the bureaucracy he managed:

> In its judgment the court naturally conceded that such a crime could be committed only by a giant bureaucracy using the resources of government. . . . If the defendant excuses himself on the ground that he acted not as a man but as a mere functionary whose functions could just as easily have been carried out by anyone else, it is as if a criminal pointed to the statistics on crime—which set forth that so-and-so many crimes per day are committed in such-and-such a place—and declared that he only did what was

---

88. Gooding, *American Dream Deferred*, 16, 62.
89. Moynihan, *Secrecy*, 59.
90. Blank, "Two Schools for Secrecy."
91. Weber, "Bureaucracy," 46–47.
92. Arendt, *Eichmann in Jerusalem*, 27.

statistically expected, that it was mere accident that he did it and not somebody else, since after all somebody had to do it.[93]

By the latter half of the twentieth century, the formerly distinct trajectories of thought represented by sociology, psychology, and administration converged in studies of bureaucracy within the emergent disciplinary genre of "social psychology." Most infamously, Stanley Milgram described his 1963 *Obedience to Authority* as an experimentalist's response to the horrors of the Holocaust and Eichmann's role in them.[94] He thus constructed a ruse in which subjects assumed the role of an experimenter (or "teacher") who would be instructed to inflict electrical shocks upon a fictitious counterpart (a "learner") in a separate room. The experiment simulated an administrative hierarchy in which failing to learn would result in physical punishment. The "expert" would authorize acts of violence, the "teacher" (i.e., the true test subject) would either follow through on the expert's instructions or refuse them, and the "learner" was subjected to the electric shocks (or not, in the case of the "teacher's" refusal). The secret was central to the experiment's success. The "teacher" had to be duped into believing that they were torturing the "learner," when, in fact, the "learner" was an insider to the experiment who played a staged recording each time the "shock" was administered. In other words, the teacher, not the learner, was the experimental subject. Milgram and his 1971 counterpart, Philip Zimbardo, demonstrated that their subjects—college students attending Yale and Stanford, respectively—were strongly willing to carry out violence when placed within an organizational hierarchy that simply instructed them to do so.[95] More importantly, however, they effectively synthesized the secret's academic formalizations across the twentieth century. Not only did they take on an institutionalized version of the secret as the focus of their social-psychological experimentation, but they also reproduced the secret's violence by inducing social and psychological trauma in their experimental groups.

The Secret as "Civic" Paranoia

Concomitant with the secret's disciplinary emergence at the start of the twentieth century, the secret also began to assume a novel political form. Merging anti-Masonic suspicion with the expansion of the administrative state, this new variant appeared at a moment during which formerly powerful

---

93. Arendt, *Eichmann in Jerusalem*, 289.
94. Milgram, *Obedience to Authority*.
95. Zimbardo, *Lucifer Effect*.

institutions of American civil society appeared increasingly willing to abdicate functions of social welfare and economic regulation to government bureaucracies. This moment saw the decline of organizations like the Freemasons and the strengthening of state bureaucracies (most significantly, police bureaucracies) at local, federal, and international levels. The intensification of a secrecy-oriented governing structure for policing is especially noteworthy for its amplification of paranoid nationalism toward newly freed Black Americans, Bolsheviks, Catholics, Jews, unions, and "sexual deviants," a catch-all category for nonmonogamy, homosexuality, and nonbinary gender expression. According to Ghassan Hage, paranoid nationalism is "an essentially narcissistic response" to local, national, and geopolitical events; it is motivated by "the worrier's sense that the nation cannot protect them from the object of their fears."[96] Building on Hage's account, Lisa M. Corrigan describes paranoid nationalism as a uniquely American mood, one that animated covert forms of white supremacy from John F. Kennedy's presidency onward:

> Paranoid nationalism uses political feelings of anxiety and concern to move people in support of or against national policies by scapegoating others. The rhetorical practice is marked by a rhetoric of scarcity and the feeling of political precarity. Values are under attack. The threat is everywhere. No one is safe. However, as a field of political emotions, paranoid nationalism obscures how nations facilitate precarity for both citizens and non-citizens, for ideal citizens, and for those whom the nation attempts to exclude formally or informally.[97]

By 1965, the fever pitch of this discourse prompted Richard Hofstadter to coin "the paranoid style" as the prevailing rhetorical pathology of anti-Masonic oratory, evangelical ministry, and anti-communist demagoguery.[98] It encouraged increasingly violent forms of law and order to punish the carpetbagger, the international communist, the community organizer, and the domestic radical while intensifying a climate of pervasive American racism and nationalist propaganda. Even as the targets of this propaganda assumed different faces and identities, secret-keeping practices among vigilantes, federal police, and international spying agencies intensified a pervasive "civic" paranoia.

Supplementing Hage's and Corrigan's respective accounts of paranoid nationalism, *"civic" paranoia* captures how, in the twentieth and twenty-first centuries, the secret manifested as a collective mood and social hermeneutics

---

96. Hage, *Against Paranoid Nationalism*, 76–78.
97. Corrigan, *Black Feelings*, 16.
98. Hofstadter, *Paranoid Style in American Politics*.

organized around emergent conspiracy theories. "Civic" appears in scare quotes because its invocation of a public interest was deceptive, functionally justifying the secret violence perpetrated by vigilantes and police while also legitimating the imaginary climate of secrecy they projected onto subversives, foreigners, and racial others. The phrase also captures a threshold moment when the anti-Masonic movements of the nineteenth century gave way to a twentieth-century state phobia, a set of "denunciatory commonplaces often directed to the state that result in the authority of the state itself being called fascist," and which "deprives its subjects of the capacity to identify the real sources of this kind of suspicion."[99] One example is Pittsburgh's Fraternal Order of Police, founded in 1915 to lobby city leadership directly about grievances related to officer labor. Amid the anti-union fervor of the time and suspicions of communist collaborators, Pittsburgh officers Martin Toole and Delbert Nagle initially elected to use a lodge system (i.e., a "fraternal order") to avoid the "union" moniker.[100] In other words, even as the suspicion of clandestine societies from the preceding century lingered in national memory, "civic" paranoia multiplied its objects and functions. On the one hand, an emergent "civic" paranoia enabled the increasingly centralized police state to spread propaganda targeting all manner of racial, political, and gendered others under the auspices of purifying the nation. As Michel Foucault argues, the chameleonic and heterogenous character of the scapegoat may be attributed to the "development of a biologico-social racism" in which "the other race is basically not the race that came from elsewhere or that was, for a time, triumphant and dominant, but . . . a race that is permanently, ceaselessly infiltrating the social body, or which is, rather, constantly being re-created in and by the social fabric."[101] Hence also the consistently white supremacist character of the secret's sprawling policing apparatus, which upheld "a race that is portrayed as the one true race, the race that holds power and is entitled to define the norm, and against those who deviate from that norm, against those who pose a threat to the biological heritage."

On the other hand, this white supremacist hegemony inured a more legitimate public paranoia of America's intensifying police bureaucracies among

---

99. M. Dean and Villadsen, *State Phobia and Civil Society*, 15.

100. "[In] April [1915], as [Toole] made his rounds, his mind was on his Brothers. If labor could organize, shouldn't the police also find a way? Not as a labor union. Toole didn't want any part of that. But an organization for 'the social welfare of all the police in Allegheny Count' need not be a labor union. 'We are banded together for the purpose of our own enjoyment,' Toole testified later. 'We have a police trial board of our own and we have a great deal of fun with it; and we discuss criminal cases in general.'" Walsh, *Fraternal Order*, 15. See also Fraternal Order of Police, "Brief History of the Fraternal Order"; and Schrader, *Badges Without Borders*.

101. Foucault, *"Society Must Be Defended,"* 61.

these targeted populations, instilling a literal paranoia in the civitas. Perhaps the most exemplary instance of paranoia's "civic" transformation occurred following the 1919 Palmer Raids, an event that inaugurated J. Edgar Hoover's ascent as a preeminent anti-communist within the Bureau of Investigation.[102] Tasked with monitoring and prosecuting political radicals, Hoover inaugurated an era of American secret policing that included the violently homophobic "sex crime panic" of the 1930s, the 1956 counterintelligence program (COINTELPRO) that infiltrated the Black Panthers, and a continuous wiretapping campaign against Martin Luther King Jr. that framed the civil rights leader for communist ties and hypocritical licentiousness.[103] Proclaiming foreign agents to have infiltrated the US government, Hoover's FBI also ushered in the 1938 House Un-American Activities Committee (HUAC), enabled Senator Joseph McCarthy's 1947 rise to prominence and McCarthy's symbolic succession by Robert Welch and the John Birch Society in 1958.[104] As Richard Gid Powers wrote in his introduction to Daniel Patrick Moynihan's *Secrecy: The American Experience*,

> McCarthy would have been nothing without government secrecy. He was able to gain hearing for his fantastic charges only because he could claim that the evidence to support them was kept hidden by the executive branch. Every time he requested classified documents from the government and they turned out to discredit his charges, he simply moved on to new and even more fantastic allegations—the supply of secrets for him to exploit was inexhaustible.[105]

Contemporaneous with the rise of sociology and psychology, the FBI situated the secret on its inside and outside. Inwardly, the secret offered a mode of expeditious time management and facilitated the speedy installation of a sprawling means of enforcing white supremacy at a grand scale. Outwardly, it projected the secret upon civic groups, political organizers, civil rights activists, and many others in a multipronged effort to free its secret policing programs from accountability.

We may attribute the rise of racist "civic" paranoia to at least three intersecting historical factors. The first is the failure of Reconstruction after the US Civil War, and subsequently, the Supreme Court's 1883 rejection of

---

102. Belknap, "Mechanics of Repression"; Ellis, "Hoover and the 'Red Summer'"; and Selden, "General Intelligence Division."

103. See also Morris, "Hoover's Sex Crime Panic"; Hoerl and Ortiz, "Organizational Secrecy"; and Maxwell, *F.B. Eyes*, 2–5, 39–41, 110–11.

104. See also Black, "Second Persona."

105. Powers, introduction, 27.

Congress's authority to desegregate public places.[106] In the years during and after Reconstruction, paranoia emerged as a weaponized affect enlisted by ex-Confederates who accused Black legislators and Republican reformers as "conspirators" against the weakened South. Following the Civil War, Southern states enshrined Black codes and lien laws in an effort "to protect the economic interests of the wealthy planter class," effectively seeking "to reimpose conditions of slavery on the freed."[107] Southern Democrats like Thomas Whitehead charged Republican proponents of desegregation with a "conspiracy" to "stir up bad blood" and thereby reignite the Civil War.[108] Although "abolitionist and antislavery reformers" stood squarely on the side of the victorious Union, they played a key role in disseminating repressive free labor ideals by proffering an "anemic vision of freedom" that "insinuated the need for compulsion when inclination failed and condoned the use of coercion, if and when it aided in the transition to free labor."[109] Reconstruction also coincided with a white supremacist "crime-wave panic" that normalized lynchings, while organizations like the Ku Klux Klan invented a "discourse of predation" to falsely project the threat of racial violence onto newly freed African Americans.[110]

Post-Reconstruction paranoia also subsisted in the legitimate suspicion of government, policing, education, and medical institutions, all of which continued antebellum patterns of racial repression under the protective shroud of new twentieth-century policies, laws, and codes. In his 1935 essay "The Propaganda of History," W. E. B. Du Bois explains that many recently composed histories whitewashed (i.e., erased) any mention of slavery or Black soldiers from accounts of the Civil War.[111] His reflections on Reconstruction elaborate on the viciousness of private efforts to prolong an antebellum status quo, project blame onto Black populations, and prolong racial enemyship, necessitating Black enclaves and protective forms of secret communication. Likewise, explaining "the plurality of resistances enacted in everyday life" enlisted by furtive Black communities in the pre-Reconstruction South, Saidiya Hartman describes "secret meetings" as involving "unlicensed movement, collective assembly, and an abrogation of the terms of subjection" that carried "life-threatening, if not fatal" consequences when discovered.[112] Black survival required "covert and chameleonic practices" to achieve even a modicum of safety.[113]

---

106. Wilson, *Reconstruction Desegregation Debate*, 1.
107. Wilson, *Reconstruction Desegregation Debate*, 79; Taylor, foreword, xxii.
108. Wilson, *Reconstruction Desegregation Debate*, 140.
109. Hartman, *Scenes of Subjection*, 242.
110. Emberton, *Beyond Redemption*, 30, 155.
111. Du Bois, "Propaganda of History," 617.
112. Hartman, *Scenes of Subjection*, 105–6, 113–14.
113. Hartman, *Scenes of Subjection*, 116.

A second factor that fueled the emergence of racist "civic" paranoia in the late nineteenth and early twentieth century was an institutional transition in which the US administrative state became newly accountable for public welfare, displacing civil society organizations with legislatively delegated bureaus.[114] Bureaus served as welfare agencies (e.g., the Freedmen's Bureau of 1865), policing agencies (e.g., the 1908 "Bureau of Investigation," later renamed the "Federal Bureau of Investigation" in 1935), and legal relief groups (e.g., the 1917 National Civil Liberties Bureau, founded in response to free speech convictions under the Wilson-era Espionage Act, later renamed the American Civil Liberties Union in 1920). Although the bureaus were a testament to the success of late nineteenth-century organizations that had lobbied for expanded government intervention, they also intensified the state's bureaucratic management of public life while minimizing the need for an unofficial "government beyond government," most traditionally represented by Masonic civil societies. As Congress delegated its authority to administrative bureaus, it expanded the "number and types of objects" under federal control.[115]

These shifts multiplied and intensified the popular nineteenth-century suspicion of Freemasons by proliferating new anti-federalist, antisemitic, and anti-communist conspiracy theories. As Hofstadter explains, "to control and humanize and moralize the great powers that had accumulated in the hands of industrialists and political bosses, it would be necessary to purify politics and build up the administrative state to the point at which it could subject the American economy to a measure of control."[116] Correspondingly, conspiracies offered a discursive resistance to this perceived "build-up." In the 1895 *The Problem of Civilization Solved*, Mary Elizabeth Lease accused Andrew Carnegie and Grover Cleveland of being agents "of Jewish bankers and British gold."[117] A similar American penchant for antisemitic conspiracy theories was evident in the widely publicized 1894–1906 Dreyfus Affair, the story of which was subsequently adapted into several feature-length films.[118] The publication of the forged *Protocols of the Elders of Zion* in the years before the 1905 Russian revolution levied charges of dangerous conspiracy against both Jews and Freemasons.[119] Anti-communist sentiments, which projected fear of

---

114. Lowi, *End of Liberalism*, 27–29.
115. Lowi, *End of Liberalism*, 105.
116. Hofstadter, *Anti-Intellectualism in American Life*, 197.
117. D. Davis, *Fear of Conspiracy*, 199–200.
118. Méliès, *Dreyfus Affair*; von Schwartzkoppen, *Les carnets de Schwartzkoppen*; Kayser, *Dreyfus Affair*; Dieterle, *Life of Emile Zola*; Zola, *La vérité en marche*; and Begley, *Why the Dreyfus Affair Matters*.
119. D. Davis, *Fear of Conspiracy*, 228–38. See also Lipset and Raab, *Politics of Unreason*; Mosse, *Toward the Final Solution*; Bennett, *Party of Fear*; Cohn, *Warrant for Genocide*; Berlet and Lyons, *Right-Wing Populism in America*; and Rice, *Awful Archives*, 118–23.

foreign influence in American labor politics, were also at a flash point. In 1884 and 1885, German-trained economist Richard Ely and Protestant clergyman Josiah Strong warned of the coming wave of socialism owing to deep economic inequalities produced and multiplied by the factory labor system.[120] In his reflections on the 1886 Haymarket Riot, Michael J. Schaack, a police officer credited with having uncovered the bombing plot, wrote that "socialism places itself beyond the pale of moral forces and arrays itself on the side of the freebooter, the bandit, the cut-throat, and the traitor."[121]

By the late nineteen-aughts, resistance to anarchism, socialism, and immigrants converged in a mass movement known as "one hundred percent Americanism," which demanded "a continuing majority of Anglo-Saxon Protestants" as a core tenet.[122] One hundred percent Americanism coincided with America's involvement with World War I and fed the resurgence of the Ku Klux Klan after D. W. Griffith's 1915 *The Birth of a Nation*, the codification of the 1917–18 Espionage and Sedition Acts, and the immigration restriction acts of 1921 and 1924.[123] The movement circulated widely. During World War I, for instance, the American Protective League encouraged public vigilantes to work alongside the police, making white racial policing into a civic mandate:

> Over 200,000 citizens enlisted in the American Protective League, described by its official historian as "a vast, silent, volunteer army organized with the approval and operated under the direction of the United States Department of Justice, Bureau of Investigation." This meant that anyone who is deprived of shooting Huns in France could at least defend his country by taking secret oaths and becoming a member of a local vigilante society; he could then spy on his neighbors, report "disloyal utterances," and perhaps send an I.W.W. sympathizer to a concentration camp.[124]

Between 1920 and 1921, Henry Ford pushed propaganda from the discredited *Protocols* in *The Dearborn Independent*, subsequently amplified by figures like "radio-priest" Charles E. Coughlin, a former populist who, following the Wilson presidency, became "an apologist for the Nazis and a leading anti-Semite."[125] The Ku Klux Klan subsequently leveraged "its own definition of one

---

120. Ely, "Identification of America's True Enemy;" and Strong, "Why America Is Particularly Vulnerable to Socialism."
121. Schaack, "Haymarket Riot," 177.
122. D. Davis, *Fear of Conspiracy*, 209.
123. Hernandez, *Ku Klux Klan and Freemasonry*, 3–4; Galison, "Secrecy in Three Acts," 941–50; Ludmerer, "Immigration Restriction Act"; Livingston, "Passage of the Immigration Act"; and Ngai, "Architecture of Race."
124. D. Davis, *Fear of Conspiracy*, 208–9.
125. D. Davis, *Fear of Conspiracy*, 249–51.

hundred percent Americanism" that "defended prohibition and immigration restriction and combated sexual freedom, 'modernist' religion, racial equality, and alien ideas."[126] Gathering nearly 4.5 million members by the mid-1920s, the organization became a "dominant political force" in Oregon, California, Texas, Indiana, and Ohio and came to "[control] the votes of governors and senators. . . . There is no clearer illustration of a movement of countersubversion becoming in itself a secret and genuinely subversive force."[127]

A third factor that contributed to the rise of America's racist "civic" paranoia was the creation of America's international intelligence agencies, facilitated in part by the dynasty of John Watson Foster, Robert Lansing, and the Dulles brothers. As Benjamin Harrison's Secretary of State, John Watson Foster directed the overthrow of the Hawai'ian monarchy and established America's first Military Intelligence Division.[128] Serving in the same role under Woodrow Wilson in 1915, Robert Lansing, Foster's son-in-law, shaped the 1917 and 1918 Espionage and Sedition Acts after insisting that the president include "some suggestion as to legislation covering foreign intrigues in our internal affairs such as conspiracies to blow up factories, to encourage strikes, to interfere with industrial operations, to gather information of this government's secrets."[129] John Foster Dulles and Alan Welch Dulles, Lansing's nephews, were not only beneficiaries of nepotism but also defined the public rhetoric of the early Cold War. Before America entered World War II, the siblings were openly sympathetic to Nazi Germany, met with Adolf Hitler, and celebrated Joseph Goebbels.[130] Both espoused the Wilsonian philosophy of "liberal internationalism," which maintained that diplomacy should occur only among aristocratic elites.[131] In 1941, Alan Dulles was appointed as Director of the Office of the Coordinator of Information (COI), an organization which was subsequently renamed the Office of Strategic Services (OSS), the Strategic Services Unit (SSU), the Central Intelligence Group (CIG), and finally, the Central Intelligence Agency (CIA). John Foster Dulles was an attorney who studied with Henri Bergson at the Sorbonne, served as the legal adviser to the delegation on arms limitation at the League of Nations, oversaw the construction of the Panama Canal, the creation of US Steel, and the consolidation of

---

126. D. Davis, *Fear of Conspiracy*, 209–10.
127. D. Davis, *Fear of Conspiracy*, 210.
128. Kinzer, *Brothers*, 21.
129. Robert Lansing to Woodrow Wilson, November 20, 1915, in *Papers of Woodrow Wilson*, 35:230. See also Lansing, "Secretary of State to President Wilson," quoted in Moynihan, *Secrecy*, 89.
130. Talbot, *Devil's Chessboard*, 19–20.
131. Kinzer, *Brothers*, 55.

small oil firms into international cartels.[132] In 1953, he was appointed Secretary of State under Dwight D. Eisenhower, one year after Alan Dulles became the first civilian Director of Central Intelligence. During their overlapping tenure, the Dulles brothers oversaw the 1960 U-2 spy plane crash and the catastrophic failure of the 1961 Bay of Pigs Invasion, the latter of which corresponded with the official end of Alan Dulles's intelligence career.[133]

American "civic" paranoia was a protracted effect of centuries-long traditions of official state secrets, over a hundred years of American secret societies, and academic understandings of the secret—social, psychological, and bureaucratic—all of which were becoming increasingly popular lenses for interpreting public and political events. "Civic" paranoia not only authorized state violence and the consolidation of power among wealthy elites; it continuously weaponized the secret against populations and movements who maintained legitimate suspicion that racism ran deep within governing institutions. As Jonathan Metzl notes in *The Protest Psychosis,* the transformation of schizophrenia from a "docile" disease that predominantly affected white, middle-class housewives to one characterized by Black "rage" correlates almost exactly with the rise of the American Civil Rights Movement in the 1960s. By the second half of the twentieth century, schizophrenia was overwhelmingly attributed to African American patients, whose legitimate paranoia was funneled through a medical hermeneutics that translated suspicion of racism into a sign of insanity.[134]

Transparency's Rise

Even as paranoia became a culturally dominant rhetorical style for policing the nation, it also gathered a new form that sought to resist the institutionalization of white supremacy under the cover of anti-communism: a demand for disclosure, commonly known as *transparency.* Both an anachronism and an ideal, *transparency* regularly describes late twentieth-century efforts to achieve legislative and judicial accountability. Its emergence as a metaphor for making concealed information visible may be attributed to the twentieth-century

---

132. In later life, John Foster Dulles frequently invoked Bergson's distinction between "dynamic" and "static" nations to defend the rise of the "dynamic powers," Germany, Italy, and Japan: "He churned out magazine and newspaper articles asserting that the "dynamic" countries of the world—Germany, Italy, and Japan—"feel within themselves potentialities which are suppressed," and that Hitler's semi-secret rearmament project simply showed that "Germany, by unilateral action, has now taken back her freedom of action." Kinzer, *Brothers,* 49–52.

133. Talbot, *Devil's Chessboard,* 366, 403.

134. Metzl, *Protest Psychosis,* xiii.

rise of cinematography, mass media, and modernist glass architecture, which naturalized the fantasy of seeing through contained and opaque spaces.[135] Before transparency, "the right to know" and "disclosure" were the prevailing terms for the moral, legal, and cultural imperative to access institutionally protected secrets. The relative recency with which "transparency" has become the default term for such significations is attested to by the 1967 Freedom of Information Act (FOIA) and Edwin Black's 1988 essay "Secrecy and Disclosure as Rhetorical Forms," which both use "disclosure" to signal the public interest in openness.[136] We might even surmise that Michael Crichton's 1994 book (and later, film) *Disclosure,* about sexual harassment in the corporate workplace, might have been titled *Transparency* if it had been released just a decade later.[137]

Transparency's rise as a political ideal in the United States coincides with a series of activist reactions to the red scare tactics of Hoover, McCarthy, and Welch in 1971. On March 8, a group of anti-war activists broke into the FBI resident agency in Media, Pennsylvania, resulting in the publication of security files documenting the COINTELPRO unit's covert actions against Black Power and anti–Vietnam War protestors.[138] On June 13, whistleblower Daniel Ellsberg published *The Pentagon Papers,* the common shorthand for the report's longer, less memorable title: *United States–Vietnam Relations, 1945–1967: A Study Prepared by the Department of Defense; A History of the American Involvement in Vietnam.*[139] Ellsberg was "convinced that the record of the government's actual policy-making in Vietnam was so greatly at variance with the government's stated rationale that, if the public had a chance to read the Papers, it would demand an end to the war."[140] The Nixon administration's fumbled pursuit of Ellsberg was as scandalous as his disclosure of the *Papers.* A covert group known as "the Plumbers" raided Ellsberg's psychiatrist's office and later became infamous as the orchestrators of "the twisted chain of events that led to Nixon's resignation in 1974."[141] Importantly, these instances of transparency were not driven by procedure or legislation. Rather, they were a deferred effect of American state violence that had been percolating for decades.

Transparency, in other words, was not the effect of legislative will or a decline in paranoid nationalism; it was a backlash to it. To legislate such an

---

135. McQuire, "From Glass Architecture to Big Brother."
136. Black, "Secrecy and Disclosure."
137. Crichton, *Disclosure*; Levinson, *Disclosure.*
138. Powers, introduction, 34.
139. United States Department of Defense, *United States–Vietnam Relations, 1945–1967.*
140. Powers, introduction, 29–30.
141. Gitelman, *Paper Knowledge,* 86.

ideal would "facilitate 'neoliberal' agendas" or "undermine deliberation, dealmaking, and institutional capacity."[142] Holding a mirror to the racist, xenophobic, and gender-repressive paranoia of the anti-communists, transparency activists and those sympathetic to them were accused by conservative and centrist critics of being led by feelings, not facts or evidence. Borrowing a turn of phrase from media theorist Marshall McLuhan, Richard Gid Powers claimed the disclosure to be the greatest illustration possible "of the medium (secrecy) being the message (conspiracy)."[143] In Powers's view, "Government secrets—not what they revealed, but the mere existence of government secrets—would now prove to have the power to change the public's mind about the most controversial political issue of the day."[144] Nuancing this dismissive view of Ellsberg's revelations, Lisa Gitelman argues that xerography, naming, and circulation transformed the document into a signifier with a life of its own, "a convenient moniker for a giant bone of contention."[145] Spilling across multiple releases, court cases, and other, unrelated scandals, the *Papers* were a metonym for the sprawling nature of malicious government secrecy, giving way to the 1972–74 Watergate scandal, Daniel Schorr's 1975 reporting on the CIA's assassination plots, and the 1975 Pike (House) and Church (Senate) Select Committees on Intelligence—the last of which was initiated by the counterintelligence tactics revealed by the 1971 raid on the FBI's Media Office.[146] Citing Arthur Schlesinger's 1973 *The Imperial Presidency*, the Pike and Church committees accused the FBI, the CIA, and the executive branch of undemocratically wielding secret policing power with unilateral impunity.[147] Little more than a decade later, the 1985 Tower Commission turned the state's gaze upon the National Security Council's (NSC) unauthorized acts of arms sales and international war, concluding with the infamous Reagan-era Iran-Contra Affair.[148]

Transparency lends civic paranoia a double inflection. The version of civic paranoia espoused by such figures as Hoover, McCarthy, Welch, and Dulles has gradually become legible as a disciplinary mechanism of the anti-communist

---

142. Pozen and Schudson, "Introduction," 1.
143. Powers, introduction, 32.
144. Powers, introduction, 30.
145. Gitelman, *Paper Knowledge*, 88.
146. The Pike and Church committees produced two reports, one of which was banned from publication but subsequently leaked in the *Village Voice*, and together they induced Gerald Ford to write an executive order banning political assassinations. They may also be credited with more permanent committees on intelligence that brought scandals like the Iran-Contra Affair to light. Schorr, "Assassins"; and Powers, introduction, 37.
147. Schlesinger provided a historical basis for the development of secret, militarized agencies under the direction of the presidency. Schlesinger, *Imperial Presidency*, 450–51.
148. Hijazi, "Hostage's Release"; and Byrne, *Iran-Contra*, 27, 42.

state used against those who expressed resistance to twentieth-century institutional racism. Its double inflection concerns how this paranoia was mirrored in the affective disposition of transparency activists and populations who had endured the paranoid nationalism of the twentieth century. In *I Heard It Through the Grapevine,* Patricia A. Turner recounts Black traditions of rumor and folklore in the United States, linking Black enclave publics' suspicion of governing institutions to covert and community-centric forms of storytelling:

> In the late twentieth century, for example, informants have pointed to the Central Intelligence Agency (CIA), the Federal Bureau of Investigation, the Centers for Disease Control (CDC), various branches of the armed services, the "administration," and the "government" generally as engaged in conspiracies detrimental to the physical well-being of African-Americans. These rumors include among others: the belief that the FBI, in cahoots with the CDC, committed the Atlanta child murders that spanned the late 1970s–early 1980s; the idea that the Reagan administration wanted the AIDS virus to flourish in order to impede the growth of third world populations; and the notion that the "government" is directing illegal drugs into minority communities to keep the urban African-American population powerless.[149]

Like transparency, the secret has retained a double character in keeping with its Roman-era beginnings. It has been an affective disposition useful for propagandizing social unrest, enshrined in the conspiracy theories propagated by vigilantes, police, and intelligence agencies. It has also been a means to signal danger among precarious publics, making transparent what has been out in the open for those audiences capable of hearing the secret through a social grapevine. In other words, the secret is a kind of knowledge that reflects back on itself. A compensatory and covert form of communicative action, the secret aims to elucidate and undermine the police state even as the latter's clandestine practices mutate over generations.

An Epistemic Franchise

Michael Rogin's *"Ronald Reagan," the Movie; and Other Episodes in Political Demonology* repeatedly alludes to the secret as a central feature of late twentieth-century political epistemology. There, the secret is both a kind of knowledge that enables its bearers to conceal their intentions and a presumed

---

149. Turner, *I Heard It*, 108.

knowledge of the enemy other's plotting. The latter conception of the secret animated the characteristic "demonology" of Reagan- and Red Scare–era conspiracy theories, which made speculation about covert foreign actors into an expeditious explanation for national and local disruptions to white Americans' expectations of the good life. Moreover, it made Reagan into a standard-bearer for the "countersubversive tradition," in which the rhetor-president-demagogue fashions themselves as the strong-man opponent of an insidious and invisible effort to bring about the downfall of the United States.[150]

> Fearing chaos and secret penetration, the countersubversive interprets local initiatives as signs of alien power. Discrete individuals and groups become, in the countersubversive imagination, members of a single political body directed by its head. The countersubversive needs monsters to give shape to his anxieties and to permit him to indulge his forbidden desires. Demonization allows the countersubversive, in the name of battling the subversive, to imitate his enemy.[151]

Certainly, the account of the secret episteme provided in this chapter echoes Rogin's synthesis of Reagan-era political demonology. Hearkening to Freud's and Simmel's distinct formulations of where we might locate the secret, Rogin notes how the Reagan-era secret was on the *inside* of "local initiatives" and came from an *outside* "alien power." A psychoanalytic extension of "civic" paranoia, the "countersubversive imagination" is a formulaic fantasy that secures the rhetor-president-demagogue's imagining of themselves as a rightly privileged hegemon who sits atop an American Great Chain of Being, all the while projecting the suspicion of illicit hiddenness onto all manner of clandestine others.[152] As president, Reagan "imagined a titanic struggle between the forces of good and an empire of evil" and accused the latter of "secret, conspiratorial meetings in which world conquest was planned."[153] And, even as he fused historical themes of political demonology with the uniquely American context of the late Cold War, Reagan imitated his imagined enemy. Not only did he authorize the national security state to undertake illegal actions against the command of Congress, but he also intensified a color-blind paranoid

---

150. Rogin, "Countersubversive Tradition."
151. Rogin, *"Ronald Reagan,"* xiii.
152. On the insistence of the Great Chain of Being and the onto-rhetorical ordering of *catacosmesis*, see Rowland, *Zoetropes*, 19–40.
153. Rogin, *"Ronald Reagan,"* xv.

nationalism that ever more openly disavowed America's legacies of racial, gendered, and colonial violence.[154]

Although Reagan stands at the figural, historical, and material conjuncture that lent racist "civic" paranoia a recognizably American brand, there is more to the secret episteme than Reagan's unique flavor of countersubversion. The secret, contingently and cross-continentally, formed at discrete threshold moments across a centuries-long episteme, lending the paranoia that Reagan so skillfully channeled the feel of eternity. Put another way, the secret episteme described in this chapter is everywhere in *"Ronald Reagan," the Movie*. It is in the personal and cinematic indebtedness of Reagan's brand to D. W. Griffith; the spy plot of Reagan's 1940 World War II flick, *Murder in the Air*; Richard Nixon's secret war in Vietnam and his exposure of Alger Hiss; Hoover's "secret political police"; the "secret order of Freemasons and Bavarian Illuminati" who conspired to destroy the early Republic; and the list goes on.[155] The difference is that whereas Rogin centers Reagan, the foregoing genealogy centers the secret, tracing its sprawling, accelerating, accumulating collision-path with the present.

The secret episteme may therefore invite an expansion of Rogin's cinematic metaphor. Unfolding across a wide temporal horizon, the secret may be more akin to an epistemic franchise than a movie, a series of ever more intense and loosely connected plots that continuously reconstellate specialized terminology, forms of social collectivity, disciplinary knowledge, and paranoid affect into new but also familiar permutations. Consider, for instance, just how many features of the secret episteme have textured the early decades of the twenty-first century, during which time American governance has been rebranded as the second coming of Imperial Rome and a reprise of the Gilded Age. Classical architecture and art are again the preferred brand for resurgent white supremacy while Silicon Valley entrepreneurs have resuscitated Roman-era philosophy, conquest, and plutocracy as mission statements for the new era.[156] Accompanying the empire fetish is an intensification of rule by secrecy. State secrets (*arcana imperii*) leak ever more frequently, in greater volume, and with grander spectacle; as much is apparent in such events as the 2022 Mar-a-Lago document scandal and the 2024 Signalgate leak.[157] At the start of Donald

---

154. See also Melamed, *Represent and Destroy*.
155. Rogin, "Ronald Reagan," 2, 57, 69, 102, 106.
156. Kodé, "Politics of Brutalism;" Pinto, "Capitalism with a Transhuman Face;" El Assar, "Masculinity Polycrisis;" Montgomery, "Zuckerberg Augustus"; and Vervaet, "Mark Zuckerberg's Admiration for Emperor Augustus."
157. Bump, "Trump's Classified Mar-a-Lago Documents"; and Green, "Fallout from Signal Group Chat Leak."

J. Trump's second presidential term in 2024, Mar-a-Lago was widely reported on as a sieve (*secretus*) for secrets, a leaky cauldron where access and intelligence were up for sale to those willing to pay for the privilege of lobbying the sitting president.[158] The 2020s coincided with renewed concern about reactionary and religious secret societies whose overt aim was to restore white, male, and heterosexual social hierarchies of post-Reconstruction America, marking a return to ever more severe dynamics of wealth inequality, conspiracy theorizing, xenophobia, binary gender normativity, eugenics, and racism.[159] Examples of such secret societies include "Project 2025," a conservative Christian–evangelical plan for dismantling federal government and intensifying policing, as well as the Society for American Civic Renewal (SACR), whose values strongly echo One Hundred Percent Americanism.[160] Trump's second occupancy of the White House was also rife with secrecy mandates, efforts to dismantle the twentieth-century structure of federal bureaucracy, mass firings reminiscent of Wilson's purge of Black public servants, and the systematic erasure of race, gender, and ability from military, educational, and governing institutions.[161] All the while, these actions have been cloaked in a mere rhetoric of transparency whose effect has been to obfuscate, confuse, and render opaque the interests driving wealthy industrialists' efforts at iconoclastic destruction.[162] The secret episteme tells us that these are recurring and converging patterns. It is less a stand-alone movie with many scenes than the most recent, utterly predictable, and over-the-top iteration of a shitty franchise. Like Imperial Rome, the Gilded Age, and even the Reagan-era United States, the new kakistocracy is composed of plutocrat-oligarchs who negotiate policy without empathy for those who suffer the mortifying consequences of their rule. True to the intellectual tradition of genealogy, the path toward this vaguely familiar authoritarianism has been wrought with contingencies, "accidents," and "petty malice."[163] Although it did not need to be this way, the path was written well in advance.

---

158. Feiger, Matsakis, and Lahut, "People Are Paying Millions."
159. Tyrrell, "Trump's Presidency Is Being Compared to America's Gilded Age."
160. Shao, Yourish, and Kim, "How Trump's Directives Echo Project 2025"; Kovensky, "Inside A Secret Society"; and Kaplan, Elliott, and Mierjeski, "Pastor's Secretive Influence Campaign."
161. Ray, "Musk's DOGE Must Make Records Public"; Barrett, "DOGE Is the Deep State"; Fowler, "Federal Agencies Plan for Mass Layoffs"; Stolberg, Jewett, and Mandavilli, "Mass Layoffs Hit Health Agencies"; Alberty, "Navajo Code Talkers Disappear"; and Copp and Baldor, "Trump Fires Chairman."
162. Lowell, "Elon Musk Appears with Trump"; and Fahrenthold and Singer-Vine, "DOGE Makes Its Latest Errors."
163. Foucault, "Nietzsche, Genealogy, History," 144.

The secret is an epistemic franchise because it has many installments that have continued well into the twenty-first century. The *arcana imperii* echoes with each presidential scandal, endlessly deferring accountability to a subsequent decade, institution, or administration. The form of the white elite secret society and its appropriation of Black signs and tokens lingers in the dog whistle, a doubled form of discourse that enforces America's racial caste system while allowing the utterer to get off on the fantasy of duping the other with their own tactics. When security leaks break onto the global public stage, America's massive intelligence bureaucracies briefly show themselves through a routine rhetoric of state-enforced transparency that sexualizes threats to the nation. Finally, the mood of "civic" paranoia continues to be transmitted through popular narrative forms like detective fiction, which continuously encourages identification with the colonialist mentality of the police. Ultimately, these forms of the secret are continuations of an episteme in which everything—and everyone—is suspect.

CHAPTER 2

The Secret in and of Discourse

Hidden Depths and Open Surfaces

> What could be more convincing, moreover, than the gesture of turning one's cards face up on the table? It is so convincing that we are momentarily persuaded that the magician has, in fact, demonstrated, as he promised he would, how his trick was performed, whereas he has only performed it anew in a purer form; this moment makes us appreciate the supremacy of the signifier in the subject.
> —Jacques Lacan, "Seminar on 'The Purloined Letter'" (14)

Reading for the Secret

The secret is more than concealed information. It exists within the rituals that maintain communal bonds and encompasses the generational transformation of language, governmentality, disciplinary knowledge, and paranoia. Michel Foucault offers one explanation of how we might read for the secret across these registers, animated by the Nietzschean dyad of *Herkunft* and *Enstehung*. *Herkunft* is "stock or *descent*" and refers to the genealogist's tracing of the "accidents," "errors," "minute deviations," and "complete reversals" that "lie at the root of what we know and what we are."[1] *Enstehung* is "emergence, the moment of arising," an irruption of forces that "leap from the wings to center stage."[2] Instead of searching for *Ursprung*, or a singular origin, Foucault insists upon mapping the contingencies of emergence and descent, which together form a complex "profusion of entangled events" that "continues its secret existence through a 'host of errors and phantasms.'"[3]

This chapter advances a similarly dyadic framework as a reading strategy for the secret. Like emergence and descent, the phrases "the secret in

---

1. Foucault, "Nietzsche, Genealogy, History," 145–46.
2. Foucault, "Nietzsche, Genealogy, History," 148–50.
3. Foucault, "Nietzsche, Genealogy, History," 140–41, 155.

discourse" and "the secret of discourse" point to the secret as a rhetorical division, split, or rift. We could imagine *in* and *of* as demarcating the secret's vertical and horizontal axes: the *in* discourse describing the secret as deeply buried, hidden, or concealed; the *of* discourse accounting for the secret as having always or already been out in the open. In the preceding chapter, for instance, footnoted nuggets of historical detail might attune us to the secret *in* discourse, in the sense of a deep archive where more information might be found. Conversely, the movement from etymology to the secret society to disciplinary knowledge to civic paranoia performs the secret *of* discourse: a series of retroactive permutations that have enabled different forms of hiddenness to merge, diverge, and unfold across different historical moments.

The above description may be too quick because, as Jacques Lacan suggests in the opening epigraph, "turning [my] cards face up on the table" risks making my reading strategy more opaque. This chapter therefore nuances the distinction between the secret *in* and *of* discourse in the following way: The secret *in* discourse is grounded *in* a past performance, history, archive, or forgotten meaning. Once this secret is out, the jig is up: The lost object is revealed—at least, until another, even more deeply hidden secret comes to light. By contrast, the secret *of* discourse describes the signifier's iterability and unpredictable futurity. Unlike the secret *in* discourse, the secret *of* discourse does not seem to end with the discovery of an erased origin or a smoking gun. Instead, it describes a retroactive shift in perspective, or *anamorphosis*, that reconfigures the significance of events that have already transpired by changing the given meaning of a discourse that is already in circulation.[4]

To develop this theoretical grounding for the secret *in* and *of* discourse, I open by reviewing how the *in-of* distinction is a feature of canonical scholarship about rhetoric, materiality, and resistance. I then situate this distinction as indebted to two traditions of critical humanism: depth reading (corresponding with the register *in* discourse) and surface reading (corresponding with the register *of* discourse). Whereas adopting one of these approaches has often meant excluding the other, I outline a reading strategy that illuminates their connection and mutual dependency. In the final section, I explore how rhetorical tropes of naming and retroaction deconstruct the opposition between depth and surface reading, using examples that preview how the secret *in* and *of* discourse are set into motion by the scandal, the settler, the leaker, and the lie.

---

4. See also Hallsby, "Recanonizing Rhetoric."

The Secret in and of Discourse

A key example of the secret *in* and *of* discourse concerns a landmark debate over the proper scope and definition of materialist criticism in rhetorical studies. In the 1994 "The Materiality of Discourse as Oxymoron," Dana L. Cloud took issue with post-structuralist theories of discourse for their "antirealist (relativist) and anti-materialist (idealist)" proclivities.[5] She proposed a third way that prioritized "the ideological power of dominant economic and political interests in structuring, framing, and setting the limits for rhetorical action."[6] Repudiating critics who would reduce hunger, war, and poverty to "mere" discursive constructions, Cloud refused to "sacrifice the notions of practical truth, bodily reality, and material oppression to the tendency to render all of experience discursive." According to this view, rhetorical criticism should expose the real forces that naturalize and obscure hegemonic power. In his 1998 rejoinder, "Another Materialist Rhetoric," Ronald Walter Greene argued that Cloud conflated power as such "with the interests of a transcendental ruling class."[7] This conflation risked ignoring "a vast assemblage of countervailing practices" that encouraged neoliberal publics to lend their assent to such injustices as economic inequality, racism, and war. According to Greene, rhetoric ought to be understood as "a technology of deliberation that allows a series of institutions to make judgments about the welfare of a population."[8] Rather than urging critics to decipher the hegemonic code embedded in widely circulating texts, he instead encouraged them to attend to the complex "logics of articulation" that organized a governing apparatus.

At the risk of oversimplification, the debate came down to whether rhetoric created hidden meanings *in* discourse or if it openly dispersed power as a function *of* discourse. Greene contended that Cloud's approach was steeped in "a hermeneutics of suspicion" that identified power with "the interests of a 'ruling class.'" Cloud's version of rhetoric might therefore be understood as dissimulating known superstructural interests by disguising their presence *in* everyday representations. Greene's rejoinder eschewed "deep structure(s)" like the ruling class or white supremacy as singular explanations of power and thus resituated rhetoric as the effect-structure *of* a material and discursive apparatus. According to the latter view, rhetoric was not just a propaganda machine that concealed the true workings of power. It was, more crucially,

---

5. Cloud, "Materiality of Discourse," 142.
6. Cloud, "Materiality of Discourse," 158–59.
7. Greene, "Another Materialist Rhetoric," 36.
8. Greene, "Another Materialist Rhetoric," 39.

the effect of "a stratified field of action": A complex of forces, institutions, and technologies that aimed to garner mass acquiescence to the contradictory imperatives of endless war and population-level surveillance.[9]

For all their disagreement, these opposed positions resembled each other in at least one important respect: Both Cloud and Greene assumed an *either/or* antinomy between their argument and its antecedents. Cloud leveraged realist materialism to displace Michael Calvin McGee's idealism and Raymie McKerrow's relativism; Greene leveraged a Foucauldian understanding of the apparatus to displace Cloud's position and that of other ideology critics. Although substantively distinct, their interventions bore a formal resemblance. In turning away from precursor understandings of materiality, both Cloud and Greene enacted trope (quite literally, a "turn") as rhetorical theory's condition of possibility, introducing a theoretical fissure or division to resolve an open-ended theoretical debate.[10] Either rhetoric was *in* discourse and reflected the truth that deep structures determine our situation, or it was *of* discourse, a complex articulation whose features emerged from a particular conjuncture of historical, institutional, and material forces.

Rather than an *either/or*, I would wager that the status of rhetoric and materiality is better conceived as a *both/and*. Conceived as a *both/and*, the critic would be authorized to name repressive structures and to refuse the wholesale reduction of structures to static interests. At once deeply hidden (*in* discourse) and a complex articulation (*of* discourse), the secret is a continuous turning. It is an alternating and iterative contradiction that "must be thought of as a series of substitutions of center for center."[11]

Two caveats: First, the *in-of* distinction is not my invention but a common motif of critical, cultural, and deconstructive reading. One precedent comes from Stuart Hall, whose theory of ideology keeps terms like "structure" and "articulation" in tension using Sartrean categories of being *in* itself and being *for* itself. As he argues, although classes often act in complicity with ideological structures, such structures do not automatically determine class ideations: "People are not irrevocably and indelibly inscribed with the ideas they *ought* to think; the politics that they ought to have are not, as it were, already imprinted on their sociological genes."[12] On the side of resistance to ideology, he similarly argues that there is no guarantee that different social

---

9. Greene, "Another Materialist Rhetoric," 37.
10. Keeling, "Of Turning and Tropes."
11. Derrida, "Structure, Sign, and Play," 279.
12. S. Hall, "Signification, Representation, Ideology," 96.

groups will "articulate into a collective will." However, such connections can and do occur:

> The dispersed conditions of practice of different social groups *can* be effectively drawn together in ways which make those social forces not simply a class "in itself," positioned by some other relations over which it has no control, *but also* capable of intervening as a historical force, a class "for itself," capable of establishing new collective projects.[13]

Hall's use of the phrases "class *in* itself" and "class *for* itself" holds the contingent determination of class subjects by ideological structure ("*in* itself") in tension with the contingency of articulating distinct classes into new modes of relation ("*for* itself"). The secret *in* and *of* discourse holds a similar tension. These prepositional phrases denote the apparent contradiction between concealed knowledge (*in* discourse) and knowledge (*of* discourse) that retroactively reveals what was always in plain view.

Second, it would be a mistake to celebrate the secret *in* discourse as more foundational or important than the secret *of* discourse, and vice versa. To paraphrase Jacques Derrida, if "coherence in contradiction expresses the force of a desire," then any sensible way of hierarchizing the secret *in* and *of* discourse should be read as marking a desire to separate, defer, and differentiate.[14] Derrida's own prepositional criticism and explicit reflections on "the secret" are the most direct inspirations for my formulation of the secret *in* and *of* discourse.[15] One of his recurring strategies is to draw out a hierarchical binary opposition from a specific text and then to read the enactment of this binary's undoing by the very text in which it is invoked. Often, he marks such oppositions with a prepositional phrase that enables the reader to grasp how a central object, presumed selfsame, is internally divided by its own locative grammar. One example is the psychoanalytic concept of *resistance*, which Derrida explains in the following way:[16]

- "Resistance *to* psychoanalysis" describes an epistemological refusal to adopt psychoanalytic terminology or methods except as a last resort. This rejection may be based, for instance, on the presumed outdatedness of

---

13. S. Hall, "Signification, Representation, Ideology," 96; italics added.
14. Derrida, "Structure, Sign, and Play," 279.
15. See also Derrida, "Remarks on Deconstruction and Pragmatism"; and Derrida and Ferraris, *Taste for the Secret*, vii–viii, 57–59, 75.
16. Derrida, *Resistances of Psychoanalysis*, vii–viii.

- psychoanalysis, its anti-empiricism, or the assumption that psychoanalysis as such rests upon regressive understandings of sexuality, subjectivity, or identity.
- "Resistance *of* psychoanalysis" describes how resistance is an ontological component of any particular psychoanalytic interpretation. According to Freud, this form of resistance is anything that obstructs the interpretive process while in the session. It can be an indecipherable dream-text, a patient's filling of their session with chatter, or their refusal to speak at all. Resistances *of* analysis capture moments of opacity that halt the process of interpretation, signaling something that the subject's unconscious seeks to keep secret, and therefore, protect.

At first glance, the two forms of resistance may seem patently antithetical. If "resistance *to*" is a preemptive refusal of Freud, Irigaray, Klein, Kristeva, Lacan, and so forth, then "resistance *of*" minimally requires the subject to be party to the analytic session. However, Derrida rewrites these prepositional polarities as mutual dependencies and seeks to undermine any hierarchy that would make self-conscious resistance (*to* analysis) merely a version of ontological resistance (*of* analysis) and vice versa. In place of these hierarchical oppositions, he elaborates a variation on resistance as an "*inviolable secret, without depth, without place, without name, without destination, hyperbolytic,* excessive destruction, and lysis without measure, without measure and *without return*, lysis without anagogy."[17] Derrida's own account of resistance—endlessly hidden, uninterpretable, and dividing—references a difference that is the precondition of any oppositional hierarchy, formal arrangement, or mode of interpretation.

To adopt a similar frame for the secret would mean that it is neither primarily a lost meaning (*in* discourse) nor an unconscious and retroactive function (*of* discourse). It is instead the dynamic difference that organizes this opposition. As the following sections illustrate, a strict *in-of* dichotomy has been perpetuated through the critical humanist traditions of depth and surface reading, which may be understood as highly partial elaborations of the registers *in* and *of* discourse, respectively. In other words, "depth" approaches tend to diminish "surface" readings and vice versa. However, with Derrida, I would maintain these are faces of the same "inviolable secret," an organizing difference-that-makes-a-difference whose effect is to lend terms provisional hierarchy, form, and explanatory power.

---

17. Derrida, *Resistances of Psychoanalysis*, 34; italics added to "inviolable secret."

Depth Reading: The Secret *in* Discourse

The secret *in* discourse describes the assumption that knowledge is locked away *in* a name, word, phrase, sentence, text, or archive. It exists as concealed content or a repressed meaning, one that comes to light when a signifier has its true referent restored. One famous example occurs in *The Twilight Zone* episode "To Serve Man," in which a book (which bears the same title as the episode) is gifted by extraterrestrials to humankind. Initially, linguists and scientists presume the book to be a guide for assisting, supporting, and advancing humankind. The book's secret significance comes to light at the episode's end when a fuller translation restores the title's actual reference, revealing *To Serve Man* as an extraterrestrial cookbook.[18] The secret *in* discourse often demands a suspicious orientation to the text, lending the reader a skeptical relationship to what words appear to say and their subtending significations. It is a reading strategy that promises to reveal what is hidden within an as-yet undeciphered text.

The secret *in* discourse is associated with the tradition of depth reading, which encompasses such innovations as depth hermeneutics, the hermeneutics of suspicion, and paranoid reading. Its general trait is to presume that a hidden signification exists beyond the everyday interpretation of a sign, representation, or text. Within the Saussurean tradition of semiotics, for instance, concealment is innate to signification because the meaning of a given sign shifts across instances of living speech. As Hans-Georg Gadamer explains, "*parole*, the speaking word in its working reality . . . involves a strange form of concealment":

> One should realize that it is a basic character of speaking that it is completely forgetful of itself. Nobody could utter one sentence if he were completely aware of what he was doing. If I were to do that, I would not find a second word after the first. And more than that: it would really prevent me from going beyond every utterance to the matters I would convey, and force me to keep to myself what I am saying. I would go mad if I were to make an attempt at complete thematization of saying in saying. I must say something in order to speak; when I do there is a forgetfulness of speech as a theme or topic.[19]

---

18. Bare, *Twilight Zone*, S3E24.
19. Gadamer, "Hermeneutics of Suspicion," 321.

Not only does living speech actively change the signifying constellation that lends signs meaning and depth. For speech to make sense, it must consign some element of the act of communication to forgetting, or else induce psychological paralysis in the communicator, who becomes overwhelmed by the surfeit of information. The recovery of such forgetful significations may, therefore, be understood as an effort to restore or resuscitate this surplus data, having been made secret because of necessity, lack of attention, or lapsed circulation over time.[20]

Redaction illustrates just this kind of signifying concealment. Redaction today intuitively describes a form of censorship using black lines that cover up officially secret words and phrases.[21] An original method of redaction did not involve crossing out but cutting out, such that an archivist would create literal holes in a document. However, even this twentieth-century version of redaction exemplifies how the term has lost its formerly dominant resonance. Dating to the fourteenth and fifteenth centuries, the now obsolete verb and adjective form of *redact* signified a bringing together that reorganized existing textual materials into a new whole.[22] Redaction was routine among medieval

---

20. One example of this "forgetful" signification concerns Edgar Allan Poe's genre-defining detective fiction. The source material for the second (1842–43) installment of Poe's Auguste Dupin trilogy, "The Mystery of Marie Rogêt," was Mary Rogers, a migrant refugee to New York who "had died during an abortion gone awry, her body dragged to the river in an attempt to cover up the crime." (6) As Amy Gilman Srebnick explains in *The Mysterious Death of Mary Rogers*:

> Poe muddled his attempt to solve the crime, but in focusing his attention on the enigma of Mary herself and the distinctly urban quality of the event—the importance of the city setting, the collection of male characters who figured prominently in the investigation—he foregrounded the important issues in the case and simultaneously established several important ingredients of the detective genre. (10)

The story of Mary Rogers's abortion became a "model" for "the urban mystery novels gaining popularity in the 1840s," particularly "its lurid and sensational aspects" (11). In other words, Mary Rogers's true story is exemplary of the secret *in* discourse, a buried reference that organizes and animates (quite literally) a larger mystery. See also Winderman, *Back Alley Abortion*.

21. "To censor (a document) by removing or blacking out certain words or passages prior to publication or release, esp. for legal, security, or confidentiality purposes; to remove or black out (words or information) in this way. Frequently in *passive*." OED Online, s.v. "redact, v.," accessed April 19, 2022, https://www.oed.com/dictionary/redact_v.

22. "Brought together in a single entity; combined, united; brought together in a written form; compiled or described in a document." OED Online, s.v. "redact, adj.," accessed April 19, 2022, https://www.oed.com/dictionary/redact_adj. "To bring together in a single entity; to combine, unite; to bring together or organize (ideas, writings, etc.) into a coherent form; to compile, arrange, or set down in a written document. Also: to put into a particular written form. Usually with prepositions, esp. *into, unto*." OED Online, s.v. "redact, v.," accessed April 19, 2022, https://www.oed.com/dictionary/redact_v.

scholastics who would selectively transcribe and combine older documents. The purpose was not for the transcriptionist to remove forbidden knowledge (as is the case today), nor to feature the redactionist's ingenuity or the novelty of their original contribution.[23] Instead, it was to duplicate and compile texts. This older form of redaction describes how versions of the Christian Bible were revised and transcribed versions of older and sometimes discarded epistolary gospels, the selection of which changed across generations.[24] Some Christian theologians retain this esoteric meaning of redaction in practicing redaction criticism, which seeks to understand the principles of biblical sourcing and rearrangement over time.[25]

Christina Sharpe's *In the Wake* likewise restores redaction's productive and creative dimensions by describing the addition of aesthetic markings to archival images and footage so as "to make Black life visible, if only momentarily, through the optic of the door."[26] For instance, Sharpe describes documentarian Julie Dash's *Daughters of the Dust* (1992) and Dash's "decision to show the traces of slavery as the indigo blue that remains on the hands of the formerly enslaved people who labored and died over the poisonous indigo pits on the Sea Islands of the coast of South Carolina." As an act of "black redaction," the addition of indigo stains as signifying elements not only departs from how slavery's violence is most frequently represented (i.e., through embodied markings of torture endured); it also "positions viewers differently in relation to the fact that the afterlives of slavery are long and that the life span of the enslaved people who labored over the pits was very short."[27] As a secret *in* discourse, redaction goes beyond crossing-out, because it restores an originary context through the addition of signifying marks and the rearrangement of materials. It is a purposeful joining-together that brings forth a forgotten, unnoticed, or hidden meaning by returning to the past.

There are many other examples of depth reading. Literary theorist Paul Ricoeur coined both "depth semantics" and "the hermeneutics of suspicion" to describe the necessity of formal, structural analysis to interpret literature

---

23. Long, *Openness, Secrecy, Authorship*.
24. For example, see S. Brown, "Longer ('Secret') Gospel of Mark"; and Vinzent, *Christ's Torah*.
25. "[After German *Redaktionsgeschichte* (19th cent.)] the analysis of biblical texts, esp. the Gospels, through an attempt to reconstruct the editorial use made by biblical authors of earlier material, typically stressing the theological and literary concerns of these authors." *OED Online*, s.v. "redaction criticism, n.," accessed April 19, 2022, https://www.oed.com/dictionary/redaction-criticism_n.
26. Sharpe, *In the Wake*, 123.
27. Sharpe, *In the Wake*, 126.

and reveal cultural myths.[28] "Depth semantics" describes an analysis that takes stock of a text's formal features to observe "the path of thought opened up by the text," thereby shunning "surface" (that is, cursory or superficial) interpretations that would reconstruct an author's intended meaning.[29] Correspondingly, Ricoeur enlists the "hermeneutics of suspicion" to describe a common feature among the critical traditions inaugurated by Marx, Nietzsche, and Freud: Namely, that "another meaning is both given and hidden in an immediate meaning."[30] In the Freudian tradition, for instance, when a dreamer encounters their boss in the dream, they can be assured that they are not a literal representation of the person they know from waking life. Instead, the dream-work disguises and displaces the traumatic secret with a less intense figure to keep the dreamer dreaming. Hence the need to remain suspicious of the overt meaning of dreams: A boss may disguise a different kind of authority, such as a father, priest, or president. Whether as "depth semantics" or the "hermeneutics of suspicion," the secret *in* discourse arises because the true meaning of symbols is buried and must be recovered through an interpretive process.

Depth reading is, finally, a strategy for exposing the ideological secret, which is determined and circulated by a ruling interest. This formulation often lends the secret (and, by extension, rhetoric) a negative moral connotation, synonymous with superstructural mystifications that overdetermine the commodity form and the substitution of truth with a kind of experiential immediacy.[31] One example of a framework designed to "unmask" such material forces is John B. Thompson's depth hermeneutics, which offers an interpretative strategy to contest and confront ideological mystifications:

> To unmask a form of consciousness is to show that it is illusory, mistaken or without rational justification; it implies not only that it can be explained by reference to socio-economic conditions, but also that it misrepresents these conditions or that it has no justification other than the empirically demonstrable fact that it expresses the particular interests of groups whose positions are determined by these conditions.[32]

---

28. "Structural analysis," he argues, is "a stage—and a necessary one—between a naïve and a critical interpretation, between a surface and a depth interpretation." Ricoeur, "What Is a Text?," 60.

29. It is important to note that Ricoeur's juxtaposition of "depth semantics" with mere "surface" reading does not carry the nuance that it does in the subsequent section of this chapter. In Ricoeur's use, the term is instead inflected with pejorative connotations such as shallowness or inattention to detail.

30. Ricoeur, *Freud and Philosophy*, 7.

31. Kornbluh, *Immediacy*.

32. J. Thompson, *Ideology and Modern Culture*, 39.

This and similar strategies implicitly theorize the secret as a contradiction between the naivete of taking "everyday" (or "surface") representations at face value and the skepticism that would lead a critic to discover concealed, ideologically determined interests. Depth hermeneutics has "the aim of disclosing meaning in the service of power" and encourages a suspicious attitude toward mass-mediated representations, which distort the true state of things.[33] Strategies like depth hermeneutics, depth semantics, and the hermeneutics of suspicion cohere as the secret *in* discourse, a quantity hidden by erasure, trauma, and mystification. Because this secret is not immediately apprehensible, some strategy is required "to grasp the real idea of the text," that is, to reveal what the secret has buried, covered up, or made imperceptible.[34]

Surface Reading: The Secret *of* Discourse

If the secret *in* discourse is hidden *in* a concealed past, then the secret *of* discourse stages hiddenness as an unpredictable futurity. As a reading strategy, the latter is akin to skipping a stone, such that the signifier makes brief, kinetic contact with different discourses in quick succession. A further feature of the secret *of* discourse is that it is always retroactively produced. It describes something that has always been in the open but which is apprehended only too late, or after the fact. Instead of being "found out," we come upon it by adopting a new point of view that reconfigures knowledge that we already possess. To say that it is *of* discourse signifies that the secret is begotten from other discourses, or that it belongs to a signifying chain where what a sign means *now* is a belated adjustment to what it has previously meant. Rephrased, the secret *of* discourse gains its retroactive inflections by skipping from one position or perspective to another and another. Each skip unsettles the shared sense that meanings are fixed or that reality conceals a deeply "true" essence.

The strategies of textual interpretation most associated with the secret *of* discourse are what literary and cultural critics of the late twentieth and early twenty-first century call *surface readings*. In cinematic, literary, historical, and cultural criticism, "surface" signifies as the formal features of text and discourse that reflect an overt arrangement of power. Resisting Ricoeur's caricature of surfaces as superficial, "weak," "ideologically complicit," "inessential," or "deceptive," surface reading is less about placing our faith in exposure and more about "bearing witness to the given."[35] It seeks "to make visible what is

---

33. J. Thompson, *Ideology and Modern Culture*, 282–88, 292.
34. Gadamer, "Hermeneutics of Suspicion," 316.
35. François, *Open Secrets*, 35.

invisible only because it is too much on the surface of things" vis-à-vis constellations of power, affect, and form.³⁶ As Eve Kosofsky Sedgwick explains, this kind of reading eschews the pretense of finding what is concealed *in, beneath, behind,* or *beyond* a textural surface.

> Without attempting to devalue such critical practices, I have tried in this project to explore some ways around the topos of depth or hiddenness, typically followed by a drama of exposure, that has been such a staple of critical work of the past four decades. *Beneath* and *behind* are hard enough to let go of; what has been even more difficult is to get a little distance from *beyond,* in particular the bossy gesture of "calling for" an imminently perfected critical or revolutionary practice that one can oneself only adumbrate.³⁷

Surface reading is also an admonition of depth readers' knee-jerk imperatives to dive below what a text explicitly states. When addressing the depth tradition of "symptomatic reading" theorized in Fredric Jameson's *The Political Unconscious,* Rita Felski takes issue with the idea that to understand what is hidden, latent, concealed—*inside*—a text, the critic must bring a specifically Marxist or Freudian lens to bear on it, thereby anticipating the very thing that they wish to demystify and expose.³⁸ Surface reading is a practice of "[looking] *at* rather than what we must train ourselves to see *through*"; it examines the overt rather than the deeply hidden.³⁹ In other words, the "deeply hidden" is a ruse: There is no secret except what the critic's theoretical framework sets out to find.

Another common claim among surface readers is that rigorous literary and textual analysis need not be routed through paranoia, the favored affective disposition of depth readers. Sedgwick's encomium to reparative reading explicitly rejects the paranoiac tendency to place faith in exposure as expressing the truest meaning of a text or as an expeditious means to social change. Although this faith may have been appropriate in a mid- to late twentieth-century context, it is not suited to the present age:

> Why bother exposing the ruses of power in a country where, at any given moment, 40 percent of young black men are enmeshed in the penal system? In the United States and internationally, while there is plenty of hidden violence that requires exposure there is also, and increasingly, an ethos

---

36. Foucault, *Foucault Live,* 57–58, quoted in Best and Marcus, "Surface Reading," 13.
37. Sedgwick, *Touching Feeling,* 8.
38. Felski, *Limits of Critique.*
39. Best and Marcus, "Surface Reading," 9.

where forms of violence that are hypervisible from the start may be offered as an exemplary spectacle rather than remain to be unveiled as a scandalous secret.[40]

Instead of a single-minded compulsion to expose, Sedgwick favors fluid "positions" that allow the critic to "interdigitate" between positive and negative affects, offering dispositions like pleasure and amelioration as productive alternatives to paranoia. For surface readers, the secret does not always have a negative valence. There are bad secrets that feel good and good secrets that feel bad; there are secrets that, instead of promising resolution through discovery, deliver ineffable intimacy and community when entrusted to another's care. It is, therefore, fitting that so many surface readers have sought to pluralize the domain of affect by offering anti-universalist accounts of, for instance, "ugly feelings" as formal dynamics that play out on the surface of contemporary culture.[41] Like the move to center "surfaces" rather than "depths," the move to formalize affect inverts the traditional priority of terms like reason and logic over emotion, pathos, and feeling. By elevating the "minor, inconsequential, secret, [and] atomic," such inversions lend renewed importance to surface-level terms as organizing agencies of discourse.

Other variations of surface reading prioritize computational means of moving across texts and refuse to settle on interpretations gotten from exemplary cases. Franco Moretti's "distant reading," for instance, insists upon digital methods that correlate textual elements like pronouns and title construction across wide textual corpora that even multiple readers would be hard-pressed to catalog and process: "Distant reading: where distance, let me repeat it, *is a condition of knowledge*: it allows you to focus on units that are much smaller or much larger than the text: devices, themes, tropes—or genres and systems."[42] Distant reading offers holistic answers to questions such as "How frequent *were* women protagonists in the British Victorian novel?" or "What was the composition of the literary marketplace in the years prior to the French Revolution?" Instead of focusing on meanings beyond or below a textual surface, it looks to surface-level forms like titles and character networks to track circulation, power, and sovereignty as reflected by an aggregate of data.[43] Such analyses open the reader to understanding the secret not as hidden but as inaccessible without the proper tools to observe a discursive surface.

---

40. Sedgwick, *Touching Feeling*, 140.
41. Ngai, *Ugly Feelings*.
42. Moretti, *Distant Reading*, 48–49.
43. Moretti, *Distant Reading*, 179–210; 214–22.

Surface reading takes on a range of foci: affective textures, epochal shifts, and mundane narrative structures. It is a kind of reading that is "close but not deep" and attends to "all shapes and configurations, all ordering principles, all patterns of repetition of difference."[44] Importantly, such readings can and do share depth readers' fascination with the secret. Caroline Levine, for instance, aligns the secret with surface-level forms when discussing the public-private boundaries of the courtroom, the surveillant structure of the graduate seminar, the literary trope of the bureaucracy, and kinship structures like love affairs or intimate family relationships.[45] When explaining how amnesia constitutes the public spectacle that supports covert US foreign policy, Michael Rogin describes forgetting as a cultural production "of surface entertainments—movies, television series, political shows."[46] The function of this culture industry is not to publicize actual secrets or conceal superstructural interests. Rather, it is a form of state exhibitionism that places the transgressive, extralegal secret on the surface of popular attention, fetishizing the state's ability to operate without civic authorization: "The government wants it known that it has the power, secretly, to intervene."[47] Such readings elaborate the secret *of* discourse because they are not hidden *in* or *beneath* anything. They sit on culture's surface, face up, waiting for a change in perspective to lend them gravity.

Deconstructing the Secret in and of Discourse

Strictly speaking, deconstruction is neither a repeatable method nor a framework that can be applied to texts. Rather, a text deconstructs itself once opened to its own contradictions and limits. Even if deconstruction is, as a rule, irreducible to a formula or set of rules, a common feature of many deconstructionist readings is the marking and displacement of a fixed opposition or hierarchy.[48] The key example of this kind of reading is *différance*, a term of art introduced in Derrida's *Speech and Phenomena*. Most crucially, the graphic "a" that distinguishes *différance* from the French *différence* is inaudible but not invisible; it remains ever "silent, *secret*, and discreet, like a tomb."[49] This "a" performs the split, schism, or separation that Derrida's essay theorizes.

---

44. C. Levine, *Forms*, 23, 3.
45. Levine, *Forms*, 21, 47, 99, 123–29.
46. Rogin, "Make My Day!," 106.
47. Rogin, "Make My Day!," 116.
48. See, for instance, Derrida, "Time Is Out of Joint," 17; and Culler, *On Deconstruction*, 156.
49. Derrida, "Différance," 132; italics added.

Is the "a" an instance of *différance,* or is *différance* an instance of the "a"? It is both: *Différance* is a "*sameness* which is not *identical.*" "Neither a *word* nor a *concept,*" it is a thematic of connection, spacing, and deferral.[50] As Barbara A. Biesecker explains, this thematic is useful for disentangling niche theoretical debates, such as whether a speaker's mastery or the situation to which they respond wields the greater force in determining rhetoric's effects:

> From within the thematic of *différance* the "rhetorical dimension" of the text signifies not only the play of the tropological figures operating on its surface level, but also the (non)originary finessing of a division that produces the meaning of the text as such. That is to say, the "rhetorical dimension" names *both* the means by which an idea or argument is expressed and the initial formative intervention that, in centering a differential situation, makes possible the production of meaning.[51]

Biesecker's deconstructionist reading marks and displaces the opposition between a "surface level" of rhetorical figures and the more deeply "formative" situation that occasions them. As she writes, "the 'rhetorical dimension' names *both.*" Another example is the hierarchical distinction between a text's print and its margins. The printed words on a page are often the de facto site of meaning-making, while the margin is blank, meaningless space.[52] Derrida reconfigures these assumptions by demonstrating how the empty margin and the blank space are each preconditions of sense-making.[53] Whether it undoes the primacy of deep causes over "surface-level" effects or resituates the primary site of meaning-making, a common feature among deconstructionist readings is their displacement of hierarchy (i.e., this, *not that*) with a relation of mutual dependency.

Tropes are well suited to deconstructing the secret *in* and *of* discourse because, like *différance,* they trouble hierarchical distinctions between depths (i.e., the terrain of hermeneutics and demystification) and surfaces (the terrain of affect and the signifier). To begin, we might say that depth reading is consistently attuned to tropes *in* discourse, or how language turns to conceal a reference, a traumatic past, instances of living speech, or the subtle, controlling influences of ideology. As stylistic choices that are the trace of an authorial intention, tropes *in* discourse are seemingly purposeful arrangements

---

50. Derrida, "Différance," 129; italics in original.
51. Biesecker, "Rethinking the Rhetorical Situation," 112.
52. Derrida, *Positions,* 4.
53. Biesecker, "Rethinking the Rhetorical Situation," 118; Derrida, *Glas*; and Spivak, "Glas-Piece," 26.

of speech and writing whose meaning can be recovered through a situated analysis of invention, history, and context. Often, this kind of recovery relies on metaphors of decoding or unveiling: Something is presumed to be deeply concealed through (mal)intention or neglect, and the critic's work is to bring it out from the depths. Hence figures such as metaphor may take the form of a secret *in* discourse when it functions as a euphemism (e.g., "loose lips sink ships"), saying one thing to veil another, truer meaning (i.e., gossip hinders national security).

Conversely, surface reading and tropes *of* discourse offer a vocabulary for how impermanent and everyday associations come to appear natural, normal, and fixed. They do not seek to reveal anything, because nothing is presumed "deeply" hidden. Rhetorically, this is a significant reversal: Speaking subjects do not use figures or tropes to craft their speech. Instead, tropes speak through the subject, ventriloquizing them like a puppeteer's dummy in defiance of a willful agent's intentions. Tropes *of* discourse evoke the open secret that *all* language is rhetorical, governed by rules of association and separation that exceed conscious awareness. These rules precede any subject's encounter with language and anticipate the possible permutations of their speech. By this reading, metaphor transforms into a heuristic, describing how contingent associations among different signs become concrete. As Christian O. Lundberg puts it, "Metaphor . . . [exerts] a regulatory role on a chain of signifiers by retroactively organizing a series of metonymic connections . . . around a central figure with substantial gravity."[54] For instance, the tacit association of a presidential declaration of war, travel advisories, and intensified airport security may point to the metaphoric production of a threat as a retroactive linkage among signifiers. Such tropes do not deflect from the truth: They explain the formation of the real.

Trope is a pivot, connection, or juncture between depth and surface reading. It holds rhetoric's capacity for deliberate concealment (*in* discourse) alongside rhetoric's prefigurative functions (*of* discourse). By extension, the secret is not just a strategy for hiding information (*in* discourse), nor is it only retroactive rules (*of* discourse). Rather, the secret is both, and the circularity of the opposition between the *in* and the *of* makes it impossible to invoke the one without also implicating its other. Put another way, the secret and trope share the characteristic of being *active* and *retroactive*: active because anticipatory acts of arrangement (*in* discourse) can have real consequences such as hiding, erasing, and concealing; retroactive because continuous rearrangements (*of* discourse) reconfigure reality in ways that only occur to a person

---

54. Lundberg, "Enjoying God's Death," 389.

or public belatedly, making the secret perceptible only after the fact. Rhetoric is *an active and retroactive* mode of organizing discourse. It creates and re-creates the secret from familiar discursive components, often in the absence of an identifiable rhetor.

There are many tropological forms that we may associate with the secret. This claim amends a common psychoanalytic premise that there are a limited number of symbolic economies that produce signification (i.e., metonymy and metaphor) and which, in turn, guide the formation of publics.[55] For that reason, in later chapters I do not refer to trope as a singular or static category but to multiple tropes that fulfill similar but nonidentical functions concerning the secret. As Jacques Lacan explains, metaphor and metonymy are only two rhetorical terms among many that organize the subject's unconscious and, by extension, their fraught relationship with reality:

> Ellipsis and pleonasm, hyperbaton or syllepsis, regression, repetition, apposition—these are the syntactical displacements; metaphor, catachresis, antonomasia, allegory, metonymy, and synecdoche—these are the semantic condensations; Freud teaches us to read in them the intentions—whether ostentatious or demonstrative, dissimulating or persuasive, retaliatory or seductive—with which the subject modulates his oneiric [dreamlike] discourse.[56]

Such variations on trope are, like *différance*, a "sameness that is not identical," a turning *in* and *of* discourse that never repeats exactly, even if an instance

---

55. I am specifically thinking of Christian Lundberg's concept of "feigned unicity," which offers a related framework. Feigned unicity is the pretense or "illusion of communion between subjects and their others." It is a pre-tense in two senses: (1) Rhetoric furnishes the illusion (or pretense) that the world can be wholly represented through human discourse. (2) Rhetoric furnishes a grammar-like structure called *trope*, which anticipates (as a pre-tense) the limited permutations of language and discourse available to create the illusion of fullness and totality. Feigned unicity is organized by *metonymy* and *metaphor*, which Lundberg argues are sufficiently exhaustive to account for all possible arrangements of language and discourse. *Metonymy* is the logic of free association, or "any contingent connection between signs or a series of signs." *Metaphor* is "function whereby certain metonymic connections become particularly significant points of investment, exerting a regulatory role on a chain of signifiers by retroactively organizing the series of metonymic connections." However, the "totality" of metonymy and metaphor logically undermine the first pre-tense by offering a seemingly complete scheme of tropes to (mis)represent reality. The tropology of *différance* therefore differs from Lundberg's because it insists on a plurality of tropes that bear a passing likeness. However, they are not identical, and rather than bringing forth the illusion of wholeness or completeness, they offer a variety of ways that absence is brought forth as presence (and vice versa). Lundberg, *Lacan in Public*, 3; and Lundberg, "Enjoying God's Death," 389.

56. Lacan, "Function and Field," 221–22, quoted in Lundberg, *Lacan in Public*, 70.

of hiddenness and patterned repetition resonates with others. The secret, by extension, bridges prepositional registers as the organizing difference that connects intentional concealment with those perspectival shifts that put the everyday in new focus. The following sections elaborate on *naming* and *retroaction* as examples of this formal-tropological patterning and illustrate how the secret is internally divided between a deeply hidden substance (*in* discourse) and a surface-level structure (*of* discourse).

Tropes of Naming

The secret has many names: Its proper names often reference events or the medium that documents the act of revelation: the Pentagon Papers (1971); the Gulf of Tonkin Hoax (1964); Watergate (1971) and the Haldeman Tapes (1973); the Iran-Contra Affair (1985–87); Don't Ask, Don't Tell (1994); the Sixteen Words (2003); the Cablegate Leaks (2010); Benghazi (2012); the Mueller Report (2019). Its improper names include (but are not limited to) *conspiracy, cover-up, false-flag, fraud, psyop, whodunit*. Names possess a mystical and life-giving quality. In the Lacanian tradition, "the name of the father" references the big-O Other, a superegoic function or position from whence the subject observes their actions to be either worthy or irredeemable.[57] The father-Other is a metonym, one free-associatively articulated to individuals like the president, the therapist, the teacher, and the workplace supervisor—but also more depersonalized entities like God, the legal code, the incest prohibition, and the rules of language.[58] Inasmuch as the "names of the father" are tropological, some tropes are also specific to naming. One subspecies of metonymy, *antonomasia*, is "the use of an epithet or a patronymic, instead of a proper name, or the reverse."[59] This particular trope lends immaterial and inhuman objects a "material substance" by making the parasite, the gestational sac, the embryo, and the fetus all appear as if they were all viable living beings, "touchable or fleshy or real."[60] Repeating the name lends it a rhetorical realness, even if the "person" to whom it refers never existed.

The overwhelming tendency is for tropes of naming to reference the secret *in* discourse, or a hidden signification concealed by deliberate obfuscation. The names of government agencies are a potent example. The sheer number of agencies dedicated to the concealment of knowledge attests to the

---

57. Žižek, *Sublime Object of Ideology*, 120–21.
58. Lacan, *On the Names-of-the-Father*, 63, 76–77.
59. Rowland, *Zoetropes*, 91.
60. Rowland, *Zoetropes*, 91.

generational accumulation of governmental anti-epistemologies (i.e., knowledge of the concealment of knowledge).⁶¹ During Alan Dulles's tenure as an intelligence officer, for instance, Franklin D. Roosevelt's 1942 Office of Strategic Services (OSS) splintered into the 1947 Central Intelligence Agency (CIA), the 1952 National Security Agency (NSA), the 1957 Bureau of Intelligence and Research (INR), the 1961 Defense Intelligence Agency (DIA), and the 1961 National Reconnaissance Office (NRO).⁶² The division and proliferation of such agencies is a prime example of what Donovan Conley and William O. Saas describe as occultatio, or the means "by which the [George W.] Bush administration actively courted the gaps between the American citizenry, the rule of law, and its own 'war on terror.'"⁶³ In 2002, George W. Bush's Secretary of Defense Donald Rumsfeld capitalized on the proliferation of agency acronyms by announcing "the existence of the infamous Office of Strategic Influence (OSI), a Pentagon propaganda office designed to use whatever informational means necessary to achieve Terror War objectives." "A few days later," however, Rumsfeld declared that "the Office had been officially dismantled."⁶⁴ In actuality, the Secretary of Defense had "kept all the actions of strategic influence, but now under different and hidden names . . . thus heightening the power of strategic influence by announcing the legerdemain as he performed it."⁶⁵

Rumsfeld's OSI and its successors illustrate how occultatio was inherent to his naming strategy. As the secret *in* discourse, it hid the Bush administration's lack of preparedness, its willingness to accept Iraqi civilian casualties, and its personal and financial interests. Other tropes, like *mnesis* and *copia*, mark a similar kind of concealment. In the aggregate, whistleblower names (e.g., "Brockovich," "Snowden," "Silkwood," or "Winner") are often stand-ins for the secret. Over time and through accumulation, however, whistleblower names can engender a form of mnesis, "a dynamic simultaneity of memory *and* its loss with no precedence for one state or another, of having remembered over having forgotten."⁶⁶ Although the leaker persona may be remembered, the specific context that gave them publicity may not, metonymically reducing the name to one act of disclosure among many. One antidote to such forgetting

---

61. Galison, "Removing Knowledge."
62. Stout, "Birth of American Intelligence Culture"; Weiner, *Legacy of Ashes*; Bamford, *Body of Secrets*; Aid, *National Security Agency*; Beck, "Bureau of Intelligence and Research," 5–8; Allen and Shellum, *At the Creation*; and R. C. Hall, *NRO at Forty*.
63. Conley and Saas, "Bush Administration's Rhetorical War," 330.
64. Bratich, "Public Secrecy," 495.
65. Bratich, "Public Secrecy," 495.
66. Stormer, "Recursivity," 31.

is to articulate the name not just to an act of disclosure but to wider movements that resist hegemonic silencing. In the discourse of the #MeToo movement, the "volume" of copious angry testimony modulated sound and space: it "amplified and diminished" the "affective intensity" of plaintiff claims and "aggregated and dispersed bodies, interests, and energies."[67] A similar imperative to name and to remember the secret *in* discourse is attached to Black, Brown, and transgender people targeted for carceral violence and state surveillance. Hence the African American Policy Forum's (AAPF) "Say Her Name" initiative, which featured an ever growing list of the Black women killed by police. The AAPF's copious naming documented "gender-specific forms of anti-Black policing that originated in the lynching era" in rebuke of the "blue wall of silence" that prevents justice for police misconduct, retaliation, and murder.[68] However, as Logan Rae Gomez argues, such acts of memorialization also "encourage a kind of erasure or 'forgetting' that seeks to 'absolve the white nation of its ongoing racial sins,' creating a temporal distancing from past racial harms."[69] The heightened circulation of some names (e.g., Breonna Taylor and Sandra Bland) commodifies, captures, and contains "popular 'figures' of a movement," while the conspicuous absence of others signals how police brutality is an open secret that white America frequently fails to remember.[70]

At the level *of* discourse, names like *criminal, terrorist,* or *traitor* mark the subject as a secret-keeper who is at the mercy of oppressive surveillance systems. When psychiatrist Frantz Fanon theorizes the colonial gaze, he recounts how repeat encounters with racist epithets ("Look, a Negro") hurled by white Europeans brought forth the realization that he had internalized a racist subjectivity that had been foisted upon him.[71] These epithets, which seemed nonsensical or incidental in the first instance, rose to the level of an undeniable pattern. As Fanon explains, the subject hailed by such colonial encounters "epidermalizes" the open secret of their racial caste: The moment of being hatefully named is "an immediate recognition of social and economic realities." Like the infamous "Hey you!" of the police in Louis Althusser's "Ideology and Ideological State Apparatuses," the subject hailed internalizes their subordinate status through a sequence of naming and tropological turning. When the subject turns to face their addressor ("Who, me?"), this tropological response retroactively affirms their recognizability before the law, even if

---

67. Winderman, "Anger's Volumes," 333, 337.
68. Ore, "Discourses of American Lynching," 513.
69. Gomez, "Temporal Containment," 184. Gomez's quotation cites Ore, *Lynching*; and Ore and Houdek, "Lynching in Times of Suffocation."
70. Gomez, "Temporal Containment," 187.
71. Fanon, "Fact of Blackness." See also Athanasopoulos, "Fanonian Slips."

they were not its intended addressee.⁷² This kind of naming evokes the secret *of* discourse because it betrays an open-ended pattern of signification. It is less about the discovery of a deeply hidden meaning than about routinely repeated speech acts that deprive the named subject of agency. It also betrays how the secret does not stop at revelation, and instead figures the knowable, graspable, and governable subject across a multitude of quotidian utterances.

Tropes of Retroactivity

Retroactivity is not one concept but many. References to this belated temporality are features of Freud's *Nachträglichkeit* (or "deferred action"), Derrida's *différance,* and Spinoza's imminent causality (in which "the cause is an effect of its effects)."⁷³ Retroactivity is also a function of many rhetorical tropes presented in this book, such as *synecdoche,* the part that retroactively refashions our perceptions of a w(hole); *megethos,* which reveals only too late how intensifying disclosures are never enough to achieve total transparency, and *analepsis,* the trope of flashbacks that lend narratives continuity, completion, and resolution. Each serves up revelation by facilitating repeat encounters with the past and reveals a meaning hidden in plain sight after the fact.

One example of retroactivity occurs in Maggie Haberman's 2022 retrospective of the Trump presidency, *Confidence Man,* which published images of the former executive disposing of documents by flushing them down a White House toilet.⁷⁴ The potty photos threw Trump's complaints from earlier years into relief: In 2019, he had complained that wasteful Americans were flushing toilets ten or fifteen times, leading to unnecessary water waste amid nationwide droughts.⁷⁵ After Haberman's book, Trump's own tell-tale flushes were revealed as having come from inside his own house, providing a new perspective upon accusations that were already part of the public record. As Davin Allen Grindstaff puts it: "The belief that secretive contents *precede* their disclosure attributes a certain 'truth' status to the contents themselves."⁷⁶ Haberman's after-the-fact view of these secret flushes gave a new perspective to Trump's old statements, retroactively making the disposed-of contents into a renewed site of public fascination.

---

72. Althusser, "Ideological State Apparatuses."
73. May, "Spinoza and Class Struggle," 205; and Kordela, *Surplus,* 1.
74. Haberman, *Confidence Man,* 294–96.
75. Picheta, Carvajal, and Wallace, "Trump Claims Americans."
76. Grindstaff, *Rhetorical Secrets,* 25.

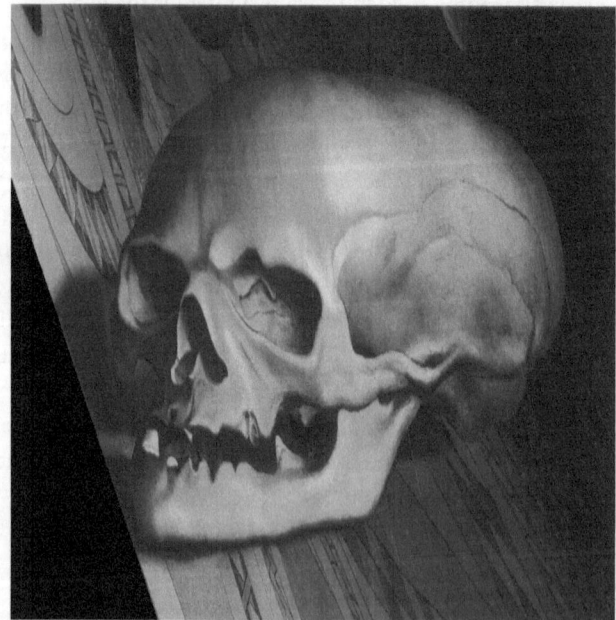

FIGURE 2.1. (top) Hans Holbein the Younger, *The Ambassadors*, 1533. Oil on oak, 207 × 209.5 cm. © The National Gallery, London. All rights reserved. (bottom) Close-up from a "corrected" angle.

If, at their most literal, tropes are turns, then retroactivity turns back time by shifting an observer's spatial and epistemic perspective. In *The Four Fundamental Concepts of Psychoanalysis*, Jacques Lacan offers a related concept in anamorphosis, a strategy used to compose *The Ambassadors*, a 1533 Tudor painting by Hans Holbein the Younger (see figure 2.1).[77] The painting depicts two ornately dressed European diplomats standing next to a table overflowing with instruments of knowledge. Viewed head-on, *The Ambassadors* depicts mandolins, measuring devices, scrolls, and globes: a comprehensive inventory of tools used to reveal Nature's hidden knowledge, its secret *in* discourse. However, as the spectator moves away from the painting's center, the stain that covers the painting's lower quadrant becomes visible as an upright skull. This is the *memento mori*: the reminder of death that appears as a large, distorted shape across the lower half of the canvas. Painted to be viewed upright only from an oblique angle, the skull is meant to be perceptible retroactively, *after* the image is viewed from the head-on position. This is the secret *of* discourse, or a retroactive recognition that is emblematic of the subjective relation to "a secret missing object" as "the cause of the subject's desire to see and understand it all: reality, truth, the world, and its own place within this world."[78] Always there, in the open, but not always perceptible, the skull stages "the veridicality of representation as 'not-whole,'" unmaking the painting's initial impression of epistemic completeness.

Holbein's anamorphosis offers several lessons about the secret's retroactivity. On the one hand, it unsettles and resituates the spectator as "as someone who is looked at from a place other than the one from which she sees."[79] What is unsettling is that the viewer observes themselves being watched from a point of view that had remained, until that point, secret. The position of the big-O Other appears to shift as "the projected point from which we take ourselves to be observed is detached from the object."[80] On the other hand, it symbolizes the secret as a tension between reality and the gaze, between the fantasy that appears "as if" it is whole and the surplus element that undermines the pretense of fullness or completion:

> In everyday reality, the gaze is normally elided. When it is not, however, its intrusion becomes a disturbing presence that destabilizes reality. This incompatibility between the gaze and reality gives Holbein's *The Ambassadors* its

---

77. Lacan, *Four Fundamental Concepts*, 86–89.
78. Finkelde, "Anamorphosis," 14.
79. Copjec, *Read My Desire*, 184.
80. Biesecker, "Prospects of Rhetoric," 27.

exemplary status, since the viewer is unable to perceive simultaneously the skull and the "reality" of what is depicted in the painting.[81]

Although the secret skull may appear to be hidden, missing, or absent on the first pass, it is always there as an excessive, unintelligible signifier. The secret is not just *in* the painting, it is a function *of* how the painting was arranged to account for the observer's shifting point of view.

Retroactivity offers several further insights about the secret *in* and *of* discourse. First, retroaction may enlist a combination of visual and verbal grammars. In Aneesh Chaganty's (2018) film *Searching*, for instance, a sequence of scenes that transpire entirely on a computer screen take the viewer through bereaved father David Kim's realization that his missing daughter, Margaret, has likely been kidnapped.[82] As Kim uploads images of Margaret to a memorial website, the camera pauses on an image of a smiling white woman thanking him for his submission. It then hesitates on the image of the woman before moving the cursor with increasing intensity to the computer's saved images of Margaret and her different social media accounts, ultimately landing on "YouCast," a fictional video chat site. There, Kim recovers a video of Margaret speaking with another user, @fish_n_chips, whose avatar matches the memorial website photo. Subsequent clicks show Kim accessing reverse-image and -address search and a voice-over in which he speaks to the model directly, confirming that the information gathered from police interviews with @fish_n_chips had been falsified. Kim's retroactive realization that he should continue "searching" for his daughter is thus communicated through a predominantly visual text in which a computer cursor performs the work of belated discovery.

Second, the secret's retroactivity describes a shift that is experienced as a realization that one lacks an independent capacity to act. The subject's recognition that they have lost their agency intensifies their sense that a watching Other was always the one in control and that their perception of free choice was a deception from the start. In the case of Fanonian epidermalization and Althusser's interpellative hail, for instance, the realization that one has been assigned a (colonial or ideological) subjectivity arrives belatedly. The subject's status before the law is uncertain until after they have already affirmed themselves as its likely addressee ("Who, me?"). In subsequent chapters, the scandal, the dog whistle, the leak, and the detective mobilize similar kinds of retroactive turning. Each foregrounds a name whose meaning turns, shifts,

---

81. Broadfoot, "Anamorphosis as Colonial Encounter," 273.
82. Chaganty, *Searching*.

and is resignified according to pre-figurative rhetorical rules that allow the loss of agency to dawn belatedly upon a named subject.

No Mere Secrets

The political secret is not a deceptive illusion. Rather, it is a rigorously constructed form of emptiness, one that furnishes the spectating subject's sense that US politics is a ceaseless game of concealment and revelation. Trope offers a way to name the formal rules of this game. It accounts for the discursive patterns that allow the secret to appear actively hidden *in* discourse and to exist at the surface-level *of* discourse, where its rhetoric retroactively unfolds. Surely, there are other ways to understand the secret's grip upon the US political imagination. What is uniquely valuable about the rhetorical approach presented here is that it offers a structural explanation for the secret's recurrence across many different instances of political discourse.

Another way of saying this is *yes, of course there are real secrets out there*. They are *in* discourse, lurking in the backdrop of public life, appearing to lie in wait until the moment of their discovery. However, reading for the secret also entails seeking a strategy for understanding how such discourse covers its own tracks, or how the work of retroaction enables data that was always and already in the open to present itself as if it were the stuff of revelation. The secret has a double force because it is both hidden and overt, both a repressed kernel and a banal, infrequently noticed signifier. The tropological readings in the following chapters offer provisional explanations of the secret's repetitions with a difference, its varied production of desire. Consistently, what we gain when we learn to read the secret rhetorically is the sense that no matter how new the information, we have been here before, transforming our encounters with the unknown into an all too familiar plot.

CHAPTER 3

The Scandal

George W. Bush and the Exposure of Valerie Plame Wilson

> [Because] every decision worthy of the name must be this exceptional scandal of a passive decision or decision of the other, the difference between the deciding decision and the undecided decision itself becomes undecidable, and then the supposed decision, the exceptionally sovereign decision looks, like two peas in a pod, just like an indecision, an unwilling, a nonliberty, a nonintention, an unconsciousness and an irrationality . . . and then the supposed sovereign subject begins, by an invincible attraction, to look like the beast he is supposed to subject to himself.
> —Jacques Derrida, *The Beast and the Sovereign, Vol. 1* (33)

The Plame Wilson Precedent

A common refrain about Donald Trump's first-term presidency (2016–20) is that it was unprecedented. His administration engaged in witness tampering; promoted a corrupt, quid-pro-quo foreign policy agenda; espoused a racist rhetoric that banned Muslim immigration; separated migrant families at the Mexico-US border; and instigated the seditious riot at the US Capitol on January 6, 2021. As Sarah Kendzior explained in 2020, the compounding effect of Trump-era scandals is a crushing affective load that intensifies collective amnesia and individual anxiety:

> In Trump's America of nonstop crises, every day brings a soul-crushing development or an earth-shattering revelation. But I can rarely pinpoint where I was for any of them without a struggle, the way the details of a nightmare fade when you awaken but your body stays tense with fright. Everyone I know who follows the news closely experiences the same exhausting disorientation. We are trapped in a reality TV autocrat's funhouse mirror, a

blurred continuum of shock and sorrow that exhausts our capacity for clarity of thought.[1]

These "non-stop crises" have led critics to attempt imperfect comparisons between Trump and prior administration-defining scandals. Nixon is a case in point: Trump's first-term campaign advisor, Roger Stone, was a former Nixon official who brokered a leak of stolen information from Hillary Clinton's campaign chair, John Podesta, just before election day in 2016.[2] In the summer of 2022, the January 6 hearings led by Bennie Thompson (D-MS) and Liz Cheney (R-WY) renewed Nixon comparisons. The testimony of former Trump staffer Cassidy Hutchinson was described as a "John Dean" moment, referencing how a former loyalist to Nixon had turned against their administration under oath.[3] Similarly, a seven-hour gap in Trump's January 6, 2021, call logs evoked comparisons to similar gaps in the Nixon-era Haldeman tapes, which had functioned as key evidence during the 1974 Watergate trial, *United States v. Mitchell*.[4]

Trump's solicitation of Ukraine president Volodymyr Zelenskyy on July 25, 2019 (also known as the "Ukrainegate" scandal), is perhaps the best example of how the 45th presidency twisted features of earlier presidential scandals together to form a recognizable genre.[5] Once again resorting to the tactic of seeking extortionary intelligence on his political adversaries, Ukrainegate showcased evidence of Trump, the sitting president, seeking *kompromat* to use against his 2020 Democratic opponent, Joseph R. Biden. Here, the telltale evidence took the form of a recorded phone call between Trump and Zelenskyy, again recalling Nixon's secretly taped conversations with advisers, members

---

1. Kendzior, *Hiding in Plain Sight*, 14–15.
2. Bank, DiMauro, and Pehme, *Get Me Roger Stone*.
3. Haberman, "Cassidy Hutchinson Stuns."
4. Shammas, "7-Hour Gap in Trump's Calls."
5. The 2019 "Ukrainegate" scandal (also known as the Trump-Ukraine scandal or the Ukraine Affair) centered around allegations that then-President Donald Trump improperly used his presidential power to pressure Ukraine to investigate his political rival Joe Biden and Biden's son Hunter, who had business dealings in Ukraine. On July 25, 2019, Trump asked Ukrainian President Volodymyr Zelenskyy to "do us a favor" by investigating the Bidens and alleged Ukrainian interference in the 2016 US election, while withholding nearly $400 million in congressionally approved military aid to Ukraine as leverage. A whistleblower complaint from a US intelligence official brought these matters to public attention in September 2019, leading to Trump's first impeachment by the House of Representatives in December 2019 on charges of abuse of power and obstruction of Congress. Trump was subsequently acquitted by the Republican-controlled Senate in February 2020. Crane, "Timeline of Key Events"; and Fandos, "Trump Acquitted."

of Congress, and foreign political leaders.[6] Ukrainegate also invited an equal share of comparisons to the Reagan-era Iran-Contra Affair.[7] Whereas Trump had threatened to withhold weapons defense systems from Ukraine amid an ongoing invasion by Russian military forces, Ronald Reagan had defied Congress by trading arms to Iran to fund anti-communist regime change in Nicaragua. Ultimately, both Trump and Reagan were subject to impotent threats of impeachment, refashioning their respective scandals as retroactive proof of each president's political resilience in the face of damning evidence.[8]

Other continuities reference the secret more explicitly. All three—Nixon, Reagan, and Trump—adopted a "paranoid style" of public address, each one fashioning themselves as uniquely attuned to a secret conspiracy of enemies who relentlessly sought to undermine not only the president but the American people.[9] During Watergate, "the paranoid style" constituted the "past motives, actions, and statements of the conspirators . . . as part of a twisted, secret world," shaping Nixon's vision of the "conflict between secrecy and democracy."[10] This speaking style has also earned Trump comparisons to Reagan: Both have been described as "Teflon Dons" (a reference originally attributed to John Gotti) for flouting congressional authority and evading legal

---

6. Rangappa, "President Is a National Security Threat"; and Conway and Katyal, "Trump Has Done Plenty."

7. The Iran-Contra Scandal spanned nearly a decade, beginning with the 1979 Iran Hostage Crisis and ending with Ronald Reagan's Address to the Nation in 1987. Seeking to fortify their global war on communism, in 1981 the Central Intelligence Agency (CIA) began to secretly sell weapons to Iran to fund anti-Sandinista Contras in Nicaragua. After becoming aware of the sales, Congressional oversight committees sought to prohibit agencies from providing financial assistance to anti-Marxist revolutionaries and secured an agreement with the CIA to discontinue its activities. However, illegal arms sales continued under the National Security Council (NSC) under the leadership of National Security Advisor Robert McFarlane, Rear Admiral John Poindexter, and Lieutenant Colonel Oliver North. In 1985, the NSC approved two separate arms sales to Iran under the pretense of releasing American hostages in Lebanon, again with the intent of funding the Contras. The following year, investigative journalist Hassan Sabra published an exposé about the sales in the Beirut magazine *Al Shiraa*. Shortly thereafter, Ronald Reagan convened the Tower Commission to investigate his own administration's role in the sales, and new, ad hoc Congressional committees were subsequently formed to investigate the covert arms transactions with Iran. During these hearings, North played an important role in defending the president's ability to authorize secret military operations. Reagan, in his 1987 address, famously evaded responsibility for the scandal with the following denial: "A few months ago I told the American people I did not trade arms for hostages. My heart and my best intentions still tell me that's true; but the facts and the evidence tell me it is not." Byrne, *Iran-Contra*, 42; Rogin, "Make My Day!"; and Rubenstein, *This Is Not a President*, 50–72.

8. Rossinow, "Politics Saved Ronald Reagan."

9. Gunn, *Political Perversion*, 83–84; Mercieca, *Demagogue for President*, 120; and Neville Shepherd, "Paranoid Style."

10. Hofstadter, *Paranoid Style in American Politics*, 16; and Goodnight and Poulakos, "Conspiracy Rhetoric," 301.

recrimination.[11] As evidenced by two failed impeachments, multiple criminal convictions that resulted in no legal penalty, and his consequence-free theft of classified national security documents, nothing has seemed to "stick" to Trump. His "Teflon" persona is attributable to the fact that he has eluded accountability for actions perpetrated in plain, public view.

Beyond Nixon and Reagan, there is another, albeit less considered, analogy to Trump's slippery evasiveness: the Valerie Plame Wilson Scandal. Like so many events during the first Trump administration, this scandal put the president's secrets brazenly out in the open but was nonetheless ineffectual when leveraged as evidence of the George W. Bush Administration's criminality. Plame Wilson's outing as a member of the CIA's counterproliferation division was widely suspected to be an act of retaliation against her spouse, US diplomat Joseph C. Wilson IV. Wilson had written loudly and publicly about Bush's baseless claim that Iraq possessed nuclear fissile materials, which the president repeatedly used to justify his ever-expanding war on terror. Another parallel to Trump's presidential scandals is that the scandal concerned the improper handling of classified information. Like the endlessly disappointing Mueller Report, it also illuminated the limitations of federal investigations into a sitting commander in chief. Most of all, the case is an exemplar of the secret scandal because it engages an escalating series of tropological and symbolic gestures whereby one secret begets another, and another, culminating in a general climate of suspicion and denial.

The many contextual displacements of Plame Wilson's secret lead me to describe this event as a *purloined letter*, a missing quantity around which different characters revolve, endlessly changing positions without ever revealing what it conceals. Additionally, the scandal and its many aftershocks illuminate how scandals are prolonged by protections of whiteness. In that regard, it is a representative anecdote for the secret's ambivalence, or how it "bites back," leaving no party unpolluted even as it protects the powerful from accountability. In retrospect, Plame Wilson's privilege as an affiliate of the national security state insulated her from public scrutiny until 2017, when she recirculated antisemitic conspiracy theories while campaigning for the US House of Representatives in New Mexico.[12] She ended a subsequent campaign in 2020 after these charges reemerged during the Democratic primary.[13] The case is a cautionary tale about the way that scandals are formative of spectacle, how the spectacle directs a public gaze, and how this gaze abets the creep of fascism.

---

11. Copjec, *Read My Desire*, 141–50.
12. Roberts, "Valerie Plame's Horrible Anti-Semitic Tweet."
13. Kessler, "Dark-Money Group Smears Valerie Plame."

Two caveats: First, there is no proof that the Plame Wilson Scandal meaningfully curbed the Bush administration's penchant for war, nor that it brought on greater accountability. To the contrary, scandals sustain the presidency. Despite his record of wartime environmental devastation, approximately 700,000 counted Afghan and Iraqi civilian casualties, and the fact that the Kuala Lumpur War Crimes Commission referred charges against Bush officials to the International Criminal Court, George W. Bush enjoyed a disturbing rehabilitation during Donald Trump's first term in office.[14] It is no accident that one of Trump's early acts was to pardon I. Scooter Libby, who was the only member of the Bush administration held responsible for the Plame Wilson scandal.[15] We should see in Bush's rehabilitation a precedent for Trump's own return to the White House in 2024.[16]

Second, the secret does not have to be especially popular to do its work. Even the biopic about the scandal, *Fair Game,* performed poorly in box office sales, grossing only 9.5 million dollars in the United States, its total profit barely exceeding production costs.[17] For most Americans, the scandal was an unremarkable episode of the Bush II years. But that is the point. While Bush waged war under the false pretense of installing democracy, the scandal concerning Plame Wilson's secret identity placed the focus back on the harms suffered by a white and American member of America's intelligence services, amounting to a domestic distraction from wartime violence perpetrated in Iraq and Afghanistan.

The Plame Wilson Scandal and the Presidential Secret

In early 2003, President George W. Bush delivered a controversial State of the Union address alleging that Iraq was conspiring with Niger to purchase raw materials for nuclear weapons. In July of the same year, Joseph Wilson IV published an opinion piece in *The New York Times* titled "What I Didn't Find in Africa."[18] A former diplomat, Wilson had been hired by the CIA in 2002 to determine whether Niger was planning to sell nuclear fissile materials to Iraq. When he returned to the United States, he informed the CIA that such a sale was "highly unlikely." Wilson's credibility was reinforced by the fact that he

---

14. Rawaf, "2003 Iraq War"; Crawford, *War-Related Death*; Falk, "Bush and Blair Guilty"; and C. Pierce, "War Criminals Among Us."
15. Raymond, "Bush Bashes Bigotry."
16. Tanenhaus, "Bush Family Image-Rehab Machine."
17. Liman, *Fair Game*; and Kroll and Harrison, "Box-Office Report," 10.
18. J. Wilson, "What I Didn't Find in Africa."

had been to Iraq and Niger and knew the political climate of both countries intimately. His editorial chastised the Bush Administration for misrepresenting the facts, accusing the executive of warmongering. Although Wilson was not the first to write about the Bush administration's false pretenses for war, his editorial became a lightning rod for the subsequent scandal.[19]

A week later, Robert Novak,[20] then a columnist for *The Washington Post*, revealed the covert identity of Wilson's spouse, CIA counterproliferation expert Valerie Plame Wilson.[21] Seeing the connection between the July 6 critique and the July 15 information leak, Joe Wilson demanded accountability, culminating in a 2005–7 federal investigation by Special Counsel Patrick Fitzgerald. During this period, Novak hinted at possible sources, including CIA spokesman Bill Harlow and Republican strategist Karl Rove.[22] The investigation concluded with the conviction of Vice-Presidential Aide I. Lewis "Scooter" Libby, who Plame Wilson claimed had outed her.[23] Libby was found guilty of obstruction of justice, perjury, and issuing false statements.[24] He was penalized with a $250,000 fine, two years of probation, and a thirty-month term in a federal prison. In 2010, the Plame Wilson story was released as a feature film starring Sean Penn and Naomi Watts. The title, *Fair Game*, referenced Karl Rove's statement that the CIA operative's covert identity had been "fair game" in Joe Wilson's flame war.[25]

When DC-based journalists, industry circles, or policy wonks invoked the Plame Wilson Scandal, it was often situated within a larger narrative arc involving George W. Bush's declaration of war in Iraq and his administration's intensification of American national security. Given how Plame Wilson's exposure was set within that larger public frame, it is sensible that

---

19. In a since-deleted tweet, independent journalist Marcy Wheeler explained that Wilson's opinion-editorial was preceded by a March 16th story in *The Washington Post*. Marcy Wheeler (@emptywheel), "The standard story behind the exposure of Plame's ID is that it was (just) retaliation for Joe Wilson's NYT op-ed. Not true. The effort started weeks before that, in response to a Walter Pincus story relying on CIA sources who knew there'd be no WMD," Twitter, March 20, 2019. See also Pincus, "U.S. Lacks Specifics on Banned Arms."

20. Robert Novak was a pivotal in facilitating journalistic leaks long before the Plame Wilson scandal. In 1976, Rowland Evans and Robert Novak publicized the leak of the "Sonnenfeldt Doctrine" as reporters with *The Washington Post*. The "Doctrine" was an unofficial foreign policy stance advanced by State Department counselor Helmut Sonnenfeldt in association with US Secretary of State Henry Kissinger; it was especially controversial because it proposed to recognize USSR sovereignty over former Soviet-bloc Baltic nations, marking a significant shift in US Cold War policy. Evans and Novak, "Soviet-East Europe 'Organic Union.'"

21. Novak, "Mission to Niger."
22. Folkenflik and Chadwick, "Novak Reveals Details."
23. Kessler, "Valerie Plame's Claim."
24. Glass, "'Scooter' Libby Convicted."
25. Liman, *Fair Game*.

Bush's justifications for how, when, and why to go to war were the dominant focus of scholarship about Bush-era rhetoric from 2001 to 2007. Precedents for the Bush administration's unwarranted expansion of secret presidential powers range from the *arcana imperii* to Vice-President Dick Cheney's twentieth-century influence and interventions.[26] Once the Bush administration entrenched such powers, they were not easily unmade: "Because much of the power given to the president is backed by new and increasing bureaucratic machinery and legal processes, it is unlikely that executive secrecy and clandestine operations will subside."[27] The George W. Bush era also produced dissonance between the interests of US government officials and what the public perceived as its most pressing concerns: "A vast chasm separated public views of national priorities from the US national security establishment's concerns about terrorism."[28] Often, the war was marketed as consonant with a vision of progressive, liberatory politics, shrouded in prosocial values promoting gender equality that implicitly justified nationalist imperatives for going to war.[29] Of course, this propaganda was also at odds with George W. Bush's escalation of airport security, his violations of human rights at Guantanamo Bay, and his efforts to legally neutralize protesting Americans' First Amendment rights.

Although there have been few academic reflections on the Plame Wilson Scandal's long-term significance, rhetorical analyses of the W. Bush administration's use of secrecy fall into three categories: (1) its improper use of evidentiary warrants, (2) its signature style that produced opacity, and (3) the creep of presidential secrecy vis-à-vis a narrow interpretation of Article II of the US Constitution. Rhetoricians who argued that the George W. Bush administration's secrecy was couched in evidentiary weaknesses frequently drew attention to his empty accusation that Iraq was harboring illegal weapons.[30] For instance, David Zarefsky's analysis of the argumentative structure of Powell's wartime appeal to the United Nations argued that the administration transmuted an absence of evidence about Iraq's nuclear program into proof of Hussein's deliberate concealment of weapons of mass destruction.[31] A second rhetorical explanation of the W. Bush Administration's secrecy involves the "occultic style," which combined redaction, esoteric language, and stonewalling to keep torture policies away from public scrutiny.[32] Stephen J. Hartnett and Jennifer

---

26. Warshaw, *Co-Presidency of Bush and Cheney*.
27. Pallitto and Weaver, *Presidential Secrecy*, 18.
28. Naftali, "Bush and the 'War on Terror,'" 60.
29. Puar, *Terrorist Assemblages*, 79–113.
30. Jamieson, "Justifying the War in Iraq."
31. Zarefsky, "Making the Case for War," 287.
32. Conley and Saas, "Bush Administration's Rhetorical War."

Mercieca label such deceptions as features of the "post-rhetorical presidency," suggesting that presidential secrecy prevents democratic exchange on the one hand and encourages public disinterest on the other.[33] Finally, some scholars understood the George W. Bush Administration's secretive rhetoric as a product of Constitutional revisionism. As Vanessa Beasley argues of the expanding definitions of the unitary executive, historically, the president's "rhetorical skill set accompanies an expansion of his office's powers," while using wartime declarations to seize control of institutions and policies that would not normally be under their control.[34] One example concerns how W. Bush used such expanded powers to restrict public access to presidential records. Referencing Executive Order 13233, Mary Stuckey claims that Bush "launched an all-out assault on the practice of preserving and opening presidential documents by reducing the power of the archivists over presidential papers and increasing the power of individual presidents—and their successors—to determine what gets opened, and more importantly, what remains closed."[35]

The US Presidency as Purloined Letter

One reason these approaches may have been an ill fit for the Plame Wilson Scandal is that it was not exactly known how presidential powers were abused in exposing her covert identity, nor who exposed it. To that end, Diane Rubenstein offers a rhetorical critique oriented specifically to presidential powers exercised in secret and for which there is no "smoking gun." In her account of the highly publicized Iran-Contra Affair, Rubenstein argues that confidential hearings, briefings, and missing intelligence reports shored up tremendous public speculation regarding President Ronald Reagan's "hidden referential content," or the clandestine knowledge that Reagan concealed.[36] Congressional proceedings never recovered hard evidence that the president had foreknowledge of illicit arms sales abroad.[37] A dismayed journalistic public instead embarked on an indefinite, obsessive, circular, and self-defeating search characterized as *enjoyment*.[38] A psychoanalytic term of art, enjoyment refers to "an indescribable compulsion toward painful pleasure *or* pleasurable

---

33. Hartnett and Mercieca, "Discovered Dissembler," 600.
34. Beasley, "Rhetorical Presidency," 27.
35. Stuckey, "Presidential Secrecy," 138. See also Parry-Giles, "Archival Research," 159–63.
36. Rubenstein, *This Is Not a President*, 52.
37. Byrne, *Iran-Contra*, 321.
38. Rubenstein, *This Is Not a President*, 20–21.

pain."³⁹ It is an ambivalent affect that produces "a subject, and the set of habits, investments, and relations that orient a subject toward its world." Enjoyment of the secret generates an endless encircling that prohibits grasping the thing itself. To borrow Rubenstein's phrasing, the secret replaces the "pursuit of happiness" with a self-defeating "pursuit of enjoyment," one whose recurring promise is that the satisfaction of accountability is just one (more) revelation away.⁴⁰

Jacques Lacan's "Seminar on 'The Purloined Letter'" offers a model for the enjoyable repetition and deferral that keeps the secret in indefinite suspense.⁴¹ The subject of the seminar is Edgar Allan Poe's "Purloined Letter," which tells the story of a royal scandal. The plot is somewhat circular: A Queen receives a compromising letter in the King's presence and conceals it by placing it face down, whereupon the Minister D- enters. The Minister D- quickly recognizes that the Queen is hiding the secret, casually drops a decoy letter on the table, and steals the dangerous document as the Queen watches, unable to act. The Queen then enlists Auguste Dupin, an "analyst," to retrieve the letter after the Prefect of the police has repeatedly failed to do so. Dupin infiltrates the Minister D-'s home, immediately sees the letter perched in plain sight, and fabricates a ruse to steal the letter back. He successfully replaces it with a fake and returns the original to the Queen. The reader never learns what is in the letter.

In Lacan's interpretation, the most important aspect of the story is how the secret puts the different characters into relation. Specifically, there are three recurring character types that appear in the two scenes of "The Purloined Letter" (see figure 3.1).⁴² The first "scene" is in the Royal Boudoir, the second in the Minister D-'s apartment.

   A. The King's oblivious gaze recurs when the Prefect of police cannot find the letter. Here, the secret is in plain sight, but the observers are "imbecilic" and cannot grasp what they are looking at.
   B. The Queen's obvious concealment recurs when the Minister D- crumples and hides the letter in a place where Auguste Dupin can easily find it.
   C. The Minister D-'s theft and substitution recurs when Auguste Dupin steals the letter and leaves his own false copy. Both purloin the letter and thereby shift a whole dynamic animated by political intrigue.

---

39. Lundberg, *Lacan in Public*, 401; italics added.
40. Rubenstein, *This Is Not a President*, 8.
41. Lacan, "Seminar on 'The Purloined Letter.'"
42. Felman, *Lacan and the Adventure of Insight*, 41–42.

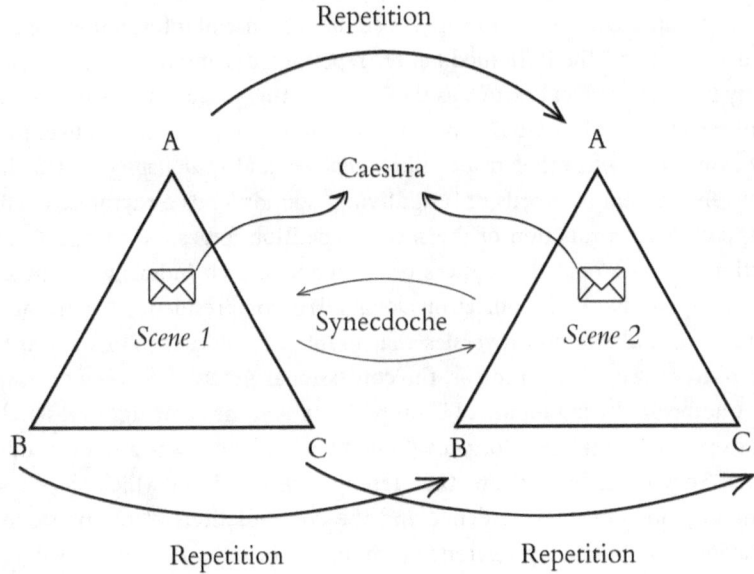

FIGURE 3.1. Repetition, caesura, and synecdoche, three rhetorical tropes that organize the narrative presentation of the scandalous secret letter in Edgar Allan Poe's "The Purloined Letter."

Lacan's interest in Poe's story is both figural and literal. The secret is the metonymic equivalent of a literal letter (i.e., the *objet petit a*) and a signifier, a nonsignifying element of language. What is important is not what is *in* the letter but how the letter-signifier allows the secret to be enjoyed as a function *of* the characters' positional repetition.

As is the case with many scandals, the contents of the letter (or the email, the report, and so on) can draw fascination, prioritizing the secret *in* discourse at the expense of attending to the secret *of* discourse. Much like the allure of the Queen's concealed document, concentrating only on what is *in* the text can mean missing the secret *of* discourse, or the retroactive, relational quality that enables it to continuously regenerate a mysterious allure. In "The Purloined Letter" and its related cases, the secret *of* discourse takes three tropological forms: repetition, caesura, and synecdoche (see figure 3.1). Put succinctly, repetition describes a repeated presencing of absence that signals the secret's existence, caesura accounts for the central, albeit contentless, character of the scandalous secret as a site of desirous fascination, and synecdoche captures the displacement of one scene, event, or emergency for another as the secret changes hands.

First, *repetition* may be understood as a variation on metonymy, a kind of free-associative connection in which a similar absence of information appears in succession. In "The Purloined Letter," repetition dictates the structural similarity between such characters as the King and the police, the Queen and the Minister D-, the Minister D- and Auguste Dupin. Repetition is conventionally associated with other tropes like *anaphora* and *epanalepsis*, in which a recurrence of similar words or "asignifying" sounds lends a rhythmic quality to speech.[43] As a function of the secret, repetition forges a contingent connection between related instances of hiddenness, each indexing a similarly obscure quantity. At the outset of Donald Trump's presidency, for instance, there were multiple controversies that pointed to hidden information: his refusal to release his tax returns, the confessional *Access Hollywood* tape, the FISA-authorized wiretapping of Trump Tower, and the campaign's close relationship to the WikiLeaks organization.[44] Each of these was a known, open secret. They described actions that Trump disavowed but which were confirmed by documentary evidence and the contradictions of the president's behavior and speech. By referencing moments of omission, disavowal, and absence, "nothing" is repeated, and it is in repeating that this "nothing" becomes conspicuous.

Second, *caesura* describes the retroactive coherence of not just any signifier but the secret. It is a gap that knits together a bigger picture and gives rise to the sense that a single, conspiratorial plot unites many different threads. In "The Purloined Letter," the letter is a caesura; it is a nodal point that, in staying unrevealed, knots together the dynamic relationships that encircle it. In the case of Donald Trump, his continuous disavowals of Project 2025 in the run-up to the 2024 presidential election allude to one such caesura: His repeated refusal to acknowledge his proximity to this set of policy proposals generated a silence in which the secret was at once out in the open and out of focus. In the scandal featured by this chapter, Valerie Plame Wilson went missing and refused to speak, both crafting a secret persona and the impression that there were still hidden details concerning her case that had yet to come out.

Finally, *synecdoche* describes a subjective transformation of the secret. This trope is operative when our understanding of a "whole" scene of relationships is undermined and refashioned. In "The Purloined Letter," the Queen, presumptively at the top of the social hierarchy, is made beholden to one of her Ministers, and vice versa. Synecdoche is the part that *is* the w(hole), or how "one particular difference assumes the representation of a totality that

---

43. Lanham, *Handlist of Rhetorical Terms*, 11, 66–67, 130, 189–90.
44. "Avoiding Taxes, Trump-Style"; "Transcript: Donald Trump's Taped Comments"; "Trump's Wiretap Allegation"; and Hallsby, "Rhetorical Algorithm."

exceeds it."⁴⁵ The hole-whole distinction accounts for the loss of one vision of social totality at the moment another is gained, a perspectival shift whereby the secret repositions the relational dynamics that encircle it. This shift is uncanny: Social reality is both the same and not the same as it once was.⁴⁶ When Donald Trump was reelected in 2024, many Democratic voters experienced this very shift: The harms of the first Trump presidency had seemed obvious, overt, and catastrophic. His stated intentions—to dismantle US institutions, take vengeance on his enemies, and destroy reproductive rights— were well known and explicitly stated. Trump's reelection alluded to a "hole" in Democrats' perception that such deficits would prevent a reelection and prompted a reimagining of the "whole" electorate that had propelled Trump to victory.

For many Americans, the secret is a fantasy of total transparency, as if *all* the executive's secret actions could be made known. This kind of fantasy is what Jacques Lacan and Joan Copjec describe as "the realist's imbecility."⁴⁷ Like the King and the Prefect of Police, the imbecile looks directly at the secret without seeing it. In practice, this phrase signals a misplaced faith in fact-checking as adequate to disabuse a voting public of its illusions. However, to prefer the referent to the signified is often a losing battle. To return to the opening example of this section, the fact-checking that sought to definitively prove Reagan had lied about his foreknowledge of the Iran-Contra Affair failed to shake the public out of their obsession with the former actor. "Fact-checking" was akin to trying to reveal the purloined letter's hidden contents, which were shrouded in government bureaucracy and denial. In becoming obsessed with the contents of the letter, the fact-checking public eschewed the relational dynamic that had bound an adoring public to Reagan:

> So absorbed were the news staffs in pinning down the president's lies and errors—his referential failures, let us call them—that they neglected to consider the intersubjective dimension of the whole affair; they forgot to take account of the strength of the American audience's *love* for Reagan. . . . Americans didn't love Reagan for what he said, but simply because he was Reagan.⁴⁸

Reagan, like Trump, successfully embodied an American je ne sais quoi, a surplus of the secret that enabled white Americans to identify with the president's

---

45. Laclau, *Rhetorical Foundations*, 72.
46. Freud, *Uncanny*, 147.
47. Lacan, "Seminar on 'The Purloined Letter,'" 17; Copjec, *Read My Desire*, 141.
48. Copjec, *Read My Desire*, 143.

frontiersman persona and color-blind rhetoric.[49] For conservative Americans, Reagan didn't keep secrets, Reagan *had* the secret, *was* the secret; he reflected the ineffable w(hole) of the nation through which they understood their own part. The Plame Wilson Scandal illuminates a related dynamic, a secret scandal that refracted the George W. Bush Administration's rationale for going to war, by continuously shifting the characters who occupied its foreground.

Repetition: Joe Wilson's Missing Link

When George W. Bush delivered his State of the Union address on January 28, 2003, he offered the following sixteen-word rationale for going to war against Iraq: "The British government has learned that Saddam Hussein recently sought significant quantities of uranium from Africa."[50] Just a week after Bush's speech, Colin Powell appeared before the United Nations to make the case for multilateral war, using the same evidence Bush cited in his speech. But in March, just days before the United States officially declared war, the International Atomic Energy Agency (IAEA) declared that the evidence supporting the sixteen words had been forged.[51] By then it was too late. Even as IAEA was delivering its public statement, the American military was "in the early stages of military operations to disarm Iraq" and Americans were decidedly in favor of war.[52] Bush and Powell claimed they had received faulty intelligence from a source named Rafid Ahmed Alwan al-Janabi—better known by the pseudonym "Curveball."[53] In the months that followed, journalists critiqued the administration's enthusiasm to go to war, but a serious investigation of the White House would not materialize for eight more months.

When an investigation *did* materialize, it was not because crucial evidence was discovered (i.e., the secret *in* discourse) but, rather, because there was a startling consistency to the information that was missing from the official record (i.e., the secret *of* discourse). This consistency is why I take up the trope of repetition. For there to be a secret, the link between what Bush said he knew and what the White House knew would have to become clear over multiple instances.[54] When Joe Wilson published his op-ed in *The New York Times*, not only did he declare Bush's sixteen words to be factually inaccurate, but he also

---

49. P. Johnson, *I the People*, 52–64.
50. White House, "White House: President Delivers."
51. Warrick, "Some Evidence on Iraq Called Fake."
52. "Bush Declares War"; and Belz, "Bush War Ratings."
53. Chulov and Pidd, "How US Was Duped."
54. Copjec, *Read My Desire*, 141–42.

asserted that the White House had known as much all along. Famously, after Hussein had threatened to take the American embassy in Baghdad hostage, Joe Wilson had confronted him before news cameras with a noose draped around his neck.[55] Billing himself as "the last American diplomat to meet with Saddam Hussein," he made clear that someone within the Bush administration had actively suppressed intelligence.[56]

The editorial spurred multiple efforts to defend the reasonableness of the president's statements. Five days after Wilson's editorial, CIA director George Tenet described Wilson's trip as unconnected to Bush's speech and claimed responsibility for the faulty intelligence himself.[57] On July 14, 2003, *Washington Post* columnist Robert Novak took the war on Joe Wilson a step further by attacking the former diplomat's credibility.[58] Suddenly, Valerie Plame Wilson entered the picture: Novak claimed that the only reason Joe Wilson had been "in Africa" was because Plame, his CIA-agent spouse, had recommended him.

Other responses to the Wilson editorial served only to make the missing identity of Novak's informant the signature feature of the scandal. On July 20, 2003, *The New York Times* described how Tenet's admission had fallen short of full disclosure by failing to name the "mystery inserter" who had quietly written the crucial phrase into Bush's speech.[59] Moreover, Novak had generated entirely new missing links by anonymously citing "two senior administration officials" who had given away confidential details about Valerie Plame Wilson's employment. Representative John Conyers (D-MI) leveraged accusations against Karl Rove, accusing him and the White House of orchestrating "a campaign to smear and intimidate truth-telling critics."[60] Senator Charles Schumer (D-NY) publicly demanded that Attorney General John Ashcroft recuse himself from the proceedings. According to Schumer, Ashcroft's close political ties with conservative strategist Karl Rove, who was accused of leaking Plame Wilson's identity,[61] would compromise a "thorough, complete and fearless" investigation.[62]

The political secret emerged as a consistent inconsistency of Bush administration speech, a disconnect between the objective reality that Iraq did not possess weapons and the speech Bush had used to sow the certainty that

---

55. Thomas and Isikoff, "Secrets and Leaks."
56. Wilson, "What I Didn't Find in Africa."
57. Tenet, "George Tenet's Statement."
58. Novak, "Mission to Niger."
59. Marquis, "How Powerful Can 16 Words Be?"
60. Isikoff and Hosenball, "Terror Watch."
61. Journalist Matthew Cooper of *Time* magazine has been cited as the source of this accusation. Lambro, "Shortsighted Tall Tales."
62. Hulse and Sanger, "New Criticism."

the weapons were there. These repeated instances of missing information took on the quality of evidence by demonstrating that something was *not* known, that information had gone undisclosed. Lacan describes these consistent inconsistencies as "the certainty of doubt": We are assured of the secret's existence when regular inconsistencies in our lived reality suggest that something remains hidden from us.[63] Whether in dreams or in presidential public address, the doubt that accompanies repeated exposure to uncertainty and revisionism marks a symbolic recoding, an effort to protect something in the form of a contradiction. The tremendous effort to disguise and resymbolize Bush's sixteen words in the wake of "What I Didn't Find in Africa" told the public nothing of what might be hidden; it signaled beyond a shadow of a doubt that something was there to protect.

Caesura: The Erasure of Valerie Plame Wilson

As the FBI investigation of the White House began, demands for "the truth" made recurring reference to a possible surplus of undisclosed information broached by the Plame Wilson story. On October 7, 2003, Bush appeared before the White House press corps, stating: "I want to know the truth. That's why I've instructed this staff of mine to cooperate fully with the investigation. Full disclosure, everything we know, the investigators will find out."[64] Soon after, former whistleblower Daniel Ellsberg urged other informants that it was their ethical obligation to come forward, no matter the professional cost. Valerie Plame Wilson, however, remained silent.

The secret endures as caesura, a rhetorical figure denoting emptiness, division, and interruption. In Greek and Latin prose, it indicates a division or gap that breaks "the flow of sound in a verse."[65] In musical language the caesura momentarily stops metrical time, often turning the piece in an entirely new direction.[66] Caesurae are gaps that appear to have no content, but which structure the content—whether prose, meter, or events—surrounding them. As a trope of the secret, it names an empty space through which other pieces of missing information are routed. Caesura knits together the secret around

---

63. Lacan, *Four Fundamental Concepts*, 35.
64. Allen, "Bush 'Willing to Cooperate'"; and Ellsberg, "Advice from a Leaker."
65. *Merriam-Webster*, s.v. "caesura, noun," accessed August 12, 2025, https://www.merriam-webster.com/dictionary/caesura.
66. "A term signifying a momentary interruption of the musical metre by silence, often indicated by a comma or 'V' above the staff." *Grove Music Online*, s.v. "caesura," accessed February 11, 2025, https://doi.org/10.1093/gmo/9781561592630.article.04537.

an explanatory node, as if to say: "If we could get to the bottom of *this*, then all the other loose ends and frayed threads would cease to be secret." By naming the presumptively unknown, it marks what is already in the open as evidence of the hidden.

Valerie Plame Wilson was an exemplary caesura because she functioned as an embodied reminder of Bush's warmongering even when she did not speak. Her first public appearance after the leak was at an award ceremony for Wilson at the National Press Club in October 2003, where he received accolades for having bravely exposed the Bush administration's lies. However, Plame Wilson "would not talk to reporters and attended the event only after receiving assurance that she would not be photographed."[67] In coverage of the event, her only mention was in reference to Wilson's speech: "Wilson was most emotional when addressing his wife's exposure. 'I'm sorry for that,' he said, looking at her and fighting back tears. 'If I could give you back your anonymity . . . I would do it in a minute.' She sat quietly, wiping away a tear."

Plame Wilson first spoke to the press in a January 2004 *Vanity Fair* exclusive titled "Double Exposure." The article's title referenced the 1944 film noir *Double Indemnity* and featured an image of the couple in a convertible, with Plame Wilson costumed in a way reminiscent of Barbara Stanwick's Phyllis Dietrichson. Dietrichson is not just a prototype for the femme fatale who lives a double life; as Joan Copjec explains, she embodies a deception that is transparently obvious to everyone except the *noir* hero.[68] Notably, Plame Wilson appears in the background of the image wearing a shawl and sunglasses, while Wilson appears in the foreground, his armed draped over the vehicle's door. This "backgrounding" carries through into the article, which narrates Plame Wilson's experience of exposure primarily through Wilson's voice. Staging a response to Novak's editorial five years after the initial exposure, *Vanity Fair* finally sought to personalize the outed spy. But strangely, Plame Wilson was quoted only twice: first, when she briefly welcomed her interviewers at the door of her home and, second, when describing how she evaded public attention in the wake of the scandal:

> When in the wake of the leak friends have asked how Plame foiled eager interlocutors, she has told them, "You just turn it around. People love to talk about themselves. There's nothing more exciting than to have someone go 'Really?'"[69]

---

67. Capps, "Paying Homage to Truth."
68. Copjec, *Read My Desire*, 198.
69. Ward, "Double Exposure."

Valerie Plame Wilson effectively symbolized an absence of discursive goods, performing the same technique of deflection that she recounts. Except for her two quotations, the remainder of the ten-page exposé was devoted to Wilson. As a caesura, she was an empty place in the record; a blank spot on the map. Even when hers was the feature story, she was not in the spotlight.

A second feature of caesura is that it is an interruption or split in the continuity of historical time. Joan Copjec describes historical continuity as the effect of erasure, the "nothing" against which a social totality forms.[70] This function is nowhere more clearly illustrated than in Plame Wilson's autobiography, *Fair Game*.[71] The book documents her life from the time she became a covert government employee until the Libby trial. The writing is heavily redacted. The publicly distributed version of the book preserves the CIA's markup of her manuscript, as roughly half of the book—words, sentences, and full pages—are covered by solid black lines. When Plame Wilson appeared on *The Daily Show* on October 30, 2007, host Jon Stewart expressed surprise at the censored content:

> They redacted things that I think are shocking. There's one that I had to get to, the most incredible one. I just want to read this to you. This is what—you were talking about your kids. "Switching between breast and syringe feedings when they took only a few ounces at each time and capturing each detail in a notebook soon took its toll. I was exhausted. . . ." Redacted! What—how is that part, "I was exhausted by spying on—" I don't understand. What could possibly be there that would be redacted?[72]

Stewart's framing of the redaction suggested a puritanical purpose behind the redactions, a wish to literally cover up Plame Wilson's maternal and medical body. However, as she underscored in reply to Stewart's question, much of what had been redacted in the book had been removed simply because she had avowed employment with the CIA. The irony was that her former employment was something everyone knew, but which she alone was forbidden from acknowledging. The redactions didn't cover up a secret but symbolized a prohibition on her speech. The mistake was to attempt to read what was behind the bar—the bars themselves created the site of fascination that compelled readers like Stewart to look for more.[73]

---

70. Copjec, *Imagine There's No Woman*, 23.
71. Plame Wilson, *Fair Game*.
72. Valerie Plame Wilson, interview by Jon Stewart, *The Daily Show*, Comedy Central, October 30, 2007.
73. Nancy and Lacoue-Labarthes, *Title of the Letter*.

A last characteristic of the caesura is that it constitutes a social whole around an empty signifier, which brings forth negative conceptions of the forces that allow the social to cohere. As Ernesto Laclau explains of "order" as an empty signifier: "In a situation of radical disorder 'order' is present as that which is absent; it becomes an empty signifier, as the signifier of that absence."[74] In her testimony before the House Oversight and Reform Committee in 2007, Plame Wilson appeared before members of the House of Representatives, offering a statement that described the consequences of her outing while appealing for stricter separation between intelligence agencies and the US executive branch:

> The harm that is done when a CIA cover is blown is grave. . . . Lives are literally at stake. Every single one of my former CIA colleagues, from my fellow covert officers to analysts to technical operations officers to even the secretaries, understand the vulnerabilities of our officers and recognize that the travesty of what happened to me could happen to them. We in the CIA always know that we might be exposed and threatened by foreign enemies. It was a terrible irony that administration officials were the ones who destroyed my cover.[75]

Suturing together foreign agents, CIA colleagues, fellow covert officers, analysts, technical operations officers, and secretaries, Plame Wilson positioned herself as a lost node in a life-giving, life-taking network of spies and technicians. She became "the signifier of . . . absence," namely the absence of separation between America's national security state and its private, political interests.

Synecdoche: George W. Bush's Speech

Over the course of the Plame Wilson Scandal, there was a dramatic shift in public attitudes toward the George W. Bush White House. During the 2000 election, Bush's campaign marketed him as a likable, trustworthy, and down-to-earth candidate: a straight shooter who couldn't mislead the public, because he tripped over his words and couldn't help but say what he meant. Following several years of the war on terror, perceptions of Bush began to change, even among Republican loyalists. Although Bush began his 2004 term "with an

---

74. Laclau, *Emancipation(s)*, 44.
75. Plame Wilson, "Statement."

approval rating of 50 percent . . . [he] saw his popularity consistently decline over the next four years."[76] A key rhetorical marker for this popularity shift is Bush's speech. There is no evidence that the former president's off-the-cuff speaking habits ever changed over time. However, a clear correlate to Bush's declining approval ratings was the way that his unfiltered blue-collar diction was described: less and less inadvertently transparent, more and more deliberately obscure. The decline of his speech was synecdoche, a part that indexed a change in his w(hole) presidency.

When Bush began campaigning for his first presidential election in 1999, he spoke with "flip, saucy playfulness," demonstrating "plenty of confidence," which was "evident in his easy swagger."[77] His preelection autobiography, *A Charge to Keep*, had a "simple, not very deep tone that rings true."[78] His anti-intellectual straight-talk even appeared to be an asset in his campaign against Al Gore. Citing Fred Greenstein, *The New York Times* suggested that voters responded better to "a normal, laid-back, colloquial style."[79] Upon ascending to the presidency, Bush displayed confidence in developing relationships with other foreign leaders, despite his lack of familiarity with international politics. As Karen DeYoung of *The Washington Post* put it, "He was confident he could 'look them in the eye' and win them over with plain talk."[80]

Admittedly, Bush's speech was criticized even before he rose to the presidency, although the focus of that discourse was his simplemindedness. In 2000, Christopher Hitchens explained "Why Dubya Can't Read."[81] In his verbal thrashing, Hitchens picked up on Bush's malapropisms like "tacular" (combining "tactical" and "nuclear") and "terriers" ("tariffs" blended with "barriers"). That same year, Bush delivered a stump speech wherein he famously noted that his opponents had "misunderestimated" him. The gaff earned him a popular neologism ("Bush-isms") that remembered his war on semantics through routinely published and widely circulated "Top 10" lists.[82] But Bush did little to correct his critics. In fact, compared to Al Gore's robotic monotone, Bush-isms were performances of authenticity. In his first presidential address to a joint session of Congress, Bush outlined a plan for tax cuts in a terse and scripted speech, pushing back against his improvisational,

---

76. Beasley, "Rhetorical Presidency," 29.
77. Bruni, "Bush Seeks Gravity."
78. Clymer, "George II."
79. Berke, "What a Mind!"
80. DeYoung, "Presidential Diplomacy."
81. Hitchens, "Why Dubya Can't Read."
82. Weisberg, "W.'s Greatest Hits." It bears noticing that these lists bear a passing resemblance to the way that public audiences in 2016 poked fun at Donald Trump's syntax with hashtags and haikus. L. Pierce, *Tense Times*, 5.

error-ridden reputation. Critics called it "a self-confident performance by a president often criticized for his inability to communicate clearly."[83] The prepared performance signaled that he was able to manage his branch, while his delivery problems confirmed that he was an ordinary American.

The first and perhaps most noteworthy sign that something was different about the president's speech came immediately after his iconic "Mission Accomplished" moment on May 1, 2003. Addressing homeward-bound soldiers, Bush declared the end of long-standing hostilities against Iraq. With a large, star-spangled marquis reading "Mission Accomplished" adorning one of the carrier's control towers, Bush announced that "the tyrant has fallen, and Iraq is free."[84] But on Memorial Day, approximately three weeks after Bush's announcement, *The Washington Post* noted an abrupt about-face by the administration as the war in Iraq was to continue without a firm end in mind.[85] On July 14, 2003—just eight days after Joseph Wilson's news release—*Newsweek* ironist Andy Borowitz lampooned Bush, suggesting that the "sixteen words" had been an obvious misreading: "Iraqi strongman Saddam Hussein did not attempt to buy uranium in Africa, as earlier alleged, but merely geraniums."[86] These comments insinuated that Bush's gaffes were a sign of the intelligence he brought to his wartime decision-making.

After the summer of 2003, reporters noticed an absence of bipartisan goodwill toward the president.[87] Following his reelection victory against Senator John Kerry, *TIME* magazine named Bush its "Person of the Year." In the issue's feature article, Bush's campaign communication director, Dan Bartlett, described the commander in chief's speech-writing process:

> "Every time we'd have a speech and attempt to scale back the liberty section, he would get mad at us," Bartlett says. Sometimes the president would simply take his black Sharpie and write the word "freedom" between two paragraphs to prompt himself to go into his extended argument for America's efforts to plant the seeds of liberty in Iraq and the rest of the Middle East.[88]

Offering his own metaphors and personalized redactions, Bush framed his discourse around goals his party found unreflective of their ideas or attitudes.

---

83. Balz, "President Begins His Toughest Sell."
84. "Text of Bush's Speech."
85. Cooperman, "U.S. Troops Are Still Dying."
86. Borowitz, "Bush: Saddam Bought Geraniums."
87. Rosenberg, "N.Y. Times Ruins Bush's Breakfast"; Down, "Gunsmoke and Mirrors"; Quindlen, "Free Pass"; Ivins, "Call Me a Bush-Hater"; and Harper, "No Holds Barred."
88. Gibbs and Dickerson, "Person of the Year."

It was, predictably, met with considerable bipartisan opposition. In contrast to his immensely popular 2003 State of the Union address, many remarked that Bush's stump speeches rehearsed tired wartime rhetoric. Not only had he failed to make good on the promises of his 2001 campaign, but the war in Iraq was ongoing, the administration had dropped the ball on its domestic policy promises, and there was no promised change of course.[89] After his January 2004 State of the Union address, *The New York Times* reported that his audience members showed serious signs of fatigue. Where listeners had been ready to hear "ambitious sounding proposals on issues like tax-free savings . . . the president shelved the big-ticket items and instead offered himself to the public as the hero of Baghdad and the scourge of terrorism."[90] After Bush's speech, *The Village Voice* noted that, despite his cowboy image, Bush "ain't no cowboy," because he "shot first," and "went back on his word," a reference to his duplicitous justifications for pre-emptive warfare.[91] Bush's former folksy appeal had been replaced with an artificial, tinny soapbox.

Bush's own discourse about his speech began to reflect an overwhelming suspicion that he was not in control of what he was saying. In 2006, after widespread concerns emerged that Donald Rumsfeld had mishandled the war, Bush issued the following statement: "I hear the voices, and I read the front page, and I know the speculation. But I'm the decider, and I decide what is best. And what's best is for Don Rumsfeld to remain as the Secretary of Defense."[92] His self-naming as the "decider" leveraged a defensive position relative to accusations that his vice-president, Dick Cheney, was truly steering the executive branch. Further evidence of this positioning appeared in 2009, when Bush released his postpresidential autobiography, *Decision Points*.[93] Valerie Plame Wilson receives a passing mention, as does Dick Cheney's advocacy on behalf of Scooter Libby:

> In the closing days of the administration, Dick [Cheney] pressed his case that Scooter should be pardoned. . . . Ultimately, I reached the same conclusion I had in 2007: The jury verdict should be respected. In one of our final meetings, I informed Dick that I would not issue a pardon. He stared at me with an intense look. "I can't believe you're going to leave a soldier on the battlefield," he said.[94]

---

89. Stolberg, "State of the Union."
90. Traub, "Way We Live Now."
91. Baard, "Bush Ain't No Cowboy."
92. "Bush: 'I'm the Decider' on Rumsfeld."
93. Bush, *Decision Points*, xii.
94. Bush, *Decision Points*, 104–5.

Paradoxically, in the end, Bush could only exercise his judgment by deciding not to exercise it. Even the title, *Decision Points,* implicitly defended that *he* had called the shots. Near the end of his presidency, Bush could not even exercise his judgment without explicitly referring to the decision-making power granted to the presidential office. He explained in words what his speech should have implicitly performed.

Jacques Derrida describes the sovereign's decisions as always implicated by a contradictory positional hierarchy. The "scandal," he writes, is that the sovereign subject's decision becomes indistinguishable from "a passive decision or the decision of the other" such that "the decider" "begins, by an invincible attraction, to look like the beast he is supposed to subject to himself."[95] The dynamic of inversion Derrida describes would appear to lend itself well to the public speculation that Dick Cheney was, in fact, the arbiter of the George W. Bush administration's major decisions, including the orchestration of the Plame Wilson Scandal. However, the parallels do not end there. Over the duration of his presidency, George W. Bush experienced a profound reputational inversion that seemed to coincide with his ever-declining popularity. In 2002, when Bush fainted in the Oval Office after choking on a pretzel, news agencies attributed the incident to his vigorous daily exercise routine. Running seven miles daily had left him with an over-healthy heart more prone to such spells.[96] But just two years later, their tune had changed. In the summer of 2004, Richard Cohen noted that "Bush's periodic two-hour midday exercise sessions and his disinclination to work nights or weekends" had made it seem that the president was missing in action.[97] Cohen called Bush's 2004 reelection campaign a "great farce" because even as the president promoted a vigilant, round-the-clock national security agenda, he only seemed to be working part-time. Instead of addressing the nation's security problems from Washington, Bush had "brought his work home with him," retreating to his ranch in Crawford, Texas. In 2005, *The Washington Post* described Bush's record-setting five-week vacation as "the longest presidential retreat in 36 years." His frequent leaves of absence "symbolize[d] a lackadaisical approach to the world's most important day job." Bush had also "spent a month at the ranch shortly before the Sept. 11, 2001, attacks, when critics asserted he should have been more attentive to warning signs."[98] The implication was that if Bush had been home, he might have seen the hijacked planes coming. Like his speech, even Bush's houses had been re-signified: An empty White House was material evidence that he had gone missing.

---

95. Derrida, *Beast and the Sovereign,* 33.
96. Sammon, "President Chokes."
97. R. Cohen, "Bush's 9/11 Farce."
98. VandeHei and Baker, "Vacationing Bush."

Everything Is Secret and Nothing Happens

The Plame Wilson Scandal offers a model of how the national security state has increasingly been captured by the executive branch, as illustrated by Plame Wilson's plaintive appeal for greater independence between intelligence institutions and the executive branch. In retrospect, her statement forecasted the possibility that a future president would seize control of such institutions to exercise their self-interested political will. This secret *of* discourse "[offered] proliferation and dispersion" rather than resolution, each of the Plame Wilson Scandal's revelations pointing to another that has yet to publicly unfold.[99] A generalizable form, the secret scandal begins as an ignorable repetition that grows into the gap, hollow, or absence of caesura. Finally, as synecdoche, the secret transforms and iterates, gesturing to a larger w(hole) of the US presidency. Bush's declining speech is the part that was the whole of his presidency. Importantly, Bush's speech never really changed. The same utterances, cadence, and content bore the marker of folksy truthfulness and intentional concealment.

Scandals are emotionally exhausting and energetically depleting because their function is to prolong a sense of not knowing. They intensify the grip of power rather than offering relief from its pressure. This, too, is why the George W. Bush administration's management of the Plame Wilson Scandal is a fitting formal precedent for Trump's presidency, one of many open-ended connections between them. At the start of Trump's second term, for instance, campaign financier Elon Musk was routinely described as the one calling the shots, spearheading the administration's effort to dismantle the legacy bureaucracies and agencies instituted in the early twentieth century. At one point, Musk even appeared at a press conference in the Oval Office, answering questions about his newly formed Department of Government Efficiency (DOGE) while standing alongside a seated Trump.[100] The scene, memorialized in a *Time* magazine cover that featured Musk behind the Resolute Desk, had the echo of earlier suspicions that Dick Cheney, and not W, was the decider in chief.[101] The connection between the Bush and Trump administrations is even more apparent when we consider how, during his first term, Trump pardoned Scooter Libby's single perjury charge, effectively finishing the job Bush had decided not to do.[102] Investigative journalist Marcy Wheeler called the Libby

---

99. Dean, *Publicity's Secret*, 77.
100. Moore, "Trump and Musk."
101. McCreesh, "Time Magazine Cover."
102. Shane and Lewis, "Bush Commutes Libby Sentence"; and Baker, "Trump Pardons Scooter Libby."

pardon "an object lesson in presidential firewalls," offering anticipatory proof that President Trump would reward his proxies for following through on illegal orders.[103]

A key difference between Bush and Trump is that the latter routinely attracted attention to his scandals, using phrases like "the deep state" to allude to an undemocratic element within government. It was for that reason that Trump was propelled by the criticism of "Anonymous"—a group of senior officials who claimed to be close to Trump (later revealed to be an individual, Department of Homeland Security chief of staff Miles Taylor)—which confirmed his paranoid belief that those around him secretly sought his downfall.[104] Such scandals proved that the executive branch could be leveraged in ways that insulated the most powerful elected officials of the US government from legal scrutiny despite the apparent openness of their wrongdoing. They also show how such events exceed the time boundary of a single event.

Since he exited office, there has been a concerted campaign to rehabilitate George W. Bush's presidential years as a more moderate or enlightened version of the zealous far-right bigotry that has subsequently gripped the United States. In 2017, George W. Bush repudiated Donald Trump during a public event, subtly alluding to his dissatisfaction with the sitting president.[105] However, in a move resonant with his backseat-driving "decider" years, he never named Trump explicitly. The unauthorized 2013 leak of Bush's self-portraits, another scandal in miniature, humanized the former president by revealing several of his private bathroom moments.[106] Curiously, Bush's gaze is averted in both images. One depicts Bush's point of view in the bathtub, looking at his feet while the tap runs. The other shows Bush in the shower, looking off into the distance, a mirror reflecting his gaze back toward the painting's observer. Both paintings have an exhibitionist feel of enjoying being looked upon, the look-back in particular seeming to affirm Bush's knowledge that he is watched. However, because these portraits were leaked without Bush's consent, the bathroom also depicts a vulnerable interiority. They show us an ex-president who, even when he looks off into the shower's corner, feels an observer's gaze upon him. For a president who saw the passage of the Patriot Act and ushered in the modern surveillance state, the irony is palpable. The leak led to *Portraits of Courage*: a 2017 installation of Bush's oil paintings "honoring the sacrifice and courage of America's military veterans" that remains accessible as a digital

---

103. Wheeler, "Libby Pardon."
104. "I Am Part of the Resistance"; Donald P. Moynihan, "Trump Has a Master Plan."
105. Siddiqui, "Bush Condemns Bigotry."
106. Byford, "Bush's Bizarre Bathroom Self-Portraits."

archive in the George W. Bush Presidential Center.[107] Both the portraits and the Plame Wilson leak are instances of the secret, managed. They present a scandal within carefully contained limits to induce the sense that one is witnessing something unauthorized, and in the case of the portraits, to humanize someone known for committing inhuman deeds. That is the key characteristic of the secret scandal: No matter how much is revealed, something always seems missing from the bigger picture.

We should not forget Bush's responsibility for mass civilian and military casualties in Iraq and Afghanistan, his authorization of torture at Guantanamo Bay and military black sites, the anti-Muslim hate that spread because of his wars, and his efforts to abridge public dissent. "Never forget" that the phrase "shock and awe," which Donald Trump used to describe his multipronged strategy of overwhelm, deportation, tariffs, and fiscal capture at the start of his second term, was popularized by the George W. Bush administration, whose "Operation Shock and Awe" comprised the opening salvo of the Iraq War.[108] That phrase so lingered in public memory that Katherine Eban titled her 2007 exposé of the CIA's "enhanced interrogation" techniques promulgated during the Bush administration's failed pursuit of al-Qaeda "Rorschach and Awe," referencing a program of psychological violence birthed from pretenses, myths, and evidence that were as faulty as that which had instigated the War on Terror.[109]

Although the Plame Wilson Scandal ostensibly ended with a federal investigation of a sitting president, it also did not end, because its rhetorical form persists. The ineffectiveness of investigations that followed the W. Bush administration (e.g., the Mueller Report and the January 6 Commission) is a warning not to be drawn too far *in* discourse, to refuse the lure of hiddenness that promises a satisfying resolution in the form of legal exposure. In the end, it did not even matter whether Libby was the one who revealed Plame Wilson's identity; in fact, there are many reasons to think that he did not act alone. Deputy Secretary of State Richard Armitage, who took responsibility for the leak in 2007, faced no repercussions.[110] Some journalists maintained that Armitage's late-presidency confession, like Libby's indictment, was cover

---

107. *Portraits of Courage*.

108. Hertling, "Shock and Awe"; Gordon, "Threats and Responses." The phrase "never forget" is in scare quotes to mark its status as a relic of the George W. Bush era, a once-frequent shorthand for the decade-long injunction to keep the trauma of September 11, 2001, alive in public memory.

109. Eban, "Rorschach and Awe." Eban's journalism was also the basis for Scott Burns's 2019 film, *The Report*, which dramatized the events leading up to the release of the 2014 *Report on Torture* by Senator Diane Feinstein and the Senate Select Committee on Intelligence.

110. Brooks, "Guide for the Perplexed."

for George W. Bush or Dick Cheney, one of whom likely ordered the leak.[111] As Marcy Wheeler explains in the concluding lines of her book, *Anatomy of Deceit*:

> Libby was charged with obstructing an investigation into the activities of a number of people, including the vice president. After his trial in 2007, Libby will either be found guilty or he will walk. Yet that verdict will not end the story. The activities of others may remain beyond the reach of Fitzgerald's investigation, because of Libby's alleged obstruction as well as constitutional limits. Cheney may continue to refuse to answer questions, and the media may stop asking the important questions. But that doesn't mean the citizens of the United States should let it rest. If the deceptions that brought us into the Iraq War have taught us anything, it is that we, as citizens, must ask the questions to reveal the truth. And there are still a lot of questions unanswered.[112]

In retrospect, Wheeler was correct: Libby's trial did not end the story. Cheney's support for Libby, whose perjury functionally screened the administration from scrutiny, left unanswered many questions about the involvement of Bush's cabinet in the scandal. Plame Wilson's own catastrophic congressional campaign reignited memories of the Bush-era scandal, only to mire her into a different one. Trump's belated pardoning of Libby created a curious continuity between the two administrations, one that signaled a kind of strategic harmony between them: Loyalists are rewarded, especially when they do the wrong thing for the right president. In failing to have its intended or anticipated effect, the scandal's form illustrates how disclosure is no guarantee that the w(hole) truth will ever be brought to light.

---

111. Wheeler, "Armitage, a Review."
112. Wheeler, *Anatomy of Deceit*, 117–18.

CHAPTER 4

The Dog Whistle

Weaponizing Saul Alinsky in the Obama Years

> They were learning the lessons of the oppressed throughout history in striking back at their oppressors; the linguistics of deception; subterfuge, to strike when least expected and then fade into the background; to hound, harass, worry and weaken the strong and whittle away at the strength and power that kept them where they were.
> —Sam Greenlee, *The Spook Who Sat by the Door* (101)

The Many Alinskys

During the last months of George W. Bush's second term, President-Elect Barack Obama announced bold plans to change the antagonistic political culture of Washington, DC.[1] Republicans began to call Obama a "Saul Alinsky radical," referencing the Jewish community organizer who had mobilized predominantly Black Chicago neighborhoods to fight housing discrimination that favored wealthy white residents. Curiously, although Alinsky's name held special significance among conservatives, it did not seem to carry any specific resonance for many on the political left. As John Cassidy of *The New Yorker* admitted, "Until Newt [Gingrich] started banging on about the Chicago radical and writer, who died in 1972, I hadn't realized what an influential figure he was."[2] Other commentators argued that the Tea Party candidates who began opposing Obama in 2009 had just discovered the spirit of 1960s radicalism a few decades late.[3] Even as the Tea Party made Alinsky a symbol of the Left's alienation from authentic American principles, they also leveraged Alinsky's organizing strategies—specifically, those recorded in his 1971 book, *Rules for Radicals*—as tools in their anti-Obama propaganda war.

---

1. Zeleny, "Initial Steps by Obama."
2. Cassidy, "Ten Things I'll Miss About Newt."
3. B. McGrath, "Movement."

From 1930 until 1965, Saul David Alinsky organized labor unions and urban communities while publicly displaying the dirty laundry of racist slumlords, greedy companies, and corrupt local governments. The founder of the Industrial Areas Foundation (IAF), he is regarded as a key figure in the history of twentieth-century community organizing. His most famous campaigns were waged in Chicago, where he assisted in the formation of the Back of the Yards Neighborhood Council (BYNC) and the Temporary Woodlawn Organization (TWO). Public responses to his interventions have ranged from celebratory to critical. Across several 1965 editions of the Black newspaper *The Chicago Defender*, columnist Brenetta Howell described Alinsky as the racist "ringmaster" of a Catholic Archdiocese–produced circus, and his organizing tactics a failed "bootstrapping operation."[4] Conversely, sociologists Donald and Dietrich Reitzes suggest that he was a model for community organizers like Fred Ross and Cesar Chavez.[5]

For members of the Tea Party, a conservative political faction that emerged after the 2008 US presidential election, Saul Alinsky was something else entirely: a dog whistle.[6] Forty-odd years after his death, his name became a centralizing signifier in conservatives' 2008 project of "refiguring social space," whereby "the new right systematically poached progressive political discourse" from the American Civil Rights Movement.[7] Alinsky represented a new horizon in the project of political refiguration. Between 2008 and 2016, Alinsky was featured in many conservative strategists' books, including *Cooking Alinsky's Goose: The New Capitalist Cookbook* (2009), *Leftist Tactics, Conservative Solutions: A Conservative Analysis of Alinsky's Rules and Other Tactics* (2010), *Rules for Radical Conservatives: Beating the Left at Its Own Game to Take Back America* (2010), *Rules for Radicals Defeated: A Practical Guide for Defeating Obama/Alinsky Tactics* (2012), *Rules for Conservatives: A Response to Rules for Radicals by Saul Alinsky* (2014), and *Rules for Patriots: How Conservatives Can Win Again* (2014). Even books that did not reference Alinsky enumerated their own "Rules for Counterradicals" with instructions for mobilizing journalistic attention and staging political events.[8] By Obama's second presidential term, conservative organizers fully embraced the effort to destroy

---

4. Howell, "Westside Roundup," *Chicago Defender*, February 17, 1965; and Howell, "Westside Roundup," *Chicago Defender*, March 2, 1965.

5. Reitzes and Reitzes, *Alinsky Legacy*, 201–29.

6. Blum, *How the Tea Party Captured the GOP.*

7. Patton, "Refiguring Social Space," 216. See also Stoneman and Packer, "American Conservativism Unmoored." Stoneman and Packer suggest that the right's co-optation of leftist strategies signals a shift whereby conservatives, who have historically "gravitated to a strategy of control," have, with increasing frequency, poached the strategies and tactics of leftist agitation.

8. O'Hara, *New American Tea Party*, 203–4; and D. Horowitz, *Take No Prisoners*, 45–46.

Alinsky's downstream generations by imitating him to the greatest extent possible. After 2008, the principal functions of the Alinsky name were to cloak the Tea Party's anti-Black racism in a principled rejection of Obama's agenda while disavowing the Tea Party's adoption of Alinsky-style tactics.

As a secret *in* discourse, Alinsky's Obama-era uptake invites us to review a complex history of organizing that was, as of 2008, largely unknown to the American political left. His critical reception in 1965 Chicago also troubles his folk status as a liberal hero. Even during his lifetime, Alinsky's worldview was ripe for conservative appropriation; it was well known that he espoused a coded racism under the guise of tactical expediency. As a secret *of* discourse, the Alinsky dog whistle was divorced from his complex reception and gained new significance through the Tea Party's intensifying repetition of his name and his principles. To that end, I theorize the dog whistle as operating through *catachresis* (or abusive misnaming) and *irony* (the inversion of mastery). Together, these feed a process of political *incorporation,* whereby a subject internalizes an object they also seek to destroy. The apotheosis of Alinskyian incorporation is gonzo pseudojournalism, an emergent genre of agitational political theater that superficially adopted the aesthetics of investigative journalism to capture community organizations, healthcare providers, and migrant shelters in the act of alleged wrongdoing. Such tactics mirror Alinsky's, not because the dog whistle deflected attention from pseudojournalists' racism but because it enabled them to justify their open racism under the auspices of making the left's obscenity visible.

Alinsky's "Hidden" History

Arguably, Saul Alinsky is most famous for organizing TWO, a community organization formed in Chicago's Woodlawn neighborhood between 1958 and 1965. Importantly, Woodlawn's history of community organizing has never been hidden—hence the scare quotes of the above section title. As documented by *The Chicago Defender,* a range of actors and institutions caricatured the neighborhood's residents as dangerous, inconvenient, and ignorable. If there is a secret *in* discourse here, it is because Alinsky's framing as Woodlawn's "Great White Father" has too often overshadowed the community's telling of its own history.[9]

Woodlawn was initially built as temporary housing for the World's Columbian Exposition in 1893: a "white city" containing the original Ferris Wheel,

---

9. Howell, "Westside Roundup," *Chicago Defender,* February 17, 1965.

a "military encampment," German and Turkish "villages," and exhibits from Harvard and the Smithsonian.[10] After World War II, the neighborhood underwent significant white flight as white residents moved out and Black residents, many from the American South, moved in:

> Between 1950 and 1960, Woodlawn changed from 86 percent white to 86 percent black. Nearly half (48.7 percent) of all housing units in Woodlawn were substandard according to the 1960 census. For this housing the new residents paid more than the median rent city-wide out of a median family income of $4,400 as compared with the $7,200 median for white families in Chicago.[11]

In 1958, clergymen Martin Farrell, Ulysses Blakeley, Charles Leber, and C. K. Proefrock formed the Woodlawn Ministers' Alliance, one of many organizations that would seek to "secure adequate law enforcement, code inspection, and other city services" for the community.[12] In partnership with other community groups, the organization headed the United Woodlawn Council (UWC). However, their efforts were hampered by damaging urban renewal plans, and groups "organized primarily in opposition to the UWC."[13] The South East Chicago Commission (SECC)—once described by University of Illinois urbanologist Pierre de Vise as "the University [of Chicago]'s own CIA"—proposed sweeping gentrification projects to enhance the area's appeal for faculty and students.[14] Many Woodlawn residents suspected it was just a matter of time before their neighborhood would be bulldozed. Although there had been proposals to hire Alinsky as early as 1954, he was controversial for, among other things, proposing "a quota system for the admission of Negroes by whites as residents in segregated communities."[15] In 1958, the prospect of involving Alinsky's IAF splintered the Minister's Alliance as Proefrock and Lutheran representatives broke with the group.[16]

---

10. D. Beck, *Unfair Labor?*, xx. See also Burg, *Chicago's White City*.
11. Fish, *Black Power / White Control*, 12–13.
12. Fish, *Black Power / White Control*, 15.
13. Fish, *Black Power / White Control*, 16.
14. Harvey, "Black P Stones"; and Harvey, "'Disorganizer' Creates Gang Climate."
15. Foster, "Other Peoples [sic] Business." According to Nicole Marie Brown, this proposal was backed by Alinsky's partners in the Roman Catholic Archdiocese, whose objective was "in securing West Woodlawn, stopping white flight and preserving the neighborhood from the fate of the neighboring deteriorating East Woodlawn, which had more black residents and suffered 'a pattern of demoralization.'" N. Brown, "Flawed Consumers," 50.
16. Fish, *Black Power / White Control*, 17.

Alinsky and the IAF became involved with Woodlawn in 1960 after Julian Levi, head of the SECC and the University of Chicago's Urban Institute, presented plans for university expansion to the Chicago Land Clearance Commission (CLCC). Levi had claimed that "the University of Chicago was threatened by an encroaching slum and crime problem . . . until it began fighting back with an urban renewal program in 1952."[17] The 1952 effort resulted in the demolition of 149 acres of Chicago's Hyde Park and Kenwood neighborhoods. As Roy Harvey stated in the *Defender*, urban renewal "meant the same old thing: black removal."[18] However, Levi's 1960 proposal spurred resistance from the CLCC, which would only consider his proposal after completing an exhaustive land survey. Levi subsequently offered $50,000 to Woodlawn community leaders, seeking a "front group to facilitate acceptance of the South Campus plan."[19] Seeing the writing on the wall, Blakeley and Leber secured financial support from the Catholic Archdiocese to hire IAF director Alinsky and his affiliate, Nicholas von Hoffman. In December, the IAF, the Ministers' Alliance, the UWC, the Knights of St. John, the Woodlawn Business Men's Association, and the Woodlawn Block Club Council formed the Temporary Woodlawn Organization (TWO), designating Rev. Arthur M. Brazier as its spokesperson.[20]

Responding to Levi's newest efforts to circumvent CLCC and Woodlawn involvement, TWO notified the Chicago Plan Commission (CPC) that Levi was seeking to build in an "area of Woodlawn which was the subject of the [CLCC's] prolonged eligibility survey," leading the CPC to delay until the "proper hearings and study would take place."[21] According to Brazier,

> This tactic put the city of Chicago in the middle of the conflict. The city had run out of funds for urban renewal programs and wanted the $14 million from Section 112 of the Housing Act of 1959. For the city to receive this money the University of Chicago had to sign certification papers. The university would not sign those papers until the city produced some kind of urban renewal program that would guarantee the university the land needed for the south campus. This the city could not do, because the people of the community were not in favor of the university's plan as it then existed and had vetoed it. At this point TWO felt that powerful segments of the white society were closing in on it.[22]

---

17. "Outlines Plan to Save Urban Universities."
18. Harvey, "'Disorganizer' Creates Gang Climate."
19. Fish, *Black Power / White Control*, 19.
20. Fish, *Black Power / White Control*, 32.
21. Fish, *Black Power / White Control*, 31.
22. Brazier, *Black Self-Determination*, 54.

In the spring of 1961, *The Christian Century,* "a well-known religious periodical," allied with the University of Chicago's Public Relations Office to attack TWO, claiming that the organization sought "to rub raw the sores of discontent and rouse dormant hostilities."[23] The *Maroon,* the University of Chicago's student newspaper, labeled TWO as a "hate group" in cahoots with the Archdiocese.[24] Rallying to support TWO, *The Chicago Defender* published a response that repudiated *The Christian Century* for "religious bigotry" and applauded Woodlawn's efforts to stop "the flight of whites."[25] The response drew thanks from Rev. Brazier, the Minister's Alliance, Catholic leaders, and Alinsky.[26]

That August, the *Defender* published "Chicago Declaration of Democracy," a full-page advertisement sponsored by the Chicago Urban League with more than 250 signatories from TWO's member organizations.[27] The "Declaration" was prelude to more than a year of organizing: By the end of 1962, TWO had mobilized rent strikes, school reforms, and a "Square Deal" campaign to hold unscrupulous businesses accountable for cheating Woodlawn customers.[28] Many, including the *Defender,* hailed Alinsky as Woodlawn's hero. In November 1962, Ernestine Cofield of the *Defender* published an interview with Alinsky titled "A General to Lead a Slum Army," which recalled Alinsky's 1939 cofounding of the BYNC, a South Side Chicago meatpacking district made famous by Upton Sinclair's *The Jungle.*[29] Alinsky also stressed the temporariness of the IAF-TWO alliance. He underscored the importance of recruiting leaders from among those who already resided within the community, which, as he claimed, would enable the community to help itself: "When we leave that neighborhood, they'll be blowing under their own steam."[30] As he wrote in response to a 1959 meeting with church leaders:

Actually, we cannot organize a community. The community does it itself. The statement may be surprising but simple arithmetic bears it out. How can four or five men walk into a place where fifty thousand people are living

---

23. Brazier, *Black Self-Determination,* 55–56.
24. K. Pierce, "Church Supports 'Hate Group.'"
25. "Christian Century in Error."
26. Brazier, "TWO Speaks"; Farrell, "Expresses Thanks"; Blakeley and Leber, "Blow at Bias"; Richards, "Newspaper Readers Laud"; E. Burke, "Courageous"; and Alinsky, "Contribution."
27. "On This We Agree."
28. Brazier, *Black Self-Determination,* 39–49; N. Brown, "Flawed Consumers," 83–112; and "Woodlawn Organization Created."
29. Cofield, "How Woodlawn Found a General."
30. Cofield, "How Woodlawn Found a General"; and Brazier, *Black Self-Determination,* 32–33.

and organize them? They cannot. Essentially what they do is get the people to organize themselves.³¹

Across different issues of the *Defender*, he argued that TWO had to employ "guerrilla tactics" because the "IAF can't afford a moral victory," while elsewhere he disparaged "organizing on an altruistic basis" as impractical and misguided.³² Statements like these reflect what Alinsky called the "realist's" attitude: "Political realists see the world as it is: an arena of power politics moved primarily by perceived immediate self-interests, where morality is rhetorical rationale for expedient action and self-interest."³³

Realism was an open secret of Alinsky's organizing philosophy because it gave him "the privilege to ignore—the right to go on not knowing or pretending not to see" the systemic nature of the racism he encountered when organizing different communities.³⁴ A cynical attitude, Alinskyian realism considered appeals to equality, justice, and freedom ineffectual and unnecessary for the accomplishment of community goals. These appeals were better understood as secondary or post hoc justifications, useful only as "a rationale to cloak a pragmatic program with a desired and essential moral cover."³⁵ In Alinsky's view, the only way to spur change was to challenge individuals at the level of their prurient self-interest.

Alinsky's brand of racial pessimism was markedly different from that of civil rights leaders. Whereas Stokely Carmichael argued that "black America is an internal colony held hostage by a white colonial superstructure" and advocated for reparations through land forfeiture and tax code reforms, Alinsky dismissed such tactics as unrealistic.³⁶ He more often sought to manipulate racists' attitudes to accomplish short-term goals. In *Rules for Radicals*, Alinsky recounts a Woodlawn rent strike outside of a white slum-landlord's home:

---

31. Saul Alinsky, "Questions and Answers Regarding the Industrial Areas Foundation," 1959, mimeographed copy, on file at First Presbyterian Church, Chicago, IL, 8, quoted in Fish, *Black Power / White Control*, 28. Nicholas von Hoffman of the IAF expressed a similar sentiment: "The organizer's first job is to organize, not right wrongs, not avenge injustice, not to win the battle for freedom. That is the task of the people who will accomplish it through the organization if it ever gets built." Von Hoffman, *Finding and Making Leaders*, handbook distributed by Students for a Democratic Society, n.d., https://www.crmvet.org/docs/630000_sds_core_ldrs.pdf, 6–7, quoted in Fish, *Black Power / White Control*, 27.

32. Cofield, "How Woodlawn Found a General"; and Harvey, "'Disorganizer' Creates Gang Climate."

33. Alinsky, *Rules for Radicals*, 12.

34. François, *Open Secrets*, 2.

35. Alinsky, *Rules for Radicals*, 38.

36. Corrigan, *Black Feelings*, 54; and "Carmichael: 'Negro Must Learn He Has Right.'"

> In its early history the organized black ghetto in the Woodlawn neighborhood in Chicago engaged in conflict with the slum landlords. It never picketed the local slum tenements or the landlord's office. It selected its blackest blacks and bused them out to the lily-white suburb of their slum landlord's residence. Their picket signs, which said, "Did you know that Jones, your neighbor, is a slum landlord?" were completely irrelevant; the point was that ... Jones would be inundated with phone calls from his [racist] neighbors.[37]

The picketing was effective not because the protesters' message was heard but because the neighborhood was eager to see Black protesters leave. Alinsky did not seek to undermine a racist structure but to create a pressure campaign among Jones and his fellow racists. The tactic was an example of one of Alinsky's "rules" in *Rules for Radicals*: "the right things [are] done for the wrong reasons."[38] Not only did the tactic affirm and intensify the racism of surrounding white neighborhoods; it put members of the Woodlawn community at risk.

Another reason to question Alinsky's status as a folk hero concerns the IAF's stated position on "indigenous" leadership (i.e., from within the community). As Nicole Marie Brown explains, the relative disorganization of the Woodlawn community was precisely what made it attractive to Alinsky in the first place:

> By engaging and centering Saul Alinsky and the IAF during their discussions about "what to do about Woodlawn," the church essentially conceded to the notion that white men must be brought into black communities to assist in their organization. White men could have just as easily been used to organize efforts to combat the racist practices of other white men which stifled the viability of communities such as Woodlawn, however, this strategy was not a consideration for the clergy. They instead opted for an organization whose program solutions did little to disrupt the status quo.[39]

Over time, it became increasingly clear that most of TWO's leadership did not reside in Woodlawn.[40] In 1965, Brenetta Howell of the *Defender* claimed that TWO had thwarted autonomous community leadership by repeatedly

---

37. Alinsky, *Rules for Radicals*, 144.
38. Alinsky, *Rules for Radicals*, 76.
39. N. Brown, "Flawed Consumers," 50–51.
40. "First Presbyterian's co-pastors, the Revs. Blakely and Leber—who had created the Woodlawn Organization and invited in Saul Alinsky to built TWO up—were kicked upstairs in the Church's national hierarchy." Harvey, "Gang Controller Is Brought In"; see also Brazier, *Black Self-Determination*, 76.

appointing leaders who were not community residents.[41] By 1966, plans were underway for Martin Luther King Jr. to take up residence in Woodlawn "to show his identification with the poor," marking a stark contrast with Alinsky and other "top civil rights leaders" who "[chose] to live in other areas."[42]

There were many more reasons Woodlawn residents were dissatisfied with Alinsky, including his rejection of "the methods of more demonstrative civil rightists," the scheduling of meetings at prohibitive hours, bad deals made with Mayor Richard Daley and the University of Chicago, lackluster support for Woodlawn's local political candidates, and the illegal appointment of eight nonresidents to the Woodlawn Community Conservation Committee. Alinsky also leveraged his visibility in Woodlawn for his own gain, seeking teaching work in Syracuse while organizing other groups like BUILD in Buffalo and FIGHT in Rochester.[43] *Defender* columnist Roy Harvey noted that things were demonstrably worse by the time Alinsky departed. One of his agreements with the University of Chicago made Woodlawn a test case in the "deschooling" education movement, which refused the idea of a "common body of academic skill and knowledge that all children should learn." Instead, it instituted a "'job training program' for 'alienated youth,' which involved the gang leadership 'in planning, design, and operation of the program.'"[44] According to Harvey, these reforms subjected Woodlawn's youth to a federally financed "sociological gang experiment" that intensified neighborhood violence for decades. By promoting "the notion that not only police but teachers were 'hostile authority figures,'" TWO's leadership had worsened educational outcomes and school attendance.[45] "Alinsky," Harvey argued, "had set up the climate of paranoia that would allow the gangs to be invited in."[46]

There is a striking dissonance between local memories of Alinsky in Woodlawn, the white activists who celebrated him as a "great pioneer," and the academics who called his organizing "a living demonstration that Negroes, even those living in the worst sort of slum, can be mobilized to help themselves."[47] Even among conservative contemporaries who considered

---

41. Howell, "Westside Roundup," *Chicago Defender*, February 17, 1965.
42. "King's Plan Wins Approval."
43. "Buffalo Unit Hires Alinsky"; "Alinsky Loses Poverty War Job"; "Kodak Fights Militant Negro Group"; and "Economic Justice."
44. Harvey, "Street Gang"; and Harvey, "University, TWO, and the Gangs."
45. Harvey, "'Disorganizer' Creates Gang Climate."
46. Harvey, "Seminary Operated Gang Hostels."
47. Heather Booth, a founder of the abortion advocacy group JANE, asserts, "Alinsky is to community organization as Freud is to psychoanalysis" (Boyte, *Backyard Revolution*, 39). For other examples of how Alinsky's memory has been celebrated in retrospect, see Boyte, *Backyard Revolution*, 48–49; and Silberman, *Crisis in Black and White*, 318. Roy Harvey quotes educator Paul Copperman's review of *Crisis in Black and White* as "one of the most damaging pieces of educational writing to have been published in the past 20 years." Harvey, "Street Gang."

Alinsky to be a political adversary, he was remembered with some fondness. William F. Buckley, the conservative founder of the *National Review*, noted in 1967 that Alinsky had a "distinctive appeal." Although they strongly disagreed on the best way to resolve the "problem of the poor," Alinsky struck a chord with conservatives because he argued that people experiencing poverty could change their own economic destinies. In his televised debate with Alinsky, Buckley stated:

> You appeal to some [people] because you have this disdain for welfarism as suggested by that ultimatum of yours, that you would rather steal than receive welfare. Now, this appeals to a lot of people who are sort of conservative-minded, who are against welfare because they do believe that there is going on in this country a sort of an institutionalization of welfare, that we ought to get out of it, and that to be essentially human, you've got to make your own way. . . . On the other you appeal to liberals and radicals, because yours is a highly non-rhetorical approach.[48]

Alinsky's bootstrapping rhetoric was, from the very beginning, ripe for conservative identification. Like Buckley, Alinsky believed in individual self-empowerment rather than institution-level interventions. Both condemned empty political gestures in favor of tactics that would allow individuals to elevate themselves from economic squalor. Alinsky's regular references to the example of the founding fathers likewise offered a key basis for his post-2008 conservative appropriation.

A final reason for Alinsky's lasting significance is that he has sometimes been touted as an exemplar of the "third" or "middle" way in liberal politics. In the late twentieth century, these phrases signaled a mean-between-extremes approach to political polarization that came to a head during the US Civil Rights Movement. "Third-way" advocates also embraced left-right compromise positions, suggesting that there was an alternative to, for instance, the extremes of bureaucracy-driven welfarism and community-driven civic rebellion. According to John Hall Fish, Alinsky was emblematic of this tradition because he maintained that targeted interventions, not structural overhaul, presented the most practical means of addressing pervasive racial and economic inequalities.[49]

> The middle way is not merely an idea but the specific incarnation of an idea at once simple and complex. The idea is that social injustice can be

---

48. Buckley, *Firing Line*, S2E79.
49. Fish, *Black Power / White Control*, 4.

overcome and excessive concentrations of power can be checked without a fundamental restructuring of the total society. It is, further, that justice can be won only through power and conflict; that oppressed groups cannot wield power or generate effective conflict without organization; and that such organization generally requires the harmonization of conflicting interests—or bargaining—in order to gain the numbers and credibility to have a substantial impact. The idea has become incarnate in a number of organizations in America; it is most clearly identified with a man, Saul Alinsky, and it attained its most forceful expression between 1960 and the present date in the Chicago community of Woodlawn.[50]

As a representative of the third way, Alinsky was distinctly unradical and nonrevolutionary, and is better characterized as a defender of the status quo. As social psychologist Frank Riessman put it, "the Alinsky model neither implies a radical view of society nor calls for radical social change"; instead, it promoted a "myth" of its own efficacy that used common tactics "employed all over the country" while leaving "no systematic evidence" that the communities he organized remained intact.[51] In 1998, Stuart Hall critiqued the "Third Way" as "The Great Moving Nowhere Show," the counterpart to conservative Britain as "The Great Moving Right Show."[52] The third way was, in other words, a barely disguised neoliberalism that stopped short of ever redressing the inequalities brought on by economic globalization. It simultaneously claimed to "transform and modernise society in a radical direction," while also failing to "disturb any existing interests."[53]

A hallmark feature of the contemporary "Third Way" is the enshrining of consensus as a way to "transcend ideological perspectives."[54] For that reason, one commentator labeled Barack Obama "the Third Way neo-liberal *par excellence*."[55] In response to the pressures of "financialization" brought on by the 2008 housing collapse, Obama presented an aspirational picture of "desired social and ecological outcomes," while seeking to "supersede a left or anti-capitalist discourse." If there is a parallel to be found between Alinsky's organizing and Obama's early presidency, this is perhaps the strongest. Rather than seeking to dismantle structures of racial inequality, both sought ways to work with and through a racist system's institutional constraints.

---

50. Fish, *Black Power / White Control*, 4.
51. Riessman, *Strategies Against Poverty*, 4–7.
52. Hall, "Great Moving Nowhere Show"; and Hall, "Great Moving Right Show."
53. Hall, "Great Moving Nowhere Show," 10.
54. Bastow and Martin, *Third Way Discourse*, 6.
55. Jutel, "Barack Obama," 1–2.

The Alinsky Dog Whistle

Between 2008 and 2016, Saul Alinsky became a signifier for the allegedly dirty tactics that had won Barack Obama the White House and reframed the party as excessively radical. As a dog whistle, Alinsky also obliquely referenced Obama's status as the first Black and biracial US president, allowing conservatives to rally racist disdain for Obama under the sign of his alleged ideological extremism. This version of Alinsky aligns his name with the secret *of* discourse: a retroactive transformation that adjusts a signifier's apparent force and meaning. As a dog whistle, post-2008 invocations of "Alinsky" signaled a recurring, intensifying contradiction between the Alinsky of Woodlawn—his literal, historical reference—and the racist surplus that the Tea Party attached to his name.

A dog whistle is like a secret password, language used against the grain of its denotation to convey a shared hidden meaning. Passwords are unique semiotic constructions: They "effect continuous variations of the common elements of language" and have "the property of being chosen in a way that is thoroughly independent from [their] signification."[56] Whether the password is "open sesame" or "Saul Alinsky," the signifier is purposely severed from a common referent to serve a specific function: to open a hidden door, to mark one's belonging to a partisan group. The dog whistle's brevity also makes it akin to a sound bite whose "textual condensation intensifies audiences' attachment to public speech."[57] The whistle metaphor is a key feature, suggestive of a signal that is widely broadcast but audible primarily to those able to pick up on the right('s) frequencies. Rhetorically, we might define the dog whistle as a relative to the fourth persona: truncated speech meant for a receiver who becomes "a collaborator in making duplicitous utterances appear legitimate before an audience of dupes."[58]

Most often, dog whistles are veiled expressions of racism, although their formal properties allow them to communicate other kinds of (e.g., gendered or ableist) enmity. Ian Haney López defines "dog whistle politics" as "coded racial appeals that carefully manipulate hostility toward non-whites."[59] Eduardo Bonilla-Silva alludes to a similar phenomenon in *Racism Without Racists*: "Whites talk about minorities in public . . . in a very careful, indirect, hesitant

---

56. Deleuze and Guattari, *Thousand Plateaus*, 97; and Lacan, *On the Names-of-the-Father*, 17–18.
57. Foley, "Sound Bites," 614, 616.
58. Morris, "Hoover's Sex Crime Panic," 241.
59. Haney López, *Dog Whistle Politics*, ix.

manner and, occasionally, even through coded language."[60] Often, dog whistles eschew overt racism through deceptively neutral appeals to color blindness, self-reliance, and merit-based achievement.[61] Many infamous examples of dog whistles come from US presidential rhetoric: Whereas López references Reagan's infamous allusion to "welfare queens" and "strapping young bucks buying T-Bone steaks with food stamps," Bonilla-Silva invokes Donald Trump's 2015 description of Mexican immigrants as "people that have lots of problems" who are "bringing drugs" and "bringing crime."[62]

In many ways, "Saul Alinsky" was a perfect dog whistle for post-2008 conservative commentators to express their rejection of the political left's policies for reasons that could only be loosely associated with Obama's Black and multiracial identity.[63] As Paul E. Johnson argues:

> Utilizing Obama as a source for white agency was fraught because many Americans tend to think about the president as an agent who rules and corrects for the defects of democracy rather than thinking about him as one agent among many. White Americans could not comfortably rely on controlling Blackness with the multiracial Obama as the symbolic sovereign of the United States.[64]

By claiming that Alinskyism—and not Obama's Blackness—was the source of their discontent, Tea Party conservatives found an alibi to evade the charge of racism. Alinsky offered a temporary means of channeling this racial libidinal animus into a name that could, in bad faith, be leveraged as the basis for rational disagreement. Over time, however, the anti-Alinsky right became the object they performatively rejected.

For the conservative public who deployed and embraced it, the Alinsky dog whistle was a racist enactment of color-blind criticism that rejected and adopted the left's (allegedly) cherished handbook for organizing, *Rules for Radicals*. Alinsky's appropriation remains significant because it anticipates related terms like "racial gaslighting" and "whataboutism" (or "both-sideism"), which refer to related tactics of equivocation that deflect accusation by aiming it back at the accuser.[65] The point of narrating the Alinsky dog whistle

---

60. Bonilla-Silva, *Racism Without Racists*, 55.
61. Harriot, "Trump's Latest Tweets."
62. Donald Trump, "Announcement of Candidacy" (speech, Trump Tower, New York, NY, June 16, 2015). See also Gabbatt, "Golden Escalator Ride"; and Kruse, "Escalator Ride."
63. For instance, see Alinsky, *Rules for Radicals*, 76–77.
64. P. Johnson, *I the People*, 123.
65. See, for instance, A. Davis and Ernst, "Racial Gaslighting"; Curtis, "Whataboutism"; and McQuade, "Dangerous Whataboutism."

alongside and against Alinsky's complex history is not to concede that "both sides" of the political spectrum were or are racist. It is to take stock of how the secret continuously justifies racism by making false equivalences between the rhetoric of the American political left and right.

Catachresis: "What's Sauce for the Goose Is Sauce for the Gander"

Catachresis (or *abusio*) is a trope of misnaming that conventionally describes how names are repurposed and reassigned to people or objects to which they previously did not belong. For instance, the phrase "the leg of the chair" attributes the term "leg," whose literal reference is a living body, to an inert object. According to Ernesto Laclau, every act of naming is an act of misnaming. Because there are fewer nouns than objects in the world, words must be casuistically stretched to cover an infinitely expansive terrain of objects and matter.[66] Importantly, Laclau's ontological elevation of catachresis sidesteps the Roman-era historical contingencies that informed its emergence as a "master" trope, namely, Cicero's celebration of catachresis as an expeditious means of (mis-)naming the peoples and territories annexed under Roman imperial rule.[67] Consequently, catachresis itself has a veiled double meaning. It is both the seemingly general, neutral act of misnaming and, more insidiously, the forced imposition of a name onto conquered peoples who had the status of objects and were presumed nameless. The dog whistle's plausible deniability similarly depends upon a shield of neutral or literal reference: Speaker and audience alike can knowingly disavow the abusive significations of speech by claiming *that's not what I/they/we meant; that's not what [the dog whistle] really refers to.*[68]

After Obama's ascension to the White House, conservative politicians and pundits loved to hate on Alinsky, asserting that both shared the same "radical-left" ideology.[69] There were real, referential connections there: Like Alinsky, Obama rose to prominence as a community organizer in Chicago and had even contributed a chapter to a 1990 edited volume entitled *After*

---

66. Laclau, *On Populist Reason*, 71.
67. Hallsby, "Recanonizing Rhetoric."
68. Joan Copjec makes a related argument about Ronald Reagan's critics: "So absorbed were the news staffs in pinning down the president's lies and errors—his referential failures, let us call them—that they neglected to consider the intersubjective dimension of the whole affair; they forgot to take account of the strength of the American audience's *love* for Reagan. . . . Americans didn't love Reagan for what he said, but simply because he was Reagan." Copjec, *Read My Desire*, 143.
69. Kovaleski, "Obama's Organizing Years"; and N. Cohen, "Know Thine Enemy."

Alinsky: Community Organizing in Illinois.[70] His secretary of state, Hillary Clinton, had written her undergraduate thesis on Alinsky and exchanged letters with the organizer in the years before his death.[71] His first-term chief of staff, Rahm Emanuel, had famously quoted Alinsky's phrase "Never let a crisis go to waste."[72] As the story went, Democrats were obsessed with the organizer. Such references track across the entirety of Obama's two terms: A 2009 *National Review* article quibbled that although Barack Obama never met Saul Alinsky, the two were distantly connected: "Three of [Obama's] mentors from his Chicago days studied at a school Alinsky founded."[73] In 2010, Sarah Palin proclaimed that the Obama administration was "all Alinsky, all the time."[74] In a 2012 primary victory speech, Newt Gingrich stated, "The centerpiece of this campaign, I believe, is American exceptionalism versus the radicalism of Saul Alinsky."[75] Andrew Breitbart made a similar accusation at the Conservative Political Action Conference (CPAC) that same year: "The anti-war movement was never about anti-war, it was a Saul Alinsky community organizing tool to get Barack Obama and the left elected."[76] The repetition of Alinsky's name suggested that the incumbent administration aspired to resuscitate the obscure 1960s radical's legacy.

As a dog whistle, however, the most literal connections between Obama and Alinsky were a screen that deflected from the Tea Party's racism and its repurposing of Alinsky's tactics. For that reason, the association of Obama with Alinsky had the character of an admission. The accusation that Obama was a covert Alinskyian offered Tea Partiers an ideological rationale for criticizing the incumbent president while also giving them a playbook for building their own coalition. Moreover, because Alinsky—who regularly instrumentalized racism—was touted as the source of the left's dirty tactics, objections to Tea Party racism were consistently met with the charge of hypocrisy. In March 2010, Tea Party demonstrators "yelled a racial epithet" and spat on US Representatives John Lewis, André Carson, and Emanuel Cleaver "as the black congressmen walked from House office buildings to the Capitol."[77] That

---

70. Obama, "Why Organize?," cited in Lizza, "Agitator."
71. Kurtz, "Hillary's Alinsky Letters"; Kruse, "First Time Hillary Clinton Was President"; Continetti, "Journalists for Hillary Clinton"; and Blankenhorn, "Clinton's Alinsky Problem."
72. Seelye, "Different Emanuel"; Jone, "Never Waste a Crisis"; Mihalopoulos, "Lifetime of Close Ties"; and Morici, "Democrats Will Never."
73. Geraghty, "Alinsky Administration."
74. Morrissey, "Video: Palin's Speech."
75. A. Horowitz, "Saul Alinsky."
76. Breitbart, "Andrew Breitbart at CPAC."
77. Hollingsworth, "NAACP Resolution." On the "birther" conspiracy theory, see also Pham, "Our Foreign President"; and Kelley-Romano and Carew, "Make America Hate Again."

year, the NAACP also released a statement repudiating "the racism within the Tea Party" and "its drive to push our country back to the pre-civil rights era." As evidence, the statement cited the movement's embrace of the conspiracy theory that Barack Obama was "born in another country," their refusal to recognize "persistent discrimination against people of color," and their belief that "the Obama Administration 'favors black people over whites.'"[78] Alinsky-inspired Tea Party organizers responded to the NAACP's accusations by denying having platformed such messaging.[79] Instead, they pointed to token Black members of the Tea Party as evidence of racial diversity, alleging that the NAACP was undermining "the cause of a colorblind society."[80] The Tea Party also alleged that Democrats and the NAACP were not just hypocrites; their accusations of racism implicated them as the true racists.

Alinsky's rhetoric also resembled the Tea Party's because both drew heavily on Revolutionary War symbols and imagery. Asserting their likeness to the white and male militants of 1776, Alinsky and Tea Partiers alike claimed a nationalist authenticity, portrayed their enemies as un-American, and favored guerrilla resistance tactics. As Alinsky wrote in *Reveille,*

> Where are America's radicals? They were with Patrick Henry in the Virginia Hall of Burgesses; they were with Sam Adams in Boston; they were with that peer of all American radicals, Tom Paine, from the distribution of Common Sense through those dark days of the American Revolution—"the times that try men's souls; the summer soldier and the sunshine patriot will, in this crisis, shrink from the service of his country; but he that stands it NOW, deserves the love and thanks of man and woman."[81]

When the Tea Party emerged as a faction within the Republican Party, it had a similarly insurrectionary connotation, seeking to undermine Republicans' prevailing power hierarchy by "ousting *Republicans* from office" and "confronting established Republican candidates in the primaries."[82] Here, too, the Tea Party laid claim to quintessentially American values in ways that were deeply and explicitly racist. When discussing the role of Charles and David Koch in forming the Tea Party as a libertarian movement, economist Bruce Bartlett stated the following:

---

78. NAACP, "Resolution: The Tea Party Movement."
79. Burghart, "Tea Party Nation."
80. Armey, "NAACP Charges of Tea Party 'Racism.'"
81. Alinsky, *Reveille for Radicals*, 13.
82. Blum, *How the Tea Party Captured the GOP,* 4.

> The problem with the whole libertarian movement is that it's been all chiefs and no Indians. There weren't any actual people, like voters, who gave a crap about it. So the problem for the Kochs has been trying to create an actual movement... everyone suddenly sees that for the first time there are Indians out there—people who can provide real ideological power.[83]

The political subordinates, foot soldiers, and on-the-ground protesters Bartlett called "Indians" were no less racist in their representations of Indigeneity. Consistent with the Tea Party's namesake, the movement's protesters frequently wore costume-like headdresses and displayed "signs and posters intended to degrade people of color generally and President Barack Obama specifically."[84] They also promoted conspiracies about white Anglo-Saxon Protestant "Extinction," used maxims like "no taxation without representation," and re-popularized the "Don't Tread On Me" Gadsden flag.[85]

Revolutionary themes were, finally, prominent in the strategies espoused by the Tea Party's "chiefs." According to Tea Party cofounder and FreedomWorks super PAC chairman Dick Armey, the postmillennium Tea Party discovered an ethos of "revolutionary participation, citizen activism, and primacy of the governed over government."[86] He proposed a return to "the period of American history leading up to the signing of the Declaration [as] the definitive case study in effective grassroots organization," hailing Samuel Adams as the first-ever community organizer.[87] When explaining his inspiration for returning to Revolutionary motifs, Armey cited Alinsky: "What's sauce for the goose is sauce for the gander. What I think of Alinsky is that he was good at what he did but what he did was not good."[88] Even as Armey excoriated Alinsky for "what he did," he avowed adopting the latter's tactics in service of his own twenty-first-century American insurrection. Catachresis was at the heart of such stratagems. Adopting Alinsky's name as an obliquely racist epithet, the movement sought to resignify Alinsky's legacy as cover for their racism and to damage Obama's reputation.

---

83. Mayer, *Dark Money*, 206.
84. Burghart, "Tea Party Nation"; and NAACP, "Resolution: The Tea Party Movement."
85. Zeskind, "Nation Dispossessed," 504; and Perrin et al., "Dimensions of Tea Party Support."
86. Armey and Kibbe, *Give Us Liberty*, 34. Paul E. Johnson describes former CNBC correspondent Rick Santelli as initiating the Tea Party movement in the United States, following from onscreen remarks made on the floor of the Chicago Mercantile Exchange on February 19, 2009, where he proposed a "Chicago Tea Party." Like Armey, Santelli also made appeals to "the founding fathers": "I'll tell you what, if you read our founding fathers, people like Benjamin Franklin and Jefferson.... What we're doing in this country now is making them roll over in their graves." P. Johnson, *I the People*, 121–48.
87. Armey and Kibbe, *Give Us Liberty*, 29.
88. Luce and Ulmer, "Obama's Foes."

Irony: "Miss the Surplus and Miss the Point"

Speaking in Palm Beach in January 2012, GOP presidential hopeful Newt Gingrich invoked Alinsky to mark differences between himself and Obama: "I am for the Declaration of Independence, he is for the writing of Saul Alinsky. I am for the Constitution, he is for European socialism."[89] According to *Washington Post* reporter Harold Meyerson, Gingrich's accusations proved just how lazy Republican pejoratives had become.[90] Alinsky explicitly stated that he was neither a communist nor a socialist and even avoided arraignment by Joseph McCarthy's anti-communist House Un-American Activities Committee.[91] Juxtaposing Alinsky to the founders and their documents also made little sense, given Alinsky's affection for the Declaration of Independence, the Constitution, and the nation's founders.[92] However, by dismissing Gingrich's reasoning as hypocrisy, Meyerson missed a larger point: how Gingrich and Alinsky resembled one another by baiting their antagonists into a self-inflicted injury.

Gingrich's doublespeak captures the Alinsky dog whistle's second organizing trope: irony. At its simplest, irony is "something said while pretending not to be saying it."[93] As an argument that relies upon deception and contradiction, irony is both a "dissembling manner of speaking typical of the educated and the upper classes" and "a marker of adept double coding" that "requires sufficient detachment from experience."[94] Although irony has pedagogical value as a method of "perspective-taking" and "perspective-revising," irony fundamentally evokes a context of competition in which a speaker feigns weakness to gain an upper hand.[95] Whereas "the *eiron* is the man who

---

89. Sugrue, "Saul Alinsky."
90. Meyerson, "GOP Misses Its Bogeyman."
91. Alinsky, *Rules for Radicals*, 11. Donald and Dietrich Reitzes recount the McCarthy episode in the following way:

> When members of McCarthy's staff threatened Alinsky with destroying his reputation, his response was: "Reputation? *What* reputation? You think I give a damn about my reputation? Call me as a witness; you won't get any Fifth Amendment from me. He [McCarthy] can force me to answer yes and no, but once I get out into the corridor with the press, then he can't stop me from talking about the way he courted Communist support for his Senate fight against Lafollette in '46. Tell McCarthy to go to hell." The McCarthy staff never called Alinsky to testify. (Alinsky, "*Playboy* Interview," 169, quoted in Reitzes and Reitzes, *Alinsky Legacy*, 10)

92. Alinsky, *Rules for Radicals*, 27.
93. Karstetter, "Rhetorical Irony," 164.
94. Swearingen, *Rhetoric and Irony*, 5; and Cloud, "Irony Bribe," 415; Cloud cites Booth, *Rhetoric of Irony*, 148, 193.
95. Steudeman, "Entelechy and Irony," 61; and Hartnett, "Fanny Fern's 1855 *Ruth Hall*," 2. Both Steudeman and Hartnett draw and build upon the epistemic interpretation of irony from K. Burke, "Four Master Tropes" (1969), 512–17.

deprecates himself" to make "himself invulnerable," irony is "a technique of appearing to be less than what one is . . . of saying as little and meaning as much as possible."[96] Irony not only has the capacity to invert the taken-for-granted meaning of words or phrases, it enacts a role reversal in which one party in a verbal conflict loses their assumed command over what that word or phrase means. Deployed with an ironic inflection, "Saul Alinsky" was resignified against the grain of how his legacy had formerly meant, using the master organizer to master those who allegedly followed in his footsteps.

One example of ironic inversion concerns the Tea Party's knowing adoption of Alinsky's strategies of naming. Alinsky regularly assigned punchy acronymic names to the groups he organized, for instance, TWO (Temporary Woodlawn Organization), BUILD (Build Unity, Independence, Liberty, and Dignity), and FIGHT (Freedom, Integration, God, Honor, Today):

> Then Alinsky told them to name the new organization. Alinsky chided them for their tame choices, saying they ought to come up with something that would play on the whites' fears. "What the hell are they most afraid of?" he asked. "And why the hell are we doing this anyway?" Somebody else said something about how the new organization should come out fighting, and one of the clergymen recalled St. Paul's words: "Fight the good fight of faith, lay hold on eternal light." "Then call it FIGHT," Alinsky said. Everybody seemed to like that, although the group had trouble finding the words for the acronym—they got as far as Freedom, Integration, Honor, Today but couldn't come up with a word beginning with "G." (The next day, Alinsky phoned Chambers with the answer. "It came to me at about 34,000 feet last night on the flight to New York. The 'G' stands for God; now God is in FIGHT.")[97]

The name FIGHT set the stage for an ongoing adversarial relationship between local government and community leaders. Newspaper editorialist Paul Miller urged the organization to select "a name somewhat less offensive to the total community," such as "WORK or LOVE or DEED," which would make it more amenable to cooperate with "other organizations, working more quietly and more usefully."[98] Alinsky "gleefully" noted that his critics were "playing right into his hands," having been baited into engagement.

According to Jane Mayer, the tactic of naming conservative political advocacy organizations, think tanks, PACs, and anonymous super PACs dates to

---

96. Frye, *Anatomy of Criticism*, 40.
97. Horwitt, *Let Them Call Me Rebel*, 461.
98. Horwitt, *Let Them Call Me Rebel*, 462.

the 1960s John Birch Society, whose rhetoric of masculine victimhood and secretive hierarchy resembled that of antecedent twentieth-century secret societies. Similar to the way the Tea Party drew their tactics from Alinsky, their figural enemy on the left, the John Birch Society "ironically... modeled itself on the Communist Party" and "set up phony front groups 'pretending to be other than what they were.'"[99] In the same decade that Alinsky organized TWO, BUILD, and FIGHT, Robert Welch created political advocacy groups with names like TRAIN (To Restore American Independence Now) and TACT (Truth About Civil Turmoil), and "wrapped the group's radical vision in mundane and unthreatening slogans" like "less government, more responsibility."[100] As the inspiration for Charles Koch, David Koch, and the Tea Party's other billionaire backers, Welch was a model for adopting the opposition's tactics. Well before the Tea Party, the Koch family employed deceptive front groups like Citizens for a Sound Economy (CSE) and the National Right to Work Legal Defense Foundation.[101] According to Tea Party strategist Matt Kibbe, a key function of CSE was to study and co-opt the political left's strategies:

> [CSE's] mission, according to one early participant, Matt Kibbe, "was to take these heavy ideas and translate them for mass America." Kibbe explained, "We read the same literature Obama did about non-violent revolutions—Saul Alinsky, Gandhi, Martin Luther King. We studied the idea of the Boston Tea Party as an example of nonviolent social change. We learned that we needed boots on the ground to sell ideas, not candidates."[102]

By 2012, Koch-backed organizations like CSE, FreedomWorks, and Americans for Prosperity (AFP) were repurposed to support Tea Party candidates against Republican incumbents, and new, candidate-centered super PACs like "Winning Our Future" gradually emerged.[103] As Armey noted of his interactions with Charles Koch, "He was half-secretive. He'd speak in cryptic tones. You'd have to think, 'What does he mean?' He'd talk about this business of trying to 'save the country' and all that.... Charles wanted to be more in control but he also wanted to be more behind the scenes. I don't get it."[104]

---

99. Mayer, *Dark Money,* 48.
100. Mayer, *Dark Money,* 49.
101. Mayer, *Dark Money,* 196.
102. Mayer, *Dark Money,* 196.
103. Mayer, "Covert Operations."
104. Mayer, *Dark Money,* 199.

Irony was also apparent in Tea Party candidates' other exposure-and-humiliation tactics—including those they used against other establishment Republicans. Weeks before Gingrich's Palm Beach comments, the pro-Gingrich super PAC, Winning Our Future, released a half-hour documentary-style advertisement entitled "The King of Bain," blasting establishment Republican candidate Mitt Romney as a "dark-hearted, vicious-minded, boodle-craving technocrat-privateer." According to the advertisement, Romney's firm, Bain Capital, actively contributed to American joblessness by stripping down companies and selling them for parts.[105] Weeks later, Romney was forced to explain how he reconciled his self-enrichment with the pressing problems of American poverty. In comments that haunted his campaign until its end, Romney confessed to CNN anchor Soledad O'Brien that he was "not concerned with the very poor."[106]

Winning Our Future did not just make Romney out to be a pirate of American industry; it did so by plundering from Alinsky's *Rules for Radicals*, specifically his maxim that "the right things are done for the wrong reasons."[107] In *Rules*, this phrase alludes to a Machiavellian attitude toward justification and political expediency. Even as Gingrich's campaign benefited from his alliances to venture capital, his campaign's super PAC used anti-corporatist arguments to depict Romney as a heartless corporate raider who would eliminate paying jobs to enrich himself. The difference was that Romney had been forced to reveal his disregard for Americans living below the poverty line. Removing Romney from contention retroactively justified the use of these claims. The right things were done for the wrong reasons: Not only did the move invert the hierarchy between establishment Republicans and fringe Tea Party candidates, but it also forced Romney to avow his lack of concern for working-class voters. No longer able to control what his speech meant for his working-class constituents, Romney's pro-capitalist stance—a frequent selling-point for conservative political candidates—suddenly became a campaign liability.

A final way that we may bear witness to the irony of Alinsky's appropriation by the Tea Party concerns their quasi-confessional discourse, which projected the charge of appropriation back upon the Left, from whom they were poaching. In 2010, then–State Representative Paul Ryan (R-WI) made the following statement:

---

105. Linkins, "'King of Bain' Attack Documentary."
106. R. Weiner, "Not Concerned About the Very Poor."
107. Alinsky, *Rules for Radicals*, 76.

We, along with the American people, were spectators while [Democrats] took this government very far left, very fast. But what became so unnerving to us and the American people is that they used *our* rhetoric. They use the rhetoric of freedom and choice and opportunity to sell an inherently statist agenda; to sell an agenda that was completely the opposite of its rhetoric. And people started to realize that they were trying to transform the country using the rhetoric of the Right to push through the substance of the Left.[108]

Given how often the Tea Party took its tactics from Alinsky, it is difficult not to read Ryan's statement as a retroactive justification for appropriating "the substance of the Left." The statement is also a quintessential illustration of the *eiron*, a feigned position of weakness that inverted the existing dynamic of appropriation. By citing Republicans' waning influence and Democrats' allegedly dirty tactics of rhetorical appropriation, Ryan sought to gain mastery and control for his fringe faction. Because Democrats controlled the White House and both legislative branches at the start of Obama's first term, Alinskyian tactics promised to invert the balance of power, making liberals into the dupes of their own organizing schemes.

Among Tea Party candidates, the Alinsky dog whistle always had a double, surplus meaning. To miss the surplus is to miss the point.[109] It would, for instance, miss the point to dwell on the contradictions between the ways that Alinsky was invoked by Tea Partiers and his well-documented history. The "surplus" of his conservative, twenty-first-century uptake is more apparent if we read his name as an oblique reference to Obama's race and the specific tactics Tea Partiers drew from the Alinsky playbook to attack his administration. To paraphrase Kenneth Burke, irony describes a dialectic in which "A(linsky) returns as non-A(linsky)."[110] Alinsky's name gained "something extra" when he returned as a dog whistle: He did not just name the dirty tactics of a liberal icon but an effort to humiliate the left and other opponents using those same "dirty tactics," all the while accusing the enemy of poaching rhetoric and strategy.[111]

---

108. Cantor and McCarthy, *Young Guns*, 7–8.
109. McDaniel, "Liberal Irony," 306.
110. Burke, "Four Master Tropes" (1941), 438.
111. Calum Matheson characterizes the related discourse of "liberal tears" similarly, as an expression of "sadistic pleasure," a zero-sum game in which the liberal other's pain is registered as an affective gain for the conservative subject while also functioning as a self-destructive "defense against threatening modes of enjoyment." Matheson, "Liberal Tears," 351.

Alinsky, Incorporated: Gonzo Pseudojournalism

In January 2001, *The New York Times* published an article on "gotcha politics," referencing a controversy preceding George W. Bush's ascension to the presidency.[112] Bush had selected Linda Chavez, a high-ranking member of the Reagan cabinet, as his secretary of labor. Chavez had sheltered an undocumented immigrant in her home and was forced to withdraw from the presidential ticket.[113] During his campaign, George W. Bush told CNN's Larry King that "a president can help purge the system of this kind of gotcha politics."[114] Like Alinsky, the phrase famously resurfaced in 2008. During an interview with CBS anchor Katie Couric, vice presidential candidate Sarah Palin defended her inability to answer questions by accusing Couric of "gotcha journalism," that is, of staging the interview to catch her off guard.[115] For a short time after, "gotcha journalism" became Tea Party shorthand for liberal media bias.

Not long after Palin's "gotcha" moment, Project Veritas founder James O'Keefe helped to popularize a new Alinsky-style tactic I call *gonzo pseudojournalism*. Like the "gonzo journalism" attributed to Hunter S. Thompson, this tactic abandoned all pretense of ideological neutrality and embraced an immersive first-person style.[116] However, O'Keefe's purpose was to produce not journalism but something that vaguely resembled it, seeking to expose, embarrass, and humiliate ideological opponents. In one instance, O'Keefe released video footage "showing the then-president of the NPR Foundation saying those affiliated with the Tea Party movement are 'really racist, racist people' and that the network would be better off without federal funding," prompting several executives and the organization's then-CEO to resign.[117] Throughout his career, O'Keefe frequently invoked *Rules for Radicals* as the key inspiration for his tactics, citing Alinsky's commitment to "making the enemy live up to its own book of rules."[118] In other words, gonzo pseudojournalism was conservative refashioning of "gotcha journalism," adopting an

---

112. Safire, "Gotcha!"
113. S. Taylor, "Smearing Linda Chavez"; Milbank and Edsall, "Chavez Pulls Out"; and del Olmo, "Don't Shed Any Tears."
114. Safire, "Gotcha!"
115. Seelye, "McCain and Palin's Interview"; Itkowitz, "History of the 'Gotcha Question'"; and J. Ross, "History of 'Gotcha' Questions."
116. Mosser, "Gonzo Journalism."
117. E. Johnson, "O'Keefe's Rules for Radicals."
118. Shane, "Political Gadfly."

aesthetic of undercover investigative reporting that involved elaborate ruses and predatory sting operations.[119]

As a variation on the Alinsky dog whistle, gonzo pseudojournalism recalls "the secret or cryptic character of *incorporation*."[120] If catachresis and irony describe the formal-rhetorical organization of dog whistles, then incorporation describes the material consequences of internalizing and distancing oneself from a love-hate object like Saul Alinsky. Incorporation is a conceptual relative to the psychoanalytic concept of enjoyment, which similarly accounts for how a subject's libidinal attachments, when repeated, function as assurance of coherent selfhood.[121] Both secure the subject's sense of identity through ritual encounters with an object that may alternately bring them pleasure, pain, or both.[122] Incorporation, however, carries the specific sense of attachment to an object that one hopes to eradicate. As Jean Laplanche and Jean-Bertrand Pontalis define it, incorporation "means to obtain pleasure by making an object penetrate oneself; it means to destroy this object; and it means, by keeping it within oneself, to appropriate the object's qualities."[123] The more one seeks the elimination of the object, the more intensely they internalize it. Incorporation is, therefore, a valuable way of understanding the function of dog whistles as speech acts that intensify the subject's object-attachment (e.g., Saul Alinsky) as they seek its extinction. Jacques Derrida describes the process as follows:

> Incorporation is a kind of theft to reappropriate the pleasure object. But that reappropriation is simultaneously rejected: which leads to the paradox of a foreign body preserved as foreign but by the same token excluded from a self that thenceforth deals not with the other, but only with itself. The more the self keeps the foreign element as a foreigner in itself, the more it excludes it.[124]

---

119. Mayer, "Sting of Myself"; and Mayer, "James O'Keefe's Call." The leaked document O'Keefe used to plan a sting of CNN reporter Abbie Boudreau is particularly damning and reads as a plot to produce revenge pornography: "I'm going to seduce [Boudreau], on camera, to use her for a video. This bubble-headed-bleach-blonde who comes on at five will get a taste of her own medicine, she'll get seduced on camera and you'll get to see the awkwardness and the aftermath." Boudreau, "Documentary Takes a Strange Detour."
120. Derrida, "*Fors*," xvii.
121. Lundberg, "Enjoying God's Death," 401–2.
122. Hallsby and Gunn, "Mirror of Enjoyment," 142–46.
123. Laplanche and Pontalis, *Language of Psychoanalysis*, 211.
124. Derrida, "*Fors*," xvii.

The Alinsky dog whistle engages in just this play of proximity and distance. *Veritas* engaged in acts of theft that sought to reappropriate Alinsky for itself, bringing the avowedly liberal organizer into the conservative fold. At the same time, they also rejected Alinsky, seeking not only to destroy his legacy but to hold him apart as "a foreign body" distinct from conservative radicalism. Incorporation, in other words, enables the subject to cling tightly to the object the dog whistle names *and* to react violently against it. Gonzo pseudojournalism became an available means of punishing Obama-era Alinskyians, while Alinsky himself authorized Veritas and O'Keefe to take pleasure in tactics of humiliation and exposure.

Two examples of gonzo pseudojournalism are especially illustrative of O'Keefe's Alinskyian incorporation. The first of these went viral in September 2009, when O'Keefe orchestrated a hidden-camera sting of the Association of Community Organizations for Reform Now (ACORN). As it was reported in *The Atlantic*, "In that film, O'Keefe and collaborator Hannah Giles pretend to be a pimp and prostitute and find some ACORN workers willing to give them advice about how to set up a brothel said to include underage prostitutes."[125] ACORN was a strategic target, one that specifically indexes Veritas's efforts to destroy Alinsky's legacy institutions. Its first chief organizer, Wade Rathke, allegedly borrowed his methods from Fred Ross, "an Alinsky co-worker who helped organize the Community Service Organization in the Mexican-American community of the southwest in the late 1940s."[126] Republican candidates had also alleged that ACORN had deep connections to Obama and had facilitated voter fraud on behalf of his first presidential campaign.[127] Most prominently, Republican presidential and vice presidential candidates John McCain and Sarah Palin had released campaign advertisements in 2008 alleging that "there were at least eleven investigations across the country involving thousands of potentially fraudulent ACORN forms," which was tantamount to "massive voter fraud."[128] During the first presidential debate, McCain accused ACORN of "perpetrating one of the greatest frauds in voter history in this country, maybe destroying the fabric of democracy."[129]

Seeking to corroborate these accusations, O'Keefe and Giles posted their pimp-and-prostitute ACORN sting on Andrew Breitbart's www.BigGovernment.com—a precursor to his more famous platform for

---

125. Friedersdorf, "What the *NYT Magazine* Doesn't Say."
126. Boyte, *Backyard Revolution*, 93.
127. Shane, "Conservatives Draw Blood."
128. Henig, "ACORN Accusations."
129. "First Presidential Debate."

conservative invective, racism, and xenophobia, *Breitbart News*. Breitbart, who was also a cofounder of the *Huffington Post*, used his journalistic credentials to endorse O'Keefe as someone who was "idealistic, right-leaning, and doesn't pretend he's a neutral and objective journalist (no one's 'objective')."[130] The footage captured ACORN staffers "who appeared to blithely encourage prostitution and tax evasion" by providing "detailed legal instructions on how to avoid problems with the police and tax authorities."[131] Although they uncovered no voter fraud, O'Keefe and Giles expressed triumph at catching ACORN in an illicit act, resulting in ACORN's shutting down in 2010. What marks this as an Alinskyian incorporation was the way that Alinsky's playbook was marshalled to shut down a community organization with distant ties to Alinsky, literally celebrating and destroying the object in one sweeping image-event. Nor did *Veritas* ever "fully" or "completely" eradicate ACORN. Rather, it left room for future destruction/internalization as conspiracy theories about how ACORN lived on in secret continued to circulate after the sting. According to a 2010 article from the right-wing *Washington Times*, many ACORN-like organizations sprouted up under the cover of new acronyms and management.[132] For years after, the US Congress employed language prohibiting federal appropriations from being routed to ACORN affiliates in must-pass spending bills.[133]

A second example concerns Veritas's continued attacks upon Planned Parenthood. In 2007, O'Keefe and Lila Rose of the anti-choice organization Live Action published videos in which Rose disguised herself as a pregnant teenager to catch staff in the act of advising her to lie about her age.[134] In 2011, Rose again published videos with the videographer disguised as a pimp seeking advice about abortions and birth control.[135] In 2015, former Live Action affiliate David R. Daleiden published a video of senior Planned Parenthood director Dr. Deborah Nucatola "discussing the collection of fetal tissue in a lunch meeting with two people posing as potential tissue buyers."[136] One of many tactics used to "[manipulate] time" and "maneuver around legal rights," such sting operations drummed up immediate public visibility for antiabortion activists, spurious evidence for government investigations of abortion

---

130. "Exposing ACORN."
131. Shane, "Conservatives Draw Blood"; and "Sensational Giles and O'Keefe."
132. "Weary Activist Group ACORN."
133. Weigel, "ACORN Funding Ban."
134. Douthat, "Pregnancy Counseling"; and Dewan, "Foes of Abortion."
135. Keiper, "Video of Planned Parenthood."
136. "Campaign of Deception."

providers, and by extension, abortion-restrictive legislation.[137] The Nucatola sting resulted in a flurry of journalistic activity about fetal tissue collection, twelve state and three federal investigations of Planned Parenthood clinics, two million dollars in fines for Daleiden, and fifteen felony charges against on-camera contributor Sandra S. Merritt for filming clinicians without their consent.[138] Gonzo pseudojournalists like Daleiden, Merritt, and O'Keefe attempted "to recast abortion as an urgent, collective, and defining moral crisis" while adopting Alinsky's tactics to accomplish their goals.[139]

As an illustration of incorporation, the racist inflections of Veritas's partnership with the antiabortion movement went beyond the pimp-and-prostitute role-play of the ACORN sting; Alinskyian tactics both justified explicit racism *and* were used in recruitment efforts to broaden the racial diversity of the antiabortion movement. O'Keefe, for instance, would seek to catch Planned Parenthood officials avowing his bigoted statements. In 2008, Rose published audio recordings in which O'Keefe had said, "You know, we just think, the less black kids out there, the better," while attempting to make a private donation to Planned Parenthood. Conversely, Rose celebrated Saul Alinsky as an antiabortion strategist at the 2008 Values Voter Summit, where she suggested that rape and racism could be instrumentally weaponized to accomplish movement goals:

> In the controversial activist handbook *Rules for Radicals*, Saul Alinsky does give some good advice. He writes, "Men don't like to step abruptly out of the security of familiar experience. They need a bridge to cross from their experience to a new way." Let's take this advice to heart. We can take positions that we all agree on: Rape and racism are both fundamentally evil, and [missing word] use them as bridges to inspire respect for human life. We need to broaden the context for people's understanding of the abortion industry and culture.[140]

Rose suggested that the anti-choice movement *could* be made palatable to a racially diverse audience, if only by shocking them. She argued that lying about rape and openly espousing racism were morally justified, so long as

---

137. Winderman, "(Never) Going Back," 287.

138. Coker, "Rhetorical Laundering," 4; Grady and St. Fleur, "Fetal Tissue"; and Pérez-Peña, "Anti-Abortion Activists Charged."

139. Although the subject of the quoted sentence concerns Crisis Pregnancy Centers' manipulation of abortion seekers to dissuade and prevent them from ending their pregnancies, I borrow this phrasing because gonzo pseudojournalists like Rose, Daleiden, and Merritt similarly instrumentalized urgency and deception to curtail abortion care. Fixmer-Oraiz, *Homeland Maternity*, 137.

140. Rose, "Values Voter Summit Speech."

these were used to coax illegal or morally reprehensible statements from abortion providers. Such propaganda would, in her words, "broaden the context" for future recruitment.

The incorporative move to reject racism and rape through disingenuous performances was even more insidious because Rose's use of the Alinsky dog whistle aimed specifically to persuade Black antiabortion activists to join her antiabortion coalition. The Rose-O'Keefe audio recordings played at the 2009 Values Voter Summit had that very effect, garnering support from Rev. Jesse Lee Peterson of Brotherhood Organization of a New Destiny (BOND), a Los Angeles–based men's rehabilitation advocacy group. According to *The New York Times*, the Rose-O'Keefe recordings also "reinvigorated old claims that the organization [Planned Parenthood] was a front for racial genocide" and that "[Margaret] Sanger," the organization's founder, "viewed blacks as undesirable."[141] Rose's citation of Alinsky signaled a desire to expand the scope of antiabortion rhetoric, encourage a conspiratorially suspicious orientation to Planned Parenthood, and stigmatize anyone who advocated for abortion as reproductive care as themselves embodying a covert racism. Hence, *incorporation*: Tea Party conservatives and activists internalized Alinsky to destroy him in effigy, embracing him to the point that they too justified leaving the structural core of racism intact.

Alinsky's Others

Sam Greenlee's 1969 *The Spook Who Sat by the Door* tells the story of Dan Freeman, the first Black CIA officer who endures more-and-less coded racism as he is used to showcase the agency's diversity. The titular "Spook" is a double entendre, both a racial epithet and a common moniker for CIA agents. What W. E. B. Du Bois calls "double-consciousness" is a recurring motif; for Greenlee's protagonist, this divided twoness harmonizes with the persona of the double agent.[142] Freeman is "the best undercover man the CIA had": He cultivates an unthreatening aura among openly bigoted white officers, politicians, and professors, while using his intelligence expertise to undermine the racist

---

141. Dewan, "Foes of Abortion."
142. In a key passage, Du Bois defines "double-consciousness" in the following way: "It is a peculiar sensation, this double-consciousness, this sense of always looking at one's self through the eyes of others, of measuring one's soul by the tape of a world that looks on in amused contempt and pity. One ever feels his two-ness,—an American, a Negro; two souls, two thoughts, two unreconciled strivings; two warring ideals in one dark body, whose dogged strength alone keeps it from being torn asunder. The history of the American Negro is the history of this strife,—this longing to attain self-conscious manhood, to merge his double self into a better and truer self." Du Bois, "Strivings," 194–95.

system they serve.¹⁴³ After studying guerrilla warfare and counterinsurrectionary tactics, he returns home to Chicago and applies his training to organize and train young Black men into a revolutionary force. After playing the role of double agent within a University of Chicago–affiliated foundation, he secretly coordinates a revolutionary uprising that spreads across major cities in the United States.¹⁴⁴ Chicago, the primary setting of Greenlee's book, marks Saul Alinsky's involvement in Woodlawn as an obvious extradiegetic foil. Published shortly after Alinsky left Chicago, *The Spook Who Sat by the Door* presents a counterhistorical fabulation of South Side organizing from the perspective of a revolutionary community organizer who, unlike Alinsky, came from within the community, refused tactical expediency, turned the tables on racist institutions, and successfully stages a community-centered revolution against a hegemonically anti-Black system by leveraging its own tactics against it. Freeman is Alinsky's unstated but obvious other: a double or doppelgänger who demonstrates just how unradical the latter really was.

This concluding anecdote presents a counterpoint to the more contemporary examples presented in this chapter. Greenlee's book is a rescripting of 1960s Chicago community organizing that is more contemporaneous with TWO's Woodlawn interventions. It offers a version of history as it could have been, unburdened by Alinsky's realist racial paradigm. Unlike Alinsky, Freeman offers a view of reality in which the moral, material, and discursive foundations of systemic racism can be shaken given the proper worldview, leaders, and tactics.

Of course, Alinsky's transformation into a conservative dog whistle during the years 2008 to 2016 attests to a different status quo, one "that has fatally limited the possibility of overcoming racism," while enabling "new kinds of normalizing and rationalizing violences."¹⁴⁵ During these years, the Tea Party adopted racist dog whistles in tandem with a rhetoric of color blindness that denied the importance or existence of race. One perverse instance of color blindness concerns how neoconservatives proudly paraded Martin Luther King's injunction to elevate "'content of character' over 'color of skin'" to appropriate the civil rights leader as a libertarian symbol, an exemplar of "placing personal morality above government, public welfare, and the law."¹⁴⁶ The sibling ideology to color blindness is "post-racialism," a narrative of overcoming or superseding racial difference that was embraced and amplified by

---

143. Greenlee, *Spook Who Sat by the Door*, 9, 34.
144. Greenlee, *Spook Who Sat by the Door*, 67, 178.
145. Melamed, *Represent and Destroy*, xi.
146. Melamed, *Represent and Destroy*, 220.

Obama's electoral campaigns.[147] And yet, as Eric King Watts notes, this fantasy of having gotten "past" or "beyond" race "depend[s] on and reanimate[s] the affective economies concurrent to the abjection of blackness" in different forms, again and again.[148]

Dog whistles are a double-coded symptom of the racism endemic to color blindness and post-racialism. They enable their wielders to evoke the historical violence of racism while denying its material existence, in one fell swoop. As much is witnessable in the metonymic substitution of "Black Lives Matter" for "Blue Lives Matter," or the effort to unmoor "Critical Race Theory" from its critical legal roots.[149] A whole series of examples may be drawn from Republican attacks on Kamala Harris and the transformation of "busing" into a dog whistle. In 2019, Harris made waves during a primary debate by making "clear to the American voters that Biden had joined Dixie Democrats in 'opposing busing' during the 1970s," and "let it be known that, as a 'little girl,' she helped 'integrate her public schools' where 'busing' proved integral to such integration."[150] To have supported busing would have meant that Biden supported civil rights; however, he had stood with the segregationists. In 2024, "busing" and other signifiers acquired the force of dog whistles after Donald Trump leveraged them as accusations to delegitimize Harris's candidacy. In July, Republican members of Congress began to describe Harris as a "DEI hire," perpetuating "a narrative that people of color and women can only be in positions of power or authority because of quotas, preferential treatment and unfair advantage given to them based on their social identities. That is: not because of their education, qualifications, training or experience."[151] The rise of the "DEI hire" dog whistle was concomitant with related instances of coded racism about diverse hiring. During his June debate against Biden, Trump claimed that "migrants were taking 'Black jobs' and 'Hispanic jobs,'" aiming to sow division between America's naturalized minorities and the newly arrived to the United States.[152] On July 31, speaking before the National Association of Black Journalists, Trump accused Harris of having lied about her race and ethnicity credentials, arguing that she was therefore unworthy of consideration for the job of president.[153] By election day, Trump campaign supporters had

---

147. Squires, *Post-Racial Mystique*, 3–5.
148. Watts, "Postracial Fantasies," 318.
149. Biesecker, "General History to Philosophy."
150. Parry-Giles, "Disciplining Kamala," 445. Parry-Giles cites Delmont, "Generational Shift."
151. McCammon, "'DEI Hire'"; and N. Burke, "'DEI Hire.'"
152. "Trump's Debate References."
153. Deggans, "Trump's Appearance."

fully weaponized "busing" against Harris, promulgating a conspiracy theory that her campaign had illegally bused voters from New York to Pennsylvania to perpetrate electoral fraud.[154] Disarticulated from the Civil Rights Movement, busing became a dog whistle much in the same way that DEI had been months earlier. What lends credence to this as a coordinated effort at resignification is that this was not the first time that Trump had encountered the racial and historical significance of busing: After Harris's comments in 2019, he had been asked about integration-era busing. His response ("there aren't that many ways you're going to get people to schools") left journalists wondering whether he was aware of the civil rights era practice.[155]

It bears asking what the significance of dog whistles is at a moment when explicit and "unsublimated" expressions of racism are increasingly common.[156] During Donald Trump's 2025 inauguration, Elon Musk delivered a "stiff-arm salute" that strongly resembled the one used by Nazi soldiers. The ambiguity of Musk's gesture initiated pointless perseveration over whether it was, in fact, a "Roman Salute": a "visual gesture" with little connection to the Roman era, "heavily deployed in silent cinema" and later adopted "by the Italian fascist dictator Benito Mussolini."[157] At some level, looking for the secret or hidden meaning of the sign was a deflection from what was obvious to the German *Die Zeit*: "A Hitler salute is a Hitler salute is a Hitler Salute."[158] Given Musk's courting of far-right parties across Europe shortly after his inauguration-day speech, it is important to note that the function of dog whistles is to lend their enunciators a sense of mastery, enabling them to communicate their racism openly at the expense of those who fumble for a true reference.[159]

Amid the global intensification of fascistic energies and symbols, what remains significant about Alinskyian dog whistles is how they seek to absorb, incorporate, and deploy the Left's rhetoric with destructive intent. Neo-fascist strategists like Steve Bannon, political advisor to Donald Trump and former chairman of Breitbart News, are reported to have read in the traditions of post-structuralism and intersectionality in anticipation of their war on "Critical Race Theory," seeking to weaponize their insights against their staunchest

---

154. Ferris, "Voter Fraud."
155. Stockler, "Busing Is Just a Way"; and Wade, "Busing Is About Transportation."
156. P. Johnson, *I the People*, 147.
157. Bennhold, "Elon Musk's Salute."
158. Jacobsen, "Ein Hitlergruß ist ein Hitlergruß ist ein Hitlergruß."
159. Bennhold, "American Interference."

defenders.[160] A similar phenomenon also characterizes the conservative appropriation of Michel Foucault.[161] For instance, the continuous appropriation of Foucault by conservatives in the early twenty-first century characterizes his critical reflections on neoliberalism as an endorsement of "third-way" centrism.[162] Biopolitics, another of Foucault's conceptual innovations, was leveraged to justify human disposability and smear government-authorized public health measures during the early COVID-19 pandemic.[163] What's striking about such examples is how those championed by the academic left, like Alinsky, have been turned against their adherents some forty-odd years after they came into vogue.

As a secret, dog whistles are both *in* and *of* discourse: both hidden (ignored, forgotten, overshadowed) and productive (a patterned re-production of racism that was always and already there). Their power derives not just from what they mean but also from what they do, the material and mortal consequence of speaking the words aloud.[164] Understanding the dog whistle's form is an integral part of the riddle. Only an auditor who did not know how to properly listen for the password would obsess over who Alinsky really was or what his deeds really signified. As Alinsky himself stated: "Conflict is the essential core of a free and open society. If one were to project the democratic way of life in the form of a musical score, its major theme would be the harmony of dissonance."[165] In keeping with Alinsky's musical metaphor, the dog whistle remains a recurring rhetorical refrain of twenty-first-century political rhetoric. It manifests not a free and open society but one based in shared enmity, white supremacy, and a pretentious claim to mastery that subjects political adversaries to weaponized versions of their own discourse.

---

160. As whistleblower Christopher Wylie recounts:

> Bannon immediately grasped all of this, even telling me that he believed, as I do, that politics and fashion are essentially products of the same phenomenon. . . . He reads about intersectional feminism or the fluidity of identity not, as I later learned, because he's open to those ideas but because he wants to invert them—to identify what people attach themselves to and then to weaponize it. What I didn't know that day was that Bannon wanted to fight a cultural war, and so he had come to the people who specialized in informational weapons to help him build his arsenal. (Wylie, *Mindf*ck*, 67; see also Scheuermann, "Searching in Europe")

161. For instance, see Paletta, "Amend and Deny"; and Douthat, "Foucault Lost the Left."
162. Zamora and Behrent, *Foucault and Neoliberalism*, 103.
163. Ganz, "Foucault and the Conservatives." See also Kotsko, "Giorgio Agamben."
164. Gunn, *Modern Occult Rhetoric*, xix.
165. Alinsky, *Rules for Radicals*, 62.

CHAPTER 5
================

The Leak

Sexual Caricature and the National Security State

> To "spy on" in order to "know"; to "tame" in order to "cure": such are the methods used by masculine reason so as to objectify feminine madness, and thereby to master it.
> —Shoshana Felman, *What Does a Woman Want?* (33)

The Fluidity Menace

In a key scene of *Dr. Strangelove* (1964), the unhinged Brigadier General Jack D. Ripper confronts Captain Lionel Mandrake about the ubiquitous threat posed by covert communist agents. After deploying nuclear weapons against the Soviet Union (and, by extension, the world), Ripper repeatedly avows his belief that communists are sapping Americans' vital potency: "It's incredibly obvious, isn't it? A foreign substance is introduced into our precious bodily fluids, without the knowledge of the individual, certainly without any choice. That's the way your hard-core commie works."[1] Ripper's speech echoed a popular conspiracy theory familiar to many US audiences in 1964: the public controversy over water fluoridation.[2] His obsession with bodily fluids also evokes a more general crisis of masculinity that has stretched from the mid-twentieth century to the mid-twenty-first. In this paranoid fantasy, an American way of life and a masculine sexual ideology are presumed to be under a ubiquitous, invisible threat.[3] Certainly, many Cold War–era "nuclear euphemisms" (e.g.,

---

1. Kubrick, *Dr. Strangelove*.
2. J. Johnson, "Man's Mouth," 1–2.
3. Kelly, *Apocalypse Man*, 2; and Sisco King, *Washed in Blood*, 5. See also Levant, "Masculinity Crisis"; Robinson, *Marked Men*; Banet-Weiser, *Empowered*; and Beckman, "Paranoid Masculinity."

"deep penetration," "spasm war," "hardening," and "bang for the buck") established a "link between sex and death" in ways that reflect a related crisis of violent masculinity.[4] Ripper's preoccupation with bodily leakiness is no exception; it is a metonym for "an emasculating humiliation that requires recouping masculinity in some other, often phallic form."[5] After all, what more phallic overcompensation is there than an atomic bomb?

National security leaks present a parallel case to Ripper's obsessive fantasy. Leaks sexualize the national and corporeal body by evoking a great, dripping secret at the heart of the national security state (hereafter NSS). Under the surveillant gaze of the NSS and its many agencies, they also evoke the crisis of waning masculinity using patriarchal, heteronormative, and cisgendered tropes.[6] Most often, such agencies attribute characteristics of masculine mastery or feminized deception to leakers.[7] Such attributions are outward expressions of what Timothy Melley terms "agency panic": An "intense anxiety about an apparent loss of autonomy or self-control" that confines leakers to one of two characterological types.[8] The masculine *spymaster*'s trope is a compensatory *megethos*, an accumulation of information whose disclosure fails to achieve its intended consequence. The femme fatale's is *apophasis*, the secret that transforms the category of the subject each time it is found. Together, these types and tropes lend leaks a form that aims to recuperate a hegemonically masculine/phallic and feminine/phatic geopolitical order. As I argue, *every* national security leak evokes this regressive sexual logic.

Before proceeding, two terminological clarifications. First, I call agents of unauthorized disclosure *leakers* and not whistleblowers. *Leaker* and *leak* convey unauthorized information flows and their facilitating agents in the broadest possible terms. This generality is why Alan Turing—who facilitated the state-sanctioned leak of the ENIGMA code—shares space with Chelsea Manning in the final sections. "Whistleblower" has force as a legal performative, describing a special, semiprotected status accorded by the US judicial system.[9] The catachresis whereby a leaker is called a whistleblower in the absence of

---

4. Matheson, *Desiring the Bomb*, 127–28.
5. Rowland, "Small Dick Problems," 26.
6. This chapter adopts a capacious understanding of "agency" informed by Kenneth Burke's metaphorical alignment of this term with clandestine security institutions and his definition of it as the "how" or "by what means" state-sponsored and -enforced sexualization transpires. An NSS "agency" includes such formal institutions as the NSA, CIA, or US State Department, but also journalistic outlets which take these institutions' word at face value, proxying for securitarian interests. K. Burke, *Grammar of Motives*, 228.
7. Beauchamp, *Going Stealth*.
8. Melley, "Agency Panic," 62. See also Melley, *Empire of Conspiracy*, 6–16.
9. See also Sagar, *Secrets and Leaks*.

such protections most often signals an endorsement of leaking as an ethical act. For instance, in Daniel Ellsberg's final interview, he places faith in "whistleblowers" who circumvent official channels to espouse his conviction that leakers deserve protections denied to them by the state.[10] I do not disagree with Ellsberg that such leakers are often deserving of protection. However, to call the leaker a whistleblower begs the question of whether *any* leaker who compromises the NSS can *ever* assume the status of a legally protected whistleblower, given their aprioristic positioning against the rule of law.

Second, this chapter purposely dwells on *sexuality* as its pivotal term. I specifically borrow Joan Copjec's formulation of the masculine and the feminine as modes of logical failure, or ways that reason comes into contradiction with itself.[11] This focus on the sexual dynamics of leaking distinguishes my rhetorical treatment of national security leakers like Edward Snowden and Chelsea Manning from that of Dana L. Cloud, who focuses on the limited media framings of leakers' gender.[12] Rather than a partial presencing or representation, sexuality is a generative absence, one that begets representation as an endless compensatory activity. As an indefinite dwelling on sex, the leaking discourses of the NSS are made intelligible as the compulsive imposition and reproduction of an unfillable lack, a state of security whose realization is constitutively prohibited.

Sexing National Security

Contemporary national security leakers are often represented to the US public in ways that continue long-standing historical patterns of sexual oppression. A blurred distinction between the act of disclosure and nonnormative sexuality has often signaled the leaker's inherent danger to national polity. In 1894, French artillery officer Alfred Dreyfus was wrongly accused of leaking secret artillery information and imprisoned for nearly a decade. The "proof" (in scare quotes) of Dreyfus's guilt consisted of little more than antisemitic stereotypes that aligned his Jewishness with inherent traits of effeminacy and deceptiveness.[13] In the United States, the policing of homosexuality extended

---

10. Hirsh, "Daniel Ellsberg Is Dying."
11. The distinction between masculine and feminine "logics" deliberately evokes the logophilic bias of sexuality in contrast to gender's theorization in affective, sensorial, and pathoscentric terms. The Lacanian inflection given to these logics is drawn from Copjec, *Read My Desire*, 201–36.
12. Cloud, "Private Manning"; and Cloud, *Reality Bites*, 75–105.
13. Carlson, "Secret Dossiers," 940.

to women and men. Whereas women who served in the military during World War II were broadly construed as undertaking "a heroically brief interlude before marriage," those who came after "were automatically suspect" of "homosexual tendencies" because "they were seen as choosing the military (as opposed to marriage) for a career."[14] Throughout the 1950s and 1960s, J. Edgar Hoover's FBI engaged in an active propaganda campaign popularly termed "the Lavender Scare," which specifically targeted gay men (or "lavender lads") for termination from government posts.[15]

Coverage of national security leaks in the twentieth century also isolated specific actors whose "abnormal behavior posed a threat not only to domestic normalcy but to national security" by linking sexuality to security.[16] In the 1940s, for instance, the scandals surrounding both Alger Hiss and Sumner Welles had a "sexual subtext" that informed their public disgrace. Whereas Welles, FDR's undersecretary of state, "resigned amid allegations of homosexuality,"[17] Hiss was accused of passing classified State Department documents to the Soviet Union via former Communist party operative Whittaker Chambers.[18] By the time of Hiss's trial, Chambers had publicly renounced his communist affiliations, but his testimony prompted speculation regarding "a past sexual relationship between Chambers and Hiss."[19] A similar bias was leveraged against "accused female spies of the Cold War," laminating ill-fitting, hypereroticized caricatures atop such scandalous figures as Elizabeth Bentley, Priscilla Hiss, Judith Coplon, and Ethel Rosenberg.[20] Transgender servicepeople were likewise subjected to public smearing, as nonnormative gender performances undermined the US military fantasy of the prototypically masculine soldier. Susan Stryker and Mia Fischer highlight the story of Christine Jorgensen, an "ex-GI"[21] who in 1952 became "the first transgender person to receive significant media coverage for her successful gender-affirmation surgery."[22] Jorgensen's transition also indexed a change in "midcentury sexual discourse," one that "raised previously buried, unmentionable, or unconfronted issues and phantoms for men."[23]

---

14. Canady, *Straight State*, 177–78.
15. Whitfield, *Culture of the Cold War*, 48–49; and Nolan, "LGBTQIA+ Diversity."
16. Davidson, *Guys Like Us*, 11.
17. Cuordileone, "'Politics in an Age of Anxiety,'" 535.
18. Cuordileone, "'Politics in an Age of Anxiety,'" 533.
19. Cuordileone, "'Politics in an Age of Anxiety,'" 534.
20. Olmsted, "Blond Queens."
21. Stryker, *Transgender History*, 48.
22. Fischer, *Terrorizing Gender*, 32.
23. Cuordileone, "'Politics in an Age of Anxiety,'" 531.

Of course, NSS sexuation also had a more positive, propagandistic face. Individuals affiliated with the twentieth-century NSS were often elevated as exemplars of heterosexual masculine potency. As Timothy Melley explains, "While the state increasingly shelters citizens from the dirty work of foreign policy, the fictions of the covert sphere compensate for this structural "feminization" with fantasies of masculinist bravado and heroic agency."[24] Such fantasies also reflected the sexual ideology of those who occupied positions of authority within the NSS. Model defenders of national security often insisted that traditional gender roles were under threat and that gender inequality was the natural order of things. Hoover, for instance, made regular reference to his impugned "manhood" and sought any opportunity to bolster a masculine persona for himself in the public eye.[25] Also striking is the example of Allen W. Dulles, who was the inaugural civilian director of the CIA, a zealous anticommunist, and an unapologetic adulterer.[26] As he stated in a 1962 interview with CBS Reports:

> The ordinary man, the man in the street, the man and woman, he doesn't know how he can contribute. He agrees as to the judgment that there is a menace, that our society is menaced by communism. But what's he to do? And that has resulted in certain aberrations that I don't need to define because you and those who are listening, hearing, seeing will probably know what I have in mind, to these aberrations and I think a great many innocent people without realizing the harm they are doing get led astray by this.[27]

After his appointment to the CIA, Dulles pursued a vehemently antigay policy in his offices. He also habitually enlisted the "aberrations" epithet (used in the preceding quotation) to reference gay servicepeople and communist agents.[28] Of course, Dulles had a different attitude toward heterosexual promiscuity, believing that he would suffer no consequences should his libertine lifestyle be publicized.[29]

One name for this dichotomous mode of sexuation is "the crisis of American masculinity."[30] Coined by Arthur M. Schlesinger, this "crisis" was

---

24. Melley, *Covert Sphere*, 14.
25. Morris, "Hoover's Sex Crime Panic," 235.
26. Kinzer, *Brothers*.
27. Allen W. Dulles, interviewed by Eric Sevareid, *The Hot and Cold Wars of Allen Dulles*, CBS Reports, April 26, 1962.
28. Dulles, *Craft of Intelligence*, 109, 234.
29. Dulles, *Craft of Intelligence*, 102.
30. Schlesinger, "Crisis of American Masculinity."

comprised of the belief that the nation was suffering from the "unmanning of American men," leaving the United States vulnerable to the "sadistic" forces of communism and totalitarianism.[31] Whereas the political right had been "emasculated" by handing its power over to the "accountants" of the administrative state, "the left-progressive never had sufficient masculinity," being instead "hopelessly and irrevocably feminine."[32] Conservative critics like Schlesinger saw masculinity under siege everywhere: in the home; by the womb-like enclosures of the group, party, organization, and collective; and by the feminizing forces of communism. Cold War–era discourse testified to the further evolution of this ideology, giving rise to metaphors like enemy "penetration," "dilettante diplomats," and the still-cited dichotomy between "hard" and "soft" approaches to security.[33]

> While rugged male agency became articulated as a defense against creeping socialism, metaphorically "leaky" forms of identity came under strict scrutiny: mothers were chastised for mollycoddling their sons; women experienced extraordinary feminizing pressures; gay and effeminate men were viewed as insufficiently tough to prevent the spread of socialism, liberalism, and even cooperation.[34]

Emerging from the shadow of the atomic bomb, Cold War–era gender oppression manifests a key precedent for what Casey Ryan Kelly calls "apocalyptic manhood." This subjectivity "constructs imminent disasters as solutions to immanent crisis," all the while oblivious to the fact that "seeking relief in imminent destruction does little to ameliorate the anomic crisis of the male self."[35] America's securitarian subjects draw implicitly upon conceptions of sexuality proclaimed to be inalienable, essential, and ontological. This amounts to a refusal to think of oneself as gendered, insofar as gender describes something that one does, performs, and enacts vis-à-vis discourse and embodiment. Instead, securitarian subjectivities reflect the belief that masculinity and femininity are preexisting things that one innately *is*, in the sense of an essence prior to discursive expression. As a material binary imposed upon national security leakers, it is a figural counterpart to other, more literal modes of carceral confinement.

---

31. Cuordileone, "'Politics in an Age of Anxiety,'" 524.
32. Cuordileone, "'Politics in an Age of Anxiety,'" 518.
33. Cuordileone, "'Politics in an Age of Anxiety,'" 515–21; Davidson, *Guys Like Us*; and Corber, *Homosexuality in Cold War America*.
34. Melley, *Covert Sphere*, 27.
35. Kelly, *Apocalypse Man*, 54–56.

Understanding leakers as sexualized also differs from other accounts that have parsed national security leaks through the lens of gender. Demonstrating how the gendered depictions of Chelsea Manning and Edward Snowden illuminate "the limits of truth telling in political culture," Cloud describes the distinct frames (e.g., public/private, agent/victim, criminal/traitor, queer/normal) that favor leakers with heteronormative desires and cisgender embodiments while vilifying their gay and transgender counterparts.[36] The former are often considered skilled, heroic, and agential, while the latter are dismissed as inexpert, mentally ill, and subject to forces beyond their control.[37] However, if Cloud operates from within the given terms of an imaginary reality by assuming access to the leaker's "raw experience," then in the following sections I propose an analysis in the register of the Real—a constitutively inaccessible register of interruption, rupture, and breakage. In psychoanalysis, the uppercased *Real* is set apart from lowercased *reality* to capture the lack of correspondence between a universe of representations, the rules that govern it, and material actuality. Sexuality is a case in point: The very idea of a "unified" male or female subjectivity is a pretense, discursive cover for an unrepresentable and unfillable gap, absence, or void that (un-)grounds subjectivity. As a theory of the NSS's carceral logic, the imposition of sexual subjectivity necessarily fails to grasp the leaker's so-called essence, even as it succeeds in disciplining them.

Tropes of Unauthorized Disclosure

National security leaks often bring forth the secret in ways that allude to an obscured whole of knowledge concealed by the state's clandestine agencies. Although the objective vastness of this knowledge alone prohibits it from being known, leaks manifest a suggestive but impossible totality of secret knowledge by deferring the promise of knowing.[38] The secret's allusion to a totality that cannot be discovered implicates it in an indefinite, regenerating process: "the secret designates that which is desired to be known, that which impels its own discovery but which hasn't yet been discovered."[39] This process also engenders a renewable relationship between the leaker and the NSS. On the one hand, the leaker and their sympathetic publics comprise a category of subject with the presumed right to know, who "desires, discovers, and knows,

---

36. Cloud, *Reality Bites*, 80, 105; italics added.
37. Cloud, "Private Manning," 81.
38. Galison, "Removing Knowledge."
39. Dean, *Publicity's Secret*, 10.

TABLE 5.1. Sexualized logics of the NSS leak

THE SECRET...	MASCULINE (PHALLIC) LOGIC	FEMININE (PHATIC) LOGIC
...*in* discourse	spymaster	femme fatale
...*of* discourse	megethos: "one more that is not enough"	apophasis: "one more that is too many"

a subject from whom nothing should be withheld." On the other, there is the NSS, "the subject supposed to know," which embodies the specular authority of determining what remains secret and what does not.[40] This relationship is always already sexualized, as the NSS and journalistic outlets routinely reconstruct the leaker's act of unauthorized disclosure using the familiar logic of binary sexuality.

The relationship between the leaker and the NSS takes shape vis-à-vis two complex tropological patterns, each one aligned with a masculine or feminine logic. Each of these sexual logics is comprised of two tropes: one *in* discourse and the other *of* discourse (see table 5.1).[41] The leaker's tropes *in* discourse describe the leaker in what Lacanian psychoanalysis describes as the imaginary register of identification. The imaginary brings forth a fantasy of the other as a character who embodies what is lacking in one's own being, creating an image (or *imago*) from within an available field of signifiers. When situated in this register, trope often refers to a recurring theme, motif, or characterological type, a version of the other who resembles the self to greater and lesser degrees. As applied to the leaker, imaginary tropes invoke two sexualized agents of unauthorized disclosure: the *spymaster*, a lascivious character who pursues the secret conspiracy, and the *femme fatale*, a character who embodies the impossibility of hiding, except in plain sight. These characters, who reside *in* the recuperative discourse about national security leaks, illuminate how sexuality pathologizes the leaker and seeps into the discourse about leaking, enveloping both in a fantasy of transgressive criminality.

When it references a specific arrangement *of* discourse, trope aligns with the Lacanian symbolic order, or the grammatical-rhetorical axioms that prefigure the leak's possible permutations. Understood in this register, trope signifies a structure *of* discourse that anticipates any given leak, the mode of arrangement that gives discourse a probable shape well before the act of disclosure transpires. Whereas the spymaster type is aligned with megethos and

---

40. Dean, *Publicity's Secret*, 11–18.
41. On the possible inflections of the term *trope* (i.e., as stylistic flourish, theme or motif, epistemic category, and arrangement *of* discourse in the symbolic register), see also Rowland, *Zoetropes*, 4–8; and Lundberg, "Enjoying God's Death," 389.

the formula "the one more that is not enough," the femme fatale is linked to apophasis, whose formula is "the one more that is too many." Phrasing the logic of these tropes as variations on the "one more" is appropriate because adding "one more" leak to the pile prefigures the act of exposure as impotent or earth-shattering: Whereas megethos fails to live up to the intended significance of the leak, apophasis references a quantity that has gone unnoticed despite its having been out in the open.

The spymaster's megethos and the femme fatale's apophasis offer tropological coordinates for the binary sexual logic that guides the characterization of the leaker. What, then, of sexuality—what could it be when put in the terms of NSS surveillance? Although sexuality conventionally signifies a false correspondence between one's biological embodiment and their performed gender identity, psychoanalytic theorist Joan Copjec redefines sexuality as a failure of reason, or "the fraudulence at the heart of every claim to positive sexual identity."[42] In other words, masculinity and femininity are not positive identities that one dons or assumes but distinct forms of contradiction by which the failure to achieve a coherent identity unfolds. The feminine side abides by a logic of addition and inclusion: There cannot be a "whole" or "totality" to the category of woman because there is no limit to the elements that may be subsumed within it. Indefinitely expanding, it captures how the subject cannot be confined to a singular set of characteristics because her being is always exceeding them: "Each and every definition ... fails somehow to 'encompass' her," exceeding the scope of available language and representation. Conversely, the masculine side abides by a logic of subtraction and exclusion, one that covers over lack-in-being through repeated acts of symbolic castration, creating a coherent category by expelling all who do not "fit." Taken together, if a wholly defined category of woman is impossible on the feminine side because of the always already "too-muchness" of what would fit under this heading, then on the masculine side, the impossibility of wholeness arises because some man's being is always excluded; for him, it is always "a matter of saying *too little*."[43]

In extending this conception of sexuality-as-failure into the domain of national security leaks, I associate the masculine mode of failure with a *phallic* logic in which the agent of disclosure takes shape as an uncanny double of the NSS, one who must be expelled for the state to regain its circumscribed unity. Correspondingly, the feminine mode of leaking aligns with a *phatic* logic, in which the leaker becomes the secret to be found. This leaker is difficult to pinpoint because her identifying characteristics are initially passed

---

42. Copjec, *Read My Desire*, 234.
43. Copjec, *Read My Desire*, 231.

over as meaningless or incoherent, or disregarded as superfluous to the act of leaking. Upon capture, however, she expands the state's conception of who a leaker might be, pointing to the unfinished, limitless expansion of this category. Whereas the masculine leaker announces themselves as the knowable counterpart to the state, the feminized leaker hides in plain sight, an excessive presence who defies surveillance by perpetrating the leak out in the open. Importantly, the adjectives phallic and phatic neither denote opposites nor a complementary pair. They instead index the regulatory-carceral imposition of the sexual binary upon different leakers, often making them knowable against the grain of their avowed gender.

The Masculine Leak: Assange and Snowden

The masculine logic theorized by psychoanalysis elaborates a fantasy of mastery over the secret, one predicated on making the subject whole through acts of exclusion. As Copjec explains, the very idea of masculinity is "an illusion fomented by prohibition: do not include everything in your all!"[44] In figure 5.1, "x" designates a successive series of either leaks or leakers who have been "expelled" from the NSS: that is, either disclosed (in the case of leaks) or neutralized (in the case of leakers). When "x" is the leak, each instance of subversive publication expels information from the contained "inside" of the NSS and demands a future leak of even greater magnitude to compensate for the weakening effect of successive disclosures (the downward-pointing arrows). When "x" is the leaker, the successive expulsion of the criminal leaker from the set of legitimate citizens leads to an intensifying search, leading to more and more expulsions that inevitably fail to seal off the NSS's porous boundary. By expelling one more (man, national security threat, or piece of classified information) from the category of "all" (men, national security threats, or secret archives), the subject fortifies the boundary between a fantasy "core" (of masculinity, national security, or public transparency) and what lies beyond it (i.e., false manhood, anarchic violence, or statist opacity). In both cases, expulsion shrinks the very domain meant to be protected, while inviting compensatory discourses of strength, grandeur, and mastery. The failure endemic to this phallic logic is that no matter how many (men, threats, or secrets) are expelled in the name of masculine totality, it is *never enough*.[45] There is always one more secret to release, another leaker to be expelled. There is no

---

44. Copjec, *Read My Desire*, 235.
45. Copjec, *Read My Desire*, 230–31.

MEGETHOS

Numbered directional arrows indicate the successive imposition of restrictive boundaries, borders, or limits upon the set (i.e., of "all men," "all leaks," and "all leakers").

Each exclusion of *X* results in a more constricted category whose claim to be the biggest, most secure, or the most important are compensatory for the category's progressive diminishment.

LET *X* BE:	AND	AND
the "one more" *man* who may always be expelled from the set of all men, those included through acts of exclusion.	the "one more" *leak* of information that will not have been enough, necessitating an even bigger subsequent leak.	the "one more" *leaker* who, having been expelled, disciplined, and confined, justifies ever more intense efforts to secure NSS against future leaks.

FIGURE 5.1. Megethos, or the masculine (phallic) logic of leaks.

specifiable limit, at least none that does not also misplace its faith in either the totally secure nation or the wholly awakened global public. Both myths are destined for failure, again and again.

Julian Assange and Edward Snowden offer clear examples of this mode of sexualization, which I align with the spymaster figure and megethos, the "one more that is not enough." Their leaks were not insignificant but impotent. Whereas both leakers adopted an imaginary spymaster persona by simultaneously evading and embodying the law, their leaks were beholden to a symbolic law in which enormity amounted to a "big nothing" in retrospect. In other words, neither achieved their promised global awakenings, despite the escalating quality and quantity of their respective disclosures. What was instead escalated was the presence of an "incel" type increasingly associated with heroized male leakers.

The Leaker as Spymaster

The first figure that masculinizes the leak is the spymaster. A purveyor of secrets who is at once the public's guardian and a threat to national security, this character pursues malevolent international conspiracies while frequently overstepping the extrajudicial authority granted them. Despite their avowed mastery of espionage, their identity is hardly ever concealed. In fact, they frequently announce themselves (e.g., "The name is Bond, James Bond") or appear openly paranoid in their awareness of surveillance. Although the spymaster is concerned with threats to an existing legal, moral, and symbolic order, they consistently disregard their own contravention of such authorities. For that reason, the spymaster-leaker is both on the lam from the nation-state and its model defender, an uncanny double of the terrorists they out: the "hero usually takes the place of the state's enemies, doing battle with the US security apparatus in an effort to save the world."[46] The spymaster routinely endeavors to expel the internal threat. And yet, there is *no* limit to the rogues who must be expelled, up to and including the spymaster themselves.

Both Julian Assange and Edward Snowden embody the recurring spymaster character-trope by undermining and evading the US national security apparatus, adopting a mastery of the secret often attributed to the NSS. Assange's spymaster persona began during the late twentieth-century cypherpunk movement, during which he personally claimed credit for hacking NASA and the US MILNET system.[47] In his 2006 manifestos "State and Terrorist Conspiracies" and "Conspiracy as Governance," Assange collapsed the distinction between democratic states and their adversaries, claiming to have developed a way to awaken the public to their corrupt plutocratic governments. As he argued, the state form was nothing more than a facade for authoritarian regimes, and the only way to purify such institutions was to purge their secrets by releasing them publicly.[48] Assange's organization, WikiLeaks, also emerged in 2006, and was pitched to aspiring leakers as the first truly anonymous hub for collating secrets, which was originally posted in an open-source "wiki" format.[49] WikiLeaks thus mounted an unprecedented war on government

---

46. Melley, *Covert Sphere*, 31.
47. Dreyfus and Assange, *Underground*; and Zetter, "Assange Hacked the Pentagon."
48. Me@iq.org, "State and Terrorist Conspiracies."
49. David Leigh and Luke Harding explain how WikiLeaks received its name, recalling the information of the early internet:

> As its name suggests, WikiLeaks began as a "wiki"—a user-editable site (which has sometimes led to confusion with the user-editable Wikipedia; there is no association). But Assange and his colleagues rapidly found that the content and need to remove dangerous or incriminating information made such a model impractical. Assange would come to revise his belief that online "citizen journalists" in their thousands would be prepared to scrutinize posted documents and discover whether they were genuine or not. (Leigh and Harding, *WikiLeaks*, 52)

secrecy, claiming responsibility for several of the largest information leaks in world history. After running afoul of the Pentagon and the US State Department, WikiLeaks was branded both a private intelligence operation and a cutout, a doppelgänger of and proxy for state-run clandestine organizations.

Edward Snowden's spymaster status is attributable to a single leak that revealed the extent of NSS surveillance in the early aughts. When he disclosed the STELLARWIND and PRISM programs in 2013, Snowden was a National Security Agency (NSA) contractor affiliated with Booz Allen Hamilton who carried high-level security clearances. STELLARWIND was a "warrantless domestic surveillance program created by Dick Cheney in late 2001," while PRISM siphoned data from private accounts with the consent of users or internet service providers (ISPs).[50] The leak was initially brokered through three individuals whom Snowden contacted individually: Barton Gellman, a winner of multiple Pulitzer Prizes for his reporting on September 11, 2001, and on US Vice President Dick Cheney's facilitation of the Iraq War; Glenn Greenwald, an ardent supporter of Julian Assange who had published a book on warrantless wiretapping; and finally, Oscar-winning documentarian Laura Poitras, whose record of anti-war filmmaking had "proved herself both a skeptic and a target of the wartime establishment."[51]

While news outlets like *The Guardian* crafted a persona for Snowden that was "intriguing, enigmatic, and courageous," his self-presentation often telegraphed familiarity with intelligence work while conveying a deep paranoia about surveillance.[52] A "supremely competent spy," he demanded that Gellman, Greenwald, and Poitras familiarize themselves with cryptography to send and receive messages and classified information.[53] These communications frequently underscored the gravity of exposing NSA surveillance programs, which could be mobilized on less evidence than required by the Foreign Intelligence Surveillance Court's (FISC) standard of probable cause.[54] More so than Assange, Snowden's spymaster persona was one that straddled the inside and outside of the policing agencies he served: "The fact that Snowden was an insider, a system administrator for the NSA, with virtually

---

50. Gellman, *Dark Mirror*, 26.

51. Gellman, *Angler*; Greenwald, *Nowhere to Hide*; quotation from Gellman, *Dark Mirror*, 11. Similar to how Benedict Cumberbatch's roles as Assange and Turing enabled these real-life leakers to occupy public attention at approximately the same moment in time, Laura Poitras's documentaries link Assange with Snowden. Her 2014 documentary *Citizenfour*, which interviews Snowden, was followed by a 2016 documentary, *Risk*, which documents Assange's self-imposed exile in London's Ecuadorean embassy. Poitras, *Citizenfour*; and Poitras, *Risk*.

52. Cloud, *Reality Bites*, 84.

53. Cloud, *Reality Bites*, 85.

54. Gellman, *Dark Mirror*, 111–12.

unrestricted access to information, gave credibility to the leaked documents, but more importantly it proved that it was not an attack by a foreign enemy."[55] This insider status also gave credence to his spymaster motives, situating him at the same level as the quasi-legal institutions he served: "Snowden undeniably violated his promise to keep the NSA's secrets. But doing so was the only way to fulfill his higher obligation to protect and defend the Constitution."[56] Such contradictory motives were eyed with suspicion by the journalists who published his leak. Gellman, for instance, refused to publish cryptographic keys provided to him, suspicious that Snowden sought to use the publication to prove his value to foreign governments while bringing NSS scrutiny on the journalists who were his proxies.[57]

Megethos: The One More That Is Not Enough

A trope of "sizing up," megethos is aligned with rhetorical terms like *copia verborum, accumulatio,* amplification, and the sublime. Even as megethos animates a vision of the nation as the static, timeless property of white settlers, digital frontiers mark its potential for growth, its surveillance apparatus a means to expand national power, discipline, and control.[58] In *Citizenfour*, Snowden exchanges the following encrypted message with Poitras, which links the size of his leaks with the quantity of the information gathered by American telecommunications and intelligence agencies:

> The truth is that the NSA has never in its history collected more than it does now. I know the location of most domestic interception points and that the largest telecommunication companies in the US are betraying the trust of their customers, which I can prove. We are building the greatest weapon for oppression in the history of man, yet its directors exempt themselves from accountability. . . . Billions of US communications are being intercepted. In gathering evidence of wrongdoing, I focused on the wronging of the American people, but believe me when I say that the surveillance we live under is the highest privilege compared to how we treat the rest of the world.[59]

---

55. Trifonov, "Performing Prudence," 34–35.
56. Friedersdorf, "Vindication of Edward Snowden," quoted in Trifonov, "Performing Prudence," 44.
57. Gellman, *Dark Mirror*, 128–30.
58. T. Farrell, "Sizing Things Up"; T. Conley, "Beauty of Lists"; Stormer, "Addressing the Sublime," 214–15; and Olson, *American Magnitude*, 13.
59. Poitras, *Citizenfour*.

Snowden wished to legitimate his leak by comparing it to the NSS's own criminal accumulation of private user data. At a more general level, however, his and other leaks may be seen as compensatory gestures that appeal to largess to make up for a felt lack. Hence the interpretation of megethos as "archival magnitude," which "sees the rhetor adding ever more evidence to archives from which he or she can draw to bolster claims."[60] In other words, the "more" of megethos is not always better, as the "obsession with size" can "become an enjoyable, apocalyptic perversion."[61]

In the case of NSS leaks, megethos abides by the shorthand "the one more that is not enough." Modeled on the phallic function of psychoanalysis, megethos amounts to a conspicuous denial that the leaker lacks anything at all.[62] Even so, the leak can always amount to a "big nothing." Even as disclosures of escalating intensity assert something unprecedentedly "extra," their patterning as a repetitive megethos begs the question of why leakers invoke enormity so incessantly. There is no better example than Julian Assange: Between 2006 and 2008, his organization, WikiLeaks, exposed small collections of classified documents and private communications that included handbooks for soldiers stationed at Guantanamo Bay, confidential bank records, and emails from Sarah Palin and the Church of Scientology. The following year saw as many releases as the previous two combined. In November 2009, WikiLeaks released an archive of 500,000 pager messages from the morning of 9/11. The following year, WikiLeaks released "The War Logs" in collaboration with *The New York Times, Der Spiegel,* and *The Guardian*. Sourced from Private First Class (PFC) Chelsea Manning, this leak contained 92,000 classified military reports from Afghanistan and 391,832 documents from Iraq. These files were accompanied by a short, WikiLeaks-curated documentary, *Collateral Murder,* which depicted American soldiers killing twelve civilians and three Reuters journalists in Baghdad.[63] Military officials quickly "domesticated" the *Collateral Murder* footage in 2010, resorting to strategies like *apologia* and recontextualization to justify soldiers' indiscriminate violence.[64] Seeking to sustain the momentum of "The War Logs," Assange released a wish list of US State Department secrets it "knew existed" to solicit more leakers

---

60. Rice, "Rhetorical Aesthetics," 27.

61. Gunn refers to a late twentieth- and early twenty-first-century obsession with "big rhetoric," which sought to redefine the academic discipline's boundaries in terms of a globalized and sprawling formulation of its central term. Gunn, "Size Matters," 85–86.

62. On the phallic function, see also Copjec, *Read My Desire,* 212–17; and Fink, *Lacanian Subject,* 101–4.

63. Cohen and Stelter, "Airstrike Video."

64. Hasian, "Wikileaks Helicopter Controversy."

to its cause.[65] Between 2011 and 2012, WikiLeaks released seven million documents ranging from private firms' intelligence data to confidential emails exchanged between members of the Syrian government. News outlets also proclaimed that Assange had assembled a "doomsday cache," an insurance policy should he be detained.[66] Reporters likened this "information bomb" to a "poison pill" and a "thermonuclear device."[67] But the "cache" was prematurely leaked without Assange's authorization.[68] This became the "Cablegate" exposé, consisting of approximately 250,000 US embassy correspondences:

> Its sheer bulk was overwhelming. If the tiny memory stick containing the cables had been a set of printed texts, it would have made up a library containing more than 2,000 sizeable books. No human diplomats would have attempted to write so much down before the coming of the digital age: if written down, no human spy would have been able to purloin copies of that much paper without using a lorry, and no human mind would have been able subsequently to analyse it without spending half a lifetime at the task.[69]

At the time, *Guardian* reporters David Leigh and Luke Harding called it the "biggest leak in history." *The Washington Post* even devoted one of its webpages to "The Anatomy of a Leak," using a graphic to show how, even when the public had been "fully" informed, only 0.1 percent of the Cablegate data had been released.[70]

After Cablegate, there was palpable WikiLeaks fatigue among Assange's former celebrants.[71] When *Saturday Night Live* buzzed on in December 2012, audiences were greeted by a larger-than-life parody of Assange by Bill Hader, who depicted the leaker as a cognac-sipping crackpot at the helm of a gossip news outfit styled after *TMZ*.[72] A growing chorus of career diplomats, NSS officials, and journalists asserted that Assange had placed lives at risk by failing

---

65. Clayton, "WikiLeaks List."
66. Zetter, "Mysterious 'Insurance' File."
67. Stahl, "Weaponizing Speech," 383.
68. Ball, "WikiLeaks Publishes Full Cache."
69. Leigh and Harding, *WikiLeaks*, 140.
70. "Anatomy of a Leak."
71. After "Cablegate," WikiLeaks drew the following criticism from Slavoj Žižek: "The only surprising thing about the WikiLeaks revelations is that they contain no surprises. Didn't we learn exactly what we expected to learn? The real disturbance was at the level of appearances: we can no longer pretend we don't know what everyone knows we know." Žižek, "Good Manners," 9–10.
72. Saturday Night Live, "WikiLeaks Cold Opening"; and Saturday Night Live, "A Message from Mark Zuckerberg."

to redact identifying information, generating a national security justification for his extradition to the United States. Seeking an escape, Assange began a seven-year shelter-in-place in London's Ecuadorean embassy.[73] During this time, WikiLeaks' disclosures again escalated. In 2016, Assange was accused of US electoral interference after leaking approximately 20,000 emails from Democratic National Committee (DNC) chair Debbie Wasserman Schultz and Clinton campaign manager John Podesta, leading to allegations that WikiLeaks was a proxy (or "cutout") for Russian intelligence.[74] Assange denied the accusations but avowed a personal feud with candidate Hillary Clinton, who as secretary of state in 2012 had been reputationally injured by Cablegate. He also claimed the DNC leak's source to be staffer Seth Rich, fueling baseless conspiracy theories that party leaders had ordered Rich's assassination.[75] In 2018, newly elected Ecuadorean President Lenín Moreno withdrew Assange's asylum, leading to his detention in London's maximum-security HM Belmarsh prison until his release in 2024.[76]

Assange and Snowden were not just aberrations because they posed security risks; they possessed a monstrous masculinity that went hand in hand with their willingness to flout the NSS. In 2010, *New York Times* journalist Eric Schmitt described Assange as a "bag lady," noting his ill-fitting clothes.[77] Harding and Leigh open their 2011 book by describing Assange as a "figure [who] might just have passed for female" and a man who "swap[ped] genders" to evade public attention.[78] Gregory Seigworth and Matthew Tiessen offer a different explanation of his masculine monstrosity, alluding to his man-spreading dance moves in a YouTube video where Assange is shown "dancing at a disco in Reykjavik.... This is a man who occupies a lot of space when he dances (Hasteley, 2011). It is the dance of someone who knows where all of the exits are located, the dance of someone who believes in the end of secrets."[79] The most credible articulation of Assange's monstrous sexuality concerned

---

73. Caselli, "Assange Will Be Granted Asylum."
74. Shear and Rosenberg, "Released Emails"; Blake, "DNC's Leaked Emails"; Naylor, "Russian Election Meddling"; Bertrand, "Stone's Secret Messages"; Packer, "Julian Assange and Donald Trump"; and Frum, "It Wasn't a Hoax."
75. Seitz-Wald, "WikiLeaks Fuels Conspiracy Theories"; and Mervosh, "Seth Rich Was Not Source."
76. Greenwald, "Ecuador Will Imminently Withdraw Asylum"; and Gilmartin and Greene, "Selling Out Julian Assange."
77. Schmitt, "WikiLeaks."
78. Leigh and Harding, *WikiLeaks*, 13–14.
79. Seigworth and Tiessen, "Mobile Affects," 71.

allegations that he had raped two Swedish nationals in 2010.[80] When the allegations broke, Assange became the target of leaks, including an image of a deliberately broken condom and speculation that Assange had infected the plaintiffs with a sexually transmitted disease.[81] After sheltering in London's Ecuadorian embassy, Assange attempted to recuperate his image by staging meetings with celebrities like Lady Gaga and Pamela Anderson.[82] During this time, WikiLeaks affiliates Renata Avila, Sarah Harrison, and Angela Richter also published *Women, Whistleblowing, WikiLeaks: A Conversation*, which criticized mainstream media for inattention to women as leaders in transparency activism.[83]

Descriptions of Snowden's monstrous masculinity were often more sparing and subtle than Assange's. Snowden played into "the straight, 'normal,' white-guy frame," displaying conventional aspects of masculinity vis-à-vis heroism and self-sacrifice.[84] While he was apprehensive about centering himself in the reporting that broke the NSA story,[85] he also claimed the role of sacrificial scapegoat:

> My personal desire is that you [Gellman, Poitras, and Greenwald] paint the target directly on my back. No one, not even my most trusted confidante, is aware of my intentions, and it would not be fair for them to fall under suspicion for my actions. You may be the only one who can prevent that, and that is by immediately nailing me to the cross rather than trying to protect me as a source.[86]

Even as Snowden offered to sacrifice himself, it was clear that the journalists brokering his story were at greatest risk. As Claire Sisco King argues, male bodies who avow their sacrificial role often align "the masculine with the allegedly immutable power of the godhead," creating a "sacrosanct authority" that is "not to be challenged or disrespected."[87] Snowden's avowed victimhood not only elevated his moral status, it legitimated putting others like Gellman, Poitras, and Greenwald in harm's way.

---

80. North, "Rape Allegation."
81. "STD Fears Sparked Assange Sex Case"; and "Julian Assange Sex Assault Allegations."
82. Stuart, "Watch Lady Gaga Question Julian Assange"; and Britton, "Pamela Anderson Visits."
83. Avila, Harrison, and Richter, *Women, Whistleblowing, WikiLeaks*.
84. Cloud, *Reality Bites*, 91–95.
85. Cloud, *Reality Bites*, 82.
86. Snowden interviewed in Poitras, *Risk*.
87. Sisco King, *Washed in Blood*, 41.

Other coverage sought to hold Snowden accountable for his destructive and toxic masculinity. Some castigated Snowden for having abandoned his partner, Lindsay Mills, without explaining his sudden departure.[88] Oliver Stone's *Snowden* overtly sexualized Mills "as a beautiful, sexy yoga instructor and pole dancer," to exaggerate Snowden's "heterosexual credentials."[89] Other stories described Snowden as a computer-obsessed loner, turncoat, and traitor.[90] Synthesizing these themes, *The Washington Post* wrote that Snowden "had a vivacious, outgoing girlfriend and boasted online about his interest in nubile, beautiful women, even as he secluded himself in a world of computer games, anime and close study of the internet's architecture."[91] Gellman's mostly sympathetic account of Snowden surfaced testimony from his teenage years that "Ed is positive that he is God's gift to women" and drew attention to sexually monstrous techniques borrowed from the NSS.[92] After fleeing to Hong Kong, he encouraged Poitras to visit him and pitched a cover story in which the two were engaged in an affair, encouraging her to bring along "a suitcase full of sex toys and lingerie."[93] Although Gellman and Poitras were taken aback ("'It is creepy, right?' Poitras wrote to me"), Gellman rationalizes the episode as "advice [that] came straight from the playbook of clandestine travel. Cover for presence. Cover for action. An embarrassing story, even as fiction, but all the better camouflage for that."[94]

The masculine logic of national security leaking takes a bivalent form: The leaker targets the state, and vice versa, each one delegitimating the other to assert their own wholeness. The repetitiveness of such exclusions gives away the fact that wholeness is *never* achieved, on either side. Even the fact that Snowden succeeds Assange as the next biggest-ever leaker alludes to the permeable boundary of national security, one that must always be discursively rescued:

> The inclusion of *all* men within the domain of phallic rule is conditioned by the fact that *at least one* escapes it. Do we count this "man escaped" among the all, or don't we? What sort of a "man" is it whose *jouissance* is not limited

---

88. Leonnig and Tate, "Snowden's Girlfriend."
89. Cloud, *Reality Bites*, 91.
90. Toobin, "Snowden Is No Hero"; Keck, "Snowden Is a Traitor"; "Kerry: Snowden a 'Coward'"; and Fick, "Was Snowden Hero or Traitor?"
91. Leonnig, Johnson, and Fisher, "Tracking Edward Snowden."
92. Gellman, *Dark Mirror*, 43.
93. Gellman, *Dark Mirror*, 136.
94. Gellman, *Dark Mirror*, 136.

to the male variety; and what sort of an "all" is it that is missing one of its elements?[95]

This missing element could equally describe the insufficiently or excessively masculine man or the criminalized leaker. To say that "*at least one* (man or leaker) escapes" suggests that a member of the apparatus, someone who embodies "desirable" characteristics (of manhood, of intelligence) exists beyond the boundary (of true manhood, the NSS) and must be excluded to fortify the opposition between inside and outside. Assange and Snowden are "men escaped" from the NSS. Their proclivity for the secret makes for a strange resemblance to the United States–authorized spymaster, though with some qualifications: If they are men, then they are pathological—either not man enough or embrace a hazardous species of masculinity; if they are leakers, then their leaks mask a terroristic intent in a mere rhetoric of openness and transparency. Megethos, the one more that is not enough, offers a temporary resolution to this situation. It asserts that the subject—sexual and national—*is* a whole, despite itself; that its boundaries are stronger than ever.

Expelling such leakers has a further effect: It creates the potential for popular and perverse identification with the leaker beyond the state, who is a leaker not just because he leaks but because of his apocalyptic manhood. His victimage is proven by the state's criminal pursuit, creating an errant character whose features include depravity, self-imposed seclusion, and bodily deprivation. This vision of masculinity is entirely harmonious with the incel "type": "these underappreciated men are morally and biologically superior to the alpha males (or Chads) they chase."[96] Rather than being emasculated by the "Chad" (the sexually lascivious, physically attractive man), the leaker is emasculated by the strongman state. With respect to Snowden and Assange, it is not a question of whether these figures truly are or are not incels but rather the coincidence of their heroic portrayal with a form of self-imposed exile and a monstrous masculinity. Not only were they not quite masculine "enough," but their disclosures were not enough to penetrate the state's veil of opacity. Correspondingly, the NSS's expulsion of "one more" leaker was not enough to stem the flow of NSS leaks once and for all. There will always be one more, and that will not be enough. Hence the escalating cycle of the masculine leak: It makes for ever more victim-monster-leakers seeking to penetrate the state's seal of secrecy, while reproducing the possibility of the leaker's being ever more subjected to the state's penetrating gaze.

---

95. Copjec, *Read My Desire*, 216.
96. Kelly and Aunspach, "Incels," 154.

The Feminine Leak: Turing and Manning

The masculine pursuit of secrets often caricatures the feminine as an indefinitely sought-after secret. As Shoshana Felman explains, masculine sexuality often shows itself as a desire to capture, tame, and control the feminized other, while the feminine manifests as the impossibility of ever doing so.[97] Across many feminist revisions of Lacanian psychoanalysis, the logic of feminine sexuality is often theorized in terms of an evasion of language, surveillance, and the law.[98] Such theorizations posit the category of "woman" as encapsulating a resistive, elusive becoming. Although "everything can be and is said about her ... none of what is said amounts to a confirmation or denial of her existence, which eludes every symbolic articulation."[99] If the masculine logic creates a definitional boundary regarding who or what may count as "man" by pushing those variations that do not fit outside of itself, then the feminine logic pulls subjects *inward,* forming an internal limit that only fails to circumscribe identity because there is always a futural "one more" woman who may yet be added to this category (see figure 5.2). In the words of Luce Irigaray, "Theoretically there would be no such thing as woman. She would not exist. The best that can be said is that she does not exist *yet.*"[100]

Alan Turing and Chelsea Manning offer parallel examples of this feminized "not yet," an excessive embodiment that is beyond the state's knowing, existing beyond hegemonic (i.e., heteronormative and cisgender) categories of womanhood. The feminine logic textures their respective national security leaks. Both received hormone replacement therapies authorized by the state: Turing by force and Manning by choice. Their distinct embodiments allude to the state's "failure to 'see' transgender women as women" unless this womanhood offers a means to enforce binary sexuality (in Turing's case) or marks the transgender person as deviating from heterosexual, cisgender differences.[101] In the sections that follow, I intertwine the leak and the feminine logic of psychoanalysis using two tropes: that of the elusive femme fatale and the symbolic structure of apophasis, which figures a quantity beyond knowability or predictive reason.

---

97. Felman, *What Does a Woman Want?*, 33.
98. For other psychoanalytic retheorizations of feminine sexuality, see also Ragland, *Logic of Sexuation*; and Ashtor, *Homo Psyche*.
99. Copjec, *Read My Desire*, 226.
100. Irigaray, *Speculum of the Other Woman*, 166.
101. Beauchamp, *Going Stealth*, 108.

APOPHASIS

Numbered directional arrows indicate the successive expansion of boundaries, borders, or limits as efforts to encompass the set (i.e., of "all women," "all leaks," and "all leakers").

Each addition of *X* results in a widened category whose claim to be the most exhaustive is cover for the impossibility of capturing the set as a totality.

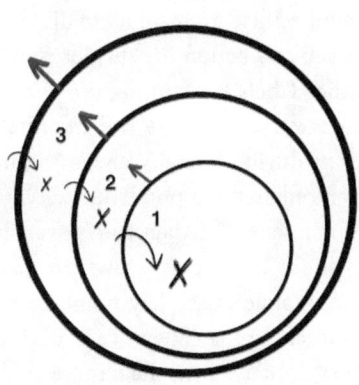

LET *X* BE:	AND	AND
the "one more" *woman* who may always be added to the category of all women, a limit that is also the absence of limit.	the "one more" *leak* of identifying data that will have been too many, leading to the leaker's incarceration by the NSS.	the "one more" *leaker* who, having initially evaded identification by the NSS, will have been too many and thus threatens to compromise the NSS once and for all.

FIGURE 5.2. Apophasis, or the feminine (phatic) logic of leaks.

The Leaker as Femme Fatale

The first figure associated with both the feminine logic and the leak is the femme fatale. In film noir, this recurring character type displays an unrestricted desire that unmakes a (prototypically masculine) protagonist's worldview. Noir's cinematic techniques and intersubjective relationships stage the impossibility of hiddenness under conditions of constant surveillance.[102] Its mise-en-scène depicts the impossibility of full or total secrecy by juxtaposing "deep" visual techniques (i.e., the "artificial replication of depth in the image" using "shadows and depth of field") with the "flat" diegetic spaces of the noir world (i.e., "a world in which nothing can lie hidden, everything must come to light").[103] The femme fatale embodies a similar contradiction: "If the femme fatale is the embodiment of deceit, it is always a deceit of this order: transparent, painted on—a deceit that does not disguise itself."[104] She evades a masculine gaze—the protagonist's or the law's—without any pretense of concealment. Although the masculine subject—the detective or the NSS—looks directly at

---

102. Copjec, *Read My Desire*, 169.
103. Copjec, *Read My Desire*, 197.
104. Copjec, *Read My Desire*, 198–99.

the femme fatale, they are oblivious to her danger until too late. This is "the realist's imbecility," an inability to discern the symbolic coordinates that would lend speech and action the surplus signification of the secret.[105]

Neither Chelsea Manning nor Alan Turing may seem to fit the mold of this character. The *fatale*'s real-life reference, Mata Hari, was a sex-worker-turned-spy during World War I, a "beautiful, doomed exotic dancer who had been manipulated by a powerful man into sleeping with other men to get their secret documents."[106] Mata Hari's overt heterosexuality made her an ill-fitting stereotype for later spies. However, the ill fit of every attempt to generalize the femme fatale is the key point: *there is always one more that will be too many*, unmaking the coherence of such categories as all women, all spies, and all leakers. Consistently, the femme fatale is discovered too late and perennially un-included in the category of what would mark a leaker as conspicuous. Thus, although neither Alan Turing nor Chelsea Manning shares the Mata Hari profile (i.e., sensuous cisgender seductress), they share the characteristic of evading an NSS gaze that claims to be all-seeing.

In addition to their roles as keepers of the secret and transgressors of national security law, Turing and Manning most overlap because of a shared historical moment between 2010 and 2014. During this time, both achieved (in Turing's case, renewed) a conspicuous public prominence. For the cryptanalyst Turing, these years corresponded with a hard-fought posthumous royal pardon and the release of Morten Tyldum's biopic, *The Imitation Game* (2014).[107] The film depicts the mathematician's celebrated wartime leak—the deciphering of the Nazi ENIGMA code in 1942—as well as the leak concerning his gender, in which Turing was convicted and physically punished for his homosexuality, criminalized in Britain until 1967. Correspondingly, Chelsea Manning became a household name following her arrest as the source of the 2010 "War Logs" leak. Manning's court-martial lasted until 2013. Soon after her conviction, Manning disclosed that she was transgender, igniting "an unprecedented public debate about the correct use of pronouns for trans-identified individuals."[108] In her pardon request to President Barack Obama, Manning wrote that her leak was motivated by the need for "public accountability," eschewing the typical pattern of electing "to hide behind the veil of

---

105. Copjec, *Read My Desire*, 142; and Lacan, "Seminar on 'The Purloined Letter,'" 40.
106. Olmsted, "Blond Queens," 79–80.
107. "Royal Pardon for Codebreaker Alan Turing"; and Tyldum, *Imitation Game*. One incidental linkage between Assange and Turing is that, during the period described, both were played by British actor Benedict Cumberbatch. Condon, *Fifth Estate*.
108. Fischer, *Terrorizing Gender*, 31.

national security and classified information."[109] Thus juxtaposed, Turing and Manning are leakers who illustrate "just how quickly nationalist discourses can turn on GLBTQ persons who seek to protect and ensure the nation."[110]

A final way that Turing and Manning are in keeping with the femme fatale archetype concerns how their distinct, nongeneralizable genders marked each as a potential threat. In 1952, following a burglary that disclosed his relationship with Arnold Murray, Turing pled guilty to charges of gross indecency and was compelled to undergo female hormone injections—a chemical castration technique devised in 1940 to decrease homosexual libido.[111] Although Turing's homosexuality had been well known among friends and colleagues, he was stripped of his security clearances and was forced to accept the injections as a condition of his probation. Despite his national security service, he was marked as a threat and subjected to the state's pseudoscientific association of femininity with the absence of sexual urge. Although Manning's case differs from Turing's because she underwent hormonal therapy as part of a desired transition, the two are also alike because she, too, did not conceal her gender or sexuality from her military superiors. Court documents from her trial "reveal not only that the army knew about Manning's struggle with her gender identity and sexual orientation in advance of the leaks, but that her chain of command deliberately chose to ignore warning signs about her mental health and failed to provide her with adequate treatment."[112] By avowing her identity as a transgender woman, Manning's trial was overdetermined by regressive narratives that aligned cisgender self-presentation with truthfulness and transgender identity with innate qualities of deception: "Imagining that a gender-nonconforming individual fundamentally has something to hide . . . helps construct the gender-nonconforming figure as an inherently deceptive object of state and public scrutiny."[113] When juxtaposed, Turing and Manning make the state's punitive understandings of sexuality visible. Although their sexuality and gender were made out to be secret signs of danger during their prosecutions, these were well known before and during their respective leaks and only retroactively used to discredit each "as troubled, confused, damaged, weak, irrational, and pathological."[114] So, too, with the femme fatale: Each leaker's avowed gender came to mark a threat despite the documented openness of their "secret."

---

109. Manning, "Heavy Price."
110. Dunn, *Queerly Remembered*, 104.
111. Hodges, *Alan Turing*, 590.
112. Fischer, *Terrorizing Gender*, 43.
113. Beauchamp, *Going Stealth*, 2.
114. Cloud, "Private Manning," 81.

Apophasis: The One More That Is Too Many

A relative to paralipsis, apophasis most often describes speech that "pretend[s] to deny what is really affirmed," stating outright that one is passing over an issue (e.g., "We don't talk about Bruno" or "I can neither confirm nor deny that statement").[115] However, unlike paralipsis (which either accentuates a topic to dismiss it or introduces a "side-track" absent from a narrative's main sequence),[116] apophasis is a form of speaking-away that emphasizes what does not exist.[117] A trope used across many scholarly disciplines, apophasis denotes a gap, lacuna, or limit. It is an articulation of what is inarticulable, "an acknowledgment that the real is more immeasurable, complex, rich, multiple, and mysterious than even a 'realist' representation of it can possibly account for."[118] Within the tradition of negative theology, it refers to "the speech of 'unsaying,' and in particular, the unsaying of God."[119] Jacques Derrida describes "democracy to come" as dependent on an apophatic "spacing before any determination and any possible reappropriation," linking the trope to a double bind in which "the desire to be inclusive of all" is at odds with "the desire to keep or entrust the secret."[120]

My proposed shorthand for apophasis is "the one more that is too many." The formula, tailored after the feminine logic of psychoanalysis, is well suited to describe the logic that feminizes leakers and leaks, which forms a limit vis-à-vis inclusion. There is always "one more" that can be added to the category of woman, making a stable or permanent boundary between "woman" and what lies beyond it impossible to discern.[121] Apophasis likewise articulates what lies beyond the limit of reality. It is the organizing logic by which the real falls short of the Real, the latter always exceeding what is presumptively contained by the former. In other words, the boundary of any stable reality is an encounter with a disruptive signifier that is both inside and outside of it, and whose straddling of this distinction poses a threat to the very sense of order the boundary seems to promise.

Apophasis is appropriate to describe information leaks for two related reasons. First, by disclosing the leaker's sexuality and gender, "one more" leak is

---

115. Lanham, *Handlist of Rhetorical Tropes*, 19.
116. Mercieca, *Demagogue for President*, 87–95; Genette, *Narrative Discourse*, 205; and Bal, *Narratology*, 177.
117. *OED Online*, s.v. "apophasis, n.," last accessed February 11, 2025, https://www.oed.com/dictionary/apophasis_n.
118. J. McGrath, *Chinese Film*, 21.
119. Keller, "Apophasis of Gender," 909.
120. Derrida, *Rogues*, 82; and Derrida, *On the Name*, 83–84.
121. Copjec, *Read My Desire*, 199.

added to the leaker's repertoire of disclosures, breaching the safe social enclosure in which they once operated. Other metaphors of this "one more" are the bridge too far, the point of no return. It is "too many" because, as a final disclosure, it signals an end to the leaker's evasion of the law. By making their gender visible in ways they did not foresee, the leak becomes the lens through which the whole of a leaker's previous statements, utterances, and writings are retroactively reinterpretable. Arguably, Turing's disclosure to police of his relationship with Arnold was just this sort of "one more that is too many": it resulted in his prosecution and enabled rereadings of Turing's early life that projected his homosexuality as the hidden subtext of his mathematical writings. However, as biographer Andrew Hodges reminds us, Turing's homosexuality was largely known to his colleagues: "exposure . . . held no intrinsic terror for him."

> For most gay men, the question of *who knew* would be of colossal significance, and life would be rigidly divided into two compartments, one for those who knew, and one for those who did not. . . . The question was important to Alan too, but in a rather different way: it was because he did not wish to be accepted or respected as the person he was not.[122]

Hodges's metaphor of compartmentalization alludes to the retroactive reading of his gender onto his most famous work, the 1936 "Test for Machine Intelligence."[123] This essay, originally written as a solution to David Hilbert's 1928 *Entscheidungsproblem* (or "decision problem"), posited that it was impossible to conceive of formal rules by which *any* mathematical formula might be parsed.[124] Before elaborating his famous "test," Turing used the analogy of a parlor game with three players: a man (A) a woman (B), and a judge of indeterminate sex (C). In the game, partygoers guess the sex of two concealed individuals, who communicate via a scrap of paper passed beneath a door. The goal is to correctly judge which of the two is male and which is female. When Turing moves from the game to his famous test, he replaces one human player with a machine.[125] Retroactively highlighted is the fact that the computer must "pass" in plain sight. Whereas in the first iteration, the man wins by passing as

---

122. Hodges, *Alan Turing*, 582.
123. For instance, see Hayles, *How We Became Posthuman*, xii–xiii.
124. Turing, "Computing Machinery."
125. According to Friedrich Kittler, the prototype of the machine operator was the female typist or stenographer, who had become a fixture of the modern workplace since the beginning of the twentieth century. Sexuality and the computer closet were thus already linked as features of the mid-century symbolic order. Kittler, *Gramophone, Film, Typewriter*, 246.

a woman (and vice versa), in the second, the machine wins the intelligence-imitation game by putting "the computer in drag as a man."[126] As apophasis, the parlor game is retroactively visible as "one" instance of Turing knowingly making reference to his own passing and closeting. Placed in that tropological frame, it anticipates the "one too many" that led to his prosecution.

Second, leakers like Turing and Manning embody "one more" security breach that is "too many" for the NSS because they signal a precarious contravention of its claim to totalizing surveillance. If the NSS consistently seeks to extinguish queer desire and scapegoat queer bodies as innately deceptive, then these leakers attest to inhabiting new, discursively made carceral enclosures stamped in the mold of state-imposed sexual failure. Whether "one more" refers to a leaker's freshly revealed gender or the newly disclosed limits of state surveillance, apophasis adds "one more" to signal the futility of an anticipatory knowing that could ever be presumed total, whole, or complete. This kind of apophasis is apparent in Turing's remembrance as a heroic cryptographer. His posthumous hagiography, the 2014 *Imitation Game*, depicts sexuality as a surplus signifier to which Turing was uniquely attuned. Applied to his cryptographic efforts, it reveals an open secret, allowing a fictionalized story about a heterosexual dynamic to spur his ingenious "cracking" of the Nazi ENIGMA code. Tyldum's Turing admits that the brilliance of the Nazi code is that it is easily intercepted but not so easily deciphered. Its impossibly numerous (1,305,093,289,500) configurations would have to be tested one by one each time the machine was reset.[127] At a crucial moment, Turing has a flash of inspiration after listening to Helen, a typist at Bletchley Park, who imagines coded intercepts as love letters. As she explains, German messages seem like intimate addresses; each bore a similar, predictable pattern (called *cillys*) she thought of as proper names. "Cillys" were indeed exploited by Bletchley Park cryptologists, referencing conspicuous character sequences that could be used to reverse engineer the ENIGMA's ciphertext key:

> For each message, the [German Enigma] operator was supposed to select a different message key, three letters chosen at random. However, in the heat of battle, rather than straining their imaginations to pick a random key, the overworked operators would sometimes pick three consecutive letters from the Enigma keyboard, such as QWE or BNM. . . . Another type of cilly was the repeated use of the same message key, perhaps the initials of the operator's girlfriend—indeed, one such set of initials, C.I.L., may have been the origin of the term.[128]

---

126. Foley, "'Prove You're Human,'" 367.
127. Hodges, *Alan Turing*, 214.
128. Singh, *Code Book* (1999), 164.

In the quasi-fictional scenario depicted in *The Imitation Game,* the heterosexual dynamic is the secret "one more" that is "too much" for the Axis powers. From Clarke's anecdote, Turing deduces a new set of rules for his computer, guided by the insight that German dispatches would *always* contain certain letter patterns. Transfiguring an indecipherable message into a love letter added the crucial something extra that secures Allied victory. This "one more" is not just any clue; it is a heterosexual dynamic retroactively added to Turing's popular memory.

Turing's and Manning's doubled apophases are most evident in their respective written correspondence, each leaker voicing a dysphoric existence within a system that made no space for them. As Pamela VanHaitsma explains, the epistolary tradition has long dismissed queer relationalities as "failures" relative to "successful" heterosexual couplings.[129] In romantic letter writing, any outcome apart from male-female courtship has typically been deemed a failure. Although the objective of the leakers' epistolary discourse was not courtship, Turing and Manning evoke queer failure because their metaphors allude to an inability to be seen despite their brilliance, as well as a "too-muchness" associated with being queer within a viciously heteronormative regime. Each leaker is *themselves* "a one more that is too many," a secret exceeding what either the state or society could tolerate.

Turing's epistolary apophases elaborate a "beyond" to what the state or science could rationalize, equating his "far-fetched" (in scare quotes) thoughts about machine intelligence with his then-criminalized sexuality. Before pleading guilty, Turing wrote a letter to colleague Norman Routledge, ending it with the following syllogism:

Turing believes machines can think
Turing lies with men
Therefore machines cannot think.[130]

The minor premise, "Turing lies with men," conveys two ideas: that Turing prevaricates *and* that he is gay. The synthesis "Therefore machines cannot think" invalidates his theory of machine intelligence—what many hold to be his most lasting contribution to computer science—by unifying it with the bigoted presumption that his gender nonconformity makes him intrinsically deceptive. In being revealed as "one" subject "too many," for Bletchley Park and the courts, Turing's leaked identity over-writes the significance of his

---

129. VanHaitsma, *Queering Romantic Engagement.*
130. Hodges, *Alan Turing,* xxx.

contributions to mathematics and national security. He *is* the extra element that is too many—for himself and for the NSS.

Manning's belatedly published chats with Adrian Lamo reveal similar sentiments. Lamo, a bisexual hacker and queer activist, is widely credited as having revealed Manning's identity as a WikiLeaks source.[131] Their dialogue paints a picture of Manning as isolated among hypermasculine peers. In one exchange, she elaborates the felt dissonance between her assigned military role and her authentic, gendered self, with a computer hardware analogy that echoes Turing's computer-themed syllogism:

> (1:14:11 PM) Manning: i've totally lost my mind . . . i make no sense . . . the CPU is not made for this motherboard . . .
> (1:30:32 PM) Manning: >sigh<
> (1:31:40 PM) Manning: i just wanted enough time to figure myself out . . . to be myself . . . and not be running around all the time, trying to meet someone else's expectations[132]

The CPU (central processing unit) is the instruction "hub" that coordinates the operation of all other components, while the motherboard is the integrated circuit that supplies power and communication between different components. A mismatch between them results in malfunction, such as when the CPU demands more power than the motherboard can supply. Manning's analogy suggests that the different components of her identity were out of balance, that her cognitive center was at odds with the body it was plugged into. Subsequent references to a life lived in plain sight ("no one took any notice of me") attest to the shift from Manning's having disclosed secrets to her having *become* the secret, too much for the surroundings into which she had been implanted.

It is no accident that Turing's—and, by extension, Manning's—apophases coincide with instances of phatic discourse. This term, phatic, describes a register of speech whose primary function is relational, and which therefore is often shunned as incidental to knowledge transmission.[133] It often references an affective, intersubjective domain that may be dismissed as formal gestures, pleasantries, or terms of endearment. However, the phatic register is not just an ignorable feature of the leaker's discourse. It is confessional, revealing, disclosive, an internal fissuring that goes beyond any specific NSS information

---

131. Manning, *Readme.txt*, 156.
132. Hansen, "Manning-Lamo Chat Logs Revealed." Ellipses in original.
133. Coupland, Coupland, and Robinson, "How Are You?"; V. Miller, "New Media"; and Rigilano, "Decline of Phatic Efficiency."

the leaker might disclose. The suffix *-phatic* itself hides in plain sight within "apophatic," elaborating the feeling of exceeding a system in which the subject has no place.[134] As Turing and Manning illustrate, apophasis feminizes the leaker by lending phatic utterances the texture of a vulnerable admission, bringing the secret forth as that which was always there, but which is simply one too many for the prevailing sexual order.

Sealing Up the Leak, Indefinitely

We now perennially live in the wake of leaks whose magnitude constitutively prohibits us from fully knowing what is disclosed. Three years after Snowden's revelations, the International Consortium of Investigative Journalists (ICIJ) released several new biggest-ever leaks: the 2016 Panama Papers (11.5 million documents), the 2017 Paradise Papers (13.4 million documents), and the 2021 Pandora Papers (11.9 million documents), exposing the offshore holdings of world leaders, billionaires, and celebrities.[135] According to the ICIJ, the 2021 leak was "larger and more global" than its 2016 counterpart, and "unprecedented" even by comparison to the quantitatively larger 2017 leak.[136] At one level, the act of leaking state and financial secrets is analogous to the visual logic of anamorphosis, which "gives a coherent representation" according to the "preconstructed viewpoint" of wealthy oligarchs and the NSS: "In the case of Edward Snowden's leaking of classified documents, an agent deviates from the focal viewpoint of what political reality is supposed to represent."[137] The function of the NSS's sexual logics is to restore a semblance of the hegemonic status quo, as if redirecting attention away from Holbein's deathlike skull and back toward a world organized by "a structure of education, rule-observance, and obedience."[138]

The repeat sexualization of leakers reinstates these normative rules and the nation's ever-penetrable securitarian boundary. At the level of the imaginary

---

134. Divided into its Greek etymological roots, *apophasis* combines the Greek prefix *apo-* (signifying "apart, away, off, completing, ceasing from, back again, standing off or away from each other") with the suffix *-phatic* (signifying "spoken" or "to say"). *OED Online*, s.v. "apo-, prefix," last accessed February 11, 2025, https://www.oed.com/dictionary/apo_prefix; *OED Online*, s.v. "phatic, adj.," last accessed February 11, 2025, https://www.oed.com/dictionary/phatic_adj.
135. Schmidt and Myers, "Panama Law Firm's Leaked Files"; Zerofsky, "German Newspaper"; Miller, Cenziper, and Whoriskey, "Billions Hidden"; and Whoriskey and Aremdariz, "Secret Trove."
136. ICIJ, "Offshore Havens and Hidden Riches."
137. Finkelde, "Anamorphosis," 7.
138. Finkelde, "Anamorphosis," 16.

(spymaster and femme fatale) and the symbolic (megethos and apophasis), sexualization wards off a political Real tantamount to the death of NSS institutions and surveillant governmentality as such. The phallic logic of leaking feeds a rhetorical economy in which megethos functions as a limit upon public transmissibility, accessibility, and comprehension. This is especially the case when considering how leaks prolong anxiety over the NSS's susceptibility to threats from within:

> When an individual or actor claims to know in advance who is or is not a member of the polity, they make this claim from a position theoretically exterior to the polity, for they must assume an Archimedean position that disavows the intersubjective, ambiguous character of personhood and community. . . . These subjects occupy positions of near-constant anxiety, since the subject has identified itself with totality, one which cannot possibly exist as a whole entity if the subject is capable of perceiving themselves in relation to it.[139]

The NSS is one such "individual or actor" who is supposed to know, a collection of agencies that assumes a point of view above and beyond what is available to citizens. Its phallic function not only polices the boundary separating the nation-state's legitimate (masculinized) insiders from its illegitimate (feminized) outsiders; it cultivates limited interpretations of sexual motive that collapse the distinction between exposure and uncloseting, as well as that between prudent securitarianism and normatively repressed sexuality. The typecasting of the national security leaker illuminates just how carceral the sexual binary can be, especially when leveraged as a neutral explanation of why those who transgress informational boundaries are inclined to do so.

This rhetoric has other dire consequences: on the masculine side, associating illicit NSS leaking with profiles of toxic masculinity—a surplus identification with monstrous, phallic manhood—risks fashioning incel masculinity as heroic or aspirational. Following the 2023 Discord Leaks (a leak of classified military information concerning Russia's incursion into Ukraine), news reports described the unlikely leaker, Jack Teixeira, as a novice spymaster.[140] In the Discord group where the leak first transpired, Texiera was "the elder leader of their tiny tribe" and "claimed to know secrets that the government withheld from ordinary people."[141] While *The Christian Science Monitor* likened Teixeira to Snowden for exposing "cracks" in American intelligence handling,

---

139. P. Johnson, *I the People*, 13.
140. Toler, "From Discord to 4chan."
141. Harris and Oakford, "Discord Member Details."

others argued that Teixeira shared Donald Trump's "combustible blend of narcissism, insecurity, troubled interpersonal relationships and grudges, along with the narcissistic belief that 'I can do whatever I want.'"[142] In the wake of his arrest, Teixeira was celebrated by "hard-line" conservatives like Marjorie Taylor Greene, who posited that the leaker had been specifically targeted for his political identity: "Jack Teixeira is white, male, Christian, and anti-war. That makes him an enemy to the Biden regime."[143] Assuming a paternal role over his Discord group, Teixeira thus created a miniaturized NSS, a purveyor of secrets for whom dissemination became a sacrificial act.

More dangerously yet, Teixeira's case portends how the monstrously masculine leaker figure enables proponents of an emergent "grievance culture" to claim ownership over transparency activism as such. As key signatories to the Westminster Declaration, a petition that accuses intelligence agencies and private enterprises of unprecedented censorship, Assange and Snowden are exemplary martyrs, having already been "canceled" by the "Censorship-Industrial Complex."[144] According to the document, petitioners "[come] from the left, right, and centre," resist *any* effort to engage in content moderation or label misinformation, and condemn "deplatforming" and "fact-checking" as an abandonment of "journalistic values of debate and intellectual inquiry." The document also testifies to an important, albeit subtle shift in the political polarities of transparency activism. For instance, it equates the movement to end the deplatforming of hate speech with "the abolition of slavery and the civil rights movement." It also employs the phrase "Censorship-Industrial Complex," hearkening to Daniel Ellsberg's *Pentagon Papers*, which exposed the excesses of the US military-industrial complex during Richard Nixon's presidency. Unlike Ellsberg's *Papers*, the petition's demands are aligned with originalist interpretations of "the founders," "laws," and "constitutions." The Declaration does not so much have the right to *know* whether information is true or false as a right to *say* what one desires without regard for the consequences. Labeling any effort to restrict, moderate, or label speech as censorship, the petitioners elaborate their own masculine logic, crafting unity by promising to expel those who would prohibit their discursive secretions.

Conversely, the feminine logic of the leak makes the leaker both the subject for whom "one more" disclosure steps past the threshold of ignorability and the subject who embodies a "one more" that breaks the leaker stereotype. However, the feminization of NSS leakers makes transgender womanhood

---

142. Robertson, "Plugging Intelligence Leaks"; and Radack, "Pentagon Leaker Jack Teixeira."
143. Drezner, "Whistleblower or Traitor?"
144. "Westminster Declaration."

invisible while marking transgender people generally as a threat to heteronational security, feeding efforts to uncloset nonnormative gender expressions in contexts ranging from bathrooms to airports to libraries.[145] This logic is destructive, in other words, because it frames any expression of "excessive" (in scare quotes) femininity as "one more that is too many," evoking a coercive and nonconsensual bringing-to-light.

The feminine side of the NSS's sexual logic also posits the impossibility of seeing "every" subject, despite the size and scope of its surveillance apparatus. In this regard, the feminized knowledge of psychoanalysis, with its fatalistic explanatory power, is not exempt from carceral sexualization. Take, for example, Julia Kristeva, who in 2018 was accused of having served as "Sabina," a Bulgarian secret agent under "the country's notorious Communist-era secret service."[146] Kristeva denied the accusation, documented in a voluminous file that, despite containing "extensive reports of alleged conversations with her handlers," had "not a single intelligence-related document written or signed by her." Still uncaptured and uncapturable, Kristeva's alleged "exposure" (in scare quotes) retroactively lends her work as a leading psychoanalytic theorist novel texture, adding a signifying surplus to her cultivated "persona of a perpetual exile, unconstrained by borders."[147] Rather than confining the suspected national security leaker to a "type," the feminine logic offers an explanation of the limitations put upon "queer" leaking in its refusal to conform with masculine or feminine sexuation.

It is not a matter of representing leakers' experiences in ways that approximate their lived realities. No matter how closely we may approach the leaker's "raw experience," the feminine logic promises us that *something* remains off-limits. This asymptotic relation to subjectivity is depicted in *Reality* (2023), which dramatizes leaker Reality Winner's interrogation by the FBI.[148] A film based on a stage play based on an official FBI transcript, *Reality* brings the audience as close as possible to the "raw experience" of Reality's confession, in which she admits to having leaked classified documents about Russia's efforts to compromise the 2016 US presidential election. Where the FBI transcript is redacted, however, the film's sound cuts out with a noise resembling the pulling of an audio jack from its socket. In those moments, Reality, too, disappears

---

145. Fixmer-Oraiz, *Homeland Maternity*.
146. Schuessler and Dzhambazova, "Bulgaria Says."
147. Kenarov, "Philosopher Julia Kristeva."
148. Satter, *Reality*. In this sentence, "asymptote" refers to a line that a curve approaches but never quite touches as the curve extends toward infinity. An "asymptotic" relation to subjectivity is one that approaches but never quite touches a subject, despite the impression of getting closer to their subtending essence.

from the screen, going missing for the duration of the classified segment. It does not matter whether we know, in retrospect or from context, what the redacted content may have been. No matter how close we are to capturing the leaker in their totality, something about Reality/reality remains beyond apprehension. After all, no matter how scrupulously the leaker is profiled for "aberrant" behavior or "illicit" desire (both in scare quotes), there is always a *next* one who will have evaded capture, another cover-up destined for repetition.

CHAPTER 6

The Detective

Settler Subjects and Neocolonial Warfare

> ANTITERRORISM experts are talking
> about us again. Some news anchor
> cussing during commercials.
> I saw your wanted ad at the subway station.
> I saw a young Taliban
> but couldn't see past his beauty,
> brows of an ancient RELIEF, to the tank
> he was riding on.
> —Solmaz Sharif, *Look* (20)

Surveillance and Its Discontents

On October 29, 2013, two auspicious events transpired. The first was a meeting held by the House Permanent Select Committee on Intelligence, which discussed the legality of National Security Agency (NSA) programs and whether amendments ought to be made to the Foreign Intelligence Surveillance Act (FISA) following the revelation by Edward Snowden earlier that year of sprawling domestic spying programs.[1] The second concerned the testimony of thirteen-year-old Zubair Rehman and his sister, Nabila, who provided testimony to Congress at a briefing organized by US Representative Alan Grayson (D-FL).[2] From Pakistan's Waziristan region, Zubair described collecting okra in preparation for Eid when a drone deployed a Hellfire missile that killed his grandmother and injured several members of his family. He described how,

---

1. Rogers, "NSA Programs."
2. There is no congressional record available for this hearing, although it was widely reported in regional and national newspapers at the time it transpired. See, for instance, Henneberger, "Drone Strike's Toll"; and "U.S. Rep. Alan Grayson."

"when the sky brightens and becomes blue, the drones return, and so does the fear."[3] Unlike the Snowden meetings, this testimony neither drew protesters nor the attention of more than a few members of Congress.[4] According to Shahzad Akbar, the Rehmans' attorney, this absence proved an important point: "If only five or six people from Congress showed up to hear from the victims of drone strikes, it just proves that it is a government and society where money and lobbying are stronger than the aim to find justice."[5]

The two meetings mark a striking incongruity. Whereas the 2013 Snowden hearings captured the interest of demonstrators and Congress alike, there was a dearth of attention paid to the concomitant testimony of drone victims. As this chapter argues, these events are connected by the figure of the settler-detective, who imagines themselves as both the discoverer of—and spectator to—acts of neocolonial violence. This figural subject is not a collection of substantive characteristics that, once summed up, allow us to know a settler when we see one. Rather, they are driven by the pretense and pursuit of a certain kind of secret, identifying with the imperative to detect neocolonial atrocities—particularly those that impact them personally. Triangulated by similar narrative tropes that center their perspective as the egoic "I" of Western popular culture, the settler and the detective alike seek out the secret as a means to remain unimplicated in a greater scene of global violence.

The settler and the detective are isomorphic figures for many reasons. Like the settler, the detective bears only a passing resemblance to the police, because they are stationed below and above the law. Beholden to the law, detectives are private citizens with unusual perceptual powers, placing their ability to discern the secret into the service of their sovereign. Above the law, the detective is one who does what the police cannot, a vigilante whose capacities and methods exceed those used by state-authorized investigators. Hence also the settler-detective's capacity for disavowal: Although they are not the police, they identify with key functions of criminal detection as they push the law's boundaries.

A further continuity between the settler and the detective is how each appears to be steered by forces beyond their control. For the detective, these forces are organized as three tropes of the detective plot: analepsis, paralipsis, and prolepsis. Although these conventionally correspond with the flashback, the plot omission, and foreshadowing, detective fiction also routes each through a specific psychoanalytic register. *Analepsis* dovetails with the symbolic order and the backwards-looking pattern of retroactive signification, in

---

3. Ahmed, "Drone Victims Testify."
4. N. Khan, "Drone Victims."
5. Ahmed, "Drone Victims Testify."

which the past is rewritten in light of recently made discoveries. *Paralipsis* is aligned with imaginary disavowal, or a mode of (dis)identification whereby the settler-detective acknowledges and distances themselves from acts they avow as wrong. Finally, *prolepsis* describes the incursion of the Real, a moment of apocalyptic forecasting that envisions the consequences of neocolonial conquest to keep the settler-detective's likely destruction at bay. Together, these tropes allude to temporal and rhetorical forms that manage an absent center of settler subjectivity to keep the settler-detective in the middle of things, the focal point in a story that is not, ostensibly, about them.

What Kind of Subject Is the Settler?

Often, subjects are imagined as an interrogative "who," a person or people with a discrete, positively enumerated identity. The framing of the subject as a "who" is prevalent among psychoanalytically informed rhetorical theorists, where a prevailing trend is to describe a certain kind of kakoethotic subject. *Kakoethos,* which references a pathologically bad character, is a feature of this white, masculine, and cisgender persona.[6] Frequently, this subject evokes conservative, nationalistic, and white supremacist ideologues who present themselves as aspirational, strong, dominating, and heroic.[7] Trapped in a fantasy of narcissistic victimhood, their affects alternate between sadism, anxiety, and rage.[8] The demagogue, who preserves rhetoric's traditional speaker-audience dichotomy, is one such type: "a complete, autonomous individual with a tantalizing, emotional power" who authorizes their followers to perpetrate open bigotry and racial violence.[9] Whether it is the evangelical public who identified with *The Passion of the Christ,* Donald Trump's death-driven pattern of speaking, cultish conspiracy theorists, or the paranoid discourse of conservative pundits and the far right, rhetoricians have pushed aside the historically privileged subjectivity Quintilian once described as the

---

6. The adverb *kakoethotic* is adapted from Jenell Johnson's account of "kakoethos," which describes the attribution of a stigmatized character. Whereas Johnson's account focuses on the unjust stigmatization that resulted from a specific scandal, my use here refers to a scholarly trend of describing rhetors' objectively bad character vis-à-vis their demagogic form of symptomatic psychopathology (e.g., narcissism, anxiety, psychosis). J. Johnson, "Skeleton on the Couch."

7. P. Johnson, "Art of Masculine Victimhood," 234.

8. Matheson, "What Does Obama Want of Me?"; and Matheson, "Liberal Tears."

9. Gunn, "Hystericizing Huey," 13.

"good man speaking well" in favor of such kakoethotic figures as the dangerous incel behaving badly.[10]

However, in the Lacanian tradition of psychoanalysis, the subject is not just a "who" but also a "what," defined by a constitutive split that cannot be resolved except by repeatedly covering up this void with different fantasies and object attachments. This subject's most consistent defining feature is the breach or interruption that gives shape to conscious thought. Written about using a symbol that resembles a dollar sign ($), this "barred subject" is inaccessible to the knowing, speaking, reflective ego except through compensatory activity.[11] The "bar" of the barred subject is written into $ as a slash that places the self-present subject under erasure, dividing the conscious ego's self-reflection from the unconscious agencies that steer its speech and action.

One way of understanding the split-ness of the barred subject concerns their always divided identifications with the little-*o* other and big-*O* Other. Synonymous with "imaginary identification," the little-*o* other describes an attachment to specific people, objects, and representations. By "imitat[ing] the other at the level of resemblance," this other reflects a fantasy of oneself as they would or would not like to be (*manqué d'être*)."[12] For the American settler, the imaginary other might be the revolutionary colonist, the cowboy, or the Pinkerton: a lawless character conscripted to bring order to the frontier.

Conversely, identification with the big-*O* Other refers to the subject's relationship to a given symbolic order, often associated with the authority of the superego, language, the law, and the father.[13] This Other defines that point from whence the subject judges its actions to be likable to itself. Should a person refuse dessert because a parent, dietician, or doctor wouldn't want them to indulge, these figural, substitutable positions of authority occupy the position of the Other. Set within the greater situation of settler colonialism, the Other is that position that issues the mandate to conquer, authorizes genocide and racism as reflective of the natural order, and erects rules of property and commerce to seize Indigenous land.

---

10. Lundberg, "Enjoying God's Death"; Gunn, *Political Perversion*; P. Johnson, *I the People*; Kelly, *Apocalypse Man*; Rice, *Awful Archives*; Bedsole, "Voice as Little Object (A)rgument"; Matheson, "What Does Obama Want of Me?"; and Chebrolu, "Racial Lens." See also Van Schenck, "'Wagecuck' Meme"; Kelly and Aunspach, "Compulsory Sexuality"; and Bratich and Banet-Weiser, "Pick-Up Artists."

11. Fink, *Lacanian Subject*, 39.

12. Žižek, *Sublime Object of Ideology*, 120–21. A Lacanian term of art, *manqué d'être* translates as "failed to be" or "missed being." It here signifies the subject as one who aspires to be (or not to be) like the other to whom they bear an imagined resemblance.

13. Žižek, *Sublime Object of Ideology*, 120–21.

Divided between these distinct modes of identification, $ names a position that is brought into contradiction by them. In other words, the barred subject is an interruptive articulation, a position between the others who we imagine (not) to resemble ourselves and the Other (e.g., God, the father, or the president) who adjudicates the correctness of our thoughts and actions. Even triangulated in this way, however, the barred subject assumes vastly different forms and purposes once situated in a colonial context. Such psychoanalytic concepts must be retranslated, revised, and adapted to suit cultural contexts beyond the colonial one in which they were birthed.[14]

It matters, for instance, how we might define the other/Other for the patients Frantz Fanon treated while resisting French colonial rule in Algeria.[15] Certainly, colonial authorities would not be the source of lawlike authorization for necessary acts of decolonial resistance. Similarly, Lara Sheehi and Stephen Sheehi argue for a "psychoanalysis under occupation" to resist the settler tendency of projecting pathology upon Palestinians. Instead, they seek "to represent [Palestinians] as they are—as full selves and not exclusively as objects of erasure or victims of racist, settler colonialism and, simultaneously, benefactors of our pity."[16] To construe Palestinians as this sort of other would recapitulate colonial modes of identification by caricaturing them as destitute or less complete than their white and Western counterparts. Freud's metaphor of the unconscious as "dark continent"—which associates the "repressed, concealed, and mysterious" of the unconscious with "colonial Africa, women, and the primitive"—must be thoroughly dismantled.[17] The settler is not "the" subject but "a" particular position triangulated by a split identification with the colonial other/Other, the function of which is to contrive a monopoly over resources, land, and even the definition of who is granted subjectivity.

Settler ($) Melodrama

As critics of the Lacanian tradition have noted, the barred subject is too often granted a negative universality on the presumption that *all* infantile subjects

---

14. See also El-Shakry, *Arabic Freud*.

15. "During his tenure at the psychiatric hospital at Blida (1953–56), there were occasions on which [Fanon] covertly trained the *fidayine* (village militias) to cope with their own attacks of terror and anxiety while they were carrying out assassination attempts; he also taught them psychological ways and physiological means of withstanding torture and resisting interrogation." Bhabha, "Foreword," xxxix.

16. Sheehi and Sheehi, *Psychoanalysis Under Occupation*, 5.

17. Khanna, *Dark Continents*, 6.

experience a similar series of traumatic splits.[18] Such developmental narratives are beset by damning exclusions. Building upon Luce Irigaray's repudiation of "the" subject of psychoanalysis as normalizing male and cisgender identity, Jules Gill-Peterson elaborates how twentieth-century psychological science was predicated upon the negation of intersex and transgender children.[19] Frantz Fanon likewise argues that white and Western European psychoanalysis excludes Blackness by default: "the Black man is denied the form of alienation so precious to subjectivity according to various European philosophers."[20] Fred Wilderson elaborates: "Spillers, Fanon, and Hartman maintain that the violence that continually repositions the Black as a void of historical movement is without analog in the suffering dynamics of the ontologically alive."[21] These scholars do not just theorize Blackness as a void-like subject that constitutes the discursive field of white supremacy; they also expose the shortcomings of any theory of the barred subject that fails to account for the exclusions granting it supposed universality. The systematic dismissal, exclusion, and abjection of these and other identity formations from philosophical and psychoanalytic accounts of subjectivity is the condition of possibility for arguing that there is such a thing as "the" subject.

Melodrama is one narrative genre that makes such exclusions possible. Often, melodramas systematically exclude minoritized identities from the nation-state under the auspices of "protecting" the white and cisgender citizen-subject.[22] First, melodrama "locates goodness in the suffering of the nation, evil in its antagonists, and heroism in sovereign acts of war and global control coded as expressions of virtue."[23] It also invites associations with the inexhaustible secret of conspiracy theories because it replicates "the cognitive 'error' so often attributed to conspiracy thinking" by aiming "to reveal

---

18. In the Lacanian tradition there is first the mirror stage, in which the ego, being split from the imago, ceases to be an "unorganized jumble of sensations and impulses. Subsequently, there is the subject's alienation in language, whereby the subject allows "him or herself to be represented by words" and which is experienced as the gain of speech via the loss of undifferentiated infantile being. Fink, *Lacanian Subject*, 36, 50. See also Hallsby, "Intimate Spaces"; and Gunn, *Political Perversion*, 59.

19. Irigaray, *Speculum*, 26; and Gill-Peterson, *Histories of the Transgender Child*.

20. Frosh, "Psychoanalysis, Colonialism, Racism," 147; Frosh cites Fanon, *Black Skin, White Masks*, 3.

21. Wilderson, *Red, White, and Black*, 37.

22. Steven Schwarze offers a conflicting account of melodrama as having "transformative and reifying possibilities" capable of critically interrupting "dominant modes of argument and appeal that obscure threats to the quality and future of life on the planet." Schwarze, "Environmental Melodrama," 240, 245.

23. Anker, *Orgies of Feeling*, 1–2.

patterns hidden in the banal surface of everyday life."[24] Presenting a simplified, good-and-evil version of the neocolonial status quo, melodramas entice their audiences to look for terrorist conspiracies and quotidian threats to the nation-state while providing cover for actual programs of population-level surveillance, land dispossession, and proxy war. Melodramas are, finally, politically ambivalent. Whereas "conservative forms of melodramatic discourse . . . promise the overcoming of unfreedom through sovereign state power," for the political left, "melodrama's appeal derives from the moral clarity it confers on the complex powers organizing politics and subjectivity, from its ability to identify the victims of these powers, . . . from the virtuous power it bestows upon conditions of subjugation, and . . . from the assurance it offers that heroic emancipation can conquer the villainous source of oppression."[25]

Settler narratives are often well suited to a melodramatic mode that features good-and-evil themes, conspiracy motifs, and chameleonic settler characters. The settler protagonist is divided by the inherent twoness of the colony: "both a political body that is dominated by an exogenous agency" (e.g., the Other of seventeenth- and eighteenth-century British monarchy) and "an exogenous entity that reproduces itself in a given environment" (a white and Western European group whose traditions erase and displace those of Indigenous others).[26] Extending the connection between the settler and psychoanalysis, Lorenzo Veracini maps the functions of settler narratives onto the tripartite Lacanian unconscious:

> First, there is an *imaginary* spectacle, an ordered community working hard and living peacefully *Little House on the Prairie* style. Then there is the *symbolic* and ideological background: a moral and regenerative world that supposedly epitomises settler democratic traditions (the "frontier," the "outback,'" the "backblocks," etc.). Finally, there is the *real*: expanding capitalist orders associated with the need to resettle a growing number of people.[27]

The settler is divided in many ways. Not only split between the colony's identifications with the other/Other, they also embrace fantasies of pastoral

---

24. Melley, "Melodramatic Mode," 61. See also Gunn, "Death by Publicity."
25. Anker, *Orgies of Feeling*, 30, 203.
26. Veracini, *Settler Colonialism*, 2. The iterative narrative structure of settler colonialism sets it apart from other, related signifiers like *post*-colonialism (which may imply a time *after* colonization), *anti*-colonialism (an oppositional stance to colonialism, "often identified exclusively, too exclusively, with a provincial nationalism"), and *decolonization* (an anti-rhetorical program that seeks the "repatriation of Indigenous land and life"). Young, *Postcolonialism*, 2; Tuck and Yang, "Decolonization," 20. See also Walter Mignolo, "De-Linking," 457.
27. Veracini, "Settler Collective," 363.

existence (imaginary) and a "moral and regenerative" set of rules that governs this context (symbolic). Finally, this subject is always faced with the possibility of material contingencies that threaten to reconfigure their status quo.

Veracini's psychoanalytic framework also follows a developmental sequence that enables settlers to transform their outward characteristics according to the "colonial political order" as it moves from one generation to the next.[28] In the first stage, the settler wipes nature of its indigenous inhabitants and lays claim to the people and territory. Next, the settler claims to be more indigenous than the Indigenous populations they subjugate. Finally, the settler waits for an impending invasion to provide them with the authorization to renew violence on another frontier. This progression offers "a story line that cannot be turned back," whereby settlers "stay and operate in a system that supersedes itself."[29] In other words, settler narratives are fantasies that encourage the historical benefactors of settler colonialism to avow the violence of colonization by imagining themselves as subjected to it, all the while legitimating future warfare.

The settler's transformation is evident in melodramas that hybridize settler narratives with other popular genres. Science fiction "invasion narratives," for instance, replicate the colonial sequence: The "peacefully settled settler" is subjected to an "invasion by the subaltern other," necessitating their "self-defensive violence in order to protect both their settler home *and* their lifestyle."[30] Such tales invite audiences "to identify with (or as) colonized victims," abetting an "imperial fantasy" designed "for those who benefit the most from modern-day conditions of empire."[31] They also function as fictional preparation for an imminent apocalypse, forecasting how real-world technological interventions like drones and spyware will be used for surveillance beyond the places where they are currently employed, namely "places like border checkpoints and airports and in immigration raids."[32] Once placed in these terms, drones and cyberweapons are legible not just as futuristic weapons derived from science fiction but as neocolonial extensions of the settler colonial project.

---

28. Lechuga, *Visions of Invasion*, 134.
29. Veracini, *Settler Colonialism*, 98, 100.
30. Lechuga, *Visions of Invasion*, 23.
31. Higgins, *Reverse Colonization*, 1.
32. Lechuga, *Visions of Invasion*, 25. See also Lechuga's discussion of "heat rays," "thermal imaging," and "predator technologies." Lechuga, *Visions of Invasion*, 44, 49–74; and Veracini, "Settler Evasions."

Settler-Detective Fiction

Like alien invasion narratives, detective fiction is a related melodramatic plot structure that fosters settler identifications. Prior to the nineteenth century, European crime narratives "reflect[ed] a society with a firm trust in Christian values, feudal order, and social cohesion. In these narratives no agent of detection [was] necessary" because "the signs of guilt naturally lead to detection."[33] With the dawn of the Enlightenment, however, the detective embodied a mastery of reason not available to archaic institutions.[34] Confronting "the atrocity of the crime with the gentleness of reason," the amateur analyst was one who made agents of the crown appear foolish.[35] While at certain times, the detective could look directly at tell-tale clues without being able to see them for what they were, at others, they possessed perceptual powers not granted to their law-enforcing counterparts. The character offers a fitting model for the settler: Both are singularly capable of discovering the state's involvement with neocolonial crimes, while being released from complicity by virtue of their distance from the sovereign's enforcers.

Settlers and detectives were even more deeply entangled in nineteenth- and twentieth-century American dime novels, where detectives were modeled on "the character of the traditional frontier hero."[36] Whereas the prototypical "Hawkeye" character of James Fenimore Cooper's frontier romances was a "White man who knows Indians so well that he can almost pass for one," the detective was "a man who knows strikers" and "a figure whose consciousness is 'darkened' by knowledge of criminality."[37] Dime novels were also informed by Allan Pinkerton, who authored many detective dime novels to propagandize his World-Wide Detective Agency. A private security firm that predated J. Edgar Hoover's Federal Bureau of Investigation, the Pinkerton Agency was "noted for both wartime counterespionage and postwar railroad work, and the only police force able to operate on the scale of the nation."[38] Early American detectives perpetrated lynchings and other forms of racist vigilantism; they "often acted as *agents provocateurs* or instigated vigilante-style violence against the criminals they hunted and the labor organizations they sought to break."[39] A character that fostered popular identification with a clandestine agency of

---

33. Martens, "Dramatic Monologue," 209.
34. Rzepka, *Detective Fiction*, 45–48.
35. Porter, *Pursuit of Crime*, 123.
36. Slotkin, *Gunfighter Nation*, 125.
37. Slotkin, *Gunfighter Nation*, 16, 126, 139.
38. Slotkin, *Gunfighter Nation*, 137.
39. Slotkin, *Gunfighter Nation*, 140.

TABLE 6.1. Tropes of the settler-detective

REGISTERS	PAST	PRESENT	FUTURE
PSYCHOANALYTIC	symbolic	imaginary	Real
NARRATIVE	flashback	omission	foreshadowing
GENERIC	forensic	epideictic	deliberative
TROPOLOGICAL	analepsis	paralipsis	prolepsis

guns for hire, "the detective defends the progressive social order, but does so *in the style* of an outlaw, always criticizing the costs of progress and often attacking the excesses of the privileged classes."[40] Hence the detective's splitness: vigilante agents who do what the police cannot, they retain a reflexive distance from the violence they are contracted to exact.

The detectives of the twentieth and twenty-first centuries display more and less conflicted attachments to white supremacist and colonial violence. W. S. Van Dyke, a popular director of 1930s detective cinema, "began as an assistant director under his mentor [D. W.] Griffith," using his medium to filter "pseudo-scientific judgments on race."[41] In twenty-first-century detective cinema, the conventional protagonist is sometimes cast as an aboriginal or Indigenous character, who is "inside" and "outside" the settler order.[42] In Ivan Sen's Australian Westerns *Mystery Road* (2013) and *Goldstone* (2016), the protagonist is "an Aboriginal detective-cowboy" whose identity is "defined by ambivalence," divided between their role as an officer of settler laws and their responsibility to their Indigenous community.[43] Such protagonists' "direct collaboration with the settler colonial state as a police detective positions him an immediate target for Aboriginal hatred," creating a character whose contradictory roles provide them with unique insight into scenes marked indelibly as sites of settler crimes.[44]

Similar to Veracini's schema of settler consciousness, the detective genre neatly maps onto the imaginary, symbolic, and Real. However, the addition of the detective to the settler type deepens this taxonomy with additional tropological, narratological, and generic forms (see table 6.1). First, what Veracini describes as the settler's symbolic "law" corresponds with the forensic *past*, in which the detective investigates and reconstructs what did or did not

---

40. Slotkin, *Gunfighter Nation*, 154.
41. Konzett, "South Pacific," 18.
42. For other examples of the ambivalent aboriginal or Indigenous detective protagonist, see also López, *True Detective: Night Country*; and Roland, *Dark Winds*.
43. Judd, "Hero or Dupe," 117–18.
44. Judd, "Hero or Dupe," 122.

happen. The detective's symbolic order abides by rules that govern the process of retroactive discovery, belatedly allowing the focal character to re-constellate clues into a coherent story of the crime. The trope most associated with the settler-detective's retroactive plot structure is analepsis, which is commonly synonymous with the "flashback" that returns the reader to a scene where neocolonial crimes were perpetrated.

Second, whereas for the settler the imaginary assumes the form of a nostalgic pastoral fantasy, for the settler-detective it corresponds with the epideictic genre (i.e., speeches of praise and blame) and inhabits a provisional "now" that is stationed between the past and the future. For the detective, this "now" concerns how details that lie in plain sight are passed over or ignored. It also concerns the detective's mirrorlike relationship to the criminal other, a persona who must resemble the protagonist at the level of their separation or distance from the law. The trope of the imaginary is paralipsis, a disavowal whose common formula is "I know very well, but nonetheless." Traditionally a way of dismissing a topic by invoking it, paralipsis enables the settler-detective to pass over what lies in plain sight: namely, the overt clues of settler colonial violence.

Finally, the Real describes the annihilation of symbolic rules and self-other identifications. Rather than having specific features or characteristics, this register has the character of a disruption; it punctures narrative's apparent coherence by featuring a "trifling detail that is suddenly invested with immense significance."[45] As discussed below, it is aligned with the genre of deliberative rhetoric, which is often oriented to policy initiatives and speaks to the managed uncertainty that comes with deciding what should or should not be done, as well as what will or will not come to pass. The trope of this register is prolepsis, which assumes the form of an apocalyptic forecast, a premonition of doom. For the settler-detective, prolepsis anticipates the subject's inevitable demise, the reversal of their fortunes, and with it, the destruction of order as such.

Analepsis: Post-Traumatic Settler ($) Disorder

Analepsis is a detour or return to the past. Often synonymous with the flashback, it recalls past "ideas, events, or persons."[46] The trope poses such questions as the following: What happened? Where did it occur? How was it done?

---

45. D. Miller, *Novel and the Police*, 27–28.
46. Lanham, *Handlist of Rhetorical Terms*, 11.

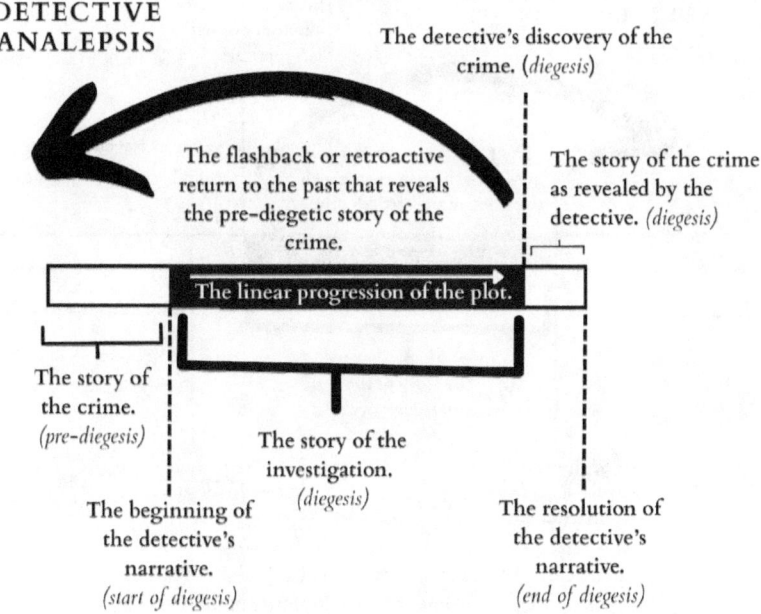

FIGURE 6.1. Detective analepsis, or the story of the crime and the story of the investigation in detective fiction.

Who was involved? Why did events transpire as they did? As a feature of detective fiction, analepsis manifests a secret in the gap between present and past. It toggles between the limited information available in the narratological now and the more complete knowledge contained in the extradiegetic past.

Scholars of detective fiction often theorize this temporal gap as a distinction between "two contiguous stories: that of the crime and that of the investigation" (see figure 6.1).[47] The story of the crime chronologically precedes the story of the investigation and is the mystery solved in the detective's concluding exposition. Situated at the narrative's beginning and end, the story of the crime is the detective's raison d'être; solving it is how they exit the narrative arc. The second story is that of the investigation, which occurs in the narratological present. It consists of the red herrings, plot twists, discoveries, and double crosses that take the reader or viewer on the detective's narrative journey. Analepsis facilitates the movement between these stories. It is the trope that facilitates the detective's anamnestic returns to the crime scene, enabling them to

---

47. Martens, "Dramatic Monologue," 201.

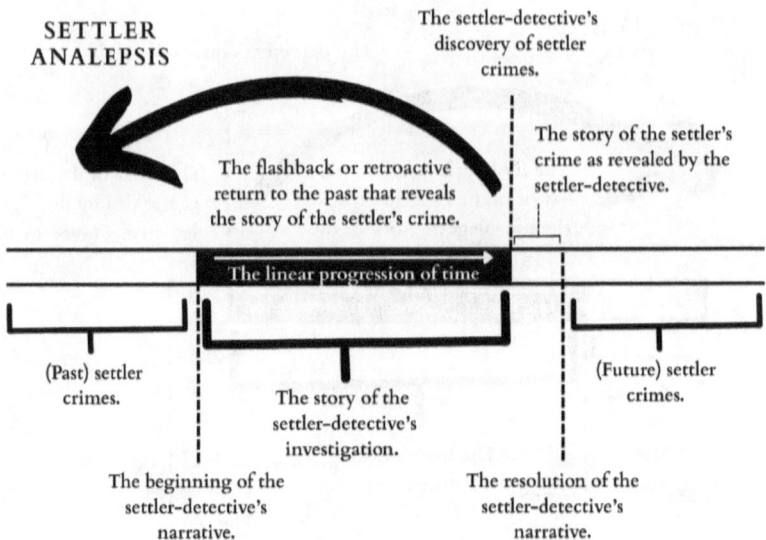

FIGURE 6.2. Settler analepsis, or the story of the crime and the story of the investigation in settler narratives.

demonstrate mastery by re-constellating disconnected past events.[48] The story ends, the crime is solved, and the detective protagonist claims their credit.

Analepsis is also an organizing logic that releases the protagonist from complicity with neocolonial atrocities. The analogy between the detective and the settler is especially apparent when it is understood that settler colonialism—the expropriation and destruction of Indigenous land, life, and culture—is understood as the story of the crime. There is one key difference: The crimes of settler colonialism are open-ended, preceding the settler's investigation and continuing after the narrative's resolution (see figure 6.2). As the story goes, the settler discovers past violence, in which they are implicated, as a secret that can be discovered, mastered, and superseded. This pattern is especially apparent in fictional renderings of neocolonial war, where settler-detective characters like therapists and drone pilots return to the scene of settler crimes to find themselves implicated in dehumanizing schemes. Their belated recognition offers them an exit from complicity, superficially purifying them as they awaken to their part in colonial violence. Such analepses comprise "a framework of excuses, distractions, and diversions," a signature form of narrative pleasure that "rigorously excludes the possibility of change, of revolution."[49]

---

48. Sargent, "Mys-Reading the Past," 289.
49. Tuck and Yang, "Decolonization," 10; and P. Brooks, *Reading for the Plot*, 70.

Finally, analepsis fosters identification with perpetrators of settler violence by centering their trauma as the secret of war, which is particularly evident in fictional narratives that invoke post-traumatic stress disorder (PTSD). Part and parcel of such narratives is an asymmetrical attention economy that prioritizes the psychological suffering of military servicepersons over that of colonized peoples subjected to military violence. Although this settler-centric narrative is often an aesthetic response to the sanitation of twenty-first-century drone warfare as "surgical strikes" and "precision targeting," the function of telling such stories is to foster identification with perpetrators of wartime violence at the expense of their targets.[50] By recovering and reliving a primal scene of PTSD, both the protagonist and the audience gain a sense of the larger settler structure and how it traumatizes settlers. In the following sections, I consider two cinematic examples, *Homecoming* and *Eye in the Sky*, both of which feature analepses that recover and replay the settler's PTSD. Although these narratives make use of analepsis in different ways, both execute the settler's moral rescue by crafting a settler-detective character retroactively awakened to their complicity with neocolonial violence.

The Forgetful Therapist

A Gimlet Media podcast (2016) adapted by Sam Esmail into a television series, *Homecoming* (2018) tells the story of a post-traumatic stress treatment facility for returning veterans.[51] The title is a double entendre: It is both the facility's name and a signifier for the analepsis that returns the listener or viewer "home," that is, to the origin of the principal character's erased memories. *Homecoming* features Heidi Bergman, a former therapist and social worker who suffers from amnesia and is unable to recall the details of her employment. After a Department of Defense investigator comes to collect Bergman's testimony, she embarks on a quest to recover her lost memories, eventually discovering her role in a military-corporate scheme to send veterans back into combat after erasing all recollection of previous wartime trauma. In the end, Bergman's plot-organizing memory gap is explained by the secret drug she once administered to make soldiers forget their psychic wounds.

Like the conventions of detective fiction, *Homecoming* tells two parallel stories. On the one hand, there is the story of the crime: the plot to erase veterans' memories and send them back into war zones where, undoubtedly, they will incur further post-traumatic stress. On the other hand, there is the

---

50. Hasian, Lawson, and McFarlane, *Rhetorical Invention*, 158.
51. Horowitz and Bloomberg, *Homecoming*; Esmail, *Homecoming*; and Ito, "Homecoming."

present-day story of the investigation, which resolves with the full exposition of how Bergman lost her memory. Narrated in fragments that toggle between past and present, the listener or viewer is made to identify with Bergman's narrative, which now has little access to the story of the crime and follows her piecemeal reconstruction of the past. Analepsis takes the form of flashbacks that gradually reveal Bergman's involvement with the psychopharmacology scheme, as well as flashbacks within flashbacks, as Bergman recalls therapy sessions in which veterans recall—with increasing difficulty—their lost companions and combat traumas.

The trope is also signaled by aesthetic choices that mark moments of temporal transition. In *Homecoming*'s podcast and televised versions, these transitions bear clear acoustical and visual markers, alerting audiences to the narrative's "back and forth" temporal movement using elements of the storytelling medium. In the original podcast version, the return to past events is signaled by tape recorder clicks, staticky cell phone conversations, and the bustle of offices and airports. These diegetic noises lend private phone calls, notes to self, and patient-doctor conversations the feel of recovered evidence, and the experience of listening the texture of eavesdropping. In the televised adaptation, flashbacks are shot in a 16:9 aspect ratio that fills the whole screen, while the present is shot in 1:1. The effect is to narrow the present-day image as if suggesting that the viewer is missing the bigger picture. Giving a form to "the spatialized configuration of time itself," *Homecoming*'s visual and acoustical storytelling media supply these signifiers to mark analepsis as organizing its plot.[52]

After many detours, analepsis finally facilitates the rescue of Bergman's own settler subjectivity in revealing the secret that she is responsible for her own forgetting. After witnessing the debilitating effects of Homecoming's drug trial, she seeks an escape for herself and one of her patients. An important aspect of this rescue concerns a countertransference that spans the entire plot, in which Bergman gradually develops a personal attachment to her patient Walter Cruz.[53] Eventually, she breaks with her employer's plan to showcase Cruz as proof of concept for Homecoming's treatment program. During a final

---

52. Stewart, *Framed Time*, 2.

53. Laplanche and Pontalis define countertransference as "the whole of the analyst's unconscious reactions to the individual analysand—especially to the analysand's [i.e., the patient's] own transference." Lacan describes transference as a resistance that arises during analysis, a projection of the analysand's existing object attachments onto the therapist, and an unconscious delay or deferral that blocks the therapeutic process. In other words, countertransference concerns the therapist's projections back upon the patient, especially once the patient has formed a resistive attachment to them. *Language of Psychoanalysis*, 92–93. See also Roudinesco, *Why Psychoanalysis*, 133; and Lacan, *Freud's Papers*, 109.

meal, in which the two discuss a fantasy cross-country road trip, Bergman serves them both food containing extra doses of the forgetting drug. The drug overdose rescues Cruz from redeployment, while Bergman is released from further collusion with her employer's dehumanizing scheme. The series ends where it began, erasing all recollections of her prior employment. Because the act of forced forgetting is the narrative climax of Bergman's many flashbacks, it offers the audience a redemptive view of the focal characters; as they forget one another, both exit the cycle of retraumatization. *Homecoming*'s analepses thus enable a redemptive view of the amnesiac settler-detective, whose deductions reveal her to have been a coconspirator within a larger settler plot.

The Disempowered Drone Operator

Analepsis is likewise essential to the plot of *Eye in the Sky* (2015), which dramatizes the vexed complicity of reluctant drone pilots with settler warfare. The film places Alia, a young Muslim girl, in the crosshairs of a US Reaper drone circling a densely populated area in Nairobi, Kenya.[54] Having unknowingly set up a vending station to sell bread in front of a house where terrorists have congregated to arm a suicide bomber, an assembly of government officials, military officers, drone pilots, and military informants dispersed across the globe watches as Alia goes about her day. In the film, every decision is subject to a ticking clock, and stress permeates every scene. The film thus places Alia at the center of a debate that balances an immediate past of gathered intelligence with a fleeting present in which that information may already be outdated. As the British attorney general notes: "If [the terrorists] kill 80 people, we win the propaganda war. If we kill one child, they do." When the first Hellfire missile is dropped, Alia is knocked thirty feet away and visibly injured. However, because one of the suspected terrorists remains alive, the drone pilots are ordered to reengage before she can make her way to safety. Just as Alia is being recovered by her parents, the drone's second strike lands. While the pilots scan the debris for human remains, Alia is carted away to a hospital with the assistance of militants, only to be pronounced deceased moments later.

Unlike *Homecoming*, which deploys analepsis as flashbacks, *Eye in the Sky* renders the return to the past as *espacement*, which captures how differences in space and temporal delays in presence provisionally lend reality structure.[55]

---

54. Hood, *Eye in the Sky*.
55. Derrida, "Différance."

A Derridean term of art, espacement captures how the ineradicable differences and deferrals that set past and present apart expose communicative immediacy (e.g., "real time" or "telepresence") as a false pretense. *Eye in the Sky* stages the contingencies of espacement vividly, with flawed collateral damage estimates (CDEs) and geospatial time delays, both of which show how decisions made with only seconds between cause and effect have unanticipated consequences. The film bears witness to such changing circumstances in the fifty sections between a missile's deployment and its detonation. When the first Hellfire missile is dropped, for instance, the government-military assemblage, helpless to change unfolding events, looks on as another small child enters the blast radius. Afterward, ranking officers order their subordinates to retroactively adjust their CDEs to indicate that the lowest possible risk of harming civilian populations was present before the strike orders were issued. The depiction captures how neither "real-time" surveillance nor calculative prediction is sufficient to resolve the contingencies of war. Satellite connections falter, spies lose cell phone contact, and strikes can only be as surgical as the delay between the issuance of a kill order and the moment of detonation. The live streamed present in which interconnected government and military institutions operate is always in Alia's past, with the most up-to-date information already unreliable by the time it is acted upon.

Despite the callousness of *Eye in the Sky*'s many military decision-makers, the analeptic return to the past also functionally rescues key members of the military assemblage—namely, drone pilots—from accountability. This film's pilots, stationed in Las Vegas, are depicted both as the ultimate arbiters of the decision to bomb and as those with the least agency to halt a kill order. After the first strike is authorized, the pilots are visibly distressed, with tears welling in their eyes. Even when it is apparent that they have seriously injured Alia, they are unable to put up resistance to the second strike, which takes her life. The film thus rescues the drone pilots from responsibility by setting them against callous superiors. It also dramatizes the unfairness of situating the trauma of having committed collateral murder with the drone pilots, who visibly carry a greater emotional burden for having caused Alia's death.

Analepsis, the return to the past, enables the rescue of settler subjects through the retrospective recovery of a trauma-instigating secret. Whereas *Homecoming* stages the stress-inducing event as the secret, *Eye in the Sky* positions the secret within the spatial-temporal gap between cause (i.e., the drone strike order) and effect (i.e., Alia's death). In both cases, sympathy for the settler is routed through post-traumatic stress induced by the characters' retroactive apprehension of past events. Even as these characters are excused from ultimate responsibility, the structures that harmed them and led them to harm others are left unchallenged and intact.

Paralipsis: The Settler ($) Double

The second trope of the settler-detective is paralipsis.[56] Traditionally a trope of disregard and omission, paralipsis often falls under the heading of *occultatio*, which is ostensibly the Ur-trope of the secret.[57] Paralipsis operates by "introducing a topic by disavowal" or by alluding to something under the pretense of not discussing it (i.e., "I'm not going to talk about X").[58] One formula for disavowal is "I know very well, but nonetheless," which enables a speaker to avow a topic that implicates them (e.g., "I know very well" that capitalist consumption contributes to climate change) before *dis*avowing this implication, dispelling it through acknowledgment (e.g., "but nonetheless" I will splurge on gifts this holiday season).[59] In detective fiction, paralipsis takes on an additional function. The detective must pass over ordinary objects that become pivotal to the story of the crime only later, observing the thing while not seeing it for what it is. For that reason, paralipsis may be considered a trope of "the realist's imbecility," in which a subject, immersed in the imaginary, can look directly at the (little-*r*) real without recognizing its significance. It enables the settler-detective to "neglect completely the 'intersubjective' or signifying space" that lends the secret its surplus value as an object attachment, or that which gives it special importance for a person or public.[60]

As a function of settler-detective narratives, paralipsis mediates the relationship between the self and specific others.[61] A vehicle for disavowal, the trope invokes a doppelgänger, or double, who resembles the settler but whose resemblance is "passed over" to establish distance from the neocolonial realities by which the latter is implicated. Michael Lechuga describes this other as the settler "antitype": a "subjective floating identifier for those deemed (or with the potential to be deemed) undesirable by the settler citizen because they pose a threat to either the settler's claim to indigeneity (Indigenous bodies that are too Native) or the settler's white supremacy (exogenous bodies that

---

56. The suffixes *-lepsis* and *-lipsis* subtly differ. Whereas "the root *-lepse* which in Greek refers to the fact of taking, ... assuming responsibility for and taking on (prolepsis: to take on something in advance; analepsis: to take on something after the event)," the suffix *-lipse* (as in ellipsis or paralipsis) refers "to the fact of leaving out, passing by without any mention." Unlike the "taking on" analepsis ("taking on" the past, such as in a flashback) and prolepsis ("taking on" of the future, such as in foreshadowing), paralipsis is a "passing over," a making someone or something absent despite their or its presence. Genette, *Narrative Discourse*, 40.

57. Lanham, *Handlist of Rhetorical Terms*, 104, 108. On *occultatio*, see also Gunn, *Modern Occult Rhetoric*; and Conley and Saas, "Bush Administration's Rhetorical War."

58. Gunn, *Political Perversion*, 73; and Mercieca, *Demagogue for President*, 87–94.

59. Žižek, *Sublime Object of Ideology*, 27–33.

60. Copjec, *Read My Desire*, 142.

61. Fink, *Lacan to the Letter*, 171.

are not white immigrants)."[62] In other words, the settler double is an antagonistic other brought forth or subdued by the settler's paraliptic utterances.

Such "fictive tale[s] of imminent threat" may be organized in two ways: Either the double's agony is imagined as a lesser, analogous version of the settler's anguish, or they are imagined as solely desiring the settler's destruction.[63] Both formulas use a strikethrough (or bar) to indicate the originating subject's erasure: In the first paraliptic mode, the colonized ~~other~~ returns as the settler, where the actual suffering endured by colonized populations is claimed as the settler's own. In the second, the ~~settler~~ returns as the colonized other, such that responsibility for neocolonial violence is projected onto those most harmed by it. In such cases, colonized others undertake tactics that deeply resemble the settler's own, but are deemed unjust, inhumane, or barbaric.

The ~~other~~ Returns as the settler

The first way that paralipsis manifests the settler double is by expropriating the suffering of colonized others from subjugated populations, making it into the unique experience of the settler (see figure 6.3). Not only does this gesture disavow the suffering of whole populations traumatized by settler violence, but it amounts to a "realist imbecility" because the settler can look directly at the other's suffering—and even suffer it themselves—but remain unable to register it as anything but their own injury.[64] Hence why the ~~other~~ is placed under erasure: expropriated, their experiences are laminated onto the settler double.

This version of paralipsis is a common feature of the asymmetrical coverage of drone pilot PTSD. Although the condition certainly affects military members *and* historically colonized populations, sympathy for the former has often overshadowed the latter. At an early stage in the twenty-first-century drone wars, the US Department of Defense speculated that drone crews experience rates of PTSD comparable to that of other combat pilots.[65] Despite prominent reporting on the dangers of PTSD among drone pilots, more recent

---

62. Lechuga, *Visions of Invasion*, 14.
63. Lechuga, *Visions of Invasion*, 22.
64. This description of paralipsis also resembles projective identifications evident throughout the COVID-19 pandemic, especially the equation of masked protestors with a "black biothreat" and claims that mask mandates and other public health measures were tantamount to "slavery." See also Watts, "Primal Scene," 4, 9, 18; and Kelly, "COVID-19 Conspiracy Rhetoric," 136–37.
65. According to *The Lancet*, "a 2013 US Department of Defense study found that drone operators are just as susceptible to mental health problems such as anxiety, depression, and PTSD, as their counterparts who pilot aircraft in conflict zones." Sachan, "Age of Drones"; Gregory, "From a View to a Kill," 198; and Wilcox, "Embodying Algorithmic War," 22.

PARALIPSIS OF THE ~~OTHER~~

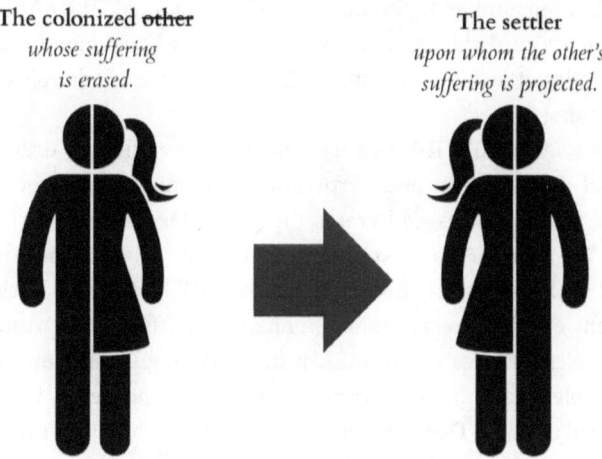

FIGURE 6.3. Paralipsis of the ~~other~~, or the appropriation and erasure of the colonized other's suffering.

studies report lower occurrences of this disorder in drone operators (1–4.3 percent) than among military personnel returning from active deployment (10–18 percent).[66] Moreover, the effects of PTSD among civilian populations subjected to drone strikes are both empirically widespread and impossible to fully document.[67] Survivor testimonials describe banal stimuli like the buzz of propellers or the sky's cerulean blue as prompting debilitating phobias, uncontrollable fear, anxiety, insomnia, loss of appetite, outbursts of anger, and suicide.[68] Drone attacks also prohibit celebration, mourning, and governance: "The targeting of community practices like *jirga*, communal prayer in mosques, mourning at funerals, and wedding celebrations spells isolation for those whose lives are already rendered precarious by drone targeting. The interruption of collective ceremonies, rituals, and kinship ties is but one of the many unseen, stultifying, and routinized effects of drone wars."[69] If, for the

---

66. For examples of popular reporting on the incidence of PTSD among drone pilots, see Sara Reardon, "I Spy"; Press, "Wounds of the Drone Warrior"; and Chappelle et al., "Analysis of Post-Traumatic Stress." Statistics drawn from Chappelle et al., "Symptoms of Psychological Distress"; and Nelson, Wilson, and Kurina, "Post-Traumatic Stress Disorder."

67. Cavallaro, Sonnenberg, and Knuckey, *Living Under Drones*, 98.

68. Hayes, *Violent Subjects*, 63–64; N. Khan, "Drone Victims"; and Beenish, "Drone Victims Testify."

69. Kapadia, "Death by Double-Tap," 209.

drone pilot, post-traumatic stress is an occupational hazard, then for those living under threat of high-tech colonization, the trauma of the drone bombing is debilitating, ambient, ubiquitous, and generational. The disproportionate representation of this stress as belonging to military members not only sidesteps reality; it fashions the drone pilot as the uncanny double of those in their crosshairs.

Senator Rand Paul's (R-KY) 2013 Senate filibuster further dramatizes the inversion of drone victim and perpetrator, imagining a hypothetical strike on US soil that displaces and erases the actual targets of American drone bombings. On March 6, just two months before the Edward Snowden disclosures, Paul spoke for nearly thirteen hours to block President Barack Obama's appointment of CIA director John Brennan. Paul's filibuster primarily concerned the secretiveness of the FISA process, calling Obama an "accuser in secret" capable of authorizing drone strikes on anyone—even US citizens.[70] Weeks earlier, a leaked Department of Justice (DOJ) white paper had revealed the executive's authorization of drone strikes on American citizens living abroad who were alleged to have terrorist affiliations.[71] Capitalizing on a burgeoning climate of state-phobic conspiracy, Paul proclaimed that the new policy infringed on citizens' right to privacy and due process:

> If there's a gentleman or woman with a grenade launcher attacking our buildings or our Capitol, we use lethal force. You don't get due process if you're involved with actively attacking us, our soldiers, or our government. You don't get due process if you're overseas in a battle shooting at our soldiers. But that's not what we're talking about. The *Wall Street Journal* reported and said that the bulk of drone attacks are signature attacks. They don't even know the name of the person. A line or a caravan is going from a place where we think there are bad people to a place we think they might commit harm, and we kill the caravan, not the person. Is that the standard that we will now use in America? Will we use a standard for killing Americans . . . that we thought you were bad, we thought you were coming from a meeting of bad people and you were in a line of traffic and so, therefore, you were fine for the killing. That is the standard we're using overseas. Is that the standard we're going to use here? I will speak today until the President responds and says no, we won't kill Americans in cafes; no, we won't kill you at home in your bed at night; no, we won't drop bombs on restaurants. Is that so hard? It's amazing that the President will not respond. I've been asking this

---

70. Little, "Rand Paul's Filibuster."
71. Department of Justice, "Lawfulness of a Lethal Operation."

question for a month. It's like pulling teeth to get the President to respond to anything. And I get no answer.⁷²

Opening with an uncanny prediction of insurrectionary violence at the US Capitol, Paul juxtaposes the possibility of domestic terrorism ("a gentleman or woman with a grenade launcher") with an admission that America's neocolonial tactics are human rights violations. Other aspects of his filibuster also adopt the other's suffering as the settler's own. Paul "knew very well" that the victims of drone war were predominantly the civilians of Muslim nations like Yemen and Pakistan. "Nonetheless," he authorized US audiences to believe they were the likeliest targets of Obama's future military interventions. Looking directly at the physical, psychic, and generational injuries inflicted by drone war, Paul found the true harm to be a conjectural violation of US citizens' rights.

One way to account for Paul's paralipsis is as *empty speech*. Superficially, empty speech is a fitting label. Not only did the filibuster fail to prevent Brennan's confirmation; after the fact, Paul admitted that his aim had been to shore up blame against Obama.⁷³ It may be tempting to apply the label of "empty speech" to any filibuster because every such speech must fill time with copious bluster. In the Lacanian tradition, however, empty speech signifies a scrupulous avoidance of reality using circular, evasive talk: "In every case, speech remains desperately 'empty'—not because it says nothing, but because its unstoppable babbling fills—and, by that same token, occults—the void of the subject."⁷⁴ Paul's filibuster fits this description because of the contradictory subject about which it speculated. Americans were both those who wield terror drones (i.e., targeting "cafes" and "restaurants" where civilians and "bad people" commingle) and those most likely to be surveilled by them. At once invoking and erasing the violence done to colonized peoples, Paul reduced these others to probabilistic abstractions, making the settler both the subject in whose name colonial violence is done and the subject most imperiled by the threat of colonization.

The ~~settler~~ Returns as the other

Paralipsis may also create a settler double by effacing the settler's role as the originator of colonial violence, projecting the charge of atrocity back upon the

---

72. Little, "Rand Paul's Filibuster."
73. Blake, "Future of GOP."
74. Borch-Jacobsen, *Lacan*, 138.

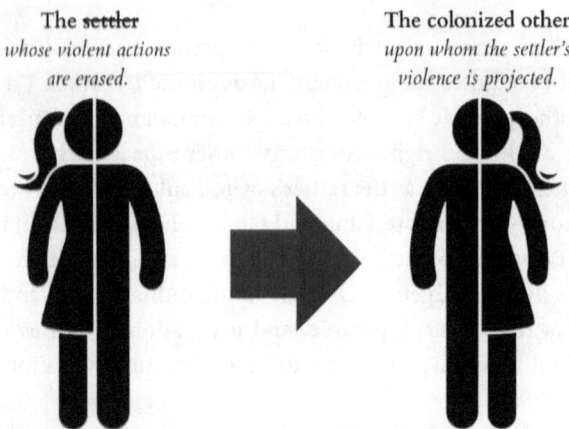

FIGURE 6.4. Paralipsis of the settler, or the projection and erasure of the settler's violence.

less-than-human other (see figure 6.4). Whereas the first version of paralipsis erases the colonized other by laying claim to their trauma, this version erases the settler's violence and rewrites it as underhanded tactics used by the colonized. The violence settlers suffer at the hands of the colonized is caricatured as barbaric, despite its resemblance to the violence they (and their forebears) justified as righteous.

In some cases, the settler's "return" is literal. Having been converted to the cause of their former enemies, such settlers are the archetype of the reprogrammed double agent who "returns" home, weaponized by the enemy. One example concerns the plot and afterlife of the television series *Homeland* (2011–20). Adapted from the two-season Israeli series *Hatufim* (2010–12, translated as *Prisoners of War* or *Abductees*), *Homeland* depicts Sgt. Nicholas Brody's return to the United States following a prolonged detention and prisoner exchange. *Homeland* centers Brody's possible sympathies with al-Qaeda, gradually revealing his secret conversion to Islam and his recruitment as a suicide bomber. In 2014, when Army Sergeant Bowe Bergdahl was released from the Taliban, CNN anchor Don Lemon compared Bergdahl's release to Brody's during an interview with *Hatufim* creator Gideon Raff.[75] Subsequent

---

75. Andone, Yan, and Valencia, "Bergdahl Gets Dishonorable Discharge"; and Coscarelli, "Comparing Bowe Bergdahl."

reporting was critical of the analogy, explaining that Bergdahl suffered from schizotypal personality disorder and had been tortured and attempted escape over a dozen times during his five years of captivity.[76] Nonetheless, the traitor motif lingered, with US President Donald Trump even encouraging Bergdahl's execution.[77] In fiction and reality, the returning settler was presumed to have become a weapon on behalf of their former enemies.

The second variation on paralipsis not only depicts the settler's return as the dangerous other. It also projects settler violence onto the other such that the latter's barbaric tactics are disarticulated from a larger context of neocolonial intelligence war. A further example of this kind of "return" concerns Central Intelligence Agency (CIA) whistleblower John Kiriakou, who became famous between 2010 and 2014 following the publication of the *Senate Intelligence Committee Report on Torture*.[78] Kiriakou was the only CIA official convicted of a crime and served approximately two years in prison for disclosing a covert operative's name to a reporter.[79] His autobiography, *The Reluctant Spy*, sought to rescue his reputation as a morally principled career officer. In it, Kiriakou explains that although "a case officer's success abroad depends upon his or her talent for recruiting agents," some assets are simply unreliable intelligence sources, making the forceful extraction of information through methods such as torture wasteful and unproductive.[80] According to Kiriakou, many of those detained during CIA raids had been unwittingly drawn into "a devil's mix of Muslim victimization, radical Islam, [and] false promises"; they were poor, desperate, and had no useful knowledge.[81] The signifier of "reluctance" marks Kiriakou's disavowal, as if he himself had only become a spy under duress. He "knew very well" what the nation was doing, but "nonetheless" he continued to celebrate the CIA's intelligence-gathering tactics, even after being punished for leaking.

Contemptuous and callously utilitarian, Kiriakou's "articulation of danger" concerning the Muslim other deserves further scrutiny.[82] His accusation that al-Qaeda makes "false promises" to recruits reads as an indirect admission of how he was the victim of the George W. Bush administration's authorization of waterboarding and the "false promises" it had made about the tactic's efficacy.[83] Moreover, his argument that the enemy had "effectively

---

76. A. Rosenberg, "Bowe Bergdahl's Return"; and Bayles, "Bowe Bergdahl."
77. Oppel, "Trump's Statements."
78. Feinstein and the Senate Select Committee on Intelligence, *Report on Torture*.
79. Coll, "Spy Who Said Too Much"; and Jouvenal, "Kiriakou Is Sentenced."
80. Kiriakou, *Reluctant Spy*, 45–46.
81. Kiriakou, *Reluctant Spy*, 144.
82. D. Campbell, *Writing Security*, 13.
83. Kiriakou, *Reluctant Spy*, 132–40, 146.

brainwashed" its foot soldiers marks a stark contrast to his earlier celebration of CIA recruitment. To "wage war against this irregular army of lunatics" was a losing battle; "the larger challenge is to win hearts and minds—to win an epic conflict fought on moral and political battlefields."[84] Kiriakou thus elevated the torture-prone, foreign-national-recruiting American agent as the moral counterpart to the degenerate terrorist. Not only did *The Reluctant Spy* invoke and avoid the continuity between the tactics that the CIA and al-Qaeda used to gather supplicants; his "very gesture of saying little [emphasized] what [he] omitted": namely, the resemblance between the cruelty of the nation he had betrayed and that of the destitute others he wished to convert to the American way of life.[85]

Prolepsis: The Settler ($) Cyberweapon

The final trope associated with the settler subject's secret is prolepsis, a gesture of oracular anticipation, narrative futurity, and fatal consequences. As a narrative trope, it is synonymous with foreshadowing, "a mark of narrative impatience" that leaps ahead to a future point in the plot.[86] In detective fiction, prolepses promise and defer the revelation of a secret, making rebus-like prophecies that allude to the mystery's unthinkable resolution. Set in the future tense of the "not yet, but soon," prolepsis assures us that the symbolic rules that lend the present its orderliness will be dissolved by some devastating eventuality. Cyberweapons are a case in point, unsettling the neat opposition between present and future by operating unnoticed, that is, until too late.

In psychoanalytic terms, the destitution of order is often aligned with "the incursion of the Real," a disruption that undermines the sense that language, narrative, and reality have a unified structure.[87] Although it is unrepresentable as such, the Real is often marked by the appearance of a discordant signifier akin to a distortion or stain that does not fit.[88] This "strange, traumatic element" is jarringly out of joint with the greater scene in which it is set.[89] A person experiencing a heart attack may begin to slur; a psychotic break may be

---

84. Kiriakou, *Reluctant Spy*, 144.
85. Rowland, *Zoetropes*, 152.
86. Genette, *Narrative Discourse*, 72.
87. This characterization of the Real's relation to the Symbolic corresponds with two psychoanalytic terms of art developed by Christian O. Lundberg: *failed unicity* and *feigned unicity*. Lundberg, *Lacan in Public*, 3; italics added. See also Matheson, *Desiring the Bomb*, 85.
88. Adams, *Emptiness of the Image*, 92.
89. Žižek, *Sublime Object of Ideology*, 147.

marked by a sudden string of disjointed speech. In narrative, the Real breaks through when strict boundaries are broken, reversed, or undone. Something that belongs inside the body could suddenly appear on its outside, what was presumed outside the image or external to the narrative diegesis suddenly "returns . . . giving rise to the fantasy of the spectral apparition that comes to occupy the place of the 'unrepresentable X.'"[90] The Real is an encounter with the cyber-Other whose lawlike force is suddenly, retroactively felt. Foregrounding a kernel of language or data that cannot be easily absorbed by fantasy, it forecasts the dissolution of stable equilibrium.[91]

The symptom of the cyberweapon is always a discordant signifier. For those affected by it, it manifests through a telltale distortion or malfunction that indicates having been there, threatening to unravel the orderly functioning of technology and society. Among its users, the cyberweapon invites "a technocratic fantasy of mastery in which we might transcend or dominate the other."[92] However, cyberweapons not only promise to colonize a digital frontier; they anticipate the demise of those who deploy them. Cyberweapons (i.e., software exploits or spyware) do not only trouble the distinction between the nation's secure interior and a menace beyond its borders. The proleptic anticipation of future cyberattacks troubles the distinction between present and future to justify continued armament.[93]

Stuxnet and Sandworm

Two cyberweapons, Stuxnet and Sandworm, offer vivid examples of signifiers that fundamentally disrupted the given order of things. Stuxnet was a 2010 cyberweapon unleashed upon a uranium enrichment facility in Natanz, Iran, to sabotage the nation's nuclear program. Its assigned name is "an alias Microsoft conjured from letters in the name of one of the driver files (mrxnet.sys) and another part of the code."[94] Its other, CIA-granted name from the early 2000s is "Olympic Games" (or "OG," which colloquially signifies "original gangster"), which both evokes the multinational scope of its spread and its

---

90. Adams, *Emptiness of the Image*, 141–59; and Broadfoot, "Anamorphosis as Colonial Encounter," 280.
91. Adams, *Emptiness of the Image*, 142.
92. Jutel, "Horror of Communication," 55.
93. Prolepsis bears a passing resemblance to justifications for preemptive war made by the W. Bush administration, most prominently, Condoleezza Rice's warning that "we don't want the smoking gun to be a mushroom cloud." Zarefsky, "Making the Case for War," 289; and Jamieson, "Justifying the War in Iraq," 262.
94. Zetter, *Countdown to Zero Day*, 14.

status as the "original" cyberweapon of the digital age. Stuxnet was developed for the singular purpose of sabotaging Siemens programmable logic controllers (PLCs) modulating the spin of uranium centrifuges. The virus caused the centrifuges to spin out of control, leading to the destruction of equipment and nuclear fissile material. By the time of its discovery by Belarusian and American antivirus firms, the virus had infected over sixty thousand computers worldwide.[95] This spread was by design. Stuxnet was meant to lay dormant, continuously affecting different connected systems until it found its sole intended target.

"Sandworm," refers to a 2015–16 virus of suspected Russian origin deployed against critical NATO and Ukrainian infrastructure.[96] Like Stuxnet, Sandworm was a name assigned to the virus by those credited with its discovery, drawn from a tag bearing the filename "arrakis02." "Arrakis" stands out as the setting of Frank Herbert's *Dune*, a famous science fiction novel that features wormlike megafauna worshipped as gods by the planet's indigenous inhabitants. However, as literary critic David Higgins explains, *Dune* is also a "reverse colonization" narrative, a genre that "imaginatively situates elite male heroes as psychically colonized victims" who "must break free from such inner limits to achieve heroic freedom and agency."[97] The name "Sandworm" thus tells us less about the computer virus than about cybersecurity experts who claimed heroic agency for themselves, at once discovering a sublime, deathly, digital creature and proving their own technological mastery.

Popular US news coverage and documentary films about Stuxnet amplified the "cyber-noir" framing of the virus's discovery, foregrounding the virus's "liminality, transgression, and tantalizing opacity."[98] For one thing, the function of Stuxnet's densely written code could not be easily deduced. At a key moment in Alex Gibney's Stuxnet documentary, *Zero Days* (2016), Control Systems Security Consultant Ralph Langner describes how he gathered clues about Stuxnet from photographs of Iranian Prime Minister Mahmoud Ahmadinejad touring the Natanz facility, matching a visual layout of 164 centrifuges clustered in six groups to a similar pattern in the attack code: "It was absolutely clear that this piece of code was attacking an array of six different groups of, let's just say, thingies, physical objects, and in those six groups,

---

95. PLCs are a category of "small computers, generally the size of a toaster, that are used in factories around the world to control things like robot arms and conveyor belts on assembly lines." Zetter, *Countdown to Zero Day*, 17; and Farwell and Rohozinski, "Stuxnet," 23.

96. Greenberg, *Sandworm*, 17.

97. Higgins, *Reverse Colonization*, 33.

98. Gibney, *Zero Days*; and Shires, "Cyber-Noir," 82. See also Wight, "60 Minutes of News-Noir."

there were 164 elements."[99] Read at the level of its code, Stuxnet was a signifier without a signified, detached from its initially intended purpose. The specific threat it posed could only be ascertained by drawing conjectural correlations between the code's form and real-world intelligence data.

Stuxnet instead left its mark through distortions and malfunctions, leaving a damage path that retroactively indicated the virus had done its work. Iran initially blamed the facility's equipment failures on its own scientists, leading to the assassinations of Majid Shahriari and Fereydoon Abbasi in 2010.[100] The Stuxnet code entered unnoticed and disrupted the facility's secure containment; only later was it realized that something from the outside had made its way in. In *Zero Days*, Symantec engineers Eric Chien and Liam O'Murchu describe how, after acquiring a Stuxnet-vulnerable PLC, they connected the device to an air pump with specific instructions to inflate a balloon, to demonstrate the virus's intended function. Without the virus, the pump would inflate for five seconds before shutting off. However, once Stuxnet was introduced, the pump would continue running, leading the balloon to overinflate and pop. Overlaying slow-motion video of balloons popping over footage of a nuclear denotation, the documentary offered an exaggerated analogy for what would happen to an infected centrifuge.[101] The earliest sign of the virus's presence was a hole in the plot, something that could not just be explained as accident or human error: PLCs that would not stop running, centrifuges that spun themselves to death, and mysterious murders that defied easy explanation.

Symantec's experts also discovered Western nations and their allies as Stuxnet's originators, that the call was coming from inside the house. In demonstrating that the code the US cybersecurity community had labeled a high-level threat had originated from their own nation's security apparatus, Symantec's engineers made Stuxnet into a signifier that had to be reassimilated into melodramatic good-evil dynamics of the existing geopolitical order. According to former CIA Director and Air Force General Michael V. Hayden, the Stuxnet program began in the Plame-Wilson years, after the George W. Bush administration failed to recover evidence of weapons of mass destruction in Iraq and military incursions abroad were becoming unpalatable to American voters.[102] Stuxnet was the preferable option: It did not require boots on the ground, eschewed attribution, and offered plausible deniability. *Zero Days* dramatizes this anonymity by compiling numerous interviews with former National Security Agency whistleblowers into a shadowy, computer-generated

---

99. Gibney, *Zero Days*, at 39 min., 55 sec.
100. Zetter, *Countdown to Zero Day*, 241.
101. Gibney, *Zero Days*, at 42 min., 50 sec.
102. Gibney, *Zero Days*, at 34 min., 12 sec.

composite who speaks through a vocal synthesizer, defying identification. The composite is an echo of Stuxnet, a computerized distortion that effects a perspectival shift concerning the existing geopolitical order:

> In the event the Israelis did attack Iran, we assumed we would be drawn into the conflict. We built in attacks on Iran's command-and-control system so the Iranians couldn't talk to each other in a fight. We infiltrated their IADs [integrated air defenses], military air defense systems, so they couldn't shoot down our planes if we flew over. We also went after their civilian support systems, power grids, transportation, communications, financial systems. We were inside waiting, watching, ready to disrupt, degrade, and destroy those systems with cyberattacks.[103]

In retrospect, the effort to shut down Natanz is widely regarded to have been a coordinated effort by the United States and Israel, which pursued the development of cyberweapons as an alternative to conventional air strikes. However, as the composite whistleblower suggests, the size and scale of cyberwar could have been—and could still be—much, much larger. Stuxnet's discovery could have spurred "potential escalatory responses" from Iran, who might have been compelled to use similar weapons against American targets.[104]

Stuxnet and Sandworm fueled other anticipatory coverage about the likely "damage and disruption" all-out cyberwar would entail.[105] Sandworm was a proof of concept: It disrupted American and Ukrainian public infrastructure—hospitals, power grids, commercial logistics, and pharmaceutical manufacturers—within the span of days.[106] However, appeals to an apocalyptic future in which the next attack would be worse, bigger, and more devastating effectively justified continued cyberweapon proliferation. Paraphrasing former Obama Administration cybersecurity coordinator J. Michael Daniel, *Sandworm* author Andy Greenberg explains: "The United States might not *want* wartime cyberattacks against critical infrastructure to be considered off-limits . . . it wants the freedom to carry out those attacks itself."[107] The statement hearkens to a classical understanding of prolepsis: "an argumentative and inventional device of anticipation" that seeks to persuade by foreseeing

---

103. Gibney, *Zero Days*, at 1 hr., 45 min., 45 sec.
104. Farwell and Rohozinski, "Stuxnet," 35.
105. Jamieson, *Cyberwar*, 8.
106. Greenberg, *Sandworm*, xi.
107. Greenberg, *Sandworm*, 287.

objections, contingencies, and risks.[108] It also evokes a contradiction in which Americans are at once subject to the threat of cyberwar and on its front lines, keeping the existing order of US cybersecurity alive and intact while reminding the reader that it is likely to be destroyed. At that level, Greenberg's ventriloquy is an effort to represent the Real in advance of its realization: to gain a sense of the size and scope of the unthinkable but inevitable future. As Calum Matheson explains:

> If the Real is the contingent eruption of nonhuman reality into a Symbolic order, then it is not deep structure with a set of laws that determine society—or, if indeed it does have a set of laws, they cannot be determined by us. The Real is what is inaccessible. It does impact our world, but it does so through distortion and disruption, not determination.[109]

It would be easy to mistake the prediction that the existing order is doomed for the Real itself. This would amount to taking Daniel at his word that he knows the end is nigh, hence the need for cyberarmament. However, Matheson's warning is that even the most well-informed preemptory effort to name and tame the Real prior to its incursion is destined to fall short of the thing itself. Having been unleashed, the only thing that is certain is that cyberweapons will return with vengeance. Per Daniel: "It will be one of those issues that will come back up. It *will* happen again."[110]

Artificial Intelligence and the Settler Future

In the waning days of 2023, two auspicious events coincided. The first was the October 30 release of President Joseph R. Biden's "Executive Order (EO) on the Safe, Secure, and Trustworthy Development and Use of Artificial Intelligence (AI)."[111] Highlighting the "promise and peril" of artificial intelligence, the EO referenced the technology's potential to amplify existing cybersecurity threats more than thirty times. The EO also instructed the directors of Homeland Security and the Cybersecurity and Infrastructure Security Agency (CISA) to assess risks, "including ways in which deploying AI may make

---

108. Besel, "Prolepsis," 238. As Besel also notes, "using prolepsis is not always a positive feature of discourse" because it "has the potential to harm the interest of the rhetors doing the anticipating." Besel, "Prolepsis," 239, 246.
109. Matheson, *Desiring the Bomb*, 52.
110. Greenberg, *Sandworm*, 289.
111. Biden, "Executive Order."

critical infrastructure systems more vulnerable to critical failures, physical attacks, and cyberattacks." The second event was the Netflix holiday release of *Leave the World Behind* (2023), a duck-and-cover film for the cyberwar era based on the book by Rumaan Alam.[112] Directed by *Homecoming*'s Sam Esmail and produced by Barack and Michelle Obama, the film depicts a white family's retreat from New York to a Hamptons countryside rental property at the very moment that a devastating cyberattack is unleashed on the United States. As the cyberattack intensifies, the rental's Black owners return home to seek shelter, only to be greeted by their renters' racist doubts about their ownership. The effects of the cyberattack are mystifying and widespread: animal migration patterns are disrupted, autonomous vehicles pile up on roads, once-friendly neighbors become ruthless survivalists, threatening leaflets written in Arabic fall from crop-dusting airplanes. At the film's conclusion, all the characters, having made temporary peace with one another, look on as plumes of smoke rise over New York City, an implicit reference to the attack on the World Trade Center on September 11, 2001.

Both texts are linked by a singular prolepsis: the imminent threat of cyberwar. Both also seek to anticipate the Real by offering inventories of what might happen *next*, should a cyberweapon be deployed against the United States. Hence the incursion of the Real: both the endpoint of the settler's current symbolic order and the start of its subsequent iteration.[113] Of course, the Real *cannot* be represented or realistically anticipated; it is a force that interrupts and reconfigures, bringing forth new settler fantasies once the current regime of resource extraction requires new resources, new territory, new colonies. Prolepsis situates the Real as both the destruction of what is and the promise of a new, inexhaustible frontier where iconoclastic destruction may recommence; it is "a future point of possibility that might retroactively justify a decision that is never guaranteed to be correct."[114] Cyberweapons like Stuxnet and Sandworm are reminders of this future frontier, forecasting the dissolution of a stable social reality while also promising the reconstitution of those categories at some moment that has yet to come.

The Un-Settling Look

The settler-detective's open secret is that the neocolonial project continues because it facilitates public audiences' enjoyment vis-à-vis the secret *in*

---

112. Esmail, *Leave the World Behind*; and Alam, *Leave the World Behind*.
113. Veracini, "Settler Collective."
114. L. Pierce, *Tense Times*, 53.

discourse: awakening, disavowal, and fear of a futural threat. My aim has been to demonstrate how we may recognize such rhetorics as they are conscripted into this subjectivity. Even the foregoing tropological analysis invites this criticism; I remain implicated as a detective of settler-detective narratives. This recursion, in which the critic of settler-detective narratives discovers themselves as a settler-detective, attests to this chapter's secret *of* discourse, a formal slippage that traverses the boundary between narrative and reality, immersing the critic in the context where they would otherwise function as a detached narrator. Even so, I would contend that naming the settler-detective as such is a first step toward breaking complacency and disavowal.

Although analepsis, paralipsis, and prolepsis correspond with a narrative past, present, and future, these tropes are not organized as a neat progression but rather as coordinates that may be experienced simultaneously or in isolation. They triangulate the settler's self as caught between a past that must be reconstructed, a present in which they are oblivious to the confessional character of their own discourse, and a future in which the secret's pursuit will be tantamount to keeping the apocalypse at bay. This sprawling, disjointed plot never brings true resolution. Instead, it defers a full accounting of the settler's crimes to the next installment of the franchise, deferring the Real by announcing the symbolic order's destruction.

I would conclude with an alternative narrative of looking: not a look that does not see but one that is always watching, introspecting, reminding us of our obligation. My hope is that we can see in its example a view that does not, at minimum, belong to an unpiloted aerial vehicle, a cyberweapon, or a settler subject. The epigraph that leads this chapter, by Solmaz Sharif, is from a poetry book titled *Look*. In Turkish, "look" may be written as *nazar*. Architectural historian Mohammed Hamdouni Alami explains that the term *nazar* is one of two ancient (CE 809–77) Arabic terms for "the look." The noun *al-baṣar*, "the sense of vision," refers to the "lucid spirit" that is reflected in the eye of the other or in the mirror. By comparison, *al-nazar* is translated as "gaze" and refers to being caught in the other's look. Unlike *al-baṣar*, *al-nazar* describes how, to see themselves as they are seen by the other, "the viewer must stand bravely and unmovable," creating a dynamic that "implies power and human will."[115]

In Turkish, the object depicted in figure 6.5 is often called the *nazar bonçuk* or *göz boncuğu*. It is a frequent adornment in Muslim homes but also across the secular Western world. I recall seeing the amulet frequently as a child. My Turkish mother described it as an "evil eye" protector, an amulet or charm that warded off those who would have bad intentions toward us. While

---

115. Hamdouni Alami, *Art and Architecture*, 223.

FIGURE 6.5. The *nazar bonçuk*.

nazar, or "gaze," is the cause of passionate love, the nazar bonçuk is meant to turn away people possessed by an envious, jealous, or evil spirit.[116] Deeply rooted in the Islamic tradition, belief in the evil eye is an absolute truth. The Qur'an references "the unbelievers who are bent on denying the truth, would all but kill you with their eyes," as well as "the mischief of the envious one as he practices envy."[117] The amulet reminds the viewer that appreciation for anyone or anything must begin with the acknowledgment and praise of Allah. It is so rooted in the Islamic faith that the gaze is understood as a fundamental mode of self-censorship. When someone cares deeply about an object or person (e.g., a home or a newborn child), they place the evil eye protector upon it.

The nazar bonçuk introduces elements of power and will, in other words, by representing the eye and symbolizing a dynamic of watching and being

---

116. R. Khan, *Self and Secrecy in Early Islam*, 80, 166; and Yun, "Evil Eye," 45–46.
117. Qur'an 68:51, 113:1–5.

watched. Of course, for the nazar bonçuk to have a felicitous effect, everyone must be "in" on what it means. It relies on the visual affirmation of those who have encountered the symbol, triangulating the relationship between the one who is watched (e.g., the guest) and the one for whom the eye watches (e.g., the host). For those protected by the charm, the eye is vigilant; for instance, it watches so that one may be a gracious host without having to wish for eyes in the back of their head. For the one whose gaze is deflected, the charm is ideally a reminder that the space they inhabit is not their own.

Once you have been seen by the nazar, you can neither be un-seen, nor can you un-see it. Hence its final, allegorical function: to foreground the constitutive function of a symbol that pushes back against the orientalist tendency to characterize Islamic art and culture primarily in terms of a lack of representation. Hence the injunction to un-settle the settler's self-centering perspective. Inviting the nazar into the home resists, for instance, the reduction of Islamic aesthetics to the prohibition on representing the Prophet Mohammad or wearing revealing clothing.[118] Such iconoclastic framing "hark[s] back to a bygone age, reinforcing the widespread [though incorrect] notion that Islamic culture is implacably hostile to anthropomorphic art."[119] To bear witness to the nazar bonçuk is a reminder of how the prima facie opposition between the Islamic world and that of the West may be undermined, to see the look as originating from not just the settler but the settler as one who is always gazed upon as well.

Like the testimony of Zubair, Nabila, and Rafique ur Rehman described at this chapter's outset, the nazar presents a look that is meant to unsettle and recalibrate the settler's taken-for-granted point of view. Both teach us that it matters where we locate the secret, whether it is presumed hidden in the settler's subjective interior or continues to unfold in plain sight. As a function of the subjectively split settler-detective, the inward gaze looks often like narcissistic self-discovery, projective disavowal, and an obsession with one's own inevitable destruction. As a function of the nazar bonçuk, the gaze is always fearlessly communicating the injunction "to delegitimate intellectualizations of what diasporic experiences should look like" by "'muddling' the borders at which racial hierarchies are drawn."[120] Put otherwise, the secret is not always waiting to be found in the search for hidden clues, buried details, or inner motives. It can also be a matter of inviting the look, standing bravely in the knowledge that we are always in the other's home.

---

118. Rashid, "Buddhas Fall"; and Buffenstein, "Monumental Loss."
119. Flood, "Between Cult and Culture," 641.
120. Aswad, "Marked Body," 243–44.

CHAPTER 7

Twisted Endings

The Secret in and of the Deep State

> I have a taste for the secret, it clearly has to do with not-belonging; I have an impulse of fear or terror in the face of a political space, for example, a public space that makes no room for the secret. For me, the demand that everything be paraded in the public square and that there be no internal forum is a glaring sign of the totalitarianization of democracy. I can rephrase this in terms of political ethics: if a right to the secret is not maintained, we are in a totalitarian space.
> —Jacques Derrida, "I Have a Taste for the Secret" (59)

Spoiler Alert!

In 2004 the television series *Lost* made the secret a central premise of its post-9/11 multicultural allegory. Opening just after an airplane crash on a tropical island, nothing is known: the disaster's cause, the other passengers' identities, the island's creaturely dangers. The survivors have limited knowledge of one another, creating a dense web of interconnected vignettes that viewers disentangled via multiepisode characterological flashbacks. Characters tended to remain alive only as long as their personal secrets remained hidden, creating literal "dead ends" throughout the show's six seasons. *Lost* referred not just to the character's literal situation but also to the show's intended effect: immersion in a bewildering, labyrinthine plot. *National Treasure* (2004) and *The Da Vinci Code* (2006) featured similar motifs, taking viewers on scavenger hunts for relics and clues absurdly inscribed on highly recognizable historical artifacts like the Declaration of Independence and the Mona Lisa. Deferred gratification was again the point: The solution to each puzzle points to another puzzle to be deciphered, taking viewers on a protracted and counterfactual historical tour of the United States and Western Europe. The *denouement* is always a more or less satisfying "reveal": a hidden cache of revolutionary war (i.e., "national") treasure, the identity of Jesus Christ's last living descendant. Like *Lost,* getting to the secret ends the narrative; once everything is out in the open, no story remains to be told. Reading for the secret is akin to becoming aware of a recurring pattern. Like a spoiler that skips ahead to the end, knowing how the secret is positioned in one of these stories furnishes a faculty of observing how they may be positioned across others.

Certainly, public audiences in the United States are routinely conditioned to expect that they lack the whole story. One salient feature of the January 6 hearings in June and July of 2022 was that the viewing public didn't know everything that had transpired behind the scenes of the 2021 insurrection at the Capitol—even though many had seen the event on live television, in real time. Admittedly, our strategies for reading the secret often look more like intuition than mathematics, a feeling rather than a formula. The secret's many emplotments cultivate the sense that the reader or viewer is participating in a process of epistemic discovery, often by identifying with a protagonist who is also out of the know. To be worthy of sustained collective attention, the secret must be partly visible but also just beyond access. The slow, steady accretion of information is like the drip, drip, drip of information leaks, prolonging our sense of approaching the hidden object. Once fully revealed, however, the story ends. Ordinary and exceptional, the secret is formative of a pervasive narrative eschatology in which it is expected that eventually, all that is hidden will be revealed.

Sovereign, Settler, Leaker, Lie argues that the secret is not just negated knowledge or concealed information. It is also a host of recurring rhetorical patterns, each one an affirmative production of absence that proliferates under different names: *scandal, detective, leak,* and *dog whistle*. Rhetorically, the secret is a renewable site of fascination and desire, capturing a dynamic that balances the negative work of the secret (i.e., hiddenness, concealment, and paranoia) with its affirmative gestures (i.e., discursive production, voluminous transparency, and viral spread) to create a spectacle that ceaselessly captures public attention. Toggling between deep contextual meanings and surface-level retroactive forms, this conclusion articulates two principles that mirror the distinction between the secret *in* and *of* discourse: (1) *there is always a "beyond" to the secret,* and (2) *the secret is there is no secret*.

The Secret's Two Principles

Two short axioms elaborate on the forms that the secret may take. The first, that *there is always a beyond to the secret,* reformulates the secret *in* discourse as a search in which attainment is endlessly deferred. This secret may be retrieved from the forgotten archive or reconstructed by attending to an understudied context. Even when we find it, however, there is always the possibility of another archive or context "beyond" the one we know, and thus also of another secret "beyond" the one we possess. The second axiom, *the secret is there is no secret*, rephrases the secret *of* discourse. This formula tells us that revelation is a discursive anamorphosis, an assemblage of already-known elements that accrues significance with the benefit of hindsight. Together, these mark the secret's rhetoric as both active (or deliberately concealed) and retroactive (or unconsciously overlooked). After briefly dwelling on each axiom, I discuss them as variations on "the deep state," a polyvalent twenty-first-century conspiracy theory.

There is always a "beyond" to the secret means that no secret ever happens in isolation from a subtending context. It also means there is always *another* subtending context that could reinvest the secret with new significance. The "beyond" enables criticism to resemble the logic of the conspiracy theorist, if only minimally: One archival document leads to another; the discovery of new evidence undermines, contradicts, and re-forms its existing assemblages. As a speculative backdrop to dominant public narratives, the secret's 'beyond' is hypothetical, futural, in scare quotes. In the words of Peter Knight, conspiracy creates "a perpetually deferred revelation" and undermines the "overt promise of uncovering What Is Really Going On."[1] Even when it does not descend into the abyssal oblivion of the conspiracy, the persistent availability of a deepened context is the condition of possibility for generating criticism as a revision (or redaction, in its oldest sense) of previous criticism, for instance, by allowing forgotten documents or testimony presumed erased to reshape a given hegemonic narrative. It gestures to something more than what the secret reveals, marking any revelation with the potential of becoming a future instance of concealment.

The secret is there is no secret is an indictment of hiddenness as the sole way of locating or understanding the secret. At its most trenchant, this principle is a critique of the spectacle whose purpose in directing attention to the hidden is to overwhelm, to create paranoia and distraction. What is speculated to hide behind, beyond, or below diverts from the overt: what is on the surface, in the open, in plain sight. Looking for hidden depths can be compulsive, leaving the brutality of the present unexamined for reasons that are unconscious, defensive, pathological, and libidinal. Like the secret *of* discourse, this principle frames concealment as a momentary pretense in which the secret gains force and meaning through a perspectival shift, a ceaseless retroactivity

---

1. Knight, "Outrageous Conspiracy Theories," 190.

TABLE 7.1. The secret's two principles

THE SECRET …	*IN* DISCOURSE (… ALWAYS HAS A BEYOND).	*OF* DISCOURSE (… IS THAT THERE IS NO SECRET).
… is real or actual.	e.g., the "signs and tokens" of the Masonic society	e.g., the plot twist or the information leak
… is a spectacle.	e.g., Elon Musk's "Roman salute"	e.g., conspiracy theories (e.g., QAnon)

whereby the secret is always sliding away from what it once meant. Whereas the principle of the "beyond" seeks deep context to discover what is hidden, to say that there is no secret hollows out the experience of revelation as a regress without resolution.

I do not advocate for privileging one of these principles over the other. Nor are they simple opposites. The indefinite, prepositional tension between the *in* and the *of* lends each a provisional coherence, stabilized by its difference from and mutual dependency upon its other (see table 7.1). Practically, this means that both the secret *in* discourse and the secret *of* discourse are *real*; neither has a lesser material existence than the other. The secret *in* discourse drives every scholarly archival expedition; it subsists in the reality of nuclear codes and classified military intelligence. It also continues to forge intracommunal bonds between others who are *in* on the secret with us, akin to those symbolized by the "signs and tokens" of the Prince Hall Lodge and other Masonic societies.[2] As indicated in earlier chapters, however, we can fully acknowledge the existence of real, hidden secrets that lurk in the beyond of public knowledge while also affirming that there are real secrets that are no secret at all. As the latter, the revelation of the secret can always amount to a "big nothing," seeming to have been known, just un-enunciated, under-reported, under-sighted. The secret may erupt as a shocking plot twist or leak, a kernel whose incorporation into the everyday threatens to reconfigure our total perception of history or a singular event. When the secret is that there is no secret, the concatenation of what a signifier means *now* with what it has always meant can be jarring or just a shrug. Neither makes the secret *of*

---

2. One recent example hearkens back to the Masons' "signs and tokens" while also attesting to the continuing relevance of the secret *in* discourse: Immediately following Superbowl LIX in February 2025, Pulitzer Prize– and Grammy Award–winning artist Kendrick Lamar's hit song "Not Like Us" was quickly re-catapulted to global top-100 lists. At least part of this popularity may be attributed to his successful mobilizations of the secret *in* discourse: As he had done in his 2024 album, *GNX*, his Super Bowl halftime show delivered a layered and coded performance replete with "easter eggs" that included double entendres and choreography that not only evoked his ongoing feud with fellow artist Drake but also "symbolized the state of America today following the election of President Trump, who was in the audience." Mier, Spanos, and Gee, "Easter Eggs."

discourse less *real*—it simply assumes the syntax of the "always has been," appearing to arrive belatedly for the subject for whom it comes as a surprise.[3]

Conversely, this also means that the secret *in* and *of* discourse can be a hallucinatory, compensatory spectacle that offers believing subjects a false sense of control or mastery in the face of its felt absence. This is the secret at its most pejorative, dangerous, and spectacular: Searching for a hidden "beyond" can function as a diversion from what happens in the open, missing the forest because one is searching for a particular tree. To draw on an example presented earlier in this book, the search for the secret significance of Elon Musk's "Roman salute" during Donald Trump's second inauguration was functionally a distraction from what others noted was a naked gesture of fascistic intent.

The secret *of* discourse can likewise be a mirage-like lure. In August 2024, *Wired* magazine published a piece on the increasing popularity of astrology as a political forecasting tool.[4] In 2020 TikTok astrologer Laurie Rivers accurately anticipated Kamala Harris's late-campaign substitution for Joe Biden on the 2024 Democratic presidential ticket. After her prediction came true, she unequivocally predicted Trump's loss that November. Following Trump's 2024 electoral victory, mediums, psychics, and spiritualists belonging to the #4amclub—a hashtag shared widely among those who claimed to have woken up in the early hours of November 6 with a sense of dread that quickly dissipated into a peaceful calm—began to promulgate the conspiracy theory that Kamala Harris had won the election.[5] Citing the hidden subtext of Democrats' postelection speeches, star charts, voting discrepancies, and a plot to arrest the incoming president before his inauguration, these influencers claimed that astrologers' earlier predictions were still correct: they just had not come true *yet*.[6] Rivers revised her predictions in light of information she claimed to have missed. However, the conspiracy theories that emerged after November 6 recalled other "deep state" conspiracy theories—most famously, QAnon—insofar as both claimed that evidence contravening official election results was out in the open if only the public just knew where to look. To call these related instances of the hallucinatory secret *of* discourse does not mean that they are

---

3. The "always has been" bears a passing resemblance to "the syntax of the 'had been,'" which "is integral for producing discourses of crisis that lay claim to the status of a trauma" (L. Pierce, *Tense Times*, 46). Although we might also witness the secret *of* discourse's "always had been" in such rhetorical and narrative forms as *peripeteia*, the red herring, and the plot twist, this retroactive form is clearly associated with the popularization of the viral "Always Has Been" meme beginning in 2016. See "Wait, It's All Ohio?"

4. Elliott, "Written in the Stars."

5. Valko, "Dead of Night."

6. Romano, "Trump 2.0."

equally damaging or violent.[7] Rather, it means that they unfolded according to a resemblant logic. By striking an epistemic bargain with reality, both sought to impose sensible order on a situation that had, for their adherents, gone unbearably wrong.

Consistent with its etymological namesake, the secret is always differentiating and dividing, sifting and separating. It dwells with the insistent difference that sets the secret *in* discourse apart from the secret *of* discourse. At some level, such fissures are the secret: a repeating but not identical difference that makes a difference, both active and retroactive. The secret *in* discourse encourages reading "beyond" the text for its hidden context. Deeply concealed, it is only available to insiders with the proper know-how. When it is *of* discourse, the secret makes the hidden legible in hindsight as never having been truly hidden at all. As the latter, we cannot *unsee* the secret; instead, we comb through familiar texts with the sense that we should have noticed what was always there, so obviously, all along. Variations on a similar theme, the secret is animated by a play of coherence and contradiction that holds together the scandal, the dog whistle, the leak, the detective—and, finally, the deep state conspiracy—as similar-but-not-the-same rhetorical partitions of the known from the unknown.

The Deep State

Like the foci of other conspiracy theories that gained prominence during Donald Trump's first administration, the deep state was a fabricated explanation of secret happenings. Deployed as a discursive weapon against adversaries, this theory treated the fact of disclosure as incontrovertible evidence and enabled the president's repeat performances of self-aggrandizing expertise.[8] Jennifer Mercieca describes conspiracy theories as "self-sealing," to account for their fluid revisionism: "holes in the story are quickly covered up," "conflicting evidence is explained away," "nonexistent confirmatory evidence is . . . suppressed," and "those who attempt to discredit . . . are stooges or conspirators."[9] Jenny Rice similarly defines the conspiracy theory as an amoebic leviathan that is always assimilating and rejecting new data: "when contrary evidence

---

7. In addition to spurring the January 6, 2021, insurrection at the US Capitol, QAnon has resulted in "dozens of bills that nod to election denialism . . . across at least twenty-five states." S. Thompson, "A.I., QAnon, and Falsehoods"; and Joffe-Block, "QAnon Hasn't Gone Away."

8. Hartelius and Gellar, "Secrecy and Pseudoscience."

9. Mercieca, *Demagogue for President*, 168. See also Sunstein and Vermeule, "Conspiracy Theories."

is offered to conspiracy theorists, that contrary evidence is often discarded as a lie or is absorbed into the larger structure of the overall theory."[10] A simple, though perhaps unsatisfying, distinction between theoretical and actual conspiracy is that the latter places conspiracy within the law's ambit. Subject to specific statutes and tests, legal definitions of conspiracy organize a theory's speculative connections into a static network whose many nodes are subject to prosecution.[11] However, conspiracy theories tend to fall outside of standards like "imminent lawless action" because their effects are often deferred and distributed, while their incitements to violence are cloaked in appeals to mere transparency.[12]

The phrase "the deep state" illustrates a confluence of the two principles described in the preceding sections. On the one hand, the deep state has the character of a secret *in* discourse, a signifier with a clear contextual "beyond." It derives from a phrase of Turkish origin (*derin devlet*) that circulated throughout the twentieth century and was regularly invoked by Prime Minister Tayyip Erdoğan in the twenty-first. In the Turkish popular imaginary, it described "a presumed clandestine network of military officers and their civilian allies who, for decades, suppressed and sometimes murdered dissidents, Communists, reporters, Islamists, Christian missionaries, and members of minority groups—anyone thought to pose a threat to the secular order, established in 1923 by Mustafa Kemal, or Atatürk."[13]

On the other hand, the deep state is a secret *of* discourse because there is often no "beyond" to it, no *there* there. The phrase's signifying mutations illustrate the absence of a true or deep meaning for this signifier, defying the control of the agents with whom it is most associated. In 2014, the phrase migrated into the American lexicon with John le Carré's international spy novel *A Delicate Truth*.[14] It was picked up by US Congress aide Mike Lofgren in an editorial published on Bill Moyers's blog and subsequently in the title

---

10. Rice, *Awful Archives*, 92.

11. A widely recognizable federal statute concerning conspiracy is the Racketeer Influenced and Corrupt Organizations Act (RICO). 18 U.S.C. §§ 1961–1968 (1970).

12. In *Brandenburg v. Ohio*, Brandenburg, a leader in the Ku Klux Klan, was convicted under an Ohio law that made "crime, sabotage, violence, or unlawful methods of terrorism as a means of accomplishing industrial or political reform" illegal. Brandenburg was protected by the First Amendment because, despite his organization's open history of racist violence, his statements were, according to the majority opinion, neither "directed at inciting or producing imminent lawless action" nor "likely to incite or produce such action." Brandenberg v. Ohio, 395 US 444, 447 (1969).

13. Filkins, "Deep State."

14. Le Carré, *Delicate Truth*.

of Lofgren's book, both of which sought to capitalize on the post-Snowden antisurveillance frenzy.[15]

> Yes, there is another government concealed behind the one that is visible at either end of Pennsylvania Avenue, a hybrid entity of public and private institutions ruling the country according to consistent patterns in season and out, connected to, but only intermittently controlled by, the visible state whose leaders we choose. My analysis of this phenomenon is *not* an exposé of a secret, conspiratorial cabal; the state within a state is hiding mostly in plain sight, and its operators mainly act in the light of day. Nor can this other government be accurately termed an "establishment." All complex societies have an establishment, a social network committed to its own enrichment and perpetuation. In terms of its scope, financial resources and sheer global reach, the American hybrid state, the Deep State, is in a class by itself. That said, it is neither omniscient nor invincible. The institution is not so much sinister (although it has highly sinister aspects) as it is relentlessly well entrenched. Far from being invincible, its failures, such as those in Iraq, Afghanistan and Libya, are routine enough that it is only the Deep State's protectiveness towards its higher-ranking personnel that allows them to escape the consequences of their frequent ineptitude.[16]

Lofgren pointed to a political ground that was being claimed in 2014, when the Snowden revelations were still fresh and WikiLeaks was still a recurring punchline on *Saturday Night Live*. More insidiously, Lofgren's use of this phrase signaled a refiguration of the political space formerly occupied by Ellsbergian appeals to transparency. Contrary to his expressed intentions, uptake of the phrase "deep state" veered toward the conspiratorial connotations he decried (i.e., not "a secret, conspiratorial cabal"), aligning with conservative claims that heteronormative, cisgender masculinity was on the wane. That was the deep state that rose to prominence with ten congressional hearings concerning Hillary Clinton's mishandling of the Benghazi scandal as US Secretary of State, Clinton's emergence as the 2016 Democratic presidential nominee, and finally, Donald J. Trump's ascendency to the US presidency.[17] Throughout Trump's first presidential term, the pretense of a deep state animated QAnon,

---

15. Lofgren, "Anatomy of the Deep State"; and Lofgren, *Deep State*.
16. Lofgren, "Anatomy of the Deep State."
17. Halper, "Republicans Release Benghazi Report"; Herszenhorn, "House Benghazi Report"; and House of Representatives, *Final Report of the Select Committee*.

a conspiracy theory group whose adherents believed the executive in chief was secretly telegraphing forthcoming events using cryptic digital clues.

Trump's deployments of "the deep state" are well documented and prolific. The phrase has referred to residual Obama-era bureaucrats in the executive branch, legislative enemies on the right and the left who opposed Trump, a judiciary that sought to punish him for his documented criminality, a disingenuous "fake news" media industry intent on his downfall, and a complex of migrant, immigrant, transgender, and racially othered populations who represented the excesses of "big government." It has been a master signifier for "a heady cocktail of mistrust not only toward immigrants and leftists but also toward what was then his own government and mainstream (or as he calls it, 'lamestream') media," a fantasy in which Trump was in the driver's seat as hidden others were trying to steer things behind the scenes.[18] As a signifier for this conspiracy, the *deep state* legitimated Trump's narrative of unfair treatment and victimage even as he portrayed himself as a strongman immune to criticism and prosecution. The phrase distanced Trump the sitting executive from the catastrophes of Trump the administration, allowing him to slough blame off to those who sought to mitigate the clear and present dangers he posed.

From Lofgren to Trump, the futile effort to bridle and control the political significance of "the deep state" uniquely illustrates how "there is no secret":

1. **There is no secret** because there is no way to fix the deep, referential meaning of "the deep state" as the stable sign for a specific kind of government overreach. Lofgren's effort to install such a reference betrays a misunderstanding of signification as such and the impotence of the effort to control this signifier. Even as he refused the deep state's resonance with authoritarian conspiracy theories, he anticipated the availability (if not the inevitability) of this catachrestic misnaming.
2. **There is no secret** because the conspiracy theories that were, following Lofgren, soon to operate under the heading of "the deep state" were concentrated around an absent center, an inexhaustible secret that sustained the Trump administration's conspiratorial machinations.[19] Like so many other conspiracy theories, "the deep state" relies upon a metonymic accumulation of evidence in which parts never *truly* add up to a whole, but continuously aggregate. This aggregation is both an aesthetic performance of archival magnitude and a symptom of the conspiracy-desiring subject's desire for mastery, accumulating ever more data as if

---

18. Beckman, *Paranoid Chronotope*, 170.
19. Gunn, "Death by Publicity."

asymptotically approaching a monopoly on the truth.[20] As a desirous expression, the conspiracy theorist's claim to have mastered this archival aggregate not only betrays their aspiration to know what they cannot; it is also symptomatic of their failure to identify with the big-O Other, that ultimate authority on the secret.

3. **There is no secret** because transparency, the rhetoric of revelation formerly synonymous with the *Pentagon Papers* and its downstream effects, is increasingly weaponized against the political left, who had once laid claim to it. There was no fixed, firm, or deep meaning to transparency that aligned it with the goals of the American political left. Even Lofgren's Republican claim to "the deep state" demonstrates the nascent realization of this partisan reversal that occurred out in the open and in plain view between 1971 and 2014. Clare Birchall describes this as the "the secret of the Left": the potential for appropriation whereby the strategies of disclosure and transparency "can always be infiltrated by the Right; its secrets are so dispersed as subjective singularities that they become permeable."[21] It is precisely because "no one governs this secret of the Left, this commons of the secret" that makes it susceptible to continuous appropriation. To say that there is no secret means that the deep state reterritorialized transparency—the ground where revelation had a potent political power—on behalf of far-right iconoclasts.

Of course, transparency-forward efforts on the left have neither ended, nor have they been fully displaced. The *Senate Intelligence Committee Report on Torture*; the Me Too and #MeToo movement; committees convened to investigate Donald Trump's Ukraine phone call and his involvement in the planning of the January 6, 2021, insurrection; and the Panama, Paradise, and Pandora Papers all continued a legislative, juridical, and journalistic quest for greater accountability. And yet, many Trump-era efforts to eradicate the deep state remain in the register of seeking to "investigate the investigators" by seeking to purify the former executive of his collusion with Russian foreign agents, rewrite his public incitements of violence, all the while capitalizing on voters captured by all-consuming racial paranoia.[22] Even those who aim to critique and control the deep state's meaning—a specific "beyond" of ideologies, institutions, and histories—perform the necessity of the secret in their efforts to undermine that system.

---

20. Rice, "Rhetorical Aesthetics."
21. Birchall, "Transparency, Interrupted," 77. See also Birchall, *Radical Secrecy,* 147–74.
22. See, for instance, Fandos and Benner, "Suspicions, Demands, and Threats"; and Lafond, "Jim Jordan."

Two concluding anecdotes drawn from the Trump era may further complicate this understanding of the deep state by illustrating the limits of its potential as a political strategy. The first concerns a related conspiracy theory: The Epstein files, which allegedly document the deeds of—and accomplices to—extortionist, child rapist, and human trafficker Jeffrey Epstein. More than Trump's other scandals, it has often seemed as though this secret *in* and *of* discourse has escaped his administration's control. In the first place, the scandalous secret allegedly contained by these files is no secret; much about Trump's connections to Epstein is well documented and widely known. As Sarah Kendzior elaborates in her 2022 book, *They Knew*, Epstein was hardly the first example of "an enigmatic, wealthy, and well-connected man" who "[rose] to prominence advising political and media elites," and who, "as their criminal connections were revealed," were lent a softened image by media outlets despite the open knowledge of their vicious deeds.[23] Indeed, Kendzior should be credited with predicting the popular resurgence of Epstein-Trump theories long before they came to a head:

> At this sick, sad point in our national history, Jeffrey Epstein may be the only thing holding Americans together. That our unity rests on shared loathing of a billionaire pedophile and his network of wealthy accomplices is an indictment of the United States itself. But it is a rare affirmation that Americans do, still, inhabit a shared political reality, even if we do not fully understand its loathsome nature.[24]

When this passage was written, it was no secret that Trump had repeatedly accompanied Epstein on his private plane.[25] Nor was Trump and Epstein's long friendship a secret.[26] Nor was Trump's propensity for sexual violence.[27] As

---

23. Kendzior, *They Knew*, 56. The Epstein antecedent Kendzior references is former Republican and foreign operative Craig Spence, who had similar connections to high-level politicians (e.g., Richard Nixon, Ronald Reagan, and Oliver North), "facilitated the abduction of minors for sexual perversion," coordinated high-level extortion schemes, and died under suspicious circumstances. Kendzior, *They Knew*, 48.

24. Kendzior, *They Knew*, 61.

25. Weider and Brown, "Maxwell Case Logs."

26. Feuer and Goldstein, "Inside the Long Friendship." One incendiary piece of evidence concerned a personal message allegedly written by Trump for Epstein's fiftieth birthday:

> The Journal described the drawing as the outline of a naked woman with Mr. Trump's signature below her waist, suggesting pubic hair. It quoted an imagined conversation between Mr. Trump and Mr. Epstein that concluded with Mr. Trump saying: "May every day be another wonderful secret." (Enrich et al., "Trump's Name")

27. Kelly, *Caught on Tape*, 110.

much has also been made apparent by Trump's predatory behavior at Elite's "Look of the Year" competition, his conviction for defamation and battery, and the leaked *Access Hollywood* tape in which he describes himself committing assault.[28] There is also a clear "beyond" to the Epstein files, that is, a secret *in* discourse brought forth by missing links in the available record. When Epstein died in 2019, the mysterious circumstances surrounding his alleged suicide were ripe for conspiracy theorizing. The footage released from New York Metropolitan Correctional Center was incomplete and showed signs of editing, despite Trump's then–Attorney General William Barr having validated it as evidence.[29] This missing video has invited significant ruminations over the possible archives that Trump's own deep state has hidden, forgotten, or destroyed.[30]

At the time of this writing, many audiences in the United States are focused on the most recent installment of the Epstein-Trump scandal. Amid widely popular and bipartisan demands to release the Epstein files in 2025, allegations of Trump's participation in Epstein's schemes echo conspiracies about Democrat pedophiles and sex traffickers that Trump's QAnon-adherent base stoked, retroactively lending the president's past support for QAnon a confessional tenor.[31] One effect of this scandal has been to produce the secret as a caesura: a complex constellation of missing links. For instance, in February 2025, Attorney General Pam Bondi confirmed the existence of an Epstein client list and Trump's appearance within it.[32] Months later, she denied the existence of *any* such list.[33] Bondi's Justice Department subsequently set meetings between Justice Department officials and Ghislane Maxwell, Epstein's convicted criminal partner, ostensibly seeking her cooperation with the Trump administration.[34] Such reversals and missing links only intensified the demands that the missing files be revealed.[35] As the Epstein-Trump scandal has reached a fever pitch, the Trump administration also released other classified files concerning John F. Kennedy and Martin Luther King.[36] As Kendzior explains, it is easy to feel as though the conspiracy is everywhere:

---

28. Osborne, Davies, and Kirchgaessner, "Teen Models, Powerful Men"; Sullivan et al., "Jury Finds Trump Liable"; and L. Nelson, "'Grab 'Em by the Pussy.'"
29. Balsamo, "AG Barr"; and Barr, *One Damn Thing After Another*.
30. Mehrotra, "FBI's Jeffrey Epstein Prison Video."
31. Sorkin, "Age of Donald Trump and Pizzagate." See also Rice, *Awful Archives*, 153–72.
32. Betts, "Jeffrey Epstein"; and Haberman and Thrush, "Attorney General Alerted Trump."
33. Lucas, "Attorney General Bondi."
34. Merlan, "How Does the Epstein Scandal End?"
35. Igielnik and Browning, "Republicans Are Breaking with Trump"; Wade, "Poll Shows Widespread Disapproval"; and Pilkington, "JD Vance's Attempt."
36. Merlan, "JFK Assassination Files"; Bailey, "Here's What We Know."

> Conspiracies are woven into the landscape of American life. They are how Americans reckon with hypocrisy and betrayal, how they feel around the edges of subjects they are not supposed to touch, how they navigate the twilight zone between principles and practice. Conspiracies structure American politics, but they are not called conspiracies when they are wrapped in the flag or stamped with bureaucracy or printed piecemeal in the papers. They are called plans or policies or "just the way things are." When the agendas of elite actors get pushed underground and you have to dig for them—that is when those agendas are called conspiracies, and facts are called theories, and you are called insane for noticing.[37]

When it comes to the conspiracy theory surrounding the Epstein files, the secret's two principles ring true. First, there is a clear "beyond" to this secret. Despite the mass public's inability to know precisely *what* the files contain, the files presumably include not only a client list but telltale evidence of wealthy elites' widespread participation in Epstein's trafficking scheme. Second, there is also no secret to the Epstein-Trump scandal: Epstein's deeds and many of his clients were widely publicized before his arrest via official testimonials, grand jury reports, and journalistic coverage. Trump's sexual assaults have been well known since before his first presidential term, and their disclosure did not prevent him from winning a second. As the secret *of* discourse, this also means that we cannot know whether the Epstein files will have been a turning point for Trump's devoted following of "deep state" conspiracy theorists until well after the fact.[38]

The second anecdote concerns Anonymous, the 2018 author of a *New York Times* editorial claiming to represent the "resistance inside the Trump administration."[39] After the editorial's publication, any number of deep readings emerged, seeking to pair Anonymous's use of key phrases (e.g., "lodestar") with recurring motifs from other cabinet members' speeches (i.e., Vice President Mike Pence).[40] Although Anonymous later self-identified as Department of Homeland Security Chief of Staff Miles Taylor, his editorial and subsequent book also lent credence to Trump's suspicions of a deep-state conspiracy against him. In the end, there was no secret; Taylor's brief stint as Anonymous only shallowly reinforced the sense that the secret was a last line of defense against executive overreach.[41]

---

37. Kendzior, *They Knew*, 203.
38. McCreesh, "Will the Conspiracists."
39. Anonymous, "I Am Part of the Resistance."
40. Azari, "Linguistic Analysis."
41. Shear, "Miles Taylor"; and Anonymous, *Warning*.

As Taylor's conspicuously enciphered "Anonymous" letter illustrates, depersonalized writing certainly can conceal hidden meanings *in* discourse, even if they are only red herrings used to throw one's targets off the scent. However, as Derrida explains, *all* writing may function as a secret *in* and *of* discourse because it "must be capable of functioning in the radical absence of every empirically determined receiver in general."[42] This is especially true of the *parrhēsiastēs*, the prototypical political truth-teller for whom "frankness puts [their own life] at risk."[43] As much is well illustrated by Tom Englehardt's post-Snowden "Letter to an Unknown Whistleblower," which applauds the heroism of a hypothetical leaker, a futurally distant *parrhēsiastēs*. Published two years before Lofgren's *Deep State*, Englehardt's letter offers a related formulation of the secret as government misdeeds that must be brought into the light. In accord with Derrida's writings on the secret, the letter addresses an anonymous, absent receiver who is called on to reveal dangerous truths on behalf of audiences that are unable to understand their sacrifice:

> Those running the government and many who write about you in the mainstream will revile you. You will be denounced as a traitor, a defector, a criminal, and your acts called treasonous, even if you're one of the last hopes of the American republic. Right now, those like you are sure to be prosecuted, jailed, or chased implacably across the planet. But this won't last forever. Someday, your country will recognize what you did—first of all for yourself, for your own sense of what's decent and right in this world, and then for us—as the acts of an upright and even heroic American.[44]

Since Englehardt's letter, many whistleblowers have suffered dire consequences for their leaks. Some were themselves adherents to the Trumpian deep-state conspiracy, others openly avowed their resistance to Trumpism as another name for an encroaching totalitarianism. What makes Englehardt's absent receiver so recognizable is not their specific political alliances but their doubled prepositionality: They exist *in* the institution whose secrets they disclose, but they are not *of* it.[45] This bifurcation between the *in* and the *of* explains Derrida's self-professed "taste for the secret." Double-edged, the secret guarantees

---

42. Derrida, "Signature, Event, Context," 8.
43. Greene, Horvath, and Browning, "Truth-Telling," 37. See also Foucault, *Fearless Speech*.
44. Englehardt, *Shadow Government*, 160–61.
45. The phrase "in but not of" is indebted to Stefano Harney and Fred Moten, who use it to describe the relationship of the fugitive undercommons to the American university: "To be in but not of—this is the path of the subversive intellectual in the modern university." Harney and Moten, *Undercommons*, 26.

both the fascist's ability to exercise violence *and* the democratic refusal of the fascist's "demand that everything be paraded in the public square."⁴⁶ This latter sense of the secret exists within and apart from the authoritarian's surveillant eye; it must be ceaselessly maintained to stave off "the totalitarianization of democracy." The anti-totalitarian secret is also what lends the addressee of Englehardt's letter a lasting familiarity. Even if we are prohibited from knowing who they are, their secret is no secret: We have seen them before, and we must expect to see them again.

A Twisted Ending

In 2024 I presented an early version of this book's argument. During one question and answer session, an audience member who had displayed enthusiastic nonverbals throughout asked why I had chosen to dismiss QAnon—a controversial and dangerous disinformation campaign—as "mere" conspiracy theorizing. Secrets like that one, I explained, are dangerous because they draw vulnerable users in by design. Hosted on fringe websites established out of a refusal to censor grotesque racist and pornographic content, QAnon uniquely gamified the secret in order to mobilize its users toward support of Donald Trump and the insurrection at the US Capitol on January 6, 2021.⁴⁷ Using "drops" of enciphered information and geocached clues, its orchestrators released puzzle after puzzle that toggled between real-world locations and virtual message boards, keeping users invested in the vain promise that some final truth would be revealed. Filling in premeditated gaps and deciphering preplanned clues, these conspiracy theorists were recruited to play a free, at-home mystery box, one that validated their sense of mastery and stoked racist resentments. With each drop linked to another and another and another, QAnon provided its adherents with the sense that they had been granted access to a highly classified point of view. Kept in near-indefinite suspense, they willingly stood in reserve until the opportune moment, when solving the final clue would authorize them to commit political violence.

QAnon is an appropriate endpoint because of how it synthesizes so many of the rhetorical-tropological forms discussed in this book: It repeated missing links, offered up metonymic free associations, created catachrestic-cryptographic rebuses, and adopted an escalating pattern akin to megethos, in which the *next* drop promised to be the biggest yet. As Karlyn Kohrs Campbell

---

46. Derrida, "I Have a Taste," 59.
47. Bortnick, "Play and Misinformation," 11.

and Kathleen Hall Jamieson argue, such rhetorical forms are *material* because they promise to bridge the perceptual with the objectively real:

> It should be apparent that these forms [i.e., repetition, refutation, crescendo, enactment, and enthymeme] are phenomena—syntheses of material that exists objectively in the rhetorical act and of perceptions in the mind of the critic, a member of the audience, or a future rhetor. The phenomenal character of forms is reflected in Kenneth Burke's reference to the "psychology of forms" and in his remark that "form is the creation of an appetite in the mind of the auditor, and the adequate satisfying of that appetite." That forms are phenomena has persuasive and critical significance because, as a result, forms can induce participation by others. This is never more evident than in the quintessentially rhetorical form, the enthymeme, whose force is explained by the fact that auditors participate in the construction of the arguments by which they are persuaded.[48]

Much like the enthymeme's missing premise, QAnon invited its users to fill in gaps and "do their own research"—even if the secret was always purposefully crafted in advance.[49] Rather than perceiving QAnon as a fragile spectacle to muddle reality and mobilize members of a growing far-right fringe toward iconoclastic violence, my listener's investment in the secret maintained QAnon to be reflective of an unalterable material reality, pointing to logical gaps that were not speculative but real. They had taken my description of the conspiracy theory's form as validation of their beliefs. In other words, they felt seen by the fact that someone else had, like them, witnessed this all-too-familiar secret.

Of course, I hope this book will have had more salubrious effects than reinforcing damaging, insurrection-spurring conspiracy theories. I wish to make the risk of becoming entrapped by the secret more intuitive—as if to say, *we have all been here before.* Akin to recognizing the patterns of the con artist, the scammer, and the bot, once we catch on to the form, we *should* be able to hang up or click out before things go too far again. These "forms" are, at a general level, those of the secret *in* and *of* discourse and, at a more granular level, the tropes of the sovereign, scandal, leaker, and lie. In his 1988 essay "Secrecy and Disclosure as Rhetorical Forms," Edwin Black argued that the public rhetoric of hiddenness and openness aligns with two distinct US publics. One is disposed to the revealing of secrets, the other to the necessity of expansive secret-keeping in the name of securing the polity:

---

48. K. Campbell and Jamieson, "Form and Genre," 402.
49. See, for instance, Hoback, *Q: Into the Storm.*

We are able finally to identify two distinct publics, each clustered about its own defining commonplaces concerning secrecy and disclosure. One public, convinced that concealment is bad, is disposed to embrace an associative plexus of values and to accede to arguments that are warranted by those values. The values include: disclosure, openness, sharing, being equal, being unacquisitive. And the other public, convinced that some knowledge can be dangerous, is disposed with equal commitment toward a plexus of values that includes: privacy, private property, hierarchy, capital accumulation, individuality. These groups differ in their politics, in their sexual attitudes, in their views of science and of art, probably even in what they eat and drink and wear on their backs. But those differences are unstable, and some of them are superficial. At a deeper, less mutable level, these publics are distinct from one another in the rhetorical forms to which they respond.[50]

The context and backdrop for Black's essay, the secret *in* discourse that we may read between its lines, concerns the aftershocks of the Iran-Contra Affair and the recalibration of the public interest with respect to newly politicized attitudes toward government secrets. The secret *of* discourse exceeds the boundaries of his argument; it is a rhetoric that has fragmented, dispersed and transformed into new, perilous possibilities for public identification. In that regard, Black was incorrect about what is immutable about the secret. Forms do not easily map onto publics; as active and retroactive modes of organizing discourse, they are dangerously open-ended. That is why scandals become useful resources for those they scandalize, dog whistles obliterate context and history to send openly hateful messages, leakers can be forcefit into state-imposed categories of binary sexuality, and the settler-detective who acknowledges their complicity with imperialism can assume the shape of a fashionable protagonist. It is, finally, how the "right to know" can transform into an injunction to believe in the conspiracy theory.

What is the secret? It is a lasting gap in meaning, a construct and a constant. Both *in* and *of* discourse, it is animated by a desire to find what is hidden, as well as the retroactive realization that nothing is hidden and everything is already out in the open. This bifurcation, *in* and *of,* belies the sense that any secret worth finding must be deeply hidden and therefore requires substantial intentional effort *and* that the experience of discovery is something that happens to a subject when signifiers whose significance was imagined as fixed become unmoored, sliding from stability. They are two registers of reading that furnish the sense that the secret, no matter how novel or exigent, is one

---

50. Black, "Secrecy and Disclosure," 149.

component of a familiar experience. Opposed, these prepositional forms can lend the secret a contradictory status, somewhere between a dangerous form of fearmongering used to recruit the perpetrators of political violence and a way of processing reality that throws the taken-for-granted into new relief. To modify an old Freudian formula, "where the secret was, there the truth shall be."[51] This final principle means that the secret is a rhetorical condition of possibility for figuring truth. Correspondingly, truth is a contingent and rhetorical effect of the secret's tropological configurations. Hopefully, knowing the secret's forms enables us to figure how our own rhetoric can shape what comes next.

---

51. The phrase is "Wo Es war, soll Ich werden," which may be alternately translated as "Where It was, there I shall be," and "Where Id was, there Ego shall be." By substituting "Id" with "secret" and "Ego" with (little-*t*) "truth," I mean to indicate the dependency of the latter on rhetoric as an organizing force that is often characterized as structureless, formless, and unknowable. Freud, "Dissection," 100; and Lacan, "Freudian Thing," 347.

ACKNOWLEDGMENTS

The behind-the-scenes action of this book is immeasurable. This project began during my time at the University of Georgia, where I benefited from the support and mentorship of Thomas R. Dunn, Thomas Lessl, Edward Panetta, Belinda Stillion-Southard, and Bjørn Stillion-Southard. I owe much to Michelle Ballif, Celeste M. Condit, and Roger Stahl, who inspired me with their theoretical prowess, interdisciplinarity, and errant love of hidden things. Barbara A. Biesecker taught me to read for form, to slow down my internal monologue, and to be responsible to the text. I hope readers benefit from these inherited lessons. Finally, I owe everything to my chosen family from UGA. Kristen Anderson, Isabel Fay, Megan Fitzmaurice, Dustin Greenwalt, Jeremy Grossman, Brittany Leach, Mikaela Malsin, Jason Myres, Lee Pierce, Eric Sloss, Sally Spalding, Leland Spencer, John Turner, Emily Winderman, and Jason Williamson taught me what a loving and supportive intellectual community can look like.

The earliest drafts took shape at North Carolina State University, where many conversations with Victoria Gallagher and Kenneth Zagacki provided material support and a sounding board for ideas. I am also grateful for the friendships I developed in Raleigh, with special thanks to Grant Bollmer, Jesse Crane-Seeber, Jean Goodwin, Katherine Guiness, Ryan Hurley, Caroline Ingraham, Chris Ingraham, Bill Kinsella, Kami Kosenko, Nicole Lee, Carolyn Miller, Elizabeth Nelson, Lynsey Romo, Sarah Stein, Nick Taylor, and Steve Wiley.

Sovereign, Settler, Leaker, Lie gained its current form at the University of Minnesota, Twin Cities. I have benefited significantly from the wisdom, mentorship, and advice of my rhetoric-area colleagues in Communication Studies: Ron Greene, Zornitsa Keremidchieva, Michael Lechuga, Rachel Presley, and Emily Winderman. These folks have been the source of countless recommendations and conversations; I am sure they will all see their mark here. I also owe much to my other communication studies colleagues, including Catherine Squires, whose questions to me during an on-campus interview reshaped the chapter on Saul Alinsky and Chicago's Woodlawn neighborhood. I have gotten similar support from conversations with Laurie Ouellette, Mary Vavrus, and Elaine Hsieh. I honed my prose in writing groups with Wendy K. Z. Anderson and Daniel Emery, while Alya Ansari, Susanne Jones, Kate Lockwood-Harris, and Jason McGrath lent me space in their classrooms to present early versions of this research and to test my ideas. Similarly, Coby Oertel, Katerina Korola, and Joshua Trey Barnett provided opportunities for me to think through the contemporary relevance of the project and to present book-adjacent work to interdisciplinary audiences. The brilliant Maggie Hennefeld, Jennifer Row, Palita Chunsaengchan, and Shir Alon have prompted me to think deeply about the project as it came to a conclusion, provided cover image advice, and pointed me in the direction of valuable university resources. I am supremely grateful for the support of my writing studies colleagues Lee-Ann Kastman Breuch, Daniel Card, Molly Kessler, Amy Lee, John Logie, Thomas Reynolds, and Liane Malinowski. They have shared a wealth of ideas, advice, and experience. Finally, so much more than this book would not have been possible without the endless help, compassion, and patience of the administrative staff members of Communication Studies: Sasha Bordeaux, Tucker Marks, Jada Pulley, Jo-Ellyn Pilarski, Carmen Sims, Hannah Trumm, and Mark Usem.

This project was supported by incredible gifts of time and resources. The Donald V. Hawkins Endowment, conferred by the Department of Communication Studies, afforded me significant resources to complete this work, including the ability to conduct research travel. A spring 2024 fellowship with the Institute for Advanced Studies at the University of Minnesota provided me with the necessary time to complete writing and revision on two chapters. More importantly, it enabled me to share a vibrant intellectual community with Lusine Bichakhchyan, Juliet Burba, Skyler Dorr, Isaac Esposto, David Gore, Zornitsa Keremidchieva, Carolina Maranon-Cobos, Laurie Moberg, Matthew Rahaim, Joanne Richardson, Treasure Tinsley, Abby Travis, and Kathryn Van Wert. I am deeply grateful to Bianet Castellanos and Susannah Smith for fostering connections and facilitating future collaborations. I also thank David La Spina of ESTO, which keeps the Ezra Stoller photographic archive, for his assistance and generosity in securing the cover image for this book.

Directly and indirectly, *Sovereign, Settler, Leaker, Lie* benefited from the hard work of undergraduate researchers and graduate scholars at the University of Minnesota. My first-ever graduate seminar, with Mark Brenden, Katlynne Davis, Stuart Deets, Austin Fleming, Brandi Fuglsby, William Heinze, Jacqueline James, Brittany Knutson, Eduardo Nevarez, Joshua Morrison, Natalie Warren, Ryan Wold, and Jessa Wood, awakened me to the potential of such spaces for working through ideas and testing new approaches. My doctoral advisees, Bill Heinze, Kristen Einertson, and Saumya Malhotra, have been endless sources of inspiration; it has been a joy to work with them and to celebrate their successes.

I have had the fortune to present early versions of this research beyond Minneapolis. Heather S. Woods and Alex McVey graciously allowed me to present this research in their 2020 and 2021 graduate seminars. They have taught me how important it is to just let a man play his tapes. The puzzle pieces that eventually became the "detective" chapter were the product of a 2023 Rhetoric Society of America workshop I led with Michael Lechuga, whose wisdom is electric and intellectual generosity is absolutely endless. I owe much to Richard Besel, my undergraduate forensics coach and a brilliant rhetoric scholar, who in spring 2024 invited me to deliver the Robert Mayberry Lecture at Grand Valley State University. I hope this book offsets the times I did not come to tournaments memorized. I am likewise grateful to Rob Asen, Allyson Gross, Jenell Johnson, Ailea Merriam-Pigg, Allison Prasch, Alicen Rushevics, and Megan L. Zahay for inviting me to present at the 2024 Midwest Winter Workshop at the University of Wisconsin, Madison. The questions I received shaped the book's final form and I am still bowled over by their generosity as hosts.

Many folks who read early drafts of this manuscript deserve special thanks. Kim Singletary of Humanities First deserves so much credit for her insightful and painstaking editing. She transformed a dense knot of rumination into an actual book. Her questions, edits, and feedback have made this text readable. Her promptings steered me to revise, rewrite, and rethink the stakes of each chapter. Ideas on Fire copyeditors Cathy Hannabach, Rachel Fudge, and Lisa Sinclair have made this book immeasurably better. Finally, Tara Cyphers, Olivia Sergent, and Elizabeth Zaleski at Ohio State University Press have put a tremendous amount of work into this book. Their labor and patience are truly the reason it can exist in the world.

Emily Winderman has likewise read every word of this book, across many iterations. Her suggestions and feedback inspired me to keep writing and kept me on track. Dan Faltesek has entertained every half-cooked idea I have had about the secret since 2010. Similarly, Dustin Greenwalt, Jeremy Grossman, Lee Pierce, and Jason Myres have been subjected to more of my tinfoil-hat rantings than I could possibly recall. Kurt Zemlicka similarly allowed me to talk through the prepositional distinction between the "in" and the "of" until it made good sense. I treasure our friendship, which we developed at a distance during the pandemic. Paul Johnson and Caitlin Bruce generously reviewed early versions of the "secret episteme" and "detective" chapters, respectively. Paul's razor-sharp ideas, source recommendations, and palimpsestic fingerprints are all over the book. It was he that pointed me in the direction of George W. Bush's use of Sharpie pens to make redactions in 2014 and who prompted me to write about Saul Alinsky. To say the least, I have benefitted from his brilliance for many years. The "dog whistle" chapter also benefited from many exchanges, over many years, with Joseph Packer. I'm grateful to Calum Matheson for his helpful thinking on "the leak" and the whistleblower, and to Timothy Barouch for creating an opportunity to present this research at the National Communication Association. Chad Vollrath's insights about *Lost* and conspiracy theories were the inspiration for the opening of "twisted endings." I hope I have done their ideas justice and that they are reminded of just how much they contributed to this project through their friendship.

Many folks in the academy have supported the writing of this book at conferences, in conversations, with board game retreats, during visiting lectures, and by supplying reading recommendations. Thank you to Ira Allen, Peter Campbell, Lisa Corrigan, Joshua Gunn, Johanna Hartelius, John Lynch, Mike Mario, Matthew May, Robert McDonald, Torin Monahan, Damien Pfister, Joshua Reeves, Jason Regnier, Marnie Richie, Nate Stormer, and Patrick W. Wade. You have helped me to believe in this work, and to see it through.

I dedicate *Sovereign, Settler, Leaker, Lie* to my family. They have given me a staggering amount of support, in visible and invisible ways. Thank you to Wayne and Eden Winderman, who freely gave me gifts of childcare, space, and time to complete this book. They are the kindest, most generous people that I know, and I do not know what I would do without them. Thank you to Celia Napton for taking such amazing care of our little ones, Isidore and Alvin, while I have brought this book to a conclusion. To my parents: Thank you to Anders Hallsby, for the kind words he has shared with me about my work. Thank you to Yasemin Ersun-Hallsby, for introducing me to the *nazar* and putting me in touch with my distant roots. To my siblings: Eli Winderman and Allison Kodan, thank you for celebrating our victories through the years; I'm so grateful to call you family. To Genghis and Rachel, I'm so glad that we get to see our little ones grow together—you truly bring everyone under one tent in the most welcoming ways imaginable. To Karl, and Tomas, I learned much of what I know about the secret's positive potential from you. Thank you also to Millie and Murray, our dogs, for your patience and companionship from the time that this book was nothing more than a blinking cursor on a blank page.

Finally, and most importantly, to the heart that I carry outside my body: Emily Winderman, you are a wellspring of care and compassion. This project could not have happened without your unceasing support. Thank you for your incredible love and your continuous belief in me, for reading my words, listening to my ramblings, and for making a home together with me. To Isidore and Alvin, thank you for retroactively reshaping my perspective in the best possible ways. You make every day a joyful adventure and remind me that my family is the greatest secret of all.

Sections of chapter 3 originally appeared as "Imagine There's No President: The Rhetorical Secret and the Exposure of Valerie Plame," *Quarterly Journal of Speech* 101, no. 2 (2015). Reprinted by permission of Taylor & Francis Ltd, http://www.tandfonline.com.

BIBLIOGRAPHY

Abraham, Nicolas, and Maria Torok. "The Topography of Reality: Sketching a Metapsychology of Secrets." In *The Shell and the Kernel,* vol. 1, edited and translated by Nicholas T. Rand, 157–61. Chicago: University of Chicago Press, 1994.

Abraham, Nicolas, and Maria Torok. *The Wolf Man's Magic Word: A Cryptonymy.* Translated by Nicholas Rand. Minneapolis: University of Minnesota Press, 1986.

Adams, Parveen. *The Emptiness of the Image: Psychoanalysis and Sexual Differences.* New York: Routledge, 1996.

Ahmed, Beenish. "Drone Victims Testify Before Congress." *Boston Review,* October 30, 2013.

Aid, Matthew M. *The Untold History of the National Security Agency.* New York: Bloomsbury, 2009.

Alam, Rumaan. *Leave the World Behind: A Novel.* New York: Ecco, 2020.

Alberty, Erin. "Exclusive: Navajo Code Talkers Disappear from Military Websites After Trump DEI Order." *Axios,* March 17, 2025. https://www.axios.com/local/salt-lake-city/2025/03/17/navajo-code-talkers-trump-dei-military-websites-wwii.

Alinsky, Saul D. "Contribution." *Chicago Defender,* July 15, 1961.

Alinsky, Saul D. "*Playboy* Interview: Saul Alinsky." Interviewed by Eric Norden. *Playboy Magazine,* March 1972, 59–78, 150–78.

Alinsky, Saul D. *Reveille for Radicals.* New York: Vintage Books, 1946.

Alinsky, Saul D. *Rules for Radicals: A Pragmatic Primer for Realistic Radicals.* New York: Vintage Books, 1989.

"Alinsky Loses Poverty War Job." *Chicago Defender,* December 23, 1965.

Al-Kadi, Ibrahim A. "Origins of Cryptography: The Arab Contributions." *Cryptologia* 16, no. 2 (1992): 97–126.

Allen, Deane J., and Brian G. Shellum. *At the Creation, 1961–1965: Origination Documents of the Defense Intelligence Agency.* Washington, DC: DIA History Office, Defense Intelligence Agency, 2002.

Allen, Ira J. *Panic Now? Tools for Humanizing.* Knoxville: University of Tennessee Press, 2024.

Allen, Mike. "Bush 'Willing to Cooperate' with Leak Probe." *Washington Post,* June 4, 2004.

Althusser, Louis. "Ideology and Ideological State Apparatuses: Notes Towards an Investigation." In *Lenin and Philosophy and Other Essays,* translated by Ben Brewster, 85–125. New York: Monthly Review Press, 2001.

"Anatomy of a Leak." *Washington Post,* December 1, 2010. http://www.washingtonpost.com/wp-srv/special/nation/wikileaks-anatomy.

Andone, Dakin, Holly Yan, and Nick Valencia. "Bowe Bergdahl Gets Dishonorable Discharge, Avoids Prison Time." *CNN,* November 4, 2017.

Andrejevic, Mark. *I Spy: Surveillance and Power in the Interactive Era.* Lawrence: University Press of Kansas, 2007.

Anker, Elisabeth R. *Orgies of Feeling: Melodrama and the Politics of Freedom.* Durham, NC: Duke University Press, 2014.

Anonymous. "I Am Part of the Resistance Inside the Trump Administration." *New York Times,* September 5, 2018.

Anonymous. *A Warning.* New York: Twelve Books, 2019.

Arendt, Hannah. *Eichmann in Jerusalem: A Report on the Banality of Evil.* New York: Penguin Classics, 2006.

Arendt, Hannah. *On Revolution.* New York: Penguin Books, 2006.

Aristotle. *The Art of Rhetoric.* Translated by John H. Freese. Cambridge, MA: Harvard University Press, 2000.

Aristotle. *On Rhetoric: A Theory of Civil Discourse.* Translated by George Kennedy. 2nd ed. New York: Oxford University Press, 2007.

Armey, Dick. "NAACP Charges of Tea Party 'Racism' Are Baseless." *Newsmax,* July 15, 2010.

Armey, Dick, and Matt Kibbe. *Give Us Liberty: A Tea Party Manifesto.* New York: HarperCollins, 2010.

Ashtor, Gila. *Homo Psyche: On Queer Theory and Erotophobia.* New York: Fordham University Press, 2021.

Aswad, Noor Ghazal. "You Are a Marked Body: Caught in the Fires of Racialization as an Arab Woman in the American Academy." In *Migrant World Making,* edited by Sergio F. Juárez, Julia Khrebtan-Höhrager, Michael Lechuga, and Arthur Soto-Vásquez, 231–49. East Lansing: Michigan State University Press, 2023.

Athanasopoulos, Charles. "Fanonian Slips: The Rhetorical Function and Field of the White Mask." *Western Journal of Communication* 87, no. 3 (2023): 471–88.

Avila, Renata, Sarah Harrison, and Angela Richter. *Women, Whistleblowing, WikiLeaks: A Conversation.* New York: OR Books, 2017.

"Avoiding Taxes, Trump-Style." *New York Times,* November 1, 2016.

Azari, Julia. "Who Wrote the Anonymous White House Op-Ed? A Linguistic Analysis." *Vox,* September 7, 2018. https://www.vox.com/mischiefs-of-faction/2018/9/7/17830304/who-wrote-anonymous-white-house-op-ed.

Azizi, Abdelmalek, and Mostafa Azizi. "Instances of Arabic Cryptography in Morocco." *Cryptologia* 35, no. 1 (2011): 47–57.

Baard, Erik. "George W. Bush Ain't No Cowboy." *Village Voice,* September 21, 2004.

Bailey, Chelsea. "Here's What We Know So Far About the MLK Files Released by the Trump Administration." *CNN,* July 22, 2025. https://www.cnn.com/2025/07/22/us/mlk-files-released-what-we-know.

Baker, Peter. "Trump Pardons Scooter Libby in a Case That Mirrors His Own." *New York Times,* April 13, 2018.

Bal, Mieke. *Narratology: Introduction to the Theory of Narrative.* Toronto: University of Toronto Press, 2009.

Ball, James. "WikiLeaks Publishes Full Cache of Unredacted Cables." *The Guardian,* September 2, 2011.

Balsamo, Michael. "AG Barr: Epstein's Death Was a 'Perfect Storm of Screw-Ups.'" Associated Press, November 22, 2019. https://apnews.com/article/ap-top-news-politics-new-york-business-suicides-4ff27f28f32d446795b65ac7dd8cc4ac.

Balz, Dan. "President Begins His Toughest Sell." *Washington Post,* February 28, 2001.

Bamford, James. *Body of Secrets: Anatomy of the Ultra-Secret National Security Agency.* New York: Knopf Doubleday, 2007.

Banet-Weiser, Sarah. *Empowered: Popular Feminism and Popular Misogyny.* Durham, NC: Duke University Press, 2018.

Bank, Dylan, Daniel DiMauro, and Morgan Pehme, dirs. *Get Me Roger Stone.* Los Gatos, CA: Netflix, 2017. https://www.netflix.com/watch/80114666.

Bare, Richard L., dir. *The Twilight Zone.* Season 3, episode 24, "To Serve Man." Written by Rod Serling. Aired March 2, 1962, on CBS. http://www.youtube.com/watch?v=6HdsO1513uE.

Barr, William P. *One Damn Thing After Another: Memoirs of an Attorney General.* New York: HarperCollins Publishers, 2022.

Barrett, Brian. "DOGE Is the Deep State." *Wired,* March 6, 2025. https://www.wired.com/story/doge-is-the-deep-state/.

Barthes, Roland. *Elements of Semiology.* Translated by Annette Lavers and Colin Smith. New York: Hill and Wang, 1977.

Bastow, Steve, and James Martin. *Third Way Discourse: European Ideologies in the Twentieth Century.* Edinburgh: Edinburgh University Press, 2003.

Bayles, Martha. "Bowe Bergdahl, 'Homeland,' and the Kindness of Strangers." *Boston Globe,* June 15, 2014.

Beasley, Vanessa B. "The Rhetorical Presidency Meets the Unitary Executive: Implications for Presidential Rhetoric on Public Policy" *Rhetoric and Public Affairs* 13, no. 1 (2010): 7–35.

Beauchamp, Toby. *Going Stealth: Transgender Politics and U.S. Surveillance Practices.* Durham, NC: Duke University Press, 2019.

Beck, Catherine. "Bureau of Intelligence and Research and Washington Politics." PhD diss., University of Georgia, 2005.

Beck, David R. M. *Unfair Labor? American Indians and the 1893 World's Columbian Exposition in Chicago.* Lincoln: University of Nebraska Press, 2019.

Beckman, Frida. *The Paranoid Chronotope: Power, Truth, Identity.* Stanford, CA: Stanford University Press, 2022.

Beckman, Frida. "Paranoid Masculinity; or, Toward a New Identity Politics." *symplokē* 29, nos. 1–2 (2021): 235–46.

Bedsole, Nathan Henry. "Voice as Little Object (A)rgument: On Hearing Gore Vidal and William F. Buckley Jr." *Argumentation and Advocacy* 54, no. 4 (2018): 323–39.

Begley, Louis. *Why the Dreyfus Affair Matters.* New Haven, CT: Yale University Press, 2009.

Belknap, Michal R. "The Mechanics of Repression: J. Edgar Hoover, the Bureau of Investigation and the Radicals, 1917–1925." *Social Justice: A Journal of Crime, Conflict and World Order,* no. 7 (Spring–Summer 1977): 49–58.

Bellman, Beryl. "The Paradox of Secrecy." *Human Studies* 4, nos. 1–2 (1981): 1–24.

Belz, Dan. "Bush War Ratings May Not Reach 9/11 Levels; Terror Attacks Brought Unity, but President Is a Polarizing Figure in Iraq Conflict." *Washington Post,* March 23, 2003.

Benbow, Mark E. "Birth of a Quotation: Woodrow Wilson and 'Like Writing History with Lightning.'" *The Journal of the Gilded Age and the Progressive Era* 9, no. 4 (2010): 509–33.

Bennett, David H. *The Party of Fear: From Nativist Movements to the New Right in American History.* New York: Knopf Doubleday, 1995.

Bennhold, Katrin. "A New Age of American Interference in Europe." *New York Times,* January 13, 2025. https://www.nytimes.com/2025/01/13/world/europe/maga-musk-europe-interference.html.

Bennhold, Katrin. "What Elon Musk's Salute Was All About." *New York Times,* January 24, 2025. https://www.nytimes.com/2025/01/24/world/europe/elon-musk-roman-salute-nazi.html.

Berke, Richard L. "What a Mind! In Politics, That's Not What Matters." *New York Times,* June 25, 2000.

Berlet, Chip, and Matthew N. Lyons. *Right-Wing Populism in America: Too Close for Comfort.* New York: Guilford, 2000.

Bertrand, Natasha. "Roger Stone's Secret Messages with WikiLeaks." *The Atlantic,* February 27, 2018.

Besel, Richard. "Prolepsis and the Environmental Rhetoric of Congressional Politics: Defeating the Climate Stewardship Act of 2003." *Environmental Communication* 6, no. 2 (2012): 233–49.

Best, Sharon, and Stephen Marcus. "Surface Reading: An Introduction." *Representations* 108, no. 1 (2009): 13.

Betts, Anna, "Jeffrey Epstein: More Files Released Related to Late Sex Offender and Financier." *The Guardian,* February 27, 2025.

Bhabha, Homi K. "Foreword: Framing Fanon." In *The Wretched of the Earth,* by Frantz Fanon, translated by Richard Philcox, vi–xlii. New York: Grove Press, 2007.

Biden, Joseph R., Jr. "Executive Order on the Safe, Secure, and Trustworthy Development and Use of Artificial Intelligence." White House, October 30, 2023. https://www.federalregister.gov/documents/2023/11/01/2023-24283/safe-secure-and-trustworthy-development-and-use-of-artificial-intelligence.

Biesecker, Barbara A. "From General History to Philosophy: Black Lives Matter, Late Neoliberal Molecular Biopolitics, and Rhetoric." *Philosophy and Rhetoric* 50, no. 4 (2017): 409–30.

Biesecker, Barbara A. "Prospects of Rhetoric for the Twenty-First Century: Speculations on Evental Rhetoric with a Note on Barack Obama and a Benediction by Jacques Lacan." In *Re-Engaging the Prospects of Rhetoric,* edited by Mark J. Porrovecchio, 16–36. New York: Routledge, 2010.

Biesecker, Barbara A. "Rethinking the Rhetorical Situation from Within the Thematic of *Différance.*" *Philosophy and Rhetoric* 22, no. 2 (1989): 110–30.

Biesecker, Barbara A. "Rhetorical Studies and the 'New' Psychoanalysis: What's the Real Problem? Or Framing the Problem of the Real." *Quarterly Journal of Speech* 84, no. 2 (1998): 222–59.

Birchall, Clare. "Aesthetics of the Secret." *New Formations* 83, no. 3 (2014): 25–46.

Birchall, Clare. *Radical Secrecy: The Ends of Transparency in Datafied America.* Minneapolis: University of Minnesota Press, 2021.

Birchall, Clare. "Transparency, Interrupted: Secrets of the Left." *Theory, Culture, and Society* 28, nos. 7–8 (2011): 60–84.

Bitzer, Lloyd F. "The Rhetorical Situation." *Philosophy and Rhetoric* 1, no. 1 (1968): 1–14.

Black, Edwin. *Rhetorical Questions: Studies of Public Discourse.* Chicago: University of Chicago Press, 1992.

Black, Edwin. "The Second Persona." *Quarterly Journal of Speech* 56, no. 2 (1970): 331–40.

Black, Edwin. "Secrecy and Disclosure as Rhetorical Forms." *Quarterly Journal of Speech* 74, no. 2 (1988): 133–50.

Blake, Aaron. "Future of GOP Blasts Its Recent Past." *Washington Post,* March 15, 2013.

Blake, Aaron. "Here Are the Latest, Most Damaging Things in the DNC's Leaked Emails." *Washington Post,* July 25, 2016.

Blakeley, Ulysses B., and Charles T. Leber Jr. "Blow at Bias." *Chicago Defender,* July 15, 1961.

Blank, Lisa. "Two Schools for Secrecy: Defining Secrecy from the Works of Max Weber, Georg Simmel, Edward Shils, and Sissela Bok." In *Government Secrecy: Classic and Contemporary Readings,* edited by Susan L. Maret and Jan Goldman, 59–68. Westport, CT: Libraries Unlimited, 2009.

Blankenhorn, David. "Clinton's Alinsky Problem—and Ours." *The American Interest,* October 11, 2016. https://www.the-american-interest.com/2016/10/11/clintons-alinsky-problem-and-ours/.

Blum, Rachel M. *How the Tea Party Captured the GOP: Insurgent Factions in American Politics.* Chicago: University of Chicago Press, 2020.

Bonilla-Silva, Eduardo. *Racism Without Racists: Color-Blind Racism and the Persistence of Racial Inequality in America.* Lanham, MD: Rowman & Littlefield, 2018.

Booth, Wayne C. *A Rhetoric of Irony.* Chicago: University of Chicago Press, 1974.

Borch-Jacobsen, Mikkel. *Lacan: The Absolute Master.* Translated by Douglas Brick. Stanford, CA: Stanford University Press, 1991.

Borowitz, Andy. "Bush: Saddam Bought Geraniums, Not Uranium." *Newsweek,* July 14, 2003.

Bortnick, Justin A. "Play and Misinformation: How America's Conspiracy Culture Became Gamified." *Games and Culture* 20, no. 2 (2025): 255–74.

Boudreau, Abbie. "Our Documentary Takes a Strange Detour." *CNN Special Investigations Unit* (blog), September 29, 2010. http://www.cnn.com/blogarchive/siu.blogs.cnn.com/2010/09/29/our-documentary-takes-a-strange-detour.

Boyte, Harry C. *The Backyard Revolution: Understanding the New Citizen Movement.* Philadelphia: Temple University Press, 1980.

Brandenberg v. Ohio, 395 U.S. 444, 447 (1969).

Bratich, Jack. "Public Secrecy and Immanent Security: A Strategic Analysis." *Cultural Studies* 20, nos. 4–5 (2006): 493–511.

Bratich, Jack, and Sarah Banet-Weiser. "From Pick-Up Artists to Incels: Con(fidence) Games, Networked Misogyny, and the Failure of Neoliberalism." *International Journal of Communication* 13 (2019): 5003–27.

Brazier, Arthur M. *Black Self-Determination: The Story of the Woodlawn Organization.* Grand Rapids, MI: William B. Eerdmans, 1969.

Brazier, Arthur M. "TWO Speaks." *Chicago Defender*, July 15, 1961.

Breitbart, Andrew. "Andrew Breitbart at CPAC Feb 10, 2012." YouTube video (13:26), posted by gvloanguy, March 1, 2012. https://www.youtube.com/watch?v=mNo99vRlCUY.

Brennan, Teresa. *The Transmission of Affect*. Ithaca, NY: Cornell University Press, 2004.

Brinkema, Eugenie. *The Forms of the Affects*. Durham, NC: Duke University Press, 2014.

Britton, Bianca. "Pamela Anderson Visits Julian Assange in Prison." *CNN*, May 7, 2019.

Broadfoot, Keith. "Anamorphosis as Colonial Encounter: The Case of Augustus Earle." *Postcolonial Studies* 25, no. 2 (2022): 270–91.

Brooks, David. "A Guide for the Perplexed." *New York Times*, September 1, 2006.

Brooks, Joanna. "The Early American Public Sphere and the Emergence of a Black Print Counterpublic." *William and Mary Quarterly*, no. 62 (January 2005): 67–92.

Brooks, Joanna. "Prince Hall, Freemasonry, and Genealogy." *African American Review* 34, no. 2 (2000): 199–200.

Brooks, Peter. *Reading for the Plot: Design and Intention in Narrative*. New York: Vintage Books, 1985.

Brown, Nicole Marie. "Flawed Consumers: Understanding the Impact of Intersectional Political Consumerism During the Chicago Welfare Rights Era." PhD diss., University of Illinois at Urbana-Champaign, 2015.

Brown, Scott G. "On the Composition History of the Longer ('Secret') Gospel of Mark." *Journal of Biblical Literature* 122, no. 1 (2003): 89–110.

Browne, Simone. *Dark Matters: On the Surveillance of Blackness*. Durham, NC: Duke University Press, 2015.

Brummett, Barry. "Some Implications of 'Process' or 'Intersubjectivity' Postmodern Rhetoric." *Philosophy and Rhetoric* 9, no. 1 (1976): 21–51.

Bruni, Frank. "Riding High, Bush Seeks Gravity." *New York Times*, September 14, 1999.

Buckley, William F., Jr. *Firing Line with William F. Buckley Jr.* Season 2, episode 79, "Mobilizing the Poor." Aired December 11, 1967, on PBS. Accessed via https://www.youtube.com/watch?v=OsfxnaFaHWI.

"Buffalo Unit Hires Alinsky." *Chicago Defender*, April 6, 1965.

Buffenstein, Alyssa. "A Monumental Loss: Here Are the Most Significant Cultural Heritage Sites That ISIS Has Destroyed to Date." *Artnet News*, May 30, 2017. https://news.artnet.com/artworld/isis-cultural-heritage-sites-destroyed-950060.

Bullock, Steven C. *Revolutionary Brotherhood: Freemasonry and the Transformation of the American Social Order, 1730–1840*. Chapel Hill: University of North Carolina Press, 1996.

Bump, Philip. "Trump's Classified Mar-a-Lago Documents, Catalogued." *Washington Post*, September 7, 2022.

Burg, David F. *Chicago's White City of 1893*. Lexington: University Press of Kentucky, 2015.

Burke, Edward M. "Courageous." *Chicago Defender*, July 15, 1961.

Burghart, Devin. "Tea Party Nation Warns of White Anglo-Saxon Protestant 'Extinction.'" *Institute for Research & Education on Human Rights*, March 29, 2011. https://irehr.org/2011/03/29/tea-party-nation-warns-of-white-anglo-saxon-protestant-extinction/.

Burke, Janet M., and Margaret C. Jacob. "French Freemasonry, Women, and Feminist Scholarship." *The Journal of Modern History* 68, no. 3 (1996): 513–49.

Burke, Kenneth. "Four Master Tropes." In *A Grammar of Motives*, 503–18. Berkeley: University of California Press, 1969.

Burke, Kenneth. "Four Master Tropes." *The Kenyon Review* 3, no. 4 (1941): 421–38.

Burke, Kenneth. *A Grammar of Motives*. Berkeley: University of California Press, 1969.

Burke, Natalie S. "The Real Reason Team Trump Keeps Trying to Call Kamala Harris a 'DEI Hire.'" *MSNBC,* August 3, 2024. https://www.msnbc.com/opinion/msnbc-opinion/team-trump-calls-kamala-harris-dei-hire-rcna164117.

Burns, Scott Z., dir. *The Report*. Culver City, CA: Amazon Studios, 2019.

Bush, George W. *Decision Points*. New York: Random House, 2010.

"Bush Declares War." *CNN Special Report,* March 19, 2003.

"Bush: 'I'm the Decider' on Rumsfeld." *CNN,* April 18, 2006.

Byford, Sam. "George W. Bush's Bizarre Bathroom Self-Portraits Laid Bare by Audacious Hack." *The Verge,* February 8, 2013. https://www.theverge.com/2013/2/8/3966678/hacker-reveals-george-w-bush-self-portraits.

Byrne, Malcolm. *Iran-Contra: Reagan's Scandal and the Unchecked Abuse of Presidential Power*. Lawrence: University Press of Kansas, 2014.

"The Campaign of Deception Against Planned Parenthood." *New York Times,* July 22, 2015. https://www.nytimes.com/2015/07/22/opinion/the-campaign-of-deception-against-planned-parenthood.html.

Campbell, David. *Writing Security: United States Foreign Policy and the Politics of Identity*. Minneapolis: University of Minnesota Press, 1998.

Campbell, Karlyn Kohrs, and Kathleen Hall Jamieson. "Form and Genre in Rhetorical Criticism." In *Readings in Rhetorical Criticism,* edited by Carl Burgchardt, 394–411. State College, PA: Strata, 1995.

Canady, Margot. *The Straight State: Sexuality and Citizenship in Twentieth-Century America*. Princeton, NJ: Princeton University Press, 2009.

Cantor, Eric, Paul Ryan, and Kevin McCarthy. *Young Guns: A New Generation of Conservative Leaders*. New York: Threshold Editions, 2010.

Capps, Reilly. "Paying Homage to Truth and Its Consequences." *Washington Post,* October 16, 2003.

Carlson, Erin G. "Secret Dossiers: Sexuality, Race, and Treason in Proust and the Dreyfus Affair." *Modern Fiction Studies* 48, no. 4 (2002): 937–68.

"Carmichael: 'Negro Must Learn He Has Right to Fight.'" *Chicago Defender,* January 21, 1967.

Caselli, Irene. "Julian Assange Will Be Granted Asylum, Says Official." *The Guardian,* August 14, 2012.

Cassidy, John. "Ten Things I'll Miss About Newt When He's Gone." *New Yorker,* April 26, 2012.

Cavallaro, James, Stephan Sonnenberg, and Sarah Knuckey. *Living Under Drones: Death, Injury, and Trauma to Civilians from US Drone Practices in Pakistan*. Stanford, CA: International Human Rights and Conflict Resolution Clinic, Stanford Law School, 2012.

Chaganty, Aneesh, dir. *Searching*. Sony Pictures Entertainment, 2018.

Chappelle, Wayne, Tanya Goodman, Laura Reardon, and William Thompson. "An Analysis of Post-Traumatic Stress Symptoms in United States Air Force Drone Operators." *Journal of Anxiety Disorders* 28, no. 5 (2014): 480–87.

Chappelle, Wayne L., Kent D. McDonald, Lillian Prince, Tanya Goodman, Bobbie N. Ray-Sannerud, and William Thompson. "Symptoms of Psychological Distress and Post-Traumatic Stress Disorder in United States Air Force 'Drone' Operators." *Military Medicine* 179, no. 8 (2014): 63–70.

Chebrolu, E. "The Racial Lens of Dylann Roof: Racial Anxiety and White Nationalist Rhetoric on New Media." *Review of Communication* 20, no. 1 (2020): 47–68.

Cherwitz, Richard A., and James W. Hikins. "Rhetorical Perspectivism." *Quarterly Journal of Speech* 69, no. 3 (1983): 249–66.

"Christian Century in Error." *Chicago Defender,* June 5, 1961.

Chulov, Martin, and Helen Pidd. "Curveball: How US Was Duped by Iraqi Fantasist Looking to Topple Saddam." *The Guardian,* February 15, 2011.

Clayton, Mark. "WikiLeaks List of 'Critical' Sites: Is It a 'Menu for Terrorists'?" *Christian Science Monitor,* December 10, 2010.

Cloud, Dana. "The Irony Bribe and Reality Television: Investment and Detachment in *The Bachelor.*" *Critical Studies in Media Communication* 27, no. 5 (2010): 413–37.

Cloud, Dana. "The Materiality of Discourse as Oxymoron: A Challenge to Critical Rhetoric." *Western Journal of Communication* 58, no. 3 (1994): 141–63.

Cloud, Dana. "Private Manning and the Chamber of Secrets." *QED: A Journal in GLBTQ Worldmaking* 1, no. 1 (2014): 80–104.

Cloud, Dana. *Reality Bites: Rhetoric and the Circulation of Truth Claims in U.S. Political Culture.* Columbus: The Ohio State University Press, 2018.

Clyner, Adam. "George II." *New York Times,* December 5, 1999.

Cofield, Ernestine. "How Woodlawn Found a General to Lead a Slum Army." *Chicago Defender,* November 20, 1962.

Cohen, Noam. "Know Thine Enemy." *New York Times,* August 23, 2009.

Cohen, Noam, and Brian Stelter. "Airstrike Video Brings Attention to Whistle-Blower Site." *New York Times,* April 7, 2010.

Cohen, Richard. "Bush's 9/11 Farce." *Washington Post,* July 27, 2004.

Cohn, Norman. *Warrant for Genocide: The Myth of the Jewish World Conspiracy and the Protocols of the Elders of Zion.* London: Serif, 1996.

Coker, Calvin R. "'Do You Think This Is Not Happening?': Rhetorical Laundering and the Federal Hearings over Planned Parenthood." *Women and Language* 46, no. 1 (2023): 3–32.

Coll, Steve. "The Spy Who Said Too Much." *New Yorker,* March 25, 2013. https://www.newyorker.com/magazine/2013/04/01/the-spy-who-said-too-much.

Condon, Bill, dir. *The Fifth Estate.* Dreamworks Pictures, 2013.

Conley, Donovan, and William O. Saas. "*Occultatio*: The Bush Administration's Rhetorical War." *Western Journal of Communication* 74, no. 4 (2010): 329–50.

Conley, Thomas M. "The Beauty of Lists: *Copia* and Argument." *Journal of the American Forensic Association* 22, no. 2 (1985): 96–103.

Continetti, Matthew. "Journalists for Hillary Clinton." *National Review,* September 27, 2014.

Conway, George T., III, and Neal Kumar Katyal. "Trump Has Done Plenty to Warrant Impeachment. But the Ukraine Allegations Are Over the Top." *Washington Post,* September 20, 2019.

Cooperman, Alan. "In Iraq, U.S. Troops Are Still Dying—One Almost Every Day; Death Rate Down, but Families of Victims Face Special Anguish." *Washington Post,* May 26, 2003.

Copjec, Joan. *Imagine There's No Woman: Ethics and Sublimation.* Cambridge, MA: MIT Press, 2004.

Copjec, Joan. *Read My Desire: Lacan Against the Historicists.* Cambridge, MA: MIT Press, 1994.

Copp, Tara, and Lolita C. Baldor. "Trump Fires Chairman of the Joint Chiefs of Staff and Two Other Military Officers." Associated Press, February 21, 2025. https://apnews.com/article/trump-brown-joint-chiefs-of-staff-firing-fa428cc1508a583b3bf5e7a5a58f6acf.

Corber, Robert J. *Homosexuality in Cold War America: Resistance and the Crisis of Masculinity.* Durham, NC: Duke University Press, 1997.

Corrigan, Lisa M. *Black Feelings: Race and Affect in the Long Sixties.* Jackson: University Press of Mississippi, 2020.

Coscarelli, Joe. "CNN Seriously Comparing Bowe Bergdahl to Brody from *Homeland.*" *New York Magazine,* June 5, 2014.

Coupland, Justine, Nikolas Coupland, and Jeffrey D. Robinson. "'How Are You?' Negotiating Phatic Communication." *Language in Society* 21, no. 2 (1992): 207–30.

Cousins, Mark, and Athar Hussein. *Michel Foucault: Traditions in Social Theory.* New York: St. Martin's Press, 1984.

Crane, Magan. "A Timeline of Key Events in the Trump-Ukraine Story." *PBS,* October 5, 2019. https://www.pbs.org/newshour/politics/a-timeline-of-key-events-in-the-trump-ukraine-story.

Crawford, Neta C. "Costs of War: War-Related Death, Injury, and Displacement in Afghanistan and Pakistan 2001–2014." Watson Institute for International Studies, Brown University, May 22, 2015.

Crichton, Michael. *Disclosure.* New York: Alfred A. Knopf, 1994.

Culler, Jonathan. *On Deconstruction: Theory and Criticism After Structuralism.* London: Routledge and Kegan Paul, 1983.

Cuordileone, K. A. "'Politics in an Age of Anxiety': Cold War Political Culture and the Crisis in American Masculinity." *The Journal of American History* 87, no. 2 (2000): 515–45.

Curtis, Benjamin. "Whataboutism: What It Is and Why It's Such a Popular Tactic in Arguments." *The Conversation,* May 20, 2022. https://theconversation.com/whataboutism-what-it-is-and-why-its-such-a-popular-tactic-in-arguments-182911.

Davidson, Michael. *Guys Like Us: Citing Masculinity in Cold War Poetics.* Chicago: University of Chicago Press, 2004.

Davis, Angelique M., and Rose Ernst. "Racial Gaslighting." *Politics, Groups, and Identities* 7, no. 4 (2019): 761–74.

Davis, Benjamin P. "The Politics of Édouard Glissant's Right to Opacity." *The CLR James Journal* 25, nos. 1–2 (2019): 59–70.

Davis, David Brion, ed. *The Fear of Conspiracy: Images of Un-American Subversion from the Revolution to the Present.* Ithaca, NY: Cornell University Press, 1971.

Davis, Murray S. "Georg Simmel and Erving Goffman: Legitimators of the Sociological Investigation of Human Experience." *Qualitative Sociology* 20, no. 3 (1997): 369–88.

Dean, Jodi. *Publicity's Secret: How Technoculture Capitalizes on Democracy.* Ithaca, NY: Cornell University Press, 2002.

Dean, Mitchell, and Kaspar Villadsen. *State Phobia and Civil Society: The Political Legacy of Michel Foucault.* Stanford, CA: Stanford University Press, 2016.

Debord, Guy. *Comments on the Society of the Spectacle: Treatise on Secrets.* Translated by Malcolm Imrie. New York: Verso, 1990.

Deggans, Eric. "5 Takeaways by a Longtime NABJ Member from Trump's Appearance Before Black Journalists." *NPR,* August 1, 2024. https://www.npr.org/2024/08/01/nx-s1-5060269/trump-nabj-appearance-controversy.

del Olmo, Frank. "Don't Shed Any Tears over Linda Chavez." *Los Angeles Times,* January 12, 2001.

Deleuze, Gilles, and Felix Guattari. *A Thousand Plateaus: Capitalism and Schizophrenia.* Minneapolis: University of Minnesota Press, 1989.

Delmont, Matthew. "There's a Generational Shift in the Debate over Busing." *Atlantic,* July 1, 2019. https://www.theatlantic.com/ideas/archive/2019/07/kamala-harris-and-busing-debate/593047/.

Department of Justice. "Lawfulness of a Lethal Operation Directed Against a U.S. Citizen Who Is a Senior Operational Leader of Al-Qa'ida or an Associated Force." White paper, draft, November 8, 2011. https://www.justice.gov/sites/default/files/oip/legacy/2014/07/23/dept-white-paper.pdf.

Der Derian, James. *Antidiplomacy: Spies, Terror, Speed, and War.* Cambridge: Blackwell, 1992.

Derrida, Jacques. *The Beast and the Sovereign, Volume 1.* Translated by Geoffrey Bennington. Chicago: University of Chicago Press, 2009.

Derrida, Jacques. "Différance." In *Speech and Phenomena and Other Essays on Husserl's Theory of Signs,* translated by David B. Allison and Newton Garver, 129–60. Evanston, IL: Northwestern University Press, 1973.

Derrida, Jacques. "Fors: The Anglish Words of Nicholas Abraham and Maria Torok." Foreword to *The Wolf Man's Magic Word,* by Nicolas Abraham and Maria Torok, translated by Nicholas Rand, xi–xlvii. Minneapolis: University of Minnesota Press, 1986.

Derrida, Jacques. *Glas.* Translated by John P. Leavey Jr. and Richard Rand. Lincoln: University of Nebraska Press, 1986.

Derrida, Jacques. "I Have a Taste for the Secret." In *A Taste for the Secret,* by Derrida and Maurizio Ferraris, edited by Giacomo Donis and David Webb, 1–92. Cambridge: Polity, 2001.

Derrida, Jacques. *On the Name.* Edited by Thomas Dutoit. Translated by David Wood, John P. Leavey Jr., and Ian McLeod. Stanford, CA: Stanford University Press, 1995.

Derrida, Jacques. *Positions.* Translated by Alan Bass. Chicago: University of Chicago Press, 1981.

Derrida, Jacques. "Remarks on Deconstruction and Pragmatism." In *Deconstruction and Pragmatism,* edited by Chantal Mouffe, 79–84. New York: Routledge, 1996.

Derrida, Jacques. *Resistances of Psychoanalysis.* Translated by Peggy Kamuf, Pascale-Anne Brault, and Michael Naas. Stanford, CA: Stanford University Press, 1998.

Derrida, Jacques. *Rogues: Two Essays on Reason.* Translated by Pascale-Anne Brault and Michael Naas. Stanford, CA: Stanford University Press, 2005.

Derrida, Jacques. "Signature, Event, Context." In *Limited Inc.,* edited by Gerald Graff, translated by Jeffrey Mehlman and Samuel Weber, 1–24. Evanston, IL: Northwestern University Press, 1988.

Derrida, Jacques. "Structure, Sign, and Play in the Discourse of the Human Sciences." In *Writing and Difference,* translated by Alan Bass, 278–94. Chicago: University of Chicago Press, 1978.

Derrida, Jacques. "The Time Is Out of Joint." Translated by Peggy Kamuf. In *Deconstruction Is/In America,* edited by Anselm Haverkamp, 14–40. New York: New York University Press, 1995.

Derrida, Jacques. "White Mythology: Metaphor in the Text of Philosophy." *New Literary History* 6, no. 1 (1974): 5–74.

Dewan, Shaila. "To Court Blacks, Foes of Abortion Make Racial Case." *New York Times,* February 26, 2010. http://www.nytimes.com/2010/02/27/us/27race.html.

DeYoung, Karen. "Presidential Diplomacy, Ranch-House Style: Bush's Personal Touch Gets Mixed Reactions in Winning and Influencing World Leaders." *Washington Post,* May 23, 2002.

Dieterle, William, dir. *The Life of Emile Zola.* Warner Bros. Pictures, 1937.

Douthat, Ross. "How Michel Foucault Lost the Left and Won the Right." *New York Times*, May 25, 2021.

Douthat, Ross. "The Politics of Pregnancy Counseling." *Ross Douthat: Evaluations* (blog), *New York Times*, December 3, 2009. https://douthat.blogs.nytimes.com/2009/12/03/the-politics-of-pregnancy-counseling.

Down, Maureen. "Gunsmoke and Mirrors." *New York Times*, September 14, 2003.

Dreyfus, Suelette, and Julian Assange. *Underground: Tales of Hacking, Madness, and Obsession on the Electronic Frontier*. Edinburgh, UK: Canongate Books, 2012.

Drezner, Daniel W. "Whistleblower or Traitor? The Thorny Politics of Leaking." *Politico*, April 30, 2023. https://www.politico.com/news/magazine/2023/04/30/national-security-leaks-political-rorschach-00094425.

Du Bois, W. E. B. "The Propaganda of History." In *Black Reconstruction in America: An Essay Toward a History of the Part Which Black Folk Played in the Attempt to Reconstruct Democracy in America, 1860–1880*, edited by Henry Louis Gates Jr., 615–29. New York: Oxford University Press, 2007.

Du Bois, W. E. B. "Strivings of the Negro People." *The Atlantic*, August 1897, 194–98. https://cdn.theatlantic.com/media/archives/1897/08/80-478/131953250.pdf.

Du Bois, W. E. B., and Isabel Eaton. *The Philadelphia Negro*. Boston: Ginn & Co., 1899.

Dulles, Allen W. *The Craft of Intelligence*. New York: Signet Books, 1965.

Dumenil, Lynn. *Freemasonry and American Culture, 1880–1930*. Princeton: Princeton University Press, 2014.

Dunbar, Paul Lawrence. "Hidden in Plain Sight: African American Secret Societies and Black Freemasonry." *Journal of African American Studies* 16, no. 4 (2012): 622–37.

Dunn, Tom. *Queerly Remembered: Rhetorics for Representing the GLBTQ Past*. Columbia: University of South Carolina Press, 2016.

Eban, Katherine. "Rorschach and Awe." *Vanity Fair*, July 17, 2007.

"Economic Justice." *Chicago Defender*, May 20, 1967.

El Assar, Mohamed. "Men Can't Stop Thinking About the Roman Empire. It's Because of the Masculinity Polycrisis." *Fortune*, September 30, 2023. https://fortune.com/2023/09/30/men-cant-stop-thinking-about-the-roman-empire-masculinity-polycrisis-culture/.

Elliott, Vittoria. "Astrologers Say 2024's Political Future May Be Written in the Stars." *Wired*, August 26, 2024. https://www.wired.com/story/political-astrology-predictions-online/.

Ellis, Mark. "J. Edgar Hoover and the 'Red Summer' of 1919." *Journal of American Studies* 28, no. 1 (1994): 39–59.

Ellsberg, Daniel. "There Are Times to Spill Secrets: Advice from a Leaker." *New York Times*, September 29, 2004.

El-Shakry, Omnia. *The Arabic Freud: Psychoanalysis and Islam in Modern Egypt*. Princeton, NJ: Princeton University Press, 2017.

Ely, Richard. "The Identification of America's True Enemy (1884)." In *The Fear of Conspiracy: Images of Un-American Subversion from the Revolution to the Present*, edited by David Brion Davis, 161–69. Ithaca, NY: Cornell University Press, 1971.

Emberton, Carole. *Beyond Redemption: Race, Violence, and the American South After the Civil War*. Chicago: University of Chicago Press, 2013.

Englehardt, Tom. *Shadow Government: Surveillance, Secret Wars, and a Global Security State in a Single-Superpower World*. Chicago: Haymarket Books, 2014.

Enrich, David, Matthew Goldstein, Jessica Silver-Greenberg, and Steve Eder. "Trump's Name Is on Contributor List for Epstein Birthday Book." *New York Times*, July 24, 2025.

Esmail, Sam. dir. *Homecoming* (TV series), Season 1. Amazon Studios. Released November 2, 2018, on Amazon Prime Video. https://www.primevideo.com/detail/Homecoming/0JP2LF83DMAYFDREZ20GAG2DAR.

Esmail, Sam. *Leave the World Behind*. Netflix, 2023. https://www.netflix.com/title/81314956.

Evans, Rowland, and Robert Novak. "A Soviet–East Europe 'Organic Union.'" *Washington Post*, March 22, 1976. Box 15, folder 21, University of Minnesota Immigration History Research Center Archives, Minneapolis, Minnesota.

"Exposing ACORN: Introducing James O'Keefe." Breitbart, September 10, 2009. http://www.breitbart.com/big-government/2009/09/10/exposing-acorn-introducing-james-o-keefe.

Fahrenthold, David A., and Jeremy Singer-Vine. "DOGE Makes Its Latest Errors Harder to Find." *New York Times*, March 13, 2025.

Falk, Richard. "Kuala Lumpur Tribunal: Bush and Blair Guilty." *Al Jazeera*, November 28, 2011.

Fandos, Nicholas. "Trump Acquitted of Two Impeachment Charges in Near Party-Line Vote." *New York Times*, February 5, 2020.

Fandos, Nicholas, and Katie Benner. "Suspicions, Demands, and Threats: Devin Nunes vs. the Justice Dept." *New York Times*, May 12, 2018.

Fanon, Frantz. *Black Skin, White Masks*. Translated by Charles Lam Markmann. London: Pluto Press, 1986.

Fanon, Frantz. "The Fact of Blackness." In *Black Skin, White Masks*, translated by Charles Lam Markmann, 109–40. London: Pluto Press, 1986.

Farrell, John J. "Expresses Thanks." *Chicago Defender*, July 15, 1961.

Farrell, Thomas. "Sizing Things Up: Colloquial Reflection as Practical Wisdom." *Argumentation* 12 (February 1998): 1–14.

Farwell, James P., and Rafal Rohozinski. "Stuxnet and the Future of Cyberwar." *Survival* 53, no. 1 (2011): 23–40.

Feiger, Leah, Louise Matsakis, and Jake Lahut, "People Are Paying Millions to Dine with Donald Trump." *Wired*, March 4, 2025. https://www.wired.com/story/people-paying-millions-donald-trump-mar-a-lago/.

Feinstein, Dianne, and the Senate Select Committee on Intelligence. *The Senate Intelligence Committee Report on Torture: Committee Study of the Central Intelligence Agency's Detention and Interrogation Program*. Academic ed. London: Melville House, 2020.

Felman, Shoshana. *Jacques Lacan and the Adventure of Insight: Psychoanalysis in Contemporary Culture*. Cambridge, MA: Harvard University Press, 1987.

Felman, Shoshana. *What Does a Woman Want? Reading and Sexual Difference*. Baltimore, MD: Johns Hopkins University Press, 1993.

Felski, Rita. *The Limits of Critique*. Chicago: University of Chicago Press, 2015.

Ferris, Layla. "Fact Checking Election Day 2024 Claims About Voter Fraud, Ballot Counting and More." *CBS News*, November 6, 2024. https://www.cbsnews.com/news/2024-election-day-fact-check/.

Feuer, Alan, and Matthew Goldstein. "Inside the Long Friendship Between Trump and Epstein." *New York Times*, July 19, 2025.

Fick, Nate. "Was Snowden Hero or Traitor? Perhaps a Little of Both." *Washington Post*, January 19, 2017.

Filkins, Dexter. "The Deep State." *New Yorker*, March 12, 2012.

Fink, Bruce. *The Lacanian Subject: Between Language and Jouissance*. Princeton, NJ: Princeton University Press, 1995.

Fink, Bruce. *Lacan to the Letter: Reading "Écrits" Closely*. Minneapolis: University of Minnesota Press, 2004.

Finkelde, Dominik. "Reason, Anamorphosis, and the Snowden Case." *Diacritics* 44, no. 3 (2016): 6–29.

"The First Presidential Debate." *New York Times*, September 26, 2008. https://www.nytimes.com/elections/2008/president/debates/transcripts/first-presidential-debate.html.

Fischer, Mia. *Terrorizing Gender: Transgender Visibility and the Surveillance Practices of the U.S. Security State*. Lincoln: University of Nebraska Press, 2019.

Fish, John Hall. *Black Power / White Control: The Struggle of the Woodlawn Organization in Chicago*. Princeton, NJ: Princeton University Press, 1973.

Fixmer-Oraiz, Natalie. *Homeland Maternity: US Security Culture and the New Reproductive Regime*. Urbana: University of Illinois Press, 2019.

Flood, Finbarr Barry. "Between Cult and Culture: Bamiyan, Islamic Iconoclasm, and the Museum." *The Art Bulletin* 84, no. 4 (2002): 641–59.

Foley, Megan. "'Prove You're Human': Fetishizing Material Embodiment and Immaterial Labor in Information Networks." *Critical Studies in Media Communication* 31, no. 5 (2014): 365–79.

Foley, Megan. "Sound Bites: Rethinking the Circulation of Speech from Fragment to Fetish." *Rhetoric and Public Affairs* 15, no. 4 (2012): 613–22.

Folkenflik, David, and Alex Chadwick. "Novak Reveals Details of CIA Identity Leak." *NPR*, July 12, 2006.

Foster, A. L. "Other Peoples [sic] Business." *Chicago Defender*, May 23, 1959.

Foucault, Michel. *Discipline and Punish: The Birth of the Prison*. New York: Vintage Books, 1995.

Foucault, Michel. *Fearless Speech*. Los Angeles: Semiotext(e), 2001.

Foucault, Michel. *Foucault Live: Interviews, 1961–84*. Edited by Sylvère Lotringer. Translated by John Johnston. New York: Semiotext(e), 1989.

Foucault, Michel. "Nietzsche, Genealogy, History." In *Language, Counter-Memory, Practice: Selected Essays and Interviews*, edited by D. F. Bouchard, 193–64. Ithaca, NY: Cornell University Press, 1977.

Foucault, Michel. *Security, Territory, Population: Lectures at the Collège de France 1977–1978*. Translated by Graham Burchell. New York: Picador, 2007.

Foucault, Michel. *"Society Must Be Defended": Lectures at the Collège de France 1975–1976*. Translated by David Macey. New York: Picador, 2003.

Fowler, Stephen. "Federal Agencies Plan for Mass Layoffs as Trump's Workforce Cuts Continue." *NPR*, March 15, 2025. https://www.npr.org/2025/03/15/nx-s1-5328721/reduction-in-force-rif-federal-workers-job-cuts-musk-doge-layoffs.

François, Anne Lise. *Open Secrets: The Literature of Uncounted Experience*. Stanford, CA: Stanford University Press, 2008.

Fraternal Order of Police. "A Brief History of the Fraternal Order of Police." Fraternal Order of Police Grand Lodge, https://fop.net/about-the-fop/history-of-the-fop. Accessed February 1, 2025.

Freud, Sigmund. *The Interpretation of Dreams*. Translated by A. A. Brill. Oxford: Oxford University Press, 1913.

Freud, Sigmund. "Part I: Parapraxes." In *Introductory Lectures on Psycho-Analysis*, edited and translated by James Strachey, 17–73. New York: W. W. Norton, 1966.

Freud, Sigmund. "Dissection of the Psychical Personality." In *New Introductory Lectures on Psycho-Analysis*. Edited and translated by James Strachey, 71–100. New York: W. W. Norton, 1989.

Freud, Sigmund. *The Psychopathology of Everyday Life*. Translated by A. A. Brill. New York: Macmillan, 1914.

Freud, Sigmund. *Totem and Taboo: Some Points of Agreement Between the Mental Lives of Savages and Neurotics*. Translated by James Strachey. New York: W. W. Norton, 1950.

Freud, Sigmund. *The Uncanny*. Translated by David McClintock. New York: Penguin Books, 2003.

Friedersdorf, Conor. "The Vindication of Edward Snowden." *The Atlantic*, May 11, 2015.

Friedersdorf, Conor. "What the *NYT Magazine* Doesn't Say About James O'Keefe." *The Atlantic*, July 29, 2011.

Frosh, Stephen. "Psychoanalysis, Colonialism, Racism." *Journal of Theoretical and Philosophical Psychology* 33, no. 3 (2013): 141–54.

Frum, David. "It Wasn't a Hoax." *The Atlantic*, November 25, 2021.

Frye, Northrop. *Anatomy of Criticism: Four Essays*. Princeton, NJ: Princeton University Press, 1973.

Gabbatt, Adam. "Golden Escalator Ride: The Surreal Day Trump Kicked Off His Bid for President." *The Guardian*, June 14, 2019.

Gadamer, Hans-Georg. "The Hermeneutics of Suspicion." *Man and World* 17, nos. 3–4 (1984): 313–23.

Galison, Peter. "Removing Knowledge: The Logic of Modern Censorship." In *Agnotology: The Making and Unmaking of Ignorance*, edited by Robert N. Proctor and Londa Schiebinger, 37–54. Stanford, CA: Stanford University Press, 2008.

Galison, Peter. "Secrecy in Three Acts." *Social Research* 77, no. 3 (2010): 941–74.

Ganz, John. "Foucault and the Conservatives: Biopolitics and the American Gothic." *Unpopular Front* (blog), June 2, 2021. https://www.unpopularfront.news/p/foucault-and-the-conservatives?utm_campaign=post&utm_medium=web.

Gellman, Barton. *Angler: The Cheney Vice-Presidency*. New York: Penguin Books, 2009.

Gellman, Barton. *Dark Mirror: Edward Snowden and the American Surveillance State*. New York: Penguin Books, 2020.

Genette, Gerard. *Narrative Discourse: An Essay in Method*. Translated by Jane E. Lewin. Ithaca, NY: Cornell University Press, 1980.

Geraghty, Jim. "The Alinsky Administration." *National Review*, May 14, 2009.

Gibbs, Nancy, and John F. Dickerson. "Person of the Year: George W. Bush." *Time*, December 19, 2004.

Gibney, Alex, dir. *Zero Days*. Magnolia Pictures, 2016.

Gill-Peterson, Jules. *Histories of the Transgender Child*. Minneapolis: University of Minnesota Press, 2018.

Gilmartin, Eoghan, and Tommy Greene. "Selling Out Julian Assange: An Interview with Txema Guijarro." *Jacobin*, July 9, 2019.

Gitelman, Lisa. *Paper Knowledge: Toward a Media History of Documents*. Durham, NC: Duke University Press, 2014.

Glass, Andrew. "'Scooter' Libby Convicted of Perjury, March 6, 2007." *Politico,* March 3, 2014. https://www.politico.com/story/2014/03/this-day-in-politics-104300.

Glissant, Édouard. *Poetics of Relation.* Translated by Betsy Wing. Ann Arbor: University of Michigan Press, 1997.

Goffman, Erving. *The Presentation of Self in Everyday Life.* New York: Anchor Books, 1959.

Goffman, Erving. *Strategic Interaction.* Philadelphia: University of Pennsylvania Press, 1970.

Gomez, Logan Rae. "Temporal Containment and the Singularity of Anti-Blackness: Saying Her Name in and Across Time." *Rhetoric Society Quarterly* 51, no. 3 (2021): 182–92.

Gooding, Frederick W. *American Dream Deferred: Black Federal Workers in Washington, D.C., 1941–1981.* Pittsburgh, PA: University of Pittsburgh Press, 2018.

Goodnight, G. Thomas, and John Poulakos. "Conspiracy Rhetoric: From Pragmatism to Fantasy in Public Discourse." *Western Journal of Speech Communication* 45, no. 4 (1981): 299–316.

Gordon, Michael R. "Threats and Responses: Military Analysis; Setting the Stage." *New York Times,* March 20, 2003. https://www.nytimes.com/2003/03/20/world/threats-and-responses-military-analysis-setting-the-stage.html.

Gorgias. *Encomium of Helen.* In *The Greek Sophists,* translated by John Dillon and Tania Gergel. New York: Penguin Books, 2003.

Grady, Denise, and Nicholas St. Fleur. "Fetal Tissue from Abortions for Research Is Traded in a Gray Area." *New York Times,* July 27, 2015. https://www.nytimes.com/2015/07/28/health/fetal-tissue-from-abortions-for-research-is-traded-in-a-gray-zone.html.

Green, Erica L. "What to Know About the Fallout from the Signal Group Chat Leak." *New York Times,* March 28, 2025.

Greenberg, Andy. *Sandworm: A New Era of Cyberwar and the Hunt for the Kremlin's Most Dangerous Hackers.* New York: Doubleday, 2019.

Greene, Ronald Walter. "Another Materialist Rhetoric." *Critical Studies in Mass Communication* 15, no. 1 (1998): 21–40.

Greene, Ronald Walter. "Rhetorical Capital: Communicative Labor, Money/Speech, and Neo-Liberal Governance." *Communication and Critical/Cultural Studies* 4, no. 3 (2007): 327–31.

Greene, Ronald Walter, Daniel Horvath, and Larry Browning. "Truth-Telling and Organizational Democracy: The Rhetoric of Whistleblowing as an Act of Parrhesia." In *Whistleblowing, Communication and Consequences: Lessons from the Norwegian National Lottery,* edited by Peer Jacob Svenkerud, Jan-Oddvar Sørnes, and Larry Browning, 31–45. New York: Routledge, 2021.

Greenlee, Sam. *The Spook Who Sat by the Door.* 2nd ed. Detroit, MI: Wayne State University Press, 2022.

Greenwald, Glenn. "Ecuador Will Imminently Withdraw Asylum for Julian Assange and Hand Him Over to the U.K. What Comes Next?" *The Intercept,* July 21, 2018. https://theintercept.com/2018/07/21/ecuador-will-imminently-withdraw-asylum-for-julian-assange-and-hand-him-over-to-the-uk-what-comes-next/.

Greenwald, Glenn. *Nowhere to Hide: Edward Snowden, the NSA, and the U.S. Surveillance State.* New York: Metropolitan Books, 2014.

Gregory, Derek. "From a View to a Kill: Drones and Late Modern War." *Theory, Culture and Society* 28, nos. 7–8 (2011): 188–215.

Griffin, Leland. "The Rhetorical Structure of the Antimasonic Movement." In *The Rhetorical Idiom: Essays in Rhetoric, Oratory, Language, and Drama,* edited by Donald C. Bryant, 145–59. Ithaca, NY: Cornell University Press, 1958.

Griffin, Leland. "The Rhetoric of Historical Movements." *Quarterly Journal of Speech* 38, no. 2 (1952): 184–88.

Grindstaff, Davin Allen. *Rhetorical Secrets: Mapping Gay Identity and Queer Resistance in Contemporary America.* Tuscaloosa: University of Alabama Press, 2013.

Gross, Alan G. "Rhetoric of Science *Is* Epistemic Rhetoric." *Quarterly Journal of Speech* 76, no. 3 (1990): 304–6.

Gross, Daniel M. *The Secret History of Emotion: From Aristotle's Rhetoric to Modern Brain Science.* Chicago: University of Chicago Press, 2006.

Gunn, Joshua. "Death by Publicity: US Freemasonry and the Public Drama of Secrecy." *Rhetoric and Public Affairs* 11, no. 2 (2008): 243–77.

Gunn, Joshua. "Hystericizing Huey: Emotional Appeals, Desire, and the Psychodynamics of Demagoguery." *Western Journal of Communication* 71, no. 1 (2007): 1–27.

Gunn, Joshua. *Modern Occult Rhetoric: Mass Media and the Drama of Secrecy in the Twentieth Century.* Tuscaloosa: University of Alabama Press, 2005.

Gunn, Joshua. "On Speech and Public Release." *Rhetoric and Public Affairs* 13, no. 2 (2010): 175–215.

Gunn, Joshua. *Political Perversion: Rhetorical Aberration in the Time of Trumpeteering.* Chicago: University of Chicago Press, 2020.

Gunn, Joshua. "Size Matters: Polytoning Rhetoric's Perverse Apocalypse." *Rhetoric Society Quarterly* 38, no. 1 (2008): 82–108.

Haberman, Maggie. "Cassidy Hutchinson Stuns with Testimony About Trump on Jan. 6." *New York Times,* June 28, 2022.

Haberman, Maggie. *Confidence Man: The Making of Donald Trump and the Breaking of America.* New York: Penguin Press, 2022.

Haberman, Maggie, and Glenn Thrush. "Attorney General Alerted Trump His Name Appeared in Epstein Files." *New York Times,* July 23, 2025.

Habermas, Jürgen. *The Structural Transformation of the Public Sphere: An Inquiry into a Category of Bourgeois Society.* Translated by Thomas Burger, with the assistance of Frederick Lawrence. Cambridge, MA: MIT Press, 1989.

Hackett, David G. *That Religion in Which All Men Agree: Freemasonry in American Culture.* Berkeley: University of California Press, 2014.

Hage, Ghassan. *Against Paranoid Nationalism: Searching for Hope in a Shrinking Society.* Sydney: Pluto Press, 2003.

Hall, R. Cargill. *The NRO at Forty: Ensuring Global Information Supremacy.* Chantilly, VA: National Reconnaissance Office, 2000.

Hall, Rachel. "Terror and the Female Grotesque: Introducing Full-Body Scanners to U.S. Airports." In *Feminist Surveillance Studies,* edited by Rachel E. Dubrofsky and Shoshana Amielle Magnet, 127–49. Durham, NC: Duke University Press, 2015.

Hall, Stuart. "The Great Moving Nowhere Show." *Marxism Today,* November/December 1998, 9–14.

Hall, Stuart. "The Great Moving Right Show." In *Selected Political Writings: The Great Moving Right Show and Other Essays,* edited by Sally Davison, David Featherstone, Michael Rustin, and Bill Schwarz, 172–86. Durham, NC: Duke University Press, 2017.

Hall, Stuart. "Signification, Representation, Ideology: Althusser and the Post-Structuralist Debates." *Critical Studies in Mass Communication* 2, no. 2 (1985): 91–114.

Hallsby, Atilla. "Intimate Spaces of Mental Wellness." *Rhetoric, Politics and Culture* 1, no. 1 (2021): 55–66.

Hallsby, Atilla. "Psychoanalysis Against WikiLeaks: Resisting the Demand for Transparency." *Review of Communication* 20, no. 1 (2020): 69–86.

Hallsby, Atilla. "Recanonizing Rhetoric: The Secret *in* and *of* Discourse." *Journal for the History of Rhetoric* 25, no. 3 (2022): 360–64.

Hallsby, Atilla. "The Rhetorical Algorithm: WikiLeaks and the Elliptical Secrets of Donald J. Trump." *Secrecy and Society* 1, no. 2 (2017): 1–41.

Hallsby, Atilla, and Joshua Gunn. "Pain, Pleasure, and the Mirror of Enjoyment." In *Pleasure and Pain in U.S. Public Culture,* edited by Christopher J. Gilbert and John Louis Lucaites, 140–63. Tuscaloosa: University of Alabama Press, 2025.

Halper, Evan. "Republicans Release Benghazi Report with No New Evidence Against Hillary Clinton." *Los Angeles Times,* June 28, 2016.

Hamdouni Alami, Mohammed. *Art and Architecture in the Islamic Tradition: Aesthetics, Politics and Desire in Early Islam.* London: I. B. Tauris, 2011.

Hamill, John. *The Craft: A History of English Freemasonry.* Wellingborough: Crucible, 1986.

Haney López, Ian. *Dog Whistle Politics: How Coded Racial Appeals Have Reinvented Racism and Wrecked the Middle Class.* New York: Oxford University Press, 2014.

Hansen, Evan. "Manning-Lamo Chat Logs Revealed." *Wired,* July 13, 2011.

Harney, Stefano, and Fred Moten. *The Undercommons: Fugitive Planning and Black Study.* New York: Minor Compositions, 2013.

Harper, Jennifer. "No Holds Barred for British Press on Bush's Visit." *Washington Times,* November 20, 2003.

Harriot, Michael. "Trump's Latest Tweets Are Dog-Whistles to White Supremacists." *The Root,* November 1, 2017. https://www.theroot.com/trumps-latest-tweets-are-dog-whistles-to-white-supremac-1820048502.

Harris, Shane, and Samuel Oakford. "Discord Member Details How Documents Leaked from Closed Chat Group." *Washington Post,* April 16, 2023.

Hartelius, E. Johanna, and Olivia S. Gellar. "Secrecy and Pseudoscience in the 'Real Battle' of COVID-19 Anti-Vaccination Arguments." *Rhetoric and Public Affairs* 26, no. 4 (2023): 95–127.

Hartman, Saidiya. *Scenes of Subjection: Terror, Slavery, and Self-Making in Nineteenth-Century America.* Rev. ed. New York: W. W. Norton, 2022.

Hartman, Saidiya. "The Time of Slavery." *South Atlantic Quarterly* 101, no. 4 (2002): 757–77.

Hartnett, Stephen. "Fanny Fern's 1855 *Ruth Hall,* the Cheerful Brutality of Capitalism, and the Irony of Sentimental Rhetoric." *Quarterly Journal of Speech* 88, no. 1 (2002): 1–18.

Hartnett, Stephen J., and Jennifer R. Mercieca. "A Discovered Dissembler Can Achieve Nothing Great; or, Four Theses on the Death of Presidential Rhetoric in an Age of Empire." *Presidential Studies Quarterly* 37, no. 4 (2009): 599–619.

Harvey, Roy. "The Black P Stones: A University Creation?" *Chicago Defender,* June 18, 1979.

Harvey, Roy. "'Disorganizer' Creates Gang Climate." *Chicago Defender,* June 19, 1979.

Harvey, Roy. "The Gang Controller Is Brought In." *Chicago Defender,* June 21, 1979.

Harvey, Roy. "Seminary Operated Gang Hostels." *Chicago Defender,* June 25, 1979.

Harvey, Roy. "The Street Gang as an Open 'Educational Experiment.'" *Chicago Defender,* June 23, 1979.

Harvey, Roy. "The University, TWO, and the Gangs." *Chicago Defender,* June 20, 1979.

Hasian, Marouf A. "Watching the Domestication of the Wikileaks Helicopter Controversy." *Communication Quarterly* 60, no. 2 (2012): 190–209.

Hasian, Marouf, Jr., Sean Lawson, and Megan D. McFarlane. *The Rhetorical Invention of America's National Security State.* Lanham, MD: Lexington Books, 2015.

Hawhee, Debra. *Rhetoric in Tooth and Claw: Animals, Language, Sensation.* Chicago: University of Chicago Press, 2017.

Hayes, Heather Ashley. *Violent Subjects and Rhetorical Cartography in the Age of the Terror Wars.* London: Palgrave Macmillan, 2016.

Hayles, N. Katherine. *How We Became Posthuman: Virtual Bodies in Cybernetics, Literature, and Informatics.* Chicago: University of Chicago Press, 1999.

Henig, Jess. "ACORN Accusations." FactCheck, October 18, 2008, http://www.factcheck.org/2008/10/acorn-accusations.

Henneberger, Melinda. "From Pakistan, Family Comes to Tell of Drone Strike's Toll." *Washington Post,* October 29, 2013.

Hernandez, Miguel. *The Ku Klux Klan and Freemasonry in 1920s America: Fighting Fraternities.* London: Routledge, 2019.

Herodotus. *The Histories.* Translated by Aubrey de Sélincourt. New York: Penguin Books, 2003.

Herszenhorn, David M. "House Benghazi Report Finds No New Evidence of Wrongdoing by Hillary Clinton." *New York Times,* June 28, 2016.

Hertling, Mark. "Team Trump Promises 'Shock and Awe.' Do They Know What That Means?" *The Bulwark,* January 17, 2025. https://www.thebulwark.com/p/team-trump-promises-shock-and-awe.

Higgins, David M. *Reverse Colonization: Science Fiction, Imperial Fantasy, and Alt-Victimhood.* Iowa City: University of Iowa Press, 2021.

Hijazi, Ihsan A. "Hostage's Release Linked to Shift in Iranian Policy." *New York Times,* November 4, 1986. https://www.nytimes.com/1986/11/04/world/hostage-s-release-is-linked-to-shift-in-iranian-policy.htm.

Hill Collins, Patricia. "A Comparison of Two Works on Black Family Life." *Signs: Journal of Women in Culture and Society* 14, no. 4 (1989): 875–84.

Hirsh, Michael. "Daniel Ellsberg Is Dying. And He Has Some Final Things to Say." *Politico,* June 4, 2023. https://www.politico.com/news/magazine/2023/06/04/daniel-ellsberg-final-advice-00099639.

Hitchens, Christopher. "Why Dubya Can't Read." *The Nation,* September 24, 2000. https://www.thenation.com/article/archive/why-dubya-cant-read/.

Hoback, Cullen, dir. *Q: Into the Storm.* HBO Documentary Films. Aired March 21–April 4, 2021, on HBO.

Hochman, Brian. *The Listeners: A History of Wiretapping in the United States.* Cambridge, MA: Harvard University Press, 2022.

Hodges, Andrew. *Alan Turing: The Enigma.* Princeton, NJ: Princeton University Press, 1983.

Hoerl, Kristen, and Erin Ortiz. "Organizational Secrecy and the FBI's COINTELPRO–Black Nationalist Hate Groups Program, 1967–1971." *Management Communication Quarterly* 29, no. 4 (2015): 590–615.

Hofstadter, Richard. *Anti-Intellectualism in American Life.* New York: Vintage Books, 1963.

Hofstadter, Richard. *The Paranoid Style in American Politics and Other Essays.* New York: Alfred A. Knopf, 1965.

Hollingsworth, Heather. "NAACP Resolution Condemns Racism in Tea Party." *Boston Globe*, July 13, 2010. https://archive.boston.com/news/nation/articles/2010/07/13/naacp_resolution_condemns_racism_in_tea_party/.

Hood, Gavin, dir. *Eye in the Sky*. Entertainment One Features and Raindog Films, 2015.

Horn, Eva. "Logics of Political Secrecy." *Theory, Culture and Society* 28, nos. 7–8 (2011): 103–22.

Horowitz, Andy. "Saul Alinsky: A True American Exceptionalist." *The Atlantic*, January 27, 2012.

Horowitz, David. *Take No Prisoners: The Battle Plan for Defeating the Left*. Washington, DC: Regnery, 2014.

Horowitz, Eli, and Micah Bloomberg. *Homecoming*. Podcast. Gimlet Media, 2016–2017. https://gimletmedia.com/shows/homecoming.

Horwitt, Sanford D. *Let Them Call Me Rebel: Saul Alinsky, His Life and Legacy*. New York: Alfred A. Knopf, 1989.

House of Representatives. *Final Report of the Select Committee on the Events Surrounding the 2012 Terrorist Attack in Benghazi*. H.R. Rep. No. 114-848, December 7, 2016. Library of Congress. https://www.congress.gov/congressional-report/114th-congress/house-report/848/1.

Howell, Brenetta. "Westside Roundup." *Chicago Defender*, February 17, 1965.

Howell, Brenetta. "Westside Roundup." *Chicago Defender*, March 2, 1965.

Hulse, Carl, and David E. Sanger. "New Criticism on Prewar Use of Intelligence." *New York Times*, September 29, 2003.

"I Am Part of the Resistance Inside the Trump Administration." *New York Times*, September 5, 2018.

ICIJ (International Consortium of Investigative Journalists). "Offshore Havens and Hidden Riches of World Leaders and Billionaires Exposed in Unprecedented Leak," ICIJ.org, October 3, 2021, https://www.icij.org/investigations/pandora-papers/global-investigation-tax-havens-offshore/.

Igielnik, Ruth, and Kellen Browning. "Republicans Are Breaking with Trump over Epstein Files, Polls Show." *New York Times*, July 23, 2025.

Igo, Sarah E. *The Known Citizen: A History of Privacy in Modern America*. Cambridge, MA: Harvard University Press, 2018.

Iraq Family Health Survey Study Group. "Violence-Related Mortality in Iraq from 2002 to 2006." *New England Journal of Medicine* 358, no. 5 (2008): 484–93. https://doi.org/10.1056/NEJMsa0707782.

Irigaray, Luce. *Speculum of the Other Woman*. Translated by Gillian C. Gill. Ithaca, NY: Cornell University Press, 1989.

Isikoff, Michael, and Mark Hosenball. "Terror Watch: Criminal or Just Plain Stupid?" *Newsweek*, October 8, 2003.

Ito, Robert. "In 'Homecoming,' a Sound Experiment Becomes Something to See." *New York Times*, October 26, 2018.

Itkowitz, Colby. "A Brief History of the 'Gotcha Question' in Politics." *Washington Post*, February 24, 2015.

Ivins, Molly. "Call Me a Bush-Hater." *The Progressive*, November 2003.

Jacob, Margaret C. *Living the Enlightenment: Freemasonry and Politics in Eighteenth-Century Europe*. Oxford: Oxford University Press, 1991.

Jacobsen, Lenz. "Ein Hitlergruß ist ein Hitlergruß ist ein Hitlergruß." *Die Zeit*, January 21, 2025. https://www.zeit.de/kultur/2025-01/elon-musk-hitlergruss-amtseinfuehrung-donald-trump.

Jamieson, Kathleen Hall. "Antecedent Genre as Rhetorical Constraint." *Quarterly Journal of Speech* 61, no. 4 (1975): 406–15.

Jamieson, Kathleen Hall. *Cyberwar: How Russian Hackers and Trolls Helped Elect a President: What We Don't, Can't and Do Know.* New York: Oxford University Press, 2021.

Jamieson, Kathleen Hall. "Justifying the War in Iraq: What the Bush Administration's Uses of Evidence Reveal." *Rhetoric and Public Affairs* 10, no. 2 (2007): 249–73. http://doi.org/10.1353/rap.2007.0038.

Jasanoff, Sheila. "Transparency in Public Science: Purposes, Reasons, Limits." *Law and Contemporary Problems* 69, no. 21 (2006): 21–45.

Jaworski, Gary D. *Erving Goffman and the Cold War.* Lanham, MD: Lexington Books, 2023.

Jay, Martin. *Downcast Eyes: The Denigration of Vision in Twentieth-Century French Thought.* Berkeley: University of California Press, 1993.

Joffe-Block, Jude. "Four Years After the Capitol Riot, Why Qanon Hasn't Gone Away." *NPR*, December 30, 2024. https://www.npr.org/2024/12/30/nx-s1-5230801/qanon-capitol-riot-social-media.

Johnson, Eliana. "James O'Keefe's Rules for Radicals." *National Review*, June 27, 2013.

Johnson, Jenell. "'A Man's Mouth Is His Castle': The Midcentury Fluoridation Controversy and the Visceral Public." *Quarterly Journal of Speech* 102, no. 1 (2016): 1–20.

Johnson, Jenell. "The Skeleton on the Couch: The Eagleton Affair, Rhetorical Disability, and the Stigma of Mental Illness." *Rhetoric Society Quarterly* 40, no. 5 (2010): 459–78.

Johnson, Lyndon B. "Remarks of the President at Howard University, June 4, 1965." In *The Moynihan Report and the Politics of Controversy*, edited by Lee Rainwater and William L. Yancey, 125–32. Cambridge, MA: MIT Press, 1967.

Johnson, Paul E. "The Art of Masculine Victimhood: Donald Trump's Demagoguery." *Women's Studies in Communication* 40, no. 3 (2017): 229–50.

Johnson, Paul E. *I the People: The Rhetoric of Conservative Populism in the United States.* Tuscaloosa: University of Alabama Press, 2022.

Jone, Saj-Nicole. "Never Waste a Crisis." *Forbes*, November 24, 2008.

Jouvenal, Justin. "Former CIA Officer John Kiriakou Is Sentenced to 30 Months in Prison for Leaks." *Washington Post*, January 25, 2013. https://www.washingtonpost.com/local/former-cia-officer-john-kiriakou-sentenced-to-30-months-in-prison-for-leaks/2013/01/25/49ea0cc0-6704-11e2-9e1b-07db1d2ccd5b_story.html.

Judd, Barry. "Hero or Dupe: Jay Swan and the Ambivalences of Aboriginal Masculinity in the Films of Ivan Sen." In *Cinematic Settlers: The Settler Colonial World in Film*, edited by Janne Lahti and Rebecca Weaver-Hightower, 115–26. New York: Routledge, 2020.

"Julian Assange Sex Assault Allegations: Timeline." *BBC News*, February 5, 2016.

Jutel, Olivier. "Barack Obama, the New Spirit of Capitalism, and the Populist Resistance." *International Journal of Žižek Studies* 6, no. 3 (2012): 1–18.

Jutel, Olivier. "The Horror of Communication." *Psychoanalysis, Culture and Society* 28 (2023): 53–71.

Kahn, David. *The Codebreakers: The Story of Secret Writing.* New York: Simon & Schuster, 1996.

Kantorowicz, Ernst H. *The King's Two Bodies: A Study in Mediaeval Political Theology.* Princeton, NJ: Princeton University Press, 2016.

Kantorowicz, Ernst H. "Mysteries of State: An Absolutist Concept and Its Late Mediaeval Origins." *The Harvard Theological Review* 48, no. 1 (1955): 65–91.

Kantrowitz, Stephen. "'Intended for the Better Government of Man': The Political History of African American Freemasonry in the Era of Emancipation." *The Journal of American History* 96, no. 4 (2010): 1005–6.

Kapadia, Ronak K. "Death by Double-Tap: (Undoing) Racial Logics in the Age of Drone Warfare." In *With Stones in Our Hands: Writings on Muslims, Racism, and Empire,* edited by Sohail Daulatzai and Junaid Rana, 201–18. Minneapolis: University of Minnesota Press, 2018.

Kapadia, Ronak K. *Insurgent Aesthetics: Security and the Queer Life of the Forever War.* Durham, NC: Duke University Press, 2019.

Kaplan, Joshua, Justin Elliott, and Alex Mierjeski. "Speaker Mike Johnson Lives in a D.C. House at the Center of a Pastor's Secretive Influence Campaign." *Tennessee Lookout* February 28, 2025. https://tennesseelookout.com/2025/02/28/speaker-mike-johnson-is-living-in-a-d-c-house-that-is-the-center-of-a-pastors-secretive-influence-campaign/.

Karstetter, Allan B. "Toward a Theory of Rhetorical Irony." *Speech Monographs* 31, no. 2 (1964): 162–78.

Kayser, Jacques. *The Dreyfus Affair.* Translated by Nora Bickley. New York: Covici, Friede, 1931.

Keck, Zachary. "Yes, Edward Snowden Is a Traitor." *The Diplomat,* December 21, 2013.

Keeling, Diane Marie. "Of Turning and Tropes." *Review of Communication* 16, no. 4 (2016): 317–33.

Keiper, Lauren. "Anti-Abortion Group Releases More Video of Planned Parenthood." *Reuters,* February 3, 2011. https://www.reuters.com/article/us-abortion-video/anti-abortion-group-releases-more-video-of-planned-parenthood-idUSTRE7130JI20110204.

Keller, Catherine. "The Apophasis of Gender: A Fourfold Unsaying of Feminist Theology." *Journal of the American Academy of Religion* 76, no. 4 (2008): 905–33.

Kelley-Romano, Stephanie, and Kathryn L. Carew. "Make America Hate Again: Donald Trump and the Birther Conspiracy." *Journal of Hate Studies* 14, no. 1 (2017): 33–52.

Kelly, Casey Ryan. *Apocalypse Man: The Death Drive and the Rhetoric of White Masculine Victimhood.* Columbus: The Ohio State University Press, 2020.

Kelly, Casey Ryan. *Caught on Tape: White Masculinity and Obscene Enjoyment.* London: Oxford University Press, 2023.

Kelly, Casey Ryan. "COVID-19 Conspiracy Theories and Other Primal Fantasies." *Quarterly Journal of Speech* 109, no. 2 (2023): 132–53.

Kelly, Casey Ryan, and Chase Aunspach. "Incels, Compulsory Sexuality, and Fascist Masculinity." *Feminist Formations* 32, no. 3 (2020): 145–72.

Kenarov, Dimeter. "Was the Philosopher Julia Kristeva a Cold War Collaborator?" *New Yorker,* September 5, 2018.

Kendzior, Sarah. *Hiding in Plain Sight: The Invention of Donald Trump and the Erosion of America.* New York: Flatiron Books, 2020.

Kendzior, Sarah. *They Knew: How a Culture of Conspiracy Keeps America Complacent.* New York: Flatiron Books, 2022.

"Kerry: Snowden a 'Coward' and 'Traitor.'" *NBC News,* May 28, 2014.

Kessler, Glenn. "Dark-Money Group Smears Valerie Plame with 'White Supremacist' Label." *Washington Post,* May 22, 2020.

Kessler, Glenn. "Valerie Plame's Claim That Scooter Libby Leaked Her Identity." *Washington Post,* September 10, 2019.

Khan, Naureen. "Drone Victims Give US Lawmakers Firsthand Account of Attack." *Al Jazeera,* October 29, 2013.

Khan, Ruqayya Yasmine. *Self and Secrecy in Early Islam.* Columbia: University of South Carolina Press, 2008.

Khanna, Ranjana. *Dark Continents: Psychoanalysis and Colonialism.* Durham, NC: Duke University Press, 2003.

"King's Plan Wins Approval." *Chicago Defender,* January 15, 1966.

Kinzer, Stephen. *The Brothers: John Foster Dulles, Allen Dulles, and Their Secret World War.* New York: Henry Holt, 2014.

Kiriakou, John. *The Reluctant Spy: My Secret Life in the CIA's War on Terror.* With Michael Ruby and with a foreword by Bruce Riedel. New York: Bantam Books, 2010.

Kittler, Friedrich. *Gramophone, Film, Typewriter.* Stanford, CA: Stanford University Press, 1999.

Klug, Sam. "The Moynihan Report Resurrected." *Dissent* 63, no. 1 (2016): 48–55.

Knight, Peter. "Outrageous Conspiracy Theories: Popular and Official Responses to 9/11 in Germany and the United States." *New German Critique* 103, no. 35 (2008): 165–93.

"Kodak Fights Militant Negro Group over Jobs." *Chicago Defender,* January 28, 1967.

Kodé, Anna. "The Politics of Brutalism." *New York Times,* February 22, 2025.

Konzett, Delia Malia. "The South Pacific as the Final Frontier: Hollywood's South Seas Fantasies, the Beachcomber, and Militarization." In *Cinematic Settlers: The Settler Colonial World in Film,* edited by Janne Lahti and Rebecca Weaver-Hightower, 13–25. New York: Routledge, 2020.

Kordela, A. Kiarina. *Surplus: Spinoza, Lacan.* Albany: State University of New York Press, 2007.

Kornbluh, Anna. *Immediacy; Or, the Style of Too-Late Capitalism.* New York: Verso, 2024.

Kotsko, Adam. "What Happened to Giorgio Agamben?" *Slate,* February 20, 2022. https://slate.com/human-interest/2022/02/giorgio-agamben-covid-holocaust-comparison-right-wing-protest.html.

Kovaleski, Serge. "Obama's Organizing Years, Guiding Others and Finding Himself." *New York Times,* July 7, 2008.

Kovensky, Josh. "Inside a Secret Society of Prominent Right-Wing Christian Men Prepping for a 'National Divorce.'" *Talking Points Memo,* March 9, 2024. https://talkingpointsmemo.com/news/inside-a-secret-society-of-prominent-right-wing-christian-men-prepping-for-a-national-divorce.

Kroll, Justin, and Alexa Harrison. "Box-Office Report." *Variety,* February 21, 2011.

Kruse, Michael. "The Escalator Ride That Changed America." *Politico,* June 14, 2019. https://www.politico.com/magazine/story/2019/06/14/donald-trump-campaign-announcement-tower-escalator-oral-history-227148/.

Kruse, Michael. "The First Time Hillary Clinton Was President." *Politico,* August 26, 2016. https://www.politico.com/magazine/story/2016/08/hillary-clinton-2016-wellesley-president-214188/.

Kubrick, Stanley, dir. *Dr. Strangelove; or, How I Learned to Stop Worrying and Love the Bomb.* Columbia Pictures, 1964.

Kurtz, Stanley. "Why Hillary's Alinsky Letters Matter." *National Review Online,* September 22, 2014. https://www.nationalreview.com/corner/why-hillarys-alinsky-letters-matter-stanley-kurtz/.

Lacan, Jacques. "The Freudian Thing." In *Écrits: The First Complete Edition in English,* translated by Bruce Fink, 334–63. New York: W. W. Norton, 2006.

Lacan, Jacques. "The Function and Field of Speech and Language in Psychoanalysis." In *Écrits: The First Complete Edition in English,* translated by Bruce Fink, 197–268. New York: W. W. Norton, 2006.

Lacan, Jacques. *On the Names-of-the-Father.* Translated by Bruce Fink. Cambridge: Polity Press, 2013.

Lacan, Jacques. *The Seminar of Jacques Lacan, Book I: Freud's Papers on Technique 1953–1954.* Translated by John Forrester. Rev. ed. New York: W. W. Norton, 1991.

Lacan, Jacques. *The Seminar of Jacques Lacan, Book XI: The Four Fundamental Concepts of Psychoanalysis.* Edited by Jacques Alain-Miller. Translated by Alan Sheridan. Rev. ed. New York: W. W. Norton, 1998.

Lacan, Jacques. "Seminar on 'The Purloined Letter.'" In *Écrits: The First Complete Edition in English,* translated by Bruce Fink, 6–48. New York: W. W. Norton, 2006.

Lacan, Jacques. "The Situation of Psychoanalysis and the Training of Psychoanalysts in 1956." *Écrits: The First Complete Edition in English,* translated by Bruce Fink, 384–407. New York: W. W. Norton, 2006.

Lacan, Jacques. "The Subversion of the Subject and the Dialectic of Desire in the Freudian Unconscious." *Écrits: The First Complete Edition in English,* translated by Bruce Fink, 671–702. New York: W. W. Norton, 2006.

Laclau, Ernesto. *Emancipation(s).* New York: Verso, 1996.

Laclau, Ernesto. *On Populist Reason.* New York: Verso, 2007.

Laclau, Ernesto. *The Rhetorical Foundations of Society.* New York: Verso, 2014.

Lafond, Nicole. "Jim Jordan Rounds Out Year Making Sure Trump Knows How Hard He's Investigating the Investigators." *Talking Points Memo,* December 21, 2023. https://talkingpointsmemo.com/where-things-stand/jim-jordan-rounds-out-year-making-sure-trump-knows-how-hard-hes-investigating-the-investigators.

Lambro, Donald. "Shortsighted Tall Tales." *Washington Times,* July 21, 2005.

Lanham, Richard A. *A Handlist of Rhetorical Terms.* 2nd ed. Berkeley: University of California Press, 1991.

Lansing, Robert. "The Secretary of State to President Wilson." In *Papers Relating to the Foreign Relations of the United States, The Lansing Papers, 1914–1920,* vol. 1. Washington, DC: Government Printing Office. https://history.state.gov/historicaldocuments/frus1914-20v01/d201.

Laplanche, Jean, and Jean-Bertrand Pontalis. *The Language of Psychoanalysis.* London: Hogarth, 1985.

Latour, Bruno. *Pandora's Hope: Essays on the Reality of Science Studies.* Cambridge, MA: Harvard University Press, 1999.

Le Bon, Gustave. *The Crowd: A Study of the Popular Mind.* New York: Macmillan, 1897.

Lebovic, Sam. "How Administrative Opposition Shaped the Freedom of Information Act." In *Troubling Transparency: The History and Future of Information,* edited by David E. Pozen and Michael Schudson, 13–33. New York: Columbia University Press, 2018.

le Carré, John. *A Delicate Truth.* New York: Penguin Books, 2014.

le Carré, John. *Tinker, Tailor, Soldier, Spy.* New York: Alfred A. Knopf, 1974.

Lechuga, Michael. *Visions of Invasion: Alien Affects, Cinema, and Citizenship in Settler Colonies.* Jackson: University Press of Mississippi, 2023.

Leigh, David, and Luke Harding. *WikiLeaks: Inside Julian Assange's War on Secrecy.* London: Guardian Books, 2011.

Leonnig, Carol D., Jenna Johnson, and Marc Fisher. "Tracking Edward Snowden, from a Maryland Classroom to a Hong Kong Hotel." *Washington Post,* June 15, 2013.

Leonnig, Carol D., and Julie Tate. "Snowden's Girlfriend—Dancer, Nature Lover—Said to Be Shocked by His Actions." *Washington Post,* June 11, 2013.

Levant, Ronald. "The Masculinity Crisis." *Journal of Men's Studies* 5, no. 3 (1997): 221–31.

Levine, Caroline. *Forms: Whole, Rhythm, Hierarchy, Network*. Princeton, NJ: Princeton University Press, 2015.

Levine, Yasha. *Surveillance Valley: The Secret Military History of the Internet*. New York: PublicAffairs, 2018.

Levinson, Barry, dir. *Disclosure*. Warner Bros., 1994.

Liman, Doug, dir. *Fair Game*. Summit Entertainment, 2010.

Linkins, Jason. "We Watch the 'King of Bain' Attack Documentary so You Don't Have To." *Huffington Post*, January 11, 2012. https://www.huffpost.com/entry/mitt-romney-newt-gingrich-attack_n_1200491.

Lipset, Seymour Martin, and Earl Raab. *The Politics of Unreason: Right Wing Extremism in America, 1790–1970*. New York: Harper & Row, 1970.

Little, Morgan. "Transcript: Rand Paul's Filibuster of John Brennan's CIA Nomination." *Los Angeles Times*, March 7, 2013.

Livingston, Gary D. "Racism and the Passage of the Immigration Act of 1924: The Beginning of the Quota System." *Journal of Borderlands Studies* 8, no. 2 (1993): 73–90.

Lizza, Ryan. "The Agitator." *New Republic*, March 18, 2007.

Lofgren, Mike. *The Deep State: The Fall of the Constitution and the Rise of a Shadow Government*. New York: Penguin Books, 2016.

Lofgren, Mike. "Essay: Anatomy of the Deep State." BillMoyers.com, February 21, 2014. https://billmoyers.com/2014/02/21/anatomy-of-the-deep-state.

Long, Pamela O. *Openness, Secrecy, Authorship: Technical Arts and the Culture of Knowledge from Antiquity to the Renaissance*. Baltimore, MA: Johns Hopkins University Press, 2004.

López, Issa, dir. *True Detective: Night Country*. Season 4. HBO Entertainment. Aired January 14–February 18, 2024, on HBO. https://www.hbo.com/true-detective.

Lowell, Hugo. "Elon Musk Appears with Trump and Tries to Claim 'Doge' Team Is Transparent." *The Guardian*, February 11, 2025. https://www.theguardian.com/us-news/2025/feb/11/elon-musk-trump-doge.

Lowi, Theodore. *The End of Liberalism: The Second Republic of the United States*. 2nd ed. New York: W. W. Norton, 1979.

Lucas, Ryan. "Attorney General Bondi Brushes Aside Questions About Her Handling of Epstein Files." *NPR*, July 15, 2025. https://www.npr.org/2025/07/15/g-s1-77698/pam-bondi-jeffrey-epstein-justice-department.

Luce, Edward, and Alexandra Ulmer. "Obama's Foes Turn to '60s Radical for Tactical Tips." *Financial Times*, August 17, 2009.

Ludmerer, Kenneth. "Genetics, Eugenics, and the Immigration Restriction Act of 1924." *Bulletin of the History of Medicine* 46, no. 1 (1972): 59–81.

Lundberg, Christian O. "Enjoying God's Death: *The Passion of the Christ* and the Practices of an Evangelical Public." *Quarterly Journal of Speech* 95, no. 4 (2009): 387–411.

Lundberg, Christian O. *Lacan in Public: Psychoanalysis and the Science of Rhetoric*. Tuscaloosa: University of Alabama Press, 2012.

Macrakis, Kristie. *Prisoners, Lovers, and Spies: The Story of Invisible Ink from Herodotus to al-Qaeda*. New Haven, CT: Yale University Press, 2014.

Manning, Chelsea. *Readme.txt*. New York: Farrar, Straus and Giroux, 2022.

Manning, Chelsea. "Sometimes You Have to Pay a Heavy Price to Live in a Free Society." *Democracy Now*, August 21, 2013.

Maret, Susan. "The Charm of Secrecy: Secrecy and Society as Secrecy Studies." *Secrecy and Society* 1, no. 1 (2016): 1–28.

Marquis, Christopher. "The World: How Powerful Can 16 Words Be?" *New York Times*, July 20, 2003.

Martens, Britta. "Dramatic Monologue, Detective Fiction, and the Search for Meaning." *Nineteenth-Century Literature* 66, no. 2 (2011): 195–218.

Martinot, Steve, and Jared Sexton. "The Avant-Garde of White Supremacy." *Social Identities* 9, no. 2 (2003): 169–81.

Marx, Gary T. *Undercover: Police Surveillance in America*. Berkeley: University of California Press, 1989.

Matheson, Calum. *Desiring the Bomb: Communication, Psychoanalysis, and the Atomic Age*. Tuscaloosa: University of Alabama Press, 2018.

Matheson, Calum. "Liberal Tears and the Rogue's Yarn of Sadistic Conservatism." *Rhetoric Society Quarterly* 52, no. 4 (2022): 341–55.

Matheson, Calum. "'What Does Obama Want of Me?' Anxiety and Jade Helm 15." *Quarterly Journal of Speech* 102, no. 2 (2016): 133–49.

Maxwell, William J. *F.B. Eyes: How J. Edgar Hoover's Ghostreaders Framed African American Literature*. Princeton, NJ: Princeton University Press, 2015.

May, Matthew. "Spinoza and Class Struggle." *Communication and Critical/Cultural Studies* 6, no. 2 (2009): 204–8.

Mayer, Jane. "Covert Operations." *New Yorker*, August 23, 2010.

Mayer, Jane. *Dark Money: The Hidden History of the Billionaires Behind the Rise of the Radical Right*. New York: Doubleday, 2016.

Mayer, Jane. "Sting of Myself." *New Yorker*, May 30, 2016. http://www.newyorker.com/magazine/2016/05/30/james-okeefe-accidentally-stings-himself.

Mayer, Jane. "The Transcript of James O'Keefe's Call to the Open Society Foundation." *New Yorker*, May 20, 2016. http://www.newyorker.com/news/news-desk/the-transcript-of-james-okeefes-call-to-the-open-society-foundations.

McCammon, Sarah. "Republicans Call Kamala Harris a 'DEI Hire' as Attacks on Her Gender and Race Increase." *NPR*, July 27, 2024. https://www.npr.org/2024/07/26/nx-s1-5049816/kamala-harris-sexism-racism-gender-jd-vance-cat-ladies.

McCreesh, Shawn. "Will a Time Magazine Cover Drive a Wedge Between Trump and Musk?" *New York Times*, February 7, 2025. https://www.nytimes.com/2025/02/07/us/politics/trump-musk-time-magazine-cover.html.

McCreesh, Shawn. "Will the Conspiracists Cultivated by Trump Turn on Him Over Epstein?" *New York Times*, July 14, 2025. https://www.nytimes.com/2025/07/14/us/politics/trump-epstein-conspiracy-theories.html.

McDaniel, James P. "Liberal Irony: A Program for Rhetoric." *Philosophy and Rhetoric* 35, no. 4 (2002): 297–327.

McGee, Michael Calvin. "A Materialist's Conception of Rhetoric." In *Rhetoric, Materiality, and Politics*, edited by Barbara A. Biesecker and John Louis Lucaites, 17–42. New York: Peter Lang, 2009.

McGrath, Ben. "The Movement: The Rise of Tea Party Activism." *New Yorker*, February 1, 2010.

McGrath, Jason. *Chinese Film: Realism and Convention from the Silent Era to the Digital Age*. Minneapolis: University of Minnesota Press, 2022.

McKittrick, Katherine. "'Freedom Is a Secret': The Future Usability of the Underground." In *Black Geographies and the Politics of Place*, edited by Katherine McKittrick and Clyde Woods, 97–114. Chico, CA: AK Press, 2007.

McLaughlin Green, Constance. *The Secret City: A History of Race Relations in the Nation's Capital*. Princeton, NJ: Princeton University Press, 1967.

McQuade, Barbara. "The Dangerous Whataboutism in the Trump Classified Docs Case." *Time*, June 12, 2023. https://time.com/6286371/trump-classified-documents-indictment-whataboutism/.

McQuire, Scott. "From Glass Architecture to Big Brother: Scenes from a Cultural History of Transparency." *Cultural Studies Review* 9, no. 1 (2013): 103–23.

Me@iq.org. "State and Terrorist Conspiracies." iq.org, November 10, 2006. http://www.iq.org/conspiracies.pdf (site discontinued).

Mehrotra, Dhruv. "The FBI's Jeffrey Epstein Prison Video Had Nearly 3 Minutes Cut Out." *Wired*, July 15, 2025.

Melamed, Jodi. *Represent and Destroy: Rationalizing Violence in the New Racial Capitalism*. Minneapolis: University of Minnesota Press, 2011.

Méliès, Georges, dir. *The Dreyfus Affair*. Star Film Company, 1899.

Melley, Timothy. "Agency Panic and the Culture of Conspiracy." In *Conspiracy Nation: The Politics of Paranoia in Postwar America*, edited by Peter Knight, 57–81. New York: New York University Press, 2002.

Melley, Timothy. *The Covert Sphere: Secrecy, Fiction, and the National Security State*. Ithaca, NY: Cornell University Press, 2012.

Melley, Timothy. *Empire of Conspiracy: The Culture of Paranoia in Postwar America*. Ithaca, NY: Cornell University Press, 1999.

Melley, Timothy. "The Melodramatic Mode in American Politics and Other Varieties of Narrative Suspicion." *symplokē* 29, nos. 1–2 (2021): 57–74.

Mercieca, Jennifer. *Demagogue for President: The Rhetorical Genius of Donald Trump*. College Station: Texas A&M University Press, 2020.

Merlan, Anna. "How Does the Epstein Scandal End?" *Mother Jones*, July 30, 2025. https://www.motherjones.com/politics/2025/07/donald-trump-jeffrey-epstein-scandal-end/.

Merlan, Anna. "The JFK Assassination Files Didn't Have a Smoking Gun, but a Very Weird Congressional Hearing Tried to Create One." *Mother Jones*, April 1, 2025. https://www.motherjones.com/politics/2025/04/jfk-assassination-files-hearing/.

Mervosh, Sarah. "Seth Rich Was Not Source of Leaked DNC Emails, Mueller Report Confirms." *New York Times*, April 20, 2019.

Messick, Graham, prod. *60 Minutes*. Season 44, episode 24, "Stuxnet." Aired March 4, 2012, on CBS. https://www.youtube.com/watch?v=6WmaZYJwJng.

Metzl, Jonathan M. *The Protest Psychosis: How Schizophrenia Became a Black Disease*. Boston: Beacon Press, 2010.

Meyerson, Harold. "The GOP Misses Its Bogeyman." *Washington Post*, February 10, 2012.

Michaels, Walter Benn. *The Shape of the Signifier: 1967 to the End of History*. Princeton, NJ: Princeton University Press, 2004.

Mier, Tomás, Brittany Spanos, and Andre Gee. "The Easter Eggs You Might Have Missed from Kendrick Lamar's Super Bowl Performance." *Rolling Stone*, February 10, 2025. https://www.rollingstone.com/music/music-features/kendrick-lamar-super-bowl-performance-serena-williams-1235262665/.

Mignolo, Walter D. "Delinking: The Rhetoric of Modernity, the Logic of Coloniality, and the Grammar of De-coloniality." *Cultural Studies* 21, nos. 2–3 (2007): 449–514.

Mihalopoulos, Dan. "A Lifetime of Close Ties and Growing Influence." *New York Times*, January 14, 2012.

Milbank, Dana, and Thomas B. Edsall. "Chavez Pulls Out as Labor Nominee." *Washington Post*, January 9, 2001.

Milgram, Stanley. *Obedience to Authority: An Experimental View*. New York: Harper and Row, 1974.

Miller, D. A. *The Novel and the Police*. Berkeley: University of California Press, 1988.

Miller, Greg, Debbie Cenziper, and Peter Whoriskey. "Billions Hidden Beyond Reach." *Washington Post*, October 3, 2021.

Miller, Jacques Alain. "Language: Much Ado About What?" in *Lacan and the Subject of Language*, edited by Ellie Ragland-Sullivan and Mark Bracher, 21–35. London: Routledge, 1991.

Miller, Vincent. "New Media, Networking and Phatic Culture." *Convergence: The International Journal of Research into New Media Technologies* 14, no. 4 (2008): 387–400.

Monahan, Torin. *Crisis Vision: Race and the Cultural Production of Surveillance*. Durham, NC: Duke University Press, 2022.

Montgomery, Blake. "Zuckerberg Augustus: Meta's Emperor Rebrands in New Clothes." *The Guardian*, September 28, 2024. https://www.theguardian.com/technology/2024/sep/28/mark-zuckeberg-revamps-public-image-style.

Moore, Elena. "Trump and Musk Appear Together in the Oval Office to Defend the Work of DOGE." *NPR*, February 11, 2025. https://www.npr.org/2025/02/11/nx-s1-5293504/trump-musk-doge-oval-office.

Moretti, Franco. *Distant Reading*. London: Verso, 2013.

Morici, Peter. "Democrats Will Never Let a Good Crisis Go to Waste." *Washington Times*, July 20, 2021.

Morin, Edgar, and Anne-Brigitte Kern. *Homeland Earth: A New Manifesto for a New Millennium*, translated by Sean M. Kelly and Roger Lapointe. Cresskill, NJ: Hampton Press, 1999.

Morris, Charles, III. "Pink Herring and the Fourth Persona: J. Edgar Hoover's Sex Crime Panic." *Quarterly Journal of Speech* 88, no. 2 (2002): 228–44.

Morrissey, Ed. "Video: Palin's Speech at the Boston Tea Party." *Hot Air*, April 14, 2010. https://hotair.com/ed-morrissey/2010/04/14/video-palins-speech-at-the-boston-tea-party-n168602.

Mosse, George L. *Toward the Final Solution: A History of European Fascism*. Madison: University of Wisconsin Press, 1985.

Mosser, Jason. "What's Gonzo About Gonzo Journalism?" *Literary Journalism Studies* 4, no. 1 (2012): 85–90.

Moynihan, Daniel Patrick. *The Negro Family: The Case for National Action*. Washington, DC: Department of Labor, Office of Policy Planning and Research, 1965.

Moynihan, Daniel Patrick. "The Negro Family and the Case for National Action." In *The Moynihan Report and the Politics of Controversy*, edited by Lee Rainwater and William L. Yancey, 41–124. Cambridge, MA: MIT Press, 1967.

Moynihan, Daniel Patrick. *Secrecy: The American Experience*. New Haven, CT: Yale University Press, 1998.

Moynihan, Donald P. "Trump Has a Master Plan for Destroying the 'Deep State.'" *New York Times*, November 27, 2023.

Muraskin, William Alan. *Middle-Class Blacks in a White Society: Prince Hall Freemasonry in America*. Berkeley: University of California Press, 1975.

NAACP. "Resolution: The Tea Party Movement." NAACP.org, 2010. https://naacp.org/resources/tea-party-movement.

Naftali, Timothy. "George W. Bush and the 'War on Terror.'" In *The Presidency of George W. Bush: A First Historical Assessment*, edited by Julian E. Zelizer, 59–87. Princeton, NJ: Princeton University Press, 2010.

Nakayama, Thomas K., and Robert L. Krizek. "Whiteness: A Strategic Rhetoric." *Quarterly Journal of Speech* 81, no. 3 (1995): 291–309.

Nancy, Jean-Luc, and Jacques Lacoue-Labarthes. *The Title of the Letter*. Translated by Francois Raffoul and David Pettigrew. New York: State University of New York Press, 1992.

Naylor, Brian. "Former CIA Director Tells Lawmakers About 'Very Aggressive' Russian Election Meddling." *NPR*, May 23, 2017.

Nelson, D. Alan, Michael Wilson, and Lianne M. Kurina. "Post-Traumatic Stress Disorder Among U.S. Army Drone Operators." *Aerospace Medicine and Human Performance* 93, no. 7 (2022): 562–70.

Nelson, John S., Allan Megill, and Deirdre N. McCloskey. "Rhetoric of Inquiry." In *Rhetoric of the Human Sciences: Language and Argument in Scholarship and Public Affairs*, edited by John S. Nelson, Allan Megill, and Deirdre N. McCloskey, 3–18. Madison: University of Wisconsin Press, 1987.

Nelson, Libby. "'Grab 'Em by the Pussy': How Trump Talked About Women in Private Is Horrifying." *Vox*, October 7, 2016. https://www.vox.com/2016/10/7/13205842/trump-secret-recording-women.

Neville Shepherd, Ryan. "Paranoid Style and Subtextual Form in Modern Conspiracy Rhetoric." *Southern Communication Journal* 83, no. 2 (2018): 119–32.

Ngai, Mae M. "The Architecture of Race in American Immigration Law: A Reexamination of the Immigration Act of 1924." In *Race, Law and Society*, edited by Ian Haney López, 351–76. New York: Routledge, 2016.

Ngai, Sianne. *Ugly Feelings*. Cambridge, MA: Harvard University Press, 2005.

Nichols, Bill. *Representing Reality: Issues and Concepts in Documentary*. Bloomington: Indiana University Press, 1991.

Nietzsche, Friedrich. *The Gay Science*. Edited by Bernard Williams. Translated by Adrian Del Caro and Josefine Nauckhoff. Cambridge, UK: Cambridge University Press, 2008.

Nolan, Bridget Rose. "From the 'Lavender Scare' to 'Out and Equal': LGBTQIA+ Diversity in the U.S. Intelligence Community." *International Journal of Intelligence and CounterIntelligence* 35, no. 4 (2022): 713–25.

North, Anna. "The Rape Allegation Against Julian Assange, Explained." *Vox*, May 13, 2019. https://www.vox.com/identities/2019/4/12/18306901/julian-assange-arrest-wikileaks-rape-sweden-embassy.

Novak, Robert D. "Mission to Niger." *Washington Post*, July 14, 2003.

Obama, Barack. "Why Organize? Problems and Promise in the Inner City." In *After Alinsky: Community Organizing in Illinois*, edited by Peg Knoepfle, 35–40. Springfield, IL: Sangamon State University, 1990.

Ochieng, Omedia. "Limit Formations: Violence, Philosophy, Rhetoric." *Philosophy and Rhetoric* 56, nos. 3–4 (2023): 330–37.

O'Hara, John M. *The New American Tea Party*. Hoboken, NJ: John Wiley & Sons, 2010.

Ohl, Jessy J. "Nothing to See or Fear: Light War and the Boring Visual Rhetoric of U.S. Drone Imagery." *Quarterly Journal of Speech* 101, no. 4 (2015): 612–32.

Olmsted, Kathryn S. "Blond Queens, Red Spiders, and Neurotic Old Maids." *Intelligence and National Security* 19, no. 1 (2004): 78–94.

Olson, Christa J. *American Magnitude: Hemispheric Vision and Public Feeling in the United States.* Columbus: The Ohio State University Press, 2021.

"On This We Agree." *Chicago Defender,* August 19, 1961.

Oppel, Richard A., Jr. "Judge Says Trump's Statements Did Not Prejudice Case Against Bergdahl." *New York Times,* February 24, 2017.

Ore, Ersula J. *Lynching: Violence, Rhetoric, and American Identity.* Jackson: University Press of Mississippi, 2019.

Ore, Ersula J. "Twenty-First Century Discourses of American Lynching." *Critical Discourse Studies* 20, no. 5 (2023): 508–23.

Ore, Ersula, and Matthew Houdek. "Lynching in Times of Suffocation: Toward a Spatiotemporal Politics of Breathing." *Women's Studies in Communication* 43, no. 4 (2020): 443–58.

Osborne, Lucy, Harry Davies, and Stephanie Kirchgaessner. "Teen Models, Powerful Men and Private Dinners: When Trump Hosted Look of the Year." *The Guardian,* March 14, 2020.

"Outlines Plan to Save Urban Universities." *Chicago Defender,* November 12, 1960.

Packer, George. "What Julian Assange and Donald Trump Have in Common." *The Atlantic,* January 13, 2019.

Paletta, Anthony. "Amend and Deny: On to Foucault." *National Review,* April 4, 2007.

Pallitto, Robert M., and William G. Weaver. *Presidential Secrecy and the Law.* Baltimore, MA: Johns Hopkins University Press, 2007.

Parry-Giles, Shawn J. "Archival Research and the American Presidency." In *The Handbook of Rhetoric and Public Address,* edited by Shawn J. Parry-Giles and J. Michael Hogan, 159–63. Malden: Blackwell, 2010.

Parry-Giles, Shawn J. "The Veeps Audition—Campaign 2020: Disciplining Kamala Harris." *Quarterly Journal of Speech* 107, no. 4 (2021): 443–50.

Patton, Cindy. "Refiguring Social Space." In *Social Postmodernism: Beyond Identity Politics,* 216–49. Cambridge: Cambridge University Press, 1995.

Pérez-Peña, Richard. "Anti-Abortion Activists Charged in Planned Parenthood Video Case." *New York Times,* March 29, 2017. https://www.nytimes.com/2017/03/29/us/planned-parenthood-video-charges.html.

Perrin, Andre J., Steven J. Tepper, Neal Caren, and Sally Morris. "Political and Cultural Dimensions of Tea Party Support, 2009–2012." *The Sociological Quarterly* 55, no. 4 (2014): 625–52.

Petronio, Sandra. *Boundaries of Privacy: Dialectics of Disclosure.* Albany: State University of New York Press, 2002.

Pham, Vincent N. "Our Foreign President Barack Obama: The Racial Logics of Birther Discourses." *Journal of International and Intercultural Communication* 8, no. 2 (2015): 86–107.

Picheta, Rob, Nikki Carvajal, and Greg Wallace. "Trump Claims Americans Have to Flush the Toilet '10 Times, 15 Times, as Opposed to Once.'" *CNN,* December 7, 2019. https://www.cnn.com/2019/12/07/politics/trump-americans-flushing-toilets-intl/index.html.

Pierce, Charles P. "War Criminals Among Us: Bush, Cheney, and the Eyes of the World." *Esquire,* June 1, 2015.

Pierce, Ken. "Church Supports 'Hate Group.'" *Maroon,* March 3, 1961.

Pierce, Lee M. *Tense Times: Rhetoric, Syntax, and Politics in U.S. Crisis Culture.* Tuscaloosa: University of Alabama Press, 2023.

Pilkington, Ed. "JD Vance's Attempt to Link Democrats to Epstein Renews Calls to 'Release the Files.'" *The Guardian*, August 10, 2025. https://www.theguardian.com/us-news/2025/aug/10/jd-vance-democrats-jeffrey-epstein-files.

Pincus, Walter. "U.S. Lacks Specifics on Banned Arms." *Washington Post*, March 16, 2003.

Pinto, Ana Teixeira. "Capitalism with a Transhuman Face: The Afterlife of Fascism and the Digital Frontier." *Third Text* 33, no. 3 (2019): 328–36.

Plame Wilson, Valerie. *Fair Game: How a Top CIA Agent Was Betrayed by Her Own Government*. New York: Simon & Schuster, 2008.

Plame Wilson, Valerie. "Statement of Valerie Plame Wilson, Former Employee, Central Intelligence Agency." In *Hearing Before the Committee on Oversight and Government Reform*, House of Representatives, 110th Congress, 17–71. Washington, DC: US Government Printing Office. https://www.govinfo.gov/content/pkg/CHRG-110hhrg38579/pdf/CHRG-110hhrg38579.pdf.

Poitras, Laura, dir. *Citizenfour*. Praxis Films, 2004.

Poitras, Laura, dir. *Risk*. Neon and Showtime Documentary Films, 2016.

Polyaenus. *Polyaenus's Stratagems of War*. Translated by R. Shepherd. London: G. Nicol, 1981. Originally published in 1793.

Popielarz, Pamela A. "Moral Dividends: Freemasonry and Finance Capitalism in Early Nineteenth-Century America." *Business History* 60, no. 5 (2018): 658–59.

Porter, Dennis. *The Pursuit of Crime: Art and Ideology in Detective Fiction*. New Haven, CT: Yale University Press, 1981.

Portraits of Courage: A Commander in Chief's Tribute to America's Warriors. George W. Bush Presidential Center, March 2–October 17, 2017. https://www.bushcenter.org/events-and-exhibits/portraits-of-courage.

Powers, Richard Gid. Introduction to *Secrecy: The American Experience*, by Daniel Patrick Moynihan, 1–58. New Haven, CT: Yale University Press, 1998.

Pozen, David E., and Michael Schudson. "Introduction: Troubling Transparency." In *Troubling Transparency: The History and Future of Freedom of Information*, edited by David E. Pozen and Michael Schudson, 1–10. New York: Columbia University Press, 2018.

Press, Eyal. "The Wounds of the Drone Warrior." *New York Times Magazine*, June 13, 2018.

Puar, Jasbir K. *Terrorist Assemblages: Homonationalism in Queer Times*. Durham, NC: Duke University Press, 2007.

Putnam, Robert D. *Bowling Alone: The Collapse and Revival of American Community*. New York: Simon & Schuster, 2000.

Quindlen, Anna. "Free Pass for the President." *Newsweek*, October 6, 2003.

Racketeer Influenced and Corrupt Organizations Act. U.S. Code. Title 18, §§ 1961–1968 (1970).

Radack, Jesselyn. "Pentagon Leaker Jack Teixeira Is Nothing Like Edward Snowden: He's More Like Donald Trump." *Salon*, May 30, 2023. https://www.salon.com/2023/05/30/pentagon-leaker-jack-teixeira-is-nothing-like-edward-snowden-hes-more-like-donald/.

Ragland, Ellie. *The Logic of Sexuation: From Aristotle to Lacan*. Albany: State University of New York Press, 2004.

Railsback, Celeste M. Condit. "Beyond Rhetorical Relativism: A Structural-Material Model of Truth and Objective Reality." *Quarterly Journal of Speech* 69, no. 4 (1983): 351–63.

Rancière, Jacques. *The Politics of Aesthetics: The Distribution of the Sensible*. London: Continuum Books, 2004.

Rangappa, Asha. "The U.S. Has No Rules for When the President Is a National Security Threat." *Washington Post*, September 20, 2019.

Rashid, Ahmed. "After 1,700 Years, Buddhas Fall to Taliban Dynamite." *Telegraph,* March 12, 2001. https://www.telegraph.co.uk/news/worldnews/asia/afghanistan/1326063/After-1700-years-Buddhas-fall-to-Taliban-dynamite.html.

Rawaf, Slaman. "The 2003 Iraq War and Avoidable Death Toll." *PLoS Medicine* 10, no. 10 (2013): e1001532. https://doi.org/10.1371/journal.pmed.1001532.

Ray, Siladitya. "Federal Judge Says Musk's DOGE Must Make Records Public—Questions 'Unusual Secrecy.'" *Forbes,* March 11, 2025. https://www.forbes.com/sites/siladityaray/2025/03/11/federal-judge-rules-doge-must-disclose-records-about-its-operation-to-comply-with-federal-transparency-law.

Raymond, Adam K. "George W. Bush Bashes Bigotry, Bullying, and Lies but Doesn't Use Trump's Name." *New York Magazine: Intelligencer,* October 19, 2017.

Reardon, Sara. "I Spy, with My Faraway Eye." *New Scientist,* January 26, 2013.

Reeves, Joshua. *Citizen Spies: The Long Rise of America's Surveillance Society.* New York: New York University Press, 2017.

Reeves, Joshua. "If You See Something, Say Something: Lateral Surveillance and the Uses of Responsibility." *Surveillance and Society* 10, nos. 3–4 (2012): 235–48.

Reitzes, Donald, and Dietrich Reitzes. *The Alinsky Legacy: Alive and Kicking.* Greenwich, CT: Jai Press, 1987.

Révauger, Cécile. "Freemasonry and Blacks." In *Handbook of Freemasonry,* edited by Henrik Bogdan and J. A. M. Snoek, 422–38. Brill, 2014.

Rice, Jenny. *Awful Archives: Conspiracy Theory, Rhetoric, and Acts of Evidence.* Columbus: The Ohio State University Press, 2020.

Rice, Jenny. "The Rhetorical Aesthetics of More: On Archival Magnitude." *Philosophy and Rhetoric* 50, no. 1 (2017): 26–49.

Richards, Joseph G. "Newspaper Readers Laud Our Editorial Stand on Housing." *Chicago Defender,* July 15, 1961.

Ricoeur, Paul. *Freud and Philosophy: An Essay on Interpretation.* Translated by Denis Savage. New Haven, CT: Yale University Press, 2008.

Ricoeur, Paul. "What Is a Text? Explanation and Understanding." In *A Ricoeur Reader: Reflection and Imagination,* edited by Mario J. Valdés, 43–64. Toronto: University of Toronto Press, 1991.

Riessman, Frank. *Strategies Against Poverty.* New York: Random House, 1969.

Rigilano, Matthew J. "The Decline of Phatic Efficiency." *Postmodern Culture* 32, no. 2 (2022). https://dx.doi.org/10.1353/pmc.2022.0003.

Roberts, Molly. "The Other Problem with Valerie Plame's Horrible Anti-Semitic Tweet." *Washington Post,* September 22, 2017.

Robertson, Noah. "Jack Teixeira, Edward Snowden, and Plugging Intelligence Leaks." *Christian Science Monitor,* May 17, 2023.

Robinson, Sally. *Marked Men: Masculinity in Crisis.* New York: Columbia University Press, 2000.

Rogers, Mike. "NSA Programs: Rep. Mike Rogers Holds a Hearing on Potential Changes to FISA." Statement on October 29, 2013, 113th Congress, House Permanent Select Committee on Intelligence, 2013. https://congressional-proquest-com.ezp2.lib.umn.edu/congressional/docview/t65.d40.10290003.s18?accountid=14585.

Rogin, Michael Paul. "The Countersubversive Tradition in American Politics." *Berkeley Journal of Sociology,* no. 31 (1986): 1–33.

Rogin, Michael Paul. "'Make My Day!': Spectacle as Amnesia in Imperial Politics." *Representations,* no. 29 (Winter 1990): 99–123.

Rogin, Michael Paul. *"Ronald Reagan," the Movie; and Other Episodes in Political Demonology.* Berkeley: University of California Press, 1987.

Roland, Graham, creator. *Dark Winds.* Seasons 1–2. AMC Studios. Aired June 12, 2022–September 3, 2023, on AMC. https://www.amc.com/shows/dark-winds--1053387.

Romano, Tricia. "The New Election Denialists Can't Cope with Trump 2.0." *Washington Post,* December 6, 2024. https://www.washingtonpost.com/style/of-interest/2024/12/06/left-election-denial/.

Rose, Lila. "Values Voter Summit Speech." Family Research Council Action Values Voter Summit, Washington, DC, September 12, 2008. YouTube video (22:45), posted by DarkLordofDebate, September 18, 2008. https://www.youtube.com/watch?v=SlzLXHZbGqE.

Rosenberg, Alyssa. "What 'Homeland' and 'The Manchurian Candidate' Tell Us About Bowe Bergdahl's Return." *Washington Post,* June 4, 2014.

Rosenberg, Scott. "Why the N.Y. Times Ruins Bush's Breakfast." *Salon,* September 8, 2003. https://www.salon.com/2003/09/08/krugman_6/.

Ross, Janell. "Donald Trump, Sarah Palin, and the History of 'Gotcha' Questions." *Washington Post,* September 5, 2015.

Ross, Kelly. "White Oversight in *The Confessions of Nat Turner, Benito Cereno,* and *The Heroic Slave.*" In *Slavery, Surveillance, and Genre in Antebellum United States Literature,* 46–71. Oxford: Oxford University Press, 2022.

Rossinow, Doug. "Politics Saved Ronald Reagan from Impeachment. That Might Happen Again for Donald Trump." *Washington Post,* October 4, 2019.

Roudinesco, Elisabeth. *Why Psychoanalysis?* Translated by Rachel Bowlby. New York: Columbia University Press, 2001.

Row, Jennifer Eun-Jung. *Queer Velocities: Time, Sex, and Biopower on the Early Modern Stage.* Evanston, IL: Northwestern University Press, 2022.

Rowland, Allison L. "Small Dick Problems: Masculine Entitlement as Rhetorical Strategy." *Quarterly Journal of Speech* 109, no. 1 (2023): 1–22.

Rowland, Allison L. *Zoetropes and the Politics of Humanhood.* Columbus: The Ohio State University Press, 2020.

"Royal Pardon for Codebreaker Alan Turing." *BBC News,* December 24, 2013, http://www.bbc.com/news/technology-25495315.

Rubenstein, Diane. *This Is Not a President: Sense, Nonsense, and the Political Imaginary.* Ithaca, NY: Cornell University Press, 2008.

Rzepka, Charles J. *Detective Fiction.* Cambridge: Polity Press, 2005.

Sachan, Dinsa. "The Age of Drones: What Might It Mean for Health?" *The Lancet* 387, no. 10030 (2016): 1803–4.

Safire, William. "Gotcha!" *New York Times,* January 28, 2001.

Sagar, Rahul. *Secrets and Leaks.* Princeton, NJ: Princeton University Press, 2013.

Sammon, Bill. "President Chokes on Pretzel, Faints." *Washington Times,* January 14, 2002.

Sargent, Neil C. "Mys-Reading the Past in Detective Fiction and Law." *Law and Literature* 22, no. 2 (2010): 288–306.

Satter, Tina, dir. *Reality.* HBO Films, 2023.

Saturday Night Live. "WikiLeaks Cold Opening." Aired December 4, 2010, YouTube video (4:12), August 14, 2013. https://www.youtube.com/watch?v=bsaz-QUDtL4.

Saturday Night Live. "A Message from Mark Zuckerberg." Aired December 18, 2010, YouTube video (2:43), August 14, 2013. https://www.youtube.com/watch?v=md3of7O02e4.

Scaff, Lawrence A. "The Mind of the Modernist: Simmel on Time." *Time and Society* 14, no. 1 (2005): 5–23.

Schaack, Michael J. "The Haymarket Riot (1886)." In *The Fear of Conspiracy: Images of Un-American Subversion from the Revolution to the Present*, edited by David Brion Davis, 50–72. Ithaca, NY: Cornell University Press, 1971.

Scheuermann, Christoph. "Searching in Europe for Glory Days Gone By." *Der Spiegel*, October 29, 2018.

Schlesinger, Arthur Meier. "Crisis of American Masculinity." *Esquire*, November 1, 1958. https://classic.esquire.com/article/1958/11/1/the-crisis-of-american-masculinity.

Schlesinger, Arthur Meier. *The Imperial Presidency*. Boston: Houghton Mifflin, 1973.

Schmidt, Michael S., and Steven Lee Myers. "Panama Law Firm's Leaked Files Detail Offshore Accounts Tied to World Leaders." *New York Times*, April 3, 2016.

Schmitt, Eric. "WikiLeaks: The Back Story." *New York Times Magazine*, February 17, 2011.

Schorr, Daniel. "The Assassins." *New York Review*, October 13, 1977.

Schrader, Stuart. *Badges Without Borders*. Oakland: University of California Press, 2019.

Schuessler, Jennifer, and Boryana Dzhambazova. "Bulgaria Says French Thinker Was a Secret Agent. She Calls It a 'Barefaced Lie.'" *New York Times*, April 1, 2018.

Schwartz, Kathryn A. "From Text to Technological Context: Medieval Arabic Cryptology's Relation to Paper, Numbers, and the Post." *Cryptologia* 38, no. 2 (2014): 133–46.

Schwarze, Steven. "Environmental Melodrama." *Quarterly Journal of Speech* 92, no. 3 (2006): 239–61.

Scott, Robert L. "On Viewing Rhetoric as Epistemic." *Central States Speech Journal* 18, no. 1 (1967): 9–17.

Sedgwick, Eve Kosofsky. *Touching Feeling: Affect, Pedagogy, Performativity*. Durham, NC: Duke University Press, 2003.

Seelye, Katharine Q. "A Different Emanuel for One Church." *New York Times*, March 17, 2009.

Seelye, Katharine Q. "McCain and Palin's Interview with Couric." *New York Times*, September 29, 2008.

Seigworth, Gregory J., and Matthew Tiessen. "Mobile Affects, Open Secrets, and Global Illiquidity: Pockets, Pools, and Plasma." *Theory, Culture, and Society* 29, no. 6 (2012): 47–77.

Seitz-Wald, Alex. "WikiLeaks Fuels Conspiracy Theories About DNC Staffer's Death." *NBC News*, August 10, 2016.

Selden, Zachary. "The General Intelligence Division: J. Edgar Hoover and the Critical Juncture of 1919." *International Journal of Intelligence and CounterIntelligence* 34, no. 2 (2021): 342–57.

"The Sensational Giles and O'Keefe." *Washington Times*, September 16, 2009. http://www.washingtontimes.com/news/2009/sep/16/the-sensational-giles-and-okeefe.

Shammas, Brittany. "A 7-Hour Gap in Trump's Calls Evokes a Missing Spot on Nixon's Tapes." *Washington Post*, March 30, 2022.

Shane, Scott. "Conservatives Draw Blood from ACORN, Favored Foe." *New York Times*, September 16, 2009. http://www.nytimes.com/2009/09/16/us/politics/16acorn.html.

Shane, Scott. "A Political Gadfly." *New York Times*, September 18, 2009.

Shane, Scott, and Neil A. Lewis. "Bush Commutes Libby Sentence, Saying 30 Months 'Is Excessive.'" *New York Times*, July 3, 2007.

Shao, Elena, Karen Yourish, and June Kim. "How Trump's Directives Echo Project 2025." *New York Times*, February 14, 2025.

Sharif, Solmaz. *Look*. Minneapolis, MN: Graywolf Press, 2016.

Sharpe, Christina. *In the Wake: On Blackness and Being.* Durham, NC: Duke University Press, 2016.

Shear, Michael D. "Miles Taylor, a Former Homeland Security Official, Reveals He Was 'Anonymous.'" *New York Times,* October 20, 2020.

Shear, Michael D., and Matthew Rosenberg. "Released Emails Suggest the DNC Derided the Sanders Campaign." *New York Times,* July 22, 2016.

Sheehi, Lara, and Stephen Sheehi. *Psychoanalysis Under Occupation: Practicing Resistance in Palestine.* New York: Routledge, 2022.

Sheldon, Rose Mary. *Ambush: Surprise Attack in Ancient Greek Warfare.* London: Frontline Books, 2012.

Shires, James. "Cyber-Noir: Cybersecurity and Popular Culture." *Contemporary Security Policy* 41, no. 1 (2020): 82–107.

Siddiqui, Sabrina. "George W. Bush Condemns Bigotry and Lies in Coded Attack on Trump." *The Guardian,* October 19, 2017.

Silberman, Charles E. *Crisis in Black and White.* New York: Random House, 1964.

Simeall, Timothy J., and Jonathan M. Spring. "Resistance Strategies: Symmetric Encryption." In *Introduction to Information Security: A Strategic-Based Approach,* 155–86. Rockland, MA: Syngress, 2014.

Simmel, Georg. *The Sociology of Georg Simmel.* Edited by Kurt H. Wolff. New York: The Free Press, 1950.

Simmel, Georg. "The Sociology of Secrets and of Secret Societies." *The American Journal of Sociology* 11, no. 4 (1906): 441–98.

Simmel, Georg. "The Stranger." In *The Sociology of Georg Simmel,* translated by Kurt H. Wolff, 402–8. New York: The Free Press, 1950.

Singh, Simon. *The Code Book: The Science of Secrecy from Ancient Egypt to Quantum Cryptography.* New York: Anchor Books, 2000.

Sisco King, Claire. *Washed in Blood: Male Sacrifice, Trauma, and the Cinema.* New Brunswick, NJ: Rutgers University Press, 2011.

Skowronek, Stephen. "The Reassociation of Ideas and Purposes: Racism, Liberalism, and the American Political Tradition." *The American Political Science Review* 100, no. 3 (2006): 385–401.

Slotkin, Richard. *Gunfighter Nation: The Myth of the Frontier in Twentieth-Century America.* Norman: University of Oklahoma Press, 1998.

Smith, Gerrit. "A Voice from the Past (1870)." In *The Fear of Conspiracy,* edited by David Brion Davis, 154–55. Ithaca, NY: Cornell University Press.

Sorkin, Amy Davidson. "The Age of Donald Trump and Pizzagate." *New Yorker,* December 6, 2016.

Spivak, Gayatri Chakravorty. "Glas-Piece: A *Compte Rendu.*" *Diacritics* 7, no. 3 (1977): 22–43.

Squires, Catherine R. *The Post-Racial Mystique.* New York: New York University Press, 2014.

Squires, Catherine R. "Rethinking the Black Public Sphere: An Alternative Vocabulary for Multiple Public Spheres." *Communication Theory* 12, no. 4 (2002): 446–68.

Srebnick, Amy Gilman. *The Mysterious Death of Mary Rogers: Sex and Culture in Nineteenth-Century New York.* New York: Oxford University Press, 1995.

Stahl, Roger. "Weaponizing Speech." *Quarterly Journal of Speech* 102, no. 4 (2016): 376–95.

"STD Fears Sparked Assange Sex Case: Swedish Women Accusing WikiLeaks Founder of Sex Crimes Wanted Him Tested, Associates Say." *Toronto Star,* December 8, 2010.

Steudeman, Michael J. "Entelechy and Irony in Political Time: The Preemptive Rhetoric of Nixon and Obama." *Rhetoric and Public Affairs* 16, no. 1 (2013): 59–96.

Stevenson, David. *The Origins of Freemasonry: Scotland's Century 1590–1710.* Cambridge, MA: Cambridge University Press, 1988.

Stewart, Garrett. *Framed Time: Toward a Post-Filmic Cinema.* Chicago: University of Chicago Press, 2007.

Stockler, Asher. "President Donald Trump Suggests Busing Is Just a Way 'to Get People to Schools.'" *Newsweek,* June 29, 2019. https://www.newsweek.com/president-donald-trump-suggests-busing-just-way-get-people-schools-1446669.

Stolberg, Sheryl Gay. "State of the Union: The Chamber; A Celebration with Prickly Undertones." *New York Times,* January 21, 2004.

Stolberg, Sheryl Gay, Christina Jewett, and Apoorva Mandavilli. "Mass Layoffs Hit Health Agencies That Track Disease and Regulate Food." *New York Times,* April 1, 2025. https://www.nytimes.com/2025/04/01/us/politics/trump-federal-layoffs-health-food.html.

Stoneman, Ethan, and Joseph Packer. "American Conservativism Unmoored: The Dissident Right's Adoption of Leftist Agitational Strategies." *Cultural Politics* 18, no. 3 (2022): 331–50.

Stormer, Nathan. "Addressing the Sublime: Space, Mass Representation, and the Unrepresentable." *Critical Studies in Media Communication* 21, no. 3 (2004): 212–40.

Stormer, Nathan. "Recursivity: A Working Paper on Rhetoric and Mnesis." *Quarterly Journal of Speech* 99, no. 1 (2013): 27–50.

Stormer, Nathan. "Rhetoric's Diverse Materiality: Polythetic Ontology and Genealogy." *Review of Communication* 16, no. 4 (2016): 299–316.

Stout, Mark. "World War I and the Birth of American Intelligence Culture." *Intelligence and National Security* 32, no. 3 (2017): 378–94.

Strong, Josiah. "Why America Is Particularly Vulnerable to Socialism (1885)." In *The Fear of Conspiracy: Images of Un-American Subversion from the Revolution to the Present,* edited by David Brion Davis, 169–76. Ithaca, NY: Cornell University Press, 1971.

Stryker, Susan. *Transgender History.* Berkeley, CA: Seal Press, 2008.

Stuart, Tessa. "Exclusive: Watch Lady Gaga Question Julian Assange in Laura Poitras' 'Risk.'" *Rolling Stone,* May 5, 2017.

Stuckey, Mary E. "Presidential Secrecy: Keeping the Archives Open." *Rhetoric and Public Affairs* 9, no. 1 (2006): 138–44.

Sugrue, Thomas J. "Saul Alinsky: The Activist Who Terrifies the Right." *Salon,* February 7, 2012. https://www.salon.com/2012/02/07/saul_alinsky_the_activist_who_terrifies_the_right/.

Sullivan, Becky, Andrea Bernstein, Ilya Marritz, and Quil Lawrence. "A Jury Finds Trump Liable for Battery and Defamation in E. Jean Carroll Trial." *NPR,* May 9, 2023. https://www.npr.org/2023/05/09/1174975870/trump-carroll-verdict.

Sunstein, Cass R., and Adrian Vermeule. "Conspiracy Theories: Causes and Cures." *Journal of Political Philosophy* 17, no. 2 (2009): 202–22.

Swearingen, C. Jan. *Rhetoric and Irony: Western Literacy and Western Lies.* Oxford: Oxford University Press, 1991.

Talbot, David. *The Devil's Chessboard.* New York: HarperCollins, 2015.

Tanenhaus, Sam. "Beware the Bush Family Image-Rehab Machine." *New York Magazine: Intelligencer,* December 1, 2018.

Taussig, Michael. *Defacement: Public Secrecy and the Labor of the Negative.* Stanford, CA: Stanford University Press, 1999, 5.

Taylor, Keeanga-Yamahtta. Foreword to *Scenes of Subjection: Terror, Slavery, and Self-Making in Nineteenth-Century America,* by Saidiya Hartman, rev. ed., x–xxiv. New York: W. W. Norton, 2022.

Taylor, Stuart, Jr. "Smearing Linda Chavez: The Poison of Partisan Thinking." *The Atlantic,* January 1, 2001.

Tenet, George. "Text of CIA Director George Tenet's Statement." *CNN,* July 11, 2003.

"Text of Bush's Speech." *CBS News,* February 11, 2009.

Thomas, Evan, and Michael Isikoff. "Secrets and Leaks." *Newsweek,* October 13, 2003.

Thompson, John B. *Ideology and Modern Culture: Critical Social Theory in the Era of Mass Communication.* Stanford, CA: Stanford University Press, 1990.

Thompson, Stuart A. "How A.I. QAnon and Falsehoods Are Reshaping the Presidential Race." *New York Times,* September 17, 2024. https://www.nytimes.com/2024/09/17/technology/election-ai-qanon-disinformation.html.

Timm, Annette F. "Introduction: Sexual Publics and Sexual Citizenship from Hirschfeld to the Present." In *Not Straight from Germany: Sexual Publics and Sexual Citizenship Since Magnus Hirschfeld,* edited by Michael Thomas Taylor, Annette F. Timm, and Ranier Herrn, 1–8. Ann Arbor: University of Michigan Press, 2017.

Toler, Aric. "From Discord to 4chan: The Improbable Journey of a US Intelligence Leak." *Bellingcat,* April 9, 2023. https://www.bellingcat.com/news/2023/04/09/from-discord-to-4chan-the-improbable-journey-of-a-us-defence-leak/.

Toobin, Jeffrey. "Edward Snowden Is No Hero." *New Yorker,* June 10, 2013.

"Transcript: Donald Trump's Taped Comments About Women." *New York Times,* October 8, 2016.

Traub, James. "The Way We Live Now: Domesticated." *New York Times,* February 8, 2004.

Trifonov, Svilen Veselinov. "Performing Prudence: Barack Obama's Defense of NSA Surveillance Programs." *Advances in the History of Rhetoric* 20, no. 1 (2017): 28–46.

"Trump's Debate References to 'Black Jobs' and 'Hispanic Jobs' Stir Democratic Anger." *Politico,* June 29, 2024. https://www.politico.com/news/2024/06/29/trumps-debate-black-jobs-democratic-anger-00165930.

"Trump's Wiretap Allegation." *National Review,* March 24, 2017.

Tuck, Eve, and K. Wayne Yang. "Decolonization Is Not a Metaphor." *Decolonization: Indigeneity, Education and Society* 1, no. 1 (2012): 1–40.

Turing, Alan Mathison. "Computing Machinery and Intelligence." *MIND: A Quarterly Review of Psychology and Philosophy* 59, no. 236 (1950): 433–60.

Turner, Patricia A. *I Heard It Through the Grapevine: Rumor in African-American Culture.* Berkeley: University of California Press, 1993.

Tyldum, Morton, dir. *The Imitation Game.* London: The Weinstein Company, 2014.

Tyrrell, Ian. "Trump's Presidency Is Being Compared to America's Gilded Age—What Was It, and What Happened Next?" *The Conversation,* March 20, 2025. https://theconversation.com/friday-essay-trumps-presidency-is-being-compared-to-americas-gilded-age-what-was-it-and-what-happened-next-251401.

United States Department of Defense. *United States-Vietnam Relations, 1945–1967: A Study Prepared by the Department of Defense.* Washington, DC: US Government Printing Office, 1971.

"U.S. Rep. Alan Grayson Stages Briefing to Attack Drone Strikes." *Orlando Sentinel,* October 29, 2013.

Valko, Alana. "A Woman Went Viral for Asking If Other Women Also Woke Up in the Dead of Night as Trump Was Elected, and Literally, Everyone Did." *Buzzfeed,* November 12, 2024. https://www.buzzfeed.com/alanavalko/women-election-night-viral-tiktok.

VandeHei, Jim, and Peter Baker. "Vacationing Bush to Set a Record: With Long Sojourn at Ranch, President on His Way to Surpassing Reagan's Total." *Washington Post,* August 3, 2005.

VanHaitsma, Pamela. *Queering Romantic Engagement in the Postal Age: A Rhetorical Education.* Columbia: University of South Carolina Press, 2019.

Van Schenck, Reed. "'Remaking the World Memetically': Interrogating White Nationalist Subject Formation Through the Circulation of the 'Wagecuck' Meme." *Communication and Critical/ Cultural Studies* 20, no. 3 (2023): 375–95.

van Wyck, Peter C. *Signs of Danger: Waste, Trauma, and Nuclear Threat.* Minneapolis: University of Minnesota Press, 2004.

Veracini, Lorenzo. *Settler Colonialism: A Theoretical Overview.* London: Palgrave Macmillan, 2010.

Veracini, Lorenzo. "Settler Collective, Founding Violence and Disavowal: The Settler Colonial Situation." *Journal of Intercultural Studies* 29, no. 4 (2008): 363–79.

Veracini, Lorenzo. "Settler Evasions in *Interstellar* and *Cowboys and Aliens*: Thinking the End of the World Is Still Easier than Thinking the End of Settler Colonialism." In *Cinematic Settlers: The Settler Colonial World in Film,* edited by Janne Lahti and Rebecca Weaver-Hightower, 203–14. New York: Routledge, 2020.

Vervaet, Frederik Juliaan. "Mark Zuckerberg's Admiration for Emperor Augustus Is Misplaced. Here's Why." *The Conversation,* January 2, 2019. https://theconversation.com/mark-zuckerbergs-admiration-for-emperor-augustus-is-misplaced-heres-why-108172.

Vinzent, Markus. *Christ's Torah: The Making of the New Testament in the Second Century.* New York: Routledge, 2024.

von Schwartzkoppen, Maximilian. *Les carnets de Schwartzkoppen (La vérité sur Dreyfus).* Edited by Bernhard Schwertfeger. Translated by A. Koyré. Paris: Éditions Rieder, 1930.

Wade, Peter. "Poll Shows Widespread Disapproval and Suspicion of Trump's Handling of Epstein Files." *Rolling Stone,* August 4, 2025. https://www.rollingstone.com/politics/politics-news/poll-disapproval-trump-handling-epstein-files-1235399381/.

Wade, Peter. "Trump, Dumb as Always, Thinks Busing Is About Transportation." *Rolling Stone,* June 29, 2019. https://www.rollingstone.com/politics/politics-news/trump-busing-853745/.

"Wait, It's All Ohio? Always Has Been." *Know Your Meme* (blog), last modified September 26, 2023. https://knowyourmeme.com/memes/wait-its-all-ohio-always-has-been.

Walker, Corey D. B. *A Noble Fight: African American Freemasonry and the Struggle for Democracy in America.* Urbana: University of Illinois Press, 2008.

Walsh, Justin. *The Fraternal Order of Police, 1915–1976: A History.* Paducah, KY: Turner Publishing Company, 2001.

Ward, Vicky. "Double Exposure." *Vanity Fair,* January 2004.

Warrick, Joby. "Some Evidence on Iraq Called Fake; U.N. Nuclear Inspector Says Documents on Purchases Were Forged." *Washington Post,* March 8, 2003.

Warshaw, Shirley Anne. *The Co-Presidency of Bush and Cheney.* Stanford, CA: Stanford University Press, 2009.

Watts, Eric King. "Postracial Fantasies, Blackness, and Zombies." *Communication and Critical/ Cultural Studies* 14, no. 4 (2017): 317–33.

Watts, Eric King. *Postracial Fantasies and Zombies: On the Racist Apocalyptic Politics Devouring the World.* Oakland: University of California Press, 2024.

Watts, Eric King. "The Primal Scene of COVID-19: 'We're All in This Together.'" *Rhetoric, Politics, and Culture* 1, no. 1 (2021): 1–26.

"Weary Activist Group ACORN Changes Affiliate Names." *Washington Times*, March 16, 2010. http://www.washingtontimes.com/news/2010/mar/16/weary-activist-group-acorn-changes-affiliate-names.

Weber, Max. "Bureaucracy: Characteristics and the Power Position of Bureaucracy (1920)." In *Government Secrecy: Classic and Contemporary Readings*, edited by Susan L. Maret and Jan Goldman, 44–49. Westport, CT: Libraries Unlimited, 2009.

Weider, Ben, and Julie K. Brown. "Maxwell Case Logs Show How Frequently Trump Flew on Epstein Jets; Bill Clinton Too." *Miami Herald*, December 21, 2021.

Weigel, David. "Congress's Undying (and Less than Effective) ACORN Funding Ban." *Acorn.org*, December 15, 2014. Site discontinued, archived copy available at: https://www.bloomberg.com/politics/articles/2014-12-15/congresss-undying-and-lessthaneffective-acorn-funding-ban.

Weiner, Rachel. "Romney, Citing Safety Net, Says He's 'Not Concerned About the Very Poor.'" *Washington Post*, February 1, 2012.

Weiner, Tim. *Legacy of Ashes: The History of the CIA*. New York: Doubleday, 2007.

Weisberg, Jacob. "W.'s Greatest Hits: The Top 25 Bushisms of All Time." *Slate*, January 21, 2009. https://slate.com/news-and-politics/2009/01/the-top-25-bushisms-of-all-time.html.

Wellerstein, Alex. *Restricted Data: The History of Nuclear Secrecy in the United States*. Chicago: University of Chicago Press, 2021.

"The Westminster Declaration." The Westminster Declaration (website). Accessed October 23, 2023. https://westminsterdeclaration.org.

Wheeler, Marcy. *Anatomy of Deceit: How the Bush Administration Used the Media to Sell the Iraq War and Out a Spy*. Berkeley, CA: Vaster Books, 2007.

Wheeler, Marcy. "Armitage, a Review." *Emptywheel* (blog), November 12, 2007. https://www.emptywheel.net/2007/11/12/armitage-a-review.

Wheeler, Marcy. "The Libby Pardon: Trump's Object Lesson in Presidential Firewalls." *Emptywheel* (blog), April 12, 2018. https://www.emptywheel.net/2018/04/12/the-libby-pardon-trumps-object-lesson-in-presidential-firewalls.

White House. "White House: President Delivers 'State of the Union.'" News release, January 28, 2003. https://georgewbush-whitehouse.archives.gov/news/releases/2003/01/20030128-19.html.

Whitfield, Stephen J. *The Culture of the Cold War*. Baltimore, MA: Johns Hopkins University Press, 2016.

Whoriskey, Peter, and Agustin Aremdariz. "Secret Trove Illuminates the Lives of Billionaires." *Washington Post*, October 6, 2021.

Wight, Julien Trey. "*60 Minutes* of News-Noir: A Study of Cyberwar Representations in News Reporting." PhD diss., University of Minnesota–Twin Cities, 2023.

Wilcox, Lauren. "Embodying Algorithmic War: Gender, Race, and the Posthuman in Drone Warfare." *Security Dialogue* 48, no. 1 (2017): 11–28.

Wilderson, Frank B., III. *Red, White and Black: Cinema and the Structure of U.S. Antagonisms*. Durham, NC: Duke University Press, 2010.

Williams, Loretta J. *Black Freemasonry and Middle-Class Realities*. Columbia: University of Missouri Press, 1980.

Wilson, Joseph C., IV. "What I Didn't Find in Africa." *New York Times*, July 6, 2003.

Wilson, Kirt H. *The Reconstruction Desegregation Debate: The Politics of Equality and the Rhetoric of Place, 1870–1875.* East Lansing: Michigan State University Press, 2002.

Wilson, Woodrow. *The Papers of Woodrow Wilson.* Vol. 35. Edited by Arthur Link Jr. Princeton, NJ: Princeton University Press, 1981.

Wilson, Woodrow. *The Study of Public Administration.* Washington, DC: Public Affairs Press, 1955.

Winderman, Emily. "Anger's Volumes: Rhetorics of Amplification and Aggregation in #MeToo." *Women's Studies in Communication* 42, no. 3 (2019): 327–46.

Winderman, Emily. *Back Alley Abortion: A Rhetorical History.* Baltimore, MD: Johns Hopkins University Press, 2025.

Winderman, Emily. "(Never) Going Back: Black Feminist Impatience for a Post-*Dobbs* Future." *Women and Language* 46, no. 1 (2023): 285–91.

Winnicott, D. W. "Communicating and Not Communicating Leading to a Study of Certain Opposites (1963)." In *Reading Winnicott,* edited by Lesley Caldwell and Angela Joyce, 184–96. London: Routledge, 2011.

"Woodlawn Organization Created from 'Melting Pot' of Different Groups." *Chicago Defender,* June 2, 1962.

Wylie, Christopher. *Mindf*ck: Cambridge Analytica and the Plot to Break America.* New York: Random House, 2019.

Young, Robert J. C. *Postcolonialism: An Historical Introduction.* Malden: Blackwell, 2001.

Yun, Safia J. "Fear of the Evil Eye: A Missional Approach Toward the Envious Gaze Among Young Jordanian Muslim Women." Eugene, OR: Wipf & Stock Publishers, 2025.

Zamora, Daniel, and Michael C. Behrent. *Foucault and Neoliberalism.* Malden: Polity Press, 2016.

Zarefsky, David. "Making the Case for War: Colin Powell at the United Nations." *Rhetoric and Public Affairs* 10, no. 2 (2007): 275–302.

Zeleny, Jeff. "Initial Steps by Obama Suggest a Bipartisan Flair." *New York Times,* November 23, 2008.

Zerofsky, Elisabeth. "How a German Newspaper Became the Go-To Place for Leaks Like the Paradise Papers." *New Yorker,* November 11, 2017.

Zeskind, Leonard. "A Nation Dispossessed: The Tea Party Movement and Race." *Critical Sociology* 38, no. 4 (2011): 495–509.

Zetter, Kim. *Countdown to Zero Day: Stuxnet and the Launch of the World's First Digital Weapon.* New York: Broadway Books, 2014.

Zetter, Kim. "The Time Julian Assange Hacked the Pentagon." *Wired,* December 20, 2010.

Zetter, Kim. "WikiLeaks Posts Mysterious 'Insurance' File." *Wired,* July 30, 2010.

Zimbardo, Philip. *The Lucifer Effect: Understanding How Good People Turn Evil.* New York: Random House, 2008.

Žižek, Slavoj. "Good Manners in the Age of WikiLeaks." *London Review of Books* 33, no. 2 (2011): 9–10.

Žižek, Slavoj. *The Sublime Object of Ideology.* 2nd ed. New York: Verso, 2008.

Zola, Émile. *La vérité en marche: L'affaire Dreyfus.* Edited by Colette Becker. Paris: Flammarion, 1969.

Zuboff, Shoshana. *The Age of Surveillance Capitalism: The Fight for a Human Future at the New Frontier of Power.* New York: PublicAffairs, 2019.

INDEX

Abbasi, Fereydoon, 201

abortion, 64n20; abortion rights activism, 116n47; attacks on abortion rights, 21, 133–35

Adams, Samuel, 123–24

aesthetics, 9, 14–16, 110, 207; of transparency, 8n35

Afghanistan, 2, 86, 106, 154, 215

African American Policy Forum (AAPF): Say Her Name, 76

agency panic, 6, 141

Ahmadinejad, Mahmoud, 200

Ahmed Alwan al-Janabi, Rafid "Curveball," 94

Akbar, Shahzad, 175

Alam, Rumaan, 204

Alinsky, Saul D.: as dog whistle, 20–21, 108–39; *Rules for Radicals*, 114–15, 128, 130, 134

Allen, Ira J., 24

Al Moetamid Ibn Abad (king), 25

al-Qaeda, 106, 196–98

Althusser, Louis, 76, 80

American Civil Rights Movement, 44, 49, 109, 114, 116–17, 136–38, 171

American Great Chain of Being, 53

American Protective League, 47

Americans for Prosperity (AFP), 127

amnesia, 70, 82, 187, 189

analepsis, 21, 77, 175, 183 table 6.1, 184–90, 191n56, 205; detective, 185 fig. 6.1; settler, 186 fig. 6.2

anamorphosis, 58, 79–90, 169, 210

anaphora, ix, 92

Anglo-Saxton Protestants, 47, 124

Anonymous (Miles Taylor), 105, 220–21

anti-Blackness: dog whistles, 20–21, 39, 76, 108–39

anti-communism, 42–44, 46, 49, 51, 84, 125, 144–45. *See also* Cold War; House Un-American Activities Committee (HUAC); Red Scare

anti-epistemology, 1, 8, 75

anti-Masonic movement, 33, 41–43

anti-Muslim hate, 106

antisemitism, 46, 47, 85, 142

273

anti-totalitarian secret, 222
antonomasia, 73–74
apophasis, 13, 21, 141, 147 table 5.1, 148, 160, 161 fig. 5.2, 164–70
arcana imperii, 27, 34, 54, 56, 88
arcanum, 26
Arendt, Hannah, 40
Aristotle, 4
Armey, Dick, 124, 127
Armitage, Richard, 106
artificial intelligence, 203–4
Ashcroft, John, 95
Assange, Julian: and national security leaks, 21, 149–59, 162, 171; sexual violence by, 157. *See also* WikiLeaks
assemblage, 5, 9, 16, 24n7, 59, 190, 210
Association of Community Organizations for Reform Now (ACORN), 132–34
astrology, 212
Atlantic, The, 132
Atomic Energy Act, 23
authoritarianism, 24, 30, 55, 151, 216, 222
Avila, Renata, 157

Back of the Yards Neighborhood Council (BYNC), 109, 113
Bannon, Steve, 138, 139n160
Barr, William, 219
barred subject, 177–79
Bartlett, Bruce, 123–24
Bartlett, Dan, 101
Bavarian Illuminati, 54
Bay of Pigs Invasion, 49
Beasley, Vanessa, 89
Benghazi scandal, 74, 215
Bentley, Elizabeth, 143
Bergdahl, Bowe, 196–97
Bergson, Henri, 48, 49n132
Besel, Richard, 203n108
Biden, Hunter, 83n5
Biden, Joseph R., 20, 83, 137, 171, 204, 212
Biesecker, Barbara A., 71
biopolitics, 13, 139

Birchall, Clare, 14, 217
Bitzer, Lloyd, 4
Black, Edwin, 10, 50, 223, 224
Black Panthers, 44
Black Power movement, 50
blackboxing, 1
Blackness, 6, 120, 137, 179
Blakeley, Ulysses, 111–12
Bland, Sandra, 76
blankness, viii–ix, 71, 98
Bletchley Park, 166–67
Bond, James, viii, 151
Bondi, Pam, 219
Bonilla-Silva, Eduardo, 119–20
Booth, Heather, 116n47
Booz Allen Hamilton, 152
Borowitz, Andy, 101
Boudreau, Abbie, 131n119
Brandenburg v. Ohio, 214n12
Bratich, Jack, 2
Brazier, Arthur M., 112–13
Breitbart, Andrew, 122, 132–33
Breitbart News, 133, 138
Brennan, John, 194–95
Brennan, Teresa, 16
Brotherhood Organization of a New Destiny (BOND), 135
Brown, Nicole Marie, 111n15, 115
Browne, Simone, 7
Buckley, William F., 117
BUILD (Build Unity, Independence, Liberty, and Dignity), 116, 126–27
Bulgaria, 172
Bullock, Steven C., 29n31
Bureau of Intelligence and Research (INR), 75
Burke, Kenneth, 129, 141n6, 223
Burns, Scott: *The Report*, 106n109
Bush, George W., 108, 130, 197, 199n93; *A Charge to Keep*, 100; *Decision Points*, 102–3; enabling Donald Trump, 20, 82–86, 104–7; George W. Bush Presidential Center, 106; "Mission Accomplished" speech, 101; *Portraits of Courage*, 105; and secrecy, 2, 11, 20, 75; "sixteen words,"

74, 94, 96, 101; speech patterns (Bushisms), 99–103; State of the Union address (2003), 86, 94, 102; State of the Union address (2004), 102; and Valerie Plame Wilson Affair, 82–107

Cablegate Leaks, 74, 155–56
caesura, 13, 20, 91 fig. 3.1, 92, 96–99, 104, 219
Campbell, Karlyn Kohrs, 222
capitalism, 14, 24n7, 128, 180, 191; racial, 5
Carmichael, Stokely, 114
Carnegie, Andrew, 46
Carson, André, 122
Cassidy, John, 108
catachresis, 13, 21, 26, 73, 110, 121–29, 131, 141, 216, 222
Catholic Archdiocese, 109, 111n15, 112
censorship, 27, 64, 64n21, 98, 171, 206, 222
Centers for Disease Control (CDC), 52
Central Intelligence Agency (CIA), 48–49, 51–52, 75, 84n7, 135, 141n6, 144, 194, 198, 199, 201; torture by, 197, 217; and Valerie Plame Wilson Affair, 82–107. *See also* Iran-Contra Affair
Central Intelligence Group (CIG), 48
certainty of doubt, 96
Chaganty, Aneesh: *Searching,* 80
Chambers, Whittaker, 143
Chavez, Cesar, 109
Chavez, Linda, 130
Cheney, Dick, 88, 102–4, 107, 152
Cheney, Liz, 83
Chicago Defender, The, 109–10, 112–16
Chicago Land Clearance Commission (CLCC), 112
Chicago Plan Commission (CPC), 112
Chicago Urban League, 113
Christianity, 33–34, 55, 65, 113, 171, 182, 214
Church of Scientology, 154
cisgender normativity, ix, 20
Citizens for a Sound Economy (CSE), 127
Civil Rights Movement. *See* American Civil Rights Movement
Cleaver, Emanuel, 122
Cleveland, Grover, 46

Clinton, Hillary, 83, 122, 156, 215
Cloud, Dana L., 59–60, 142, 146
Cofield, Ernestine, 113
Cohen, Richard, 103
Cold War, x, 48, 53, 87n20, 140, 143, 145. *See also* House Un-American Activities Committee (HUAC); Lavender Scare; Red Scare
color-blind discourse, 53, 94, 120, 136. *See also* post-racialism
communism, 42–44, 125, 127, 140, 143–45, 172. *See also* House Un-American Activities Committee (HUAC)
Confederacy, 45
Conley, Donovan, 10, 75
Connecticut, 33
Conservative Political Action Conference (CPAC), 122
conspiracies, viii–ix, 1, 10, 13, 17, 24, 48, 51–52, 54–55, 74, 84–86, 92, 135, 140, 147, 151, 156, 176, 189, 194, 210, 211 table 7.1, 219–24; anti-Christian, 33; anti-communist, 46; antisemitic, 46, 85; and civic paranoia, 42; deep state, 212–16; of Donald Trump, 21, 197, 213, 215–18, 221; and melodrama, 179–80; racist, 45, 123–24, 133, 138; rise of, 3; and spectacle, 6
Control Systems, 200
Conyers, John, 95
Cooper, James Fenimore, 182
copia, 75; *copia verborum,* 153
Copjec, Joan, 93, 97–98, 121n68, 142, 148–49
Coplon, Judith, 143
Copperman, Paul, 116n47
Corrigan, Lisa M., 42
Coughlin, Charles E., 47
Couric, Katie, 130
COVID-19 pandemic, 3, 139, 192n64
Crichton, Michael, 50
Crisis Pregnancy Centers, 134n139
critical humanism, 58, 62
cryptography, 23, 25–26, 152–53, 162, 166, 222
cryptology, 166
cryptos, 25
Cumberbatch, Benedict, 152n51, 163n107

cyberweapons, 2, 181, 199–205

Da Vinci Code, The, 208
Daily Show, The, 98
Daleiden, David R., 133–34
Daley, Richard, 116
Daniel, J. Michael, 202–3
Darius I, 25
dark money, 3
dark sousveillance, 7
Dash, Julie, 65
de Vise, Pierre, 111
Dean, Jodi, 17
Debord, Guy, 5–6
deconstruction, 70–71
deep state, viii, 21, 105, 208–25
Defense Intelligence Agency (DIA), 75
Deleuze, Gilles, 16
Demaratus, 25
Democratic National Committee (DNC), 156
Democratic Party, 45, 83, 85, 93, 122–23, 129, 156, 212, 215; Dixie Democrats, 137
depth reading, 58, 62–68, 70–71. *See also* secret *in* discourse
depth semantics, 65–67
Der Spiegel, 154
Derrida, Jacques, 61–62, 70–71, 77, 82, 103, 131, 208, 221
DeYoung, Karen, 100
différance, 70–71, 73, 77
disavowal, 21, 54, 92, 110, 121, 170, 175–76, 184, 191–92, 197, 205, 207
disclosure, 2, 7, 51, 95–96, 194, 197, 221, 224; demand for, 24, 49–50; and depth hermeneutics, 67; and Freemasons, 34; and leaking, 75, 141–42, 146–69, 171; limits of, 107, 213, 217, 220; and naming, 76; and retroaction, 77. *See also* right to know; transparency
Discord Leaks, 170–71
disinformation, viii, 3, 222
distant reading, 69
dog whistles, viii, x, 10, 13, 24, 80, 209, 213, 224; "busing," 137–38; "Critical Race Theory," 138; "DEI hire," 137–38; Nazi salute, 138, 211 table 7.1, 212; racism of, 19–21, 56, 108–39

Don't Ask, Don't Tell, 74
Double Indemnity, 97
double-consciousness, 135
Dr. Strangelove, 140
Drake, 211n2
Dreyfus Affair, 46, 142
drone strikes, 2, 174–75, 181, 186–87, 189–90, 192–95
Du Bois, W. E. B., 32, 135
Dulles, Alan Welch, 48–49, 51, 75, 144
Dulles, John Foster, 48–49

Eban, Katherine, 106
Ecuador: embassy in London, 152n51, 156–57
Eichmann, Adolf, 40–41
Eisenhower, Dwight D., 49
election, US presidential: 2000, 99; 2004, 103; 2008, 109, 132; 2016, 83, 172, 215
elision, 3, 10, 18, 79
Ellsberg, Daniel, 50–51, 96, 142, 171, 215. *See also* Pentagon Papers
Ely, Richard, 47
Emanuel, Rahm, 122
empty speech, 195
Englehardt, Tom, 221–22
enhanced interrogation, 106. *See also* torture
ENIGMA code, 141, 162, 166
Enlightenment, 28, 30, 182
Enstehung, 57
epanalepsis, 92
episteme, 5, 19, 22–56
Epstein-Trump scandal, 218–20
Erdoğan, Tayyip, 214
Esmail, Sam, 187, 204
espacement, 189–90
Espionage Act, 23, 46–48
Evans, Rowland, 87n20
Executive Order 8802, 39
Executive Order 13233, 89
Executive Order 14110, 203
Eye in the Sky, 187, 189–90

fact-checking, 93, 171
Fair Game, 86–87
"fake news," 216
false-flags, 74
Fanon, Frantz, 38–39, 76, 80, 178–79
Farrell, Martin, 111
fascism, 4, 43, 85, 138, 212, 222
Federal Bureau of Investigation (FBI), 10, 46, 51–52, 96, 143, 172, 182; COINTELPRO, 44, 50. *See also* US Bureau of Investigation
feigned unicity, 73n55, 198n87
Feinstein, Diane, 106n109
Felman, Shoshana, 140, 160
Felski, Rita, 68
femininity, 140–42, 145, 147 table 5.1, 148, 160–64, 161 fig. 5.2, 171–72
femme fatale, 97, 141, 147 table 5.1, 148, 160–63, 170
FIGHT (Freedom, Integration, God, Honor, Today), 116, 126–27
Fischer, Mia, 143
Fish, John Hall, 117
Fitzgerald, Patrick, 87
flashbacks, 77, 183 fig. 6.1, 184, 185 fig. 6.1, 185 table 6.1, 188–89, 191n56, 208
Ford, Gerald, 40, 51n146
Ford, Henry, 47
Foreign Intelligence Surveillance Act (FISA), 174, 194
Foreign Intelligence Surveillance Court (FISC), 152
forgetting, 5–6, 22, 63–64, 70, 75–76, 106, 187–89
Foster, John Watson, 48
Foucault, Michel, 13, 22–23, 26, 43, 57, 139
#4amClub, 212
Fourth Estate, 2
Franklin, Benjamin, 29
Freedmen's Bureau, 46
Freedom of Information Act (FOIA), 50
FreedomWorks, 124
Freemasons, 27–29, 34–43, 46, 54, 211 table 7.1; Black, 30–33, 211
French Revolution, 30, 69

Freud, Sigmund, 34–38, 53, 62, 66, 68, 73, 77, 116n47, 178, 225

Gadamer, Hans-Georg, 63
Galison, Peter, 8–9, 23
Gellman, Barton, 152–53, 157–58
genealogy, 9, 19, 22–57
Germany, 40, 47–48, 49n132, 111, 166–67
Gibney, Alex: *Zero Days*, 200
Giles, Hannah, 132–33
Gill-Peterson, Jules, 179
Gimlet Media, 187
Gingrich, Newt, 108, 122, 125, 128
Gitelman, Lisa, 51
Glissant, Édouard, 38–39
Goebbels, Joseph, 48
Goffman, Erving, 35–36
Gomez, Logan Rae, 76
gonzo pseudojournalism, 110, 130–35
Gore, Al, 100
Gorgias of Leontini, 4n15
gotcha politics, 130
Gotti, John, 84
Grand Lodge of England, 29, 31
Grayson, Alan, 174
Great Britain, 31, 69, 94, 118, 162, 180, 189
Great Depression, 34
Greenberg, Andy, 202–3
Greene, Marjorie Taylor, 171
Greene, Ronald Walter, 59–60
Greenlee, Sam, 108, 135–36
Greenstein, Fred, 100
Greenwald, Glen, 152, 157
grievance culture, 171
Griffith, D. W., 47, 54, 183
Grimshaw, William H., 31
Grindstaff, David Allen, 3, 77
Guantanamo Bay Naval Base, 88, 106, 154
Guardian, The, 152, 154
Guattari, Félix, 16
Gulf of Tonkin Hoax, 74
Gunn, Joshua, 10, 34, 154n61

Haberman, Maggie, 77
Habermas, Jürgen, 28
Hackett, David G., 33
Hader, Bill, 155
Hage, Ghassan, 42
Haldeman Tapes, 74, 83
Hall, Prince, 30–31
Hall, Rachel, 8n35
Hall, Stuart, 60, 118
Hallsby, Karl, 3n14
Hamdouni Alami, Mohammed, 205
Harding, Luke, 151n49, 155
Hari, Mata, 162
Hariman, Robert, 10
Harlow, Bill, 87
Harney, Stefano, 221n45
Harris, Kamala, 137–38, 212
Harrison, Benjamin, 48
Harrison, Sarah, 157
Hartman, Saidiya, 39, 45, 179
Hartnett, Stephen J., 88
Harvey, Roy, 112, 116n47
Hawai'ian monarchy, 48
Hawhee, Debra, 4n15
Hayden, Michael, 201
Haymarket Riot, 47
Helen of Troy, 4n15
Herbert, Frank: *Dune*, 200
Herkunft, 57
hermeneutics, 9, 14, 42, 49, 71; of suspicion, 59, 63, 65–67
Herodotus, 25
Herrn, Ranier, ix n9
heteronormativity, 3, 6, 141, 146, 160, 167, 172, 215
Higgins, David, 200
Hilbert, David, 165
Hirschfeld, Magnus, ix
Hiss, Alger, 54, 143
Hiss, Priscilla, 143
Histiaeus, 25

Hitchens, Christopher, 100
Hitler, Adolf, 48, 49n132. *See also* Nazis
HM Belmarsh, 156
Hochman, Brian, 23
Hodges, Andrew, 165
Hofstadter, Richard, 42, 46
Holbein, Hans: *The Ambassadors*, 78 fig. 2.1, 79, 169
Holocaust, 40–41
Homecoming, 187–90, 204
Homeland, 196
homosexuality, 10, 42, 142–43, 162–63, 165
Hoover, J. Edgar, 10, 44, 50–51, 54, 143–44, 182
House Un-American Activities Committee (HUAC), 44, 125
Housing Act, 112
Howell, Brenetta, 109, 115
Huffington Post, 133
Hussein, Saddam, 88, 94–95, 101
Hutchinson, Cassidy, 83

Igo, Sarah E., 23
Illinois, 111; Chicago, 20, 108, 121–22, 124n86; Woodlawn (Chicago), 20, 109–19, 126, 136
Imaginary (Lacanian), 21, 147, 169, 177, 180–81, 183 table 6.1, 184, 191
Imperial Rome, 54
in but not of, 221n45
incels, 150, 159, 170, 177
incorporation, 110, 131–35
Indiana, 33, 48
Indigenous people, 34–35
Industrial Areas Foundation (IAF), 109
Institute for Sexology, ix
International Atomic Energy Agency (IAEA), 94
International Consortium of Investigative Journalists (ICIJ), 169
International Criminal Court, 86
invisibility, vii, 1–2, 5, 14, 53, 68, 70, 140, 172; threat of, 140
Iran, 84n7, 199; Natanz, 202

Iran-Contra Affair, 51, 74, 84, 89, 93, 224
Iraq, 2, 20, 75, 85–88, 94–95, 101–2, 106–7, 152, 154, 201, 215
Iraq War, 106
Irigaray, Luce, 62, 160, 179
Irish Military Lodge, 31
irony, 13, 98–99, 101, 105; and dog whistles, 21, 110, 125–29, 131
Islam, 196–97, 206–7, 214. *See also* Muslims

Jacob, Margaret C., 28
Jameson, Fredric, 68
Jamieson, Kathleen Hall, 223
JANE, 116n47
January 6 attack, 82–83, 195, 209, 213n7, 217, 222
January 6 Commission, 83, 106, 209
Jefferson, Thomas, 31, 124n86
Jewish people, 42, 46, 108, 142
John Birch Society, 10, 44, 126
John of Salisbury, 29n28
Johnson, Jenell, 176n6
Johnson, Paul E., 120, 124n86
Jorgensen, Christine, 143

kakistocracy, 55
kakoethos, 176–77
Kant, Immanuel, 28
Kapadia, Ronak K., 15
Kelly, Casey Ryan, 7, 145
Kemal, Mustafa (Atatürk), 214
Kendzior, Sarah, 82, 218–19
Kennedy, George, 4n17
Kennedy, John F., 42, 219
Kern, Anne Brigitte, 24n7
Kerry, John, 101
Kibbe, Matt, 127
King, Larry, 130
King, Martin Luther, Jr., 44, 116, 127, 136, 219
Kiriakou, John, 197–98
Kittler, Friedrich, 165n125
Klein, Melanie, 62

Knight, Peter, 210
Koch, Charles and David, 123–24, 127
kompromat, 83
Kristeva, Julia, 62, 172
Kuala Lumpur War Crimes Commission, 86
Ku Klux Klan, 45, 47, 214n12

Lacan, Jacques, 12, 14, 37, 57–58, 62, 73–74, 79, 90–91, 93, 96, 142, 147, 160, 177–78, 179n18, 180, 188n53, 195
Laclau, Ernesto, 99, 121
Lamar, Kendrick: "Not Like Us," 211
Lamo, Adrian, 168
Langner, Ralph, 200
Lansing, Robert, 48
Laplanche, Jean, 131, 188n53
Lavender Scare, 143
Le Bon, Gustave, 35
le Carré, John: *A Delicate Truth*, 214; *Tinker, Tailor, Soldier, Spy*, x
League of Nations, 48
leaker/leaking, viii, x, 16, 24, 51n146, 58, 75, 83, 131n119, 197, 209, 211 table 7.1, 213, 219, 221, 223–24; under George W. Bush, 82–107; and masculinity, 21, 140–61, 168, 170, 171–72; mega-, 21; and national security, 2, 19, 56, 140–73; and retroaction, 80; and sexuality, 20, 21, 140–73; and state secrets, 54–55, 194; and transness, 143, 146–47, 160, 162–63, 171–72; vs. whistleblowers, 141–42. *See also* WikiLeaks
Lease, Mary Elizabeth, 46
Leave the World Behind, 204
Lebanon, 84n7
Leber, Charles, 111–12, 115n40
Lechuga, Michael, 191
Leigh, David, 151n49, 155–56
Lemon, Don, 196
Levi, Julian, 112
Levine, Caroline, 70
Lewis, John, 122
Libby, I. Scooter, 87, 98, 102, 106; pardon by Trump, 86, 104–5, 107
liberal internationalism, 48

liberalism, 110, 129–30, 132, 145; Third Way, 117–18, 139
libertarianism, 123–24, 136
lie, 58, 133, 137, 214, 223; dog whistles as, x; presidential, 93, 97, 121n68
Live Action, 133
Locke, John, 30
Lofgren, Mike, 214–17, 221
López, Ian Haney, 119–20
Lost, 208
Lundberg, Christian O., 72, 73n55, 198n87

Manning, Chelsea, 21, 141, 142, 146, 154, 160–63, 166–69
Mar-a-Lago document scandal, 54–55
Maret, Susan, 3
Martinot, Steven, 6
Marx, Karl, 66
Marxism, 11, 40, 68, 84n7
masculinity, 3, 127, 215; and agency panic, 6; crisis of, 140–41, 144–45; and leaker, 21, 140–61, 168, 170, 171–72; as mode of logical failure, 142; toxic, 158, 170; white, 18, 176
Massachusetts, 31, 33
Matheson, Calum, 129n111, 203
Maxwell, Ghislane, 219
Mayer, Jane, 126
McCain, John, 132
McCarthy, Joseph, 44, 50–51, 125. See also House Un-American Activities Committee (HUAC)
McFarlane, Robert, 84n7
McGee, Michael Calvin, 60
McKittrick, Katherine, 2
McLuhan, Marshall, 51
Me Too movement, 76, 217
megaleakers, 21
megethos, 21, 77, 141, 147 table 5.1, 148, 150 fig. 5.1, 153–59, 170, 222
Melley, Timothy, 141, 144
melodrama, 201; settler, 178–82
memento mori, 79
Mercieca, Jennifer, 88–89, 213

Merritt, Sandra S., 134
metaphor, 37n74, 49, 54, 72–73, 101, 119, 139, 141n6, 145, 165, 167
metonymy, 51, 72–75, 92, 137, 141, 222
Metzl, Jonathan, 49
Meyerson, Harold, 125
Michigan, 33
Milgram, Stanley, 41
Military Intelligence Division, 48
Miller, Paul, 126
Mills, Lindsay, 158
mnesis, 75
Moreno, Lenín, 156
Moretti, Franco, 69
Morin, Edgar, 24n7
Morris, Charles E., III, 10
Moten, Fred, 221n45
Moyers, Bill, 214
Moynihan, Daniel Patrick, 44
Moynihan Report, 38
Mueller Report, 74–75, 85, 106
Murder in the Air, 54
Murray, Arnold, 163
Musk, Elon, 104; Nazi salute, 138, 211 table 7.1, 212
Muslims, 15, 82, 189, 195, 196–97, 205; anti-Muslim hate, 106. See also Islam
mysterium, 26

NAACP, 123
Nachträglichkeit, 36, 77
Nagle, Delbert, 43
naming, tropes of, 20, 74–77
NASA, 151
National Association of Black Journalists, 137
National Civil Liberties Bureau, 46
National Press Club, 97
National Reconnaissance Office (NRO), 75
National Right to Work Legal Defense Foundation, 127
national security, 72, 85, 87–88, 103; and leaking, x, 2, 19, 21, 56, 140–73

National Security Agency (NSA), 75, 141n6, 152–53, 157, 174, 201
National Security Council (NSC), 51, 84n7
national security state, 2, 6, 8n35, 13, 53, 85, 99, 104, 140–73
National Treasure, 208
nationalism, 88, 123, 163, 176, 180n26; paranoid, 42, 50, 52–54; white, 24
NATO, 200
nazar bonçuk, 205–7, 206 fig. 6.5
Nazis, 40, 47–48, 162, 166; Nazi salute, 138, 211 table 7.1, 212
neocolonialism, 21, 174–207
neoliberalism, 4–5, 51, 59, 118, 139
"never forget," 106
New Mexico, 85
New York City, 64n20, 138, 204
New York State: Batavia, 33
New York Times, 86, 94–95, 101–2, 130, 154, 156
Newsweek, 101
Nicaragua, 84. *See also* Iran-Contra Affair
Nichols, Bill, 15
Nietzsche, Friedrich, ix, 57, 66
Niger, 86–87
9/11 attacks, 1–2, 8n35, 103, 106n108, 152, 154, 204, 208
Nixon, Richard, 50, 54, 83–85, 171, 218n23. *See also* Watergate scandal
North, Oliver, 84n7, 218n23
Novak, Robert, 87, 95, 97
Nucatola, Deborah, 133–34

Obama, Barack, 162, 194–95, 202, 204, 216; and Alinsky dog whistle, 21, 108–39
Obama, Michelle, 204
O'Brien, Soledad, 128
occultatio, 3, 10–11, 75, 191
Office of Strategic Influence (OSI), 75
Office of Strategic Services (OSS), 75
Office of the Coordinator of Information (COI), 48
O'Keefe, James, 130, 131n119, 132–35
omission, 3, 21, 92, 175, 183 table 6.1, 191

One Hundred Percent Americanism, 47, 55
opacity, 15, 36, 38, 50, 55, 58, 62, 88, 149, 159, 200; right to, 39
open secret, 16, 72, 76, 92, 114, 166, 204
Operation Shock and Awe, 106
order-words, 3
Other, 177–78, 180

Packer, Joseph, 109n7
Pakistan, 174, 195
Palestinians, 178
Palin, Sarah, 122, 130, 132, 154
Palmer Raids, 44
Panama Canal, 48
Panama Papers, 169, 217
Pandora Papers, 169, 217
Paradise Papers, 169, 217
paralepsis, 11, 13
paralipsis, 21, 164, 176, 183 table 6.1, 184, 191–98, 205
paranoia, viii, 3, 22, 56–57, 68–69, 105, 116, 140, 151, 176, 209–10, 217; civic, 24, 41–54, 58; paranoid criticism, 17; paranoid reading, 63; paranoid style, 42, 84; racist, 42–48, 54–55
parrhēsiastēs, 221
Paul, Rand, 194–95
Pence, Mike, 220
Penn, Sean, 87
Pentagon, 75, 152
Pentagon Papers, 50, 74, 171, 217
Peterson, Jesse Lee, 135
phallic logic, 141, 147 table 5.1, 148, 149, 150 fig. 5.1, 154, 158, 170
phatic logic, 141, 147 table 5.1, 148–49, 161 fig. 5.2, 168–69
Pierce, Lee, 17
pink herrings, 10
Pinkerton Agency, 177, 182
Pittsburgh Fraternal Order of Police, 43
Plame Wilson, Valerie, 20, 82–107, 201
Planned Parenthood, 133–35
Podesta, John, 83, 156

Poe, Edgar Allan, 64; "The Purloined Letter," 1, 16, 37n74, 90, 91 fig. 3.1, 92–93
Poindexter, John, 84n7
Poitras, Laura: *Citizenfour*, 152–53, 157–58
political whataboutism, ix, 120
polycrisis, 24
Pontalis, Jean-Bertrand, 131, 188n53
post-racialism, 6, 136–37. *See also* color-blind discourse
post-rhetorical presidency, 89
post-traumatic stress disorder (PTSD), 184–98
Powell, Colin, 88, 94
Powers, Richard Gid, 44, 51
presidential secret, 20, 86–89
Prince Hall African Lodge, 30–32, 211
PRISM, 152
Proefrock, C. K., 111
Project 2025, 55, 92
Project Veritas, 130, 132–34
prolepsis, 21, 175–76, 183 table 6.1, 184, 191n56, 198–205, 199n93
propaganda, 42–43, 47, 59, 75, 88, 108, 135, 143–44, 182, 189
Protocols of the Elders of Zion, 46–47
psyops, 74
publicity's secret, 17
purloined letter, 85, 89–103

QAnon, 3, 211 table 7.1, 212, 215, 219, 222–23
queer failure, 167
queer theory, 3
Qur'an, 206

racial capitalism, 5
racial gaslighting, 120
racism, 12, 37–38, 51, 59, 177–78, 182, 204, 214n12, 222; anti-Black, 20–21, 39, 76, 108–9; dog whistles, 19–21, 108–39; of Donald Trump, 82, 120, 137–38; and paranoia, 42–48, 54–55; of Ronald Reagan, 120; systemic, 6, 52; of Tea Party, 21, 108–39; white nationalism, 24. *See also* antisemitism; white supremacy

Raff, Gideon, 196
raison d'état, 26–27, 185
Rancière, Jacques, 14
Rathke, Wade, 132
Reagan, Ronald, 51, 52–55, 84–85, 89, 93–94, 121n68, 218n23; racist dog whistles, 120. *See also* Iran-Contra Affair
Real (Lacanian), 21, 146, 170, 183–84, 198–99, 203–5
realist's imbecility, 93, 162, 191–92
Reality, 172
Reconstruction, 32, 38–39, 44–45, 55
Red Scare, 50, 53. *See also* anti-communism; House Un-American Activities Committee (HUAC)
redaction, viii, 15, 64–65, 88, 98, 101, 156, 172–73, 210
Rehman, Nabila, 174, 207
Rehman, Zubair, 174, 207
Reitzes, Donald and Dietrich, 109, 125n91
repetition, 12, 19–20, 70, 73–74, 81, 90, 91 fig. 3.1, 92, 94–104, 110, 122, 173, 210, 223
Republican Party, 45, 83, 87, 99, 108, 123, 125, 127–29, 132, 137, 217, 218n23
retroaction, 18, 30, 73, 76, 84, 128–29, 163, 165–67, 172, 190, 199, 201, 204, 219; and action, viii; and analepsis, 175; and caesura, 92; in psychoanalysis, 36–37; and secret *of* discourse, 9, 62, 67, 72, 91, 119, 209, 212n3, 213, 224; and settler-detective, 184, 187; of talking cure, 12; tropes of, 20, 58, 77–81
Révauger, Cécile, 30
Revolutionary War (US), 29, 123–24
rhetoric of science/inquiry, 11
rhetorical materialism, 11, 13
rhetorical studies, 3, 59
Rice, Condoleezza, 199n93
Rice, Jenny, 213
Rich, Seth, 156
Richter, Angela, 157
Ricoeur, Paul, 65–67
Riessman, Frank, 118
right to know, 50, 146, 171, 224. *See also* disclosure; transparency

Rivers, Laurie, 212
Rogin, Michael, 1, 6, 52–54, 70
Romney, Mitt, 128
"Ronald Reagan," the Movie, 54
Roosevelt, Franklin D., 39, 75
Rose, Lila, 133–34
Rosenberg, Ethel, 143
Ross, Fred, 109, 132
Rousseau, Jean-Jacques, 30
Routledge, Norman, 167
Rove, Karl, 87, 95
Row, Jennifer, 16–17
Rowland, Allison L., 18
Rubenstein, Diane, 89–90
Rumsfeld, Donald, 75, 102
Russia, 46, 156, 200; invasion of Ukraine, 84, 170; Trump's collusion with, 217; US election interference, 172. See also Sandworm
Ryan, Paul, 128–29

Saas, William O., 10, 75
Sandinistas, 84
Sandworm, 199–202, 204
Sanger, Margaret, 135
Santelli, Rick, 124n86
scandal, viii, x, 19, 24, 27, 50, 56, 58, 69, 80, 143, 176n6, 209, 213, 223; Benghazi, 74, 215; Epstein-Trump, 218–20; Iran-Contra, 51, 74, 84, 89, 93, 224; Mar-a-Lago, 54–55; Trump's, 54–55, 82–84, 85, 92; Ukrainegate, 83–84; Valerie Plame Wilson, 20, 82–107, 201; Watergate, 51, 74, 83–84; William Morgan, 33
Schaack, Michael J., 47
Schlesinger, Arthur, 51, 144–45
Schmitt, Eric, 156
Schorr, Daniel, 51
Schumer, Charles, 95
Schwarze, Steven, 179n22
Scott, Robert L., 11
secrecy, definition, 18–19
secrecy studies, 1–4
secret, the: definition, 18–19, 224–25

secret administration, 40
secret episteme, 22–57, 75
secret *in* discourse, 8–9, 58, 61, 63–67, 72, 74–76, 91, 94, 110, 147 table 5.1, 204–5, 209–18, 224. See also depth reading
secret *of* discourse, 8–9, 58, 61, 67–70, 91, 94, 104, 110, 119, 147 table 5.1, 205, 209–18, 220, 224. See also surface reading
secret societies, 3, 24, 27–34, 38, 49, 55–56, 58. See also Freemasons
secret-keepers, 33, 42, 76, 223
secrets, definition, 18–19
secretum, 26
Sedgwick, Eve Kosofsky, 17, 68–69
Sedition Act, 47–48
Seigworth, Gregory, 16, 156
Sen, Ivan, 183
Senate Intelligence Committee Report on Torture, 106n109, 197, 217
settler-detective, viii, x, 11, 19–20, 24, 207, 209, 213, 224; and analepsis, 185 fig. 6.1; detective fiction, 56, 64n20; gendered, 161; and neocolonialism, 174–207; and paranoia, 56; and retroaction, 80, 184, 187; and surveillance, 174–76, 180–81, 190, 195; and trauma, 184–99; tropes of, 21, 175–76, 183 table 6.1, 184–85, 188, 191, 198
sex crime panic, 44
Sexton, Jared, 6
sexual violence, 50, 131n119, 134–35, 218; by Donald Trump, 218–20; by Jeffrey Epstein, 218–20; by Julian Assange, 157
sexuality, ix, 10, 224; and national security, 20–21, 140–73; and paranoia, 42, 56; in psychoanalysis, 62; racialized, 6, 32, 48, 55
sexuation, 144, 172
Shahriari, Majid, 201
Sharif, Solmaz: *Look*, 174, 205
Sharpe, Christina, 65
Sheehi, Lara, 178
Sheehi, Stephen, 178
Signalgate, 54
Simmel, Georg, 34–38, 53
Sinclair, Upton, 113

Sisco King, Claire, 157

situation, 4–7

slavery, 2–3, 24n7, 25, 30–32, 39, 45, 65, 171, 192n64

Snowden, Edward, 2, 21, 75, 142, 146, 149–54, 156–59, 169–71, 174–75, 194, 215, 221

socialism, 47, 125, 145

Society for American Civic Renewal (SACR), 55

Sonnenfelt Doctrine, 87n20

South East Chicago Commission (SECC), 111

sovereign power, 20, 22, 24, 26–29, 69, 82, 87n20, 103, 120, 175, 179–80, 182, 223

Soviet Union, 87n20, 140, 143

spectacle, 1, 5–10, 24, 54, 69–70, 85, 180, 209–12

Spence, Craig, 218n23

spies/spying, 49, 143, 155, 162, 190, 197–98, 209, 214; domestic spying, 174; outed, 82–107; spy films, 54; spying agencies, 42; spyware, 181, 199

Spinoza, Baruch, 77

spymaster, 141, 147 table 5.1, 148, 150–53, 159, 170

Squires, Catherine, 2

state secrets, 49, 54

steganos, 25

STELLARWIND, 152

Stewart, Jon, 98

Stone, Oliver: *Snowden*, 158

Stone, Roger, 83

Stoneman, Ethan, 109n7

Strong, Josiah, 47

Stryker, Susan, 143

Stuckey, Mary, 89

Stuxnet, 199–202, 204

surface reading, 20, 58, 62, 67–70, 72. See also secret *of* discourse

surveillance, viii, 4, 15, 24, 60, 141, 215, 222; and 9/11 aftermath, 2, 105; biopolitical, 13; gendered, 141, 148–49, 151–53, 160–61, 166, 170, 172; and graduate seminars, 70; as order-word, 3; police, 10; racialized, 76; and settler-detective, 174–76, 180–81, 190, 195; state, 2, 76, 105. See also national security state; USA Patriot Act

suspicion, 10, 13, 17, 153, 218n23; and anti-Masonism, 41, 46; and communism, 43; and deep state, 220; and dog whistles, 135; and George W. Bush, 85, 102, 104; hermeneutics of, 59, 63, 65–67; and psychoanalysis, 37–38, 53; and racism, 37–38, 45, 49, 52

Symbolic (Lacanian), 21, 37n74, 147, 170, 181, 183 table 6.1, 184, 198n87, 203–5

symbolic order, 6, 37, 147, 165n125, 177, 184, 204–5

synecdoche, 13, 20, 73, 77, 91 fig. 3.1, 92, 99–104

Syria, 155

Tacitus, Publius Cornelius, 26–27

Taft, William Howard, 39

Taliban, 174, 196

Taylor, Breonna, 76

Taylor, Miles, 105, 220–21

Tea Party: racist dog whistles, 21, 108–10, 119–30, 135, 136

Teflon Dons, 84

Teixeira, Jack, 170–71

Temporary Woodlawn Organization (TWO), 109–10, 112–16, 126–27

Tenet, George, 95

terrorism, 15, 75–76, 85, 88, 102, 151, 159, 174, 178n15, 180, 189, 194–95, 198, 214n12. See also 9/11 attacks; January 6 attack; war on terror

Test for Machine Intelligence (Turing Test), 165

Texas, 48; Crawford, 103

there is no secret, 68, 209–11, 216–17

Third Way politics, 117–18, 139

"this page intentionally left blank," vii

Thompson, Bennie, 83

Thompson, Hunter S., 130

Thompson, John B., 66

Tiessen, Matthew, 16, 156

Time magazine, 95n61, 101, 104

Toole, Martin, 43

torture, 41, 65, 88, 106, 178n15, 197–98, 217

Tower Commission, 51, 84n7

INDEX · 285

trans people, 179, 216; and leaker, 143, 146–47, 160, 162–63, 171–72

transparency, ix, 24, 55, 149, 171, 209, 214, 217; dangers of, 8, 15, 38, 56; under Donald Trump, 21; under George W. Bush, 11, 100; and *megethos*, 77, 159; rise of, 49–52; and the secret, 7, 93. *See also* disclosure; right to know

Transportation Security Administration (TSA), 8n35

trauma, 17, 35–36, 41, 66–67, 71, 106, 179, 212n3; and settler-detective, 184–99

tropes, 20, 60, 125, 141, 205, 223; of bureaucracy, 70; definition, viii–ix; and distant reading, 69; of misnaming, 121; of naming, 74–77; and *occultatio*, 11; of purloined letter, 91 fig. 3.1, 92; of repetition, 92, 94; of retroaction, 58, 77–81; of the secret, 13, 18, 73, 96; and secret *in/of* discourse, 71–72; of settler-detective, 21, 175–76, 183 table 6.1, 184–85, 188, 191, 198; of unauthorized disclosure, 21, 146–69. *See also individual tropes*

Trump, Donald, 20, 77, 85, 93, 171, 211n2, 222; conspiracy theories of, 21, 197, 213, 215–18, 221; and Elon Musk, 104, 138, 212; and George W. Bush, 104–7; pardon of Scooter Libby, 86, 104–5, 107; racism of, 82, 120, 137–38; scandals, 54–55, 82–84, 85, 92, 218–20; sexual violence by, 218–20; speech patterns, 84, 100n82, 176. *See also* January 6 attack

Turing, Alan, 21, 141, 152, 160, 162–69

Turkey, 111, 205, 214

Turner, Patricia A., 52

Twilight Zone, The, 63

Tyldum, Morten: *Imitation Game*, 162, 166–67

Ukraine, 83, 217; Russian invasion, 84, 170

Ukrainegate scandal, 83–84

uncloseting, 13, 170, 172

unconscious (psychoanalytic), 36–37, 62, 73, 177–78, 180, 188n53. *See also* Imaginary (Lacanian); Real (Lacanian); Symbolic (Lacanian)

Underground Railroad, 2

Union (Civil War), 45

United Nations, 88, 94

United States v. Mitchell, 83

United Woodlawn Council (UWC), 111–12

University, 113, 116, 136

University of Chicago, 111; Urban Institute, 112

US Bureau of Investigation, 44, 46–47. *See also* Federal Bureau of Investigation (FBI)

US Capitol attack (2021). *See* January 6 attack

US Congress, 45–46, 53, 84, 89, 100, 133, 137, 174–75, 214; Benghazi hearings, 215; House of Representatives, 83n5, 85, 99, 125; House Oversight and Reform Committee, 99; House Permanent Select Committee on Intelligence, 51, 174; House Un-American Activities Committee, 44, 125; January 6 Commission, 83, 106, 209; Senate, 83n5, 125, 194; Senate Select Committee on Intelligence, 51. *See also Senate Intelligence Committee Report on Torture*

US Constitution, 89, 107, 153, 171; Article II, 88; Fifth Amendment, 125n91; First Amendment, 88, 214n12; Fourth Amendment, 2

US Cybersecurity and Infrastructure Security Agency (CISA), 203

US Department of Defense, 187, 192. *See also* Pentagon; Pentagon Papers

US Department of Government Efficiency (DOGE), 104

US Department of Homeland Security, 105, 203, 220

US Department of Justice, 47, 194, 219

US Department of State, 87n20, 141n6, 143, 152, 154

US MILNET, 151

US Navy, 39

US Post Office, 39

US Steel, 48

US Supreme Court, 44

US Treasury, 39

USA Patriot Act, 2, 23, 105

U-2 spy plane crash (1960), 49

Valerie Plame Wilson scandal, 20, 82–107, 201

Values Voter Summit, 134–35

Van Dyke, W. S., 183

VanHaitsma, Pamela, 167
Vanity Fair, 97
Veracini, Lorenzo, 180–81, 183
Vermont, 33
Vietnam War, 50, 54
visibility, 15, 26, 28, 40, 49, 68, 110, 116, 133, 166, 209, 215; gendered, 163, 165; hyper-, 69; racialized, 65; as trap, 13; visible secrecy, 16. *See also* invisibility
Voltaire, 30
von Hoffman, Nicholas, 112, 114n31

Walker, Corey D. B., 31
war on terror, 75, 85, 99, 106
Washington Post, 87, 95, 100–101, 103, 125, 155, 158
Wasserman Schultz, Debbie, 156
Watergate scandal, 51, 74, 83–84
Watts, Eric King, 137
Watts, Naomi, 87
Weber, Max, 40
Welch, Robert, 44, 50–51, 127
Welles, Sumner, 143
Westminster Declaration, 171
Wheeler, Marcy, 87, 104, 107
whistleblowers, 50, 75, 83n5, 96, 139, 197, 201–2, 221; vs. leakers, 141–42
white nationalism, 24
white racial hegemony, ix

white supremacy, 2, 7, 20, 32–33, 42–45, 49, 54, 57, 59, 139, 176, 179, 183, 191
Whitehead, Thomas, 45
WikiLeaks, 92, 151–52, 155–57, 168, 215; *Collateral Murder*, 154; "The War Logs," 154, 162
Wilderson, Fred, 179
William Morgan affair, 33
Wilson, Joseph C., IV, 85–86, 94, 101
Wilson, Woodrow, 39, 46–48, 55
Winner, Reality, 172
Winning Our Future, 127
Wired, 212
Woodlawn Community Conservation Committee, 116
Woodlawn Ministers' Alliance, 111–12
World Trade Cener, 2
World War I, 34, 47, 162
World War II, ix, 10, 34, 40, 48, 54, 111, 143
World's Columbia Exposition, 110–11
Wylie, Christopher, 139n160

X (trope), ix
Xerxes, 25

Yemen, 195

Zarefsky, David, 88
Zelenskyy, Volodymyr, 83
Zimbardo, Philip, 41
Žižek, Slavoj, 155n71

NEW DIRECTIONS IN RHETORIC AND MATERIALITY
ALLISON L. ROWLAND, CHRISTA TESTON, AND SHUI-YIN SHARON YAM,
SERIES EDITORS

Current conversations about rhetoric signal ongoing attentiveness to and critical appraisal of material-discursive phenomena. New Directions in Rhetoric and Materiality provides a forum for responding to and extending such conversations, but also asks that books published in the series attend to social events of consequence unfolding around the world—such as violence based on misinformation, continued police brutality, immigration legislation and migration crises, and more. The series therefore seeks to amplify books that examine rhetoric's relationship to materiality while also confronting material-rhetorical forces of oppression, power imbalances, and differential vulnerabilities.

Sovereign, Settler, Leaker, Lie: Forms of the Secret in US Political Rhetoric
    ATILLA HALLSBY
Olfactory Rhetoric: Sniffing Out Environmental Problems
    LISA L. PHILLIPS
Patient Sense: Rhetorical Body Work in the Age of Technology
    LILLIAN CAMPBELL
Trafficking Rhetoric: Race, Migration, and the Making of Modern-Day Slavery
    ANNIE HILL
Nuclear Decolonization: Indigenous Resistance to High-Level Nuclear Waste Siting
    DANIELLE ENDRES
Decolonial Conversations in Posthuman and New Material Rhetorics
    EDITED BY JENNIFER CLARY-LEMON AND DAVID M. GRANT
Untimely Women: Radically Recasting Feminist Rhetorical History
    JASON BARRETT-FOX
Violent Exceptions: Children's Human Rights and Humanitarian Rhetorics
    WENDY S. HESFORD
Zoetropes and the Politics of Humanhood
    ALLISON L. ROWLAND
Ecologies of Harm: Rhetorics of Violence in the United States
    MEGAN EATMAN
Raveling the Brain: Toward a Transdisciplinary Neurorhetoric
    JORDYNN JACK
Post-Digital Rhetoric and the New Aesthetic
    JUSTIN HODGSON
Not One More! Feminicidio on the Border
    NINA MARIA LOZANO
Visualizing Posthuman Conservation in the Age of the Anthropocene
    AMY D. PROPEN
Precarious Rhetorics
    EDITED BY WENDY S. HESFORD, ADELA C. LICONA, AND CHRISTA TESTON

www.ingramcontent.com/pod-product-compliance
Lightning Source LLC
Chambersburg PA
CBHW020639230426
43665CB00008B/245